Preface

Title: Lean Six Sigma and Minitab (5th Edition)
Sub-Title: The Complete Toolbox Guide for Business Improvement

Author: Quentin Brook

ISBN-13: 978–0–9957899–0–6

Publisher: OPEX Resources Ltd

Publication Date: 1st September 2017

Previous (4th) Edition published as 'Lean Six Sigma and Minitab'
by OPEX Resources, May 2014, ISBN 978-0-9546813-8-8.

Published by OPEX Resources Ltd:

Contact us or visit our website for more information, volume discounts, online sales, errata, and Lean Six Sigma training material licensing.

E-mail:	info@opexresources.com
Web:	www.opexresources.com
Tel:	UK +44 (0)845 388 5835

With over 150,000 copies sold worldwide and now in its 5th edition, this book is firmly established as **the** guide of choice for process improvement professionals worldwide. The text explains Lean Six Sigma in a down-to-earth, practical and user friendly format, by cutting through its strange terminology and consultancy speak.

Key features include:

- **Practical examples** covering a range of industries.
- **Structured around DMAIC** with sub-steps for each phase.
- **Minitab® screenshots** and instructions for each tool (version 18).
- **Free data files and templates** available online (see page 13).
- **Routemaps** provide a logical flow through each DMAIC phase.

What's new in Edition 5?

This 5th edition has been fully updated for Minitab 18, while still compatible with previous versions. New tools have been added (incl. Bubble Plots, Trend Analysis and Laney Charts), existing material improved (incl. Time Series analysis and data transformations) and many other improvements made.

Who should use this book?

- Lean Six Sigma trainees.
- Improvement practitioners delivering real life projects.
- Project Sponsors overseeing improvement projects.
- Senior managers requiring an introduction to Lean and Six Sigma

Who Should Use This Book

This book is ideal as an introduction to Lean Six Sigma, a training companion and as a reference text for improvement practitioners who are delivering real life projects. Here are some key points of focus for different readers:

For managers and project sponsors:

- The DMAIC process is broken down into clear sub-steps.
- A down-to-earth summary of each tool is provided.
- Numerous 'non-statistical', process based tools.
- Reviewers questions at the end of each DMAIC phase (useful when attending project reviews and tollgates).

For Lean Six Sigma trainees:

- Use alongside your classroom training manuals.
- Step-by-step instructions for each tool and technique.
- Data files and templates are available online, so you can work through examples yourself for maximum learning.

For Lean Six Sigma practitioners:

- Portable format – keep it in your briefcase after training!
- Key outputs summarised for each Minitab tool, in order to refresh your memory after training.
- Numerous routemaps to help find the right tools rapidly.
- Project checklist at the end of each DMAIC phase.

Don't forget to download the free data files and templates!
See page 13 for more information.

The Author

Quentin Brook

Having graduated from the University of Bath (UK) in 1994 with a 1st Class Engineering and Management degree, Quentin developed his experience of process improvement statistical quality tools in the automotive industry of Detroit and aerospace industry in the UK.

He trained in Six Sigma with General Electric Aircraft Engines in Cincinnati, USA, before becoming Managing Director of QSB Consulting, where he has helped a broad range of clients deploy continuous improvement initiatives in a wide range of industries.

OPEX Resources was formed in 2010 as a niche provider of practical, down-to-earth support tools for professionals in the operational excellence industry, specifically Lean and Six Sigma.

Quentin Brook lives in Hampshire, UK.

Acknowledgements

Many thanks to the team of reviewers who have 'user tested' this book and provided invaluable feedback in its development. Thanks also to my family and friends for their support, and particular thanks to:

Kate Adams, Alex Fenton, Vijay Patel,

Holly Brook-Piper (editing), Marianne Hughes (layout and design),

Cathy Leonard-Hall, Monica Meagher and the team at Minitab.

Contents

Contents (cont.)

Contents (cont.)

What is Six Sigma?

There are many descriptions of Six Sigma, ranging from it being a quality level of 3.4 rejects per million, to a life changing philosophy! A more practical definition is **'data driven problem solving'**.

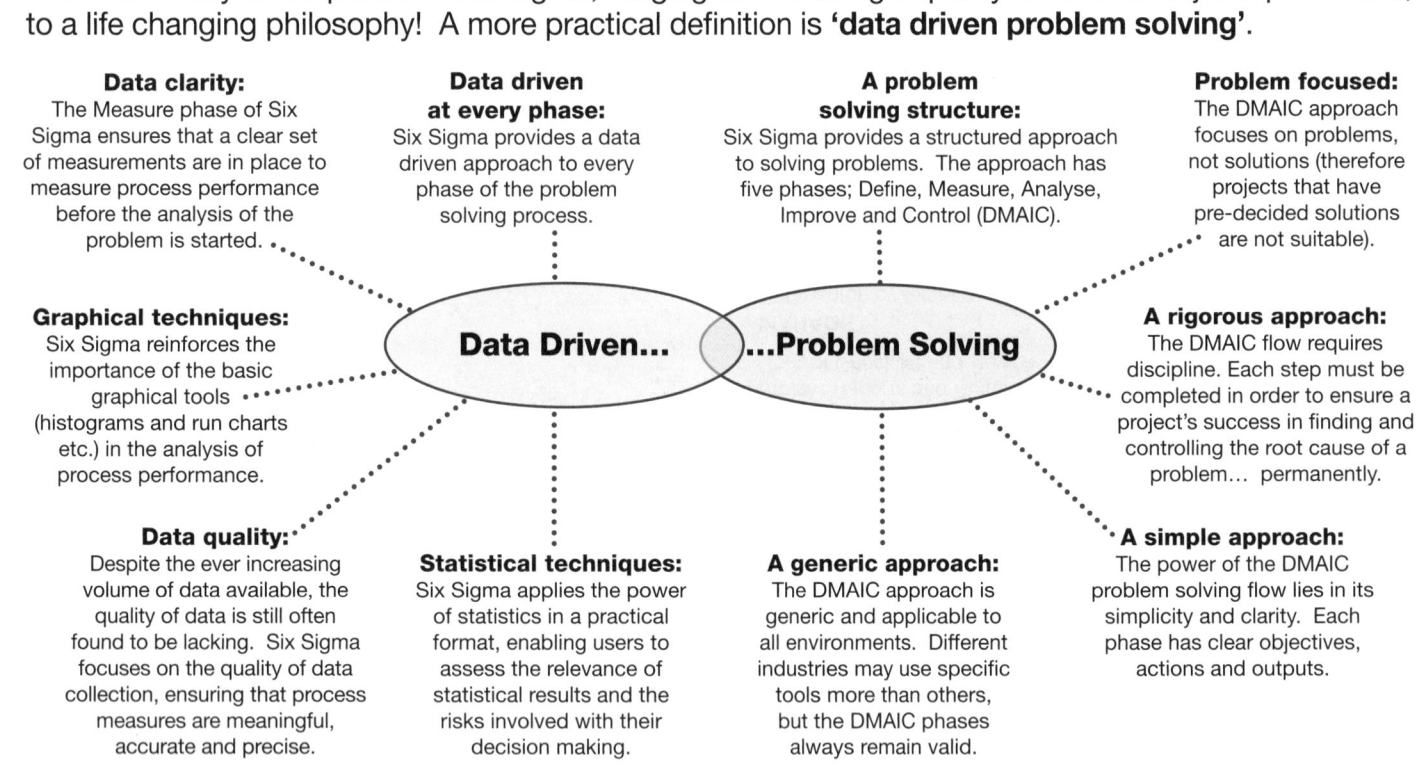

Data clarity:
The Measure phase of Six Sigma ensures that a clear set of measurements are in place to measure process performance before the analysis of the problem is started.

Data driven at every phase:
Six Sigma provides a data driven approach to every phase of the problem solving process.

A problem solving structure:
Six Sigma provides a structured approach to solving problems. The approach has five phases; Define, Measure, Analyse, Improve and Control (DMAIC).

Problem focused:
The DMAIC approach focuses on problems, not solutions (therefore projects that have pre-decided solutions are not suitable).

Graphical techniques:
Six Sigma reinforces the importance of the basic graphical tools (histograms and run charts etc.) in the analysis of process performance.

Data Driven...

...Problem Solving

A rigorous approach:
The DMAIC flow requires discipline. Each step must be completed in order to ensure a project's success in finding and controlling the root cause of a problem... permanently.

Data quality:
Despite the ever increasing volume of data available, the quality of data is still often found to be lacking. Six Sigma focuses on the quality of data collection, ensuring that process measures are meaningful, accurate and precise.

Statistical techniques:
Six Sigma applies the power of statistics in a practical format, enabling users to assess the relevance of statistical results and the risks involved with their decision making.

A generic approach:
The DMAIC approach is generic and applicable to all environments. Different industries may use specific tools more than others, but the DMAIC phases always remain valid.

A simple approach:
The power of the DMAIC problem solving flow lies in its simplicity and clarity. Each phase has clear objectives, actions and outputs.

DMAIC – A Logical Flow To Problem Solving

Six Sigma's DMAIC problem solving approach is simple and logical. Understanding and adhering to its simplistic nature is the key to a successful Lean Six Sigma project.

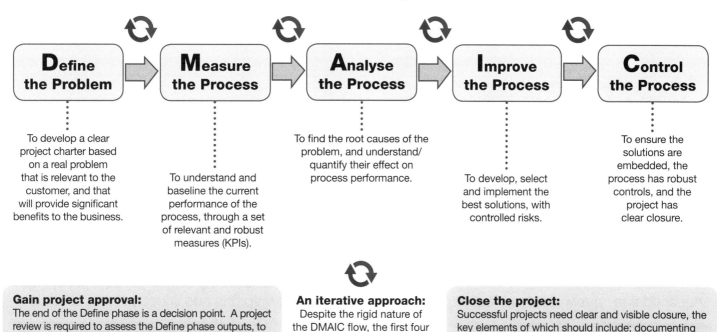

Define the Problem

To develop a clear project charter based on a real problem that is relevant to the customer, and that will provide significant benefits to the business.

Measure the Process

To understand and baseline the current performance of the process, through a set of relevant and robust measures (KPIs).

Analyse the Process

To find the root causes of the problem, and understand/ quantify their effect on process performance.

Improve the Process

To develop, select and implement the best solutions, with controlled risks.

Control the Process

To ensure the solutions are embedded, the process has robust controls, and the project has clear closure.

Gain project approval:
The end of the Define phase is a decision point. A project review is required to assess the Define phase outputs, to gain a consensus that the project is worth doing, and to commit the resources required for it to succeed.

An iterative approach:
Despite the rigid nature of the DMAIC flow, the first four phases (Define through to Improve) are often iterative in their application.

Close the project:
Successful projects need clear and visible closure, the key elements of which should include; documenting lessons learnt, transfer of the process back to 'business as usual', and finally, celebrating success!

What is Lean?

A process that is Lean is one that delivers products or services that the customer wants, at a price that reflects only the value that the customer is willing to pay for.

So what does the customer want?

They usually want things immediately!

- So a Lean process must be **fast**.

And they usually want things just how they like them!

- So a Lean process must be **flexible** in order to deliver products and services to the customers exact needs.

And what are they willing to pay for (or not)?

Customers are **not** willing to pay for the costs of:

- Making too many products before they are needed.
- Throwing away or fixing faulty products or services.
- Delays or unclear communication in the process.
- Wasted energy during the provision of products and services etc.

These costs are all examples of waste in a process, which is a key focus when creating leaner processes - see page 107.

And how do you achieve a Lean process?

In brief, developing a Lean process starts with understanding the value stream of the product or service from the customers perspective.

This can then help you to identify and eliminate waste that the customer will not pay for, and to identify the critical path for products and services to reach the customer quicker.

Recommended further reading:

The Lean approach encompasses a massive area of work and techniques, and inevitably far more than we can present in this text as part of Lean Six Sigma. For further reading on Lean, we would recommend texts by J. Womack and D. Jones.

Lean Thinking: Free Press, 7 July 2003
Lean Solutions: Simon and Schuster, 4 June 2007

Lean and the Six Sigma DMAIC structure

The Lean toolkit provides additional tools that can be deployed within the DMAIC structure.

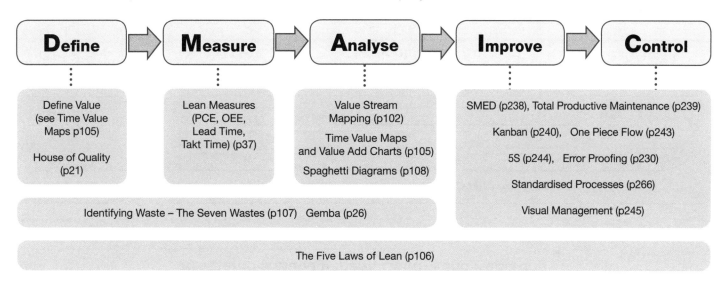

Define

Define Value
(see Time Value
Maps p105)

House of Quality
(p21)

Measure

Lean Measures
(PCE, OEE,
Lead Time,
Takt Time) (p37)

Analyse

Value Stream
Mapping (p102)

Time Value Maps
and Value Add Charts (p105)

Spaghetti Diagrams (p108)

Improve

SMED (p238), Total Productive Maintenance (p239)

Kanban (p240),   One Piece Flow (p243)

5S (p244),   Error Proofing (p230)

Standardised Processes (p266)

Visual Management (p245)

Control

Identifying Waste – The Seven Wastes (p107)   Gemba (p26)

The Five Laws of Lean (p106)

Lean versus DMAIC:

If you are looking for a discussion of the conflicts between Lean and Six Sigma, then you'll be disappointed, because we don't think there are any!

The two approaches contain a complementary range of tools and techniques. In reality, most projects, will inevitably require a range of both Lean and Six Sigma techniques. DMAIC is an effective problem solving structure that helps you to be clear about what you are trying to achieve. For that reason, we would recommend combining Lean and Six Sigma techniques as and when they are needed within a DMAIC structure, as shown above.

Building a Lean Six Sigma Programme

Using Lean Six Sigma as the backbone of your organisational improvement requires an infrastructure that is focused on supporting and managing the projects that will deliver the benefit.

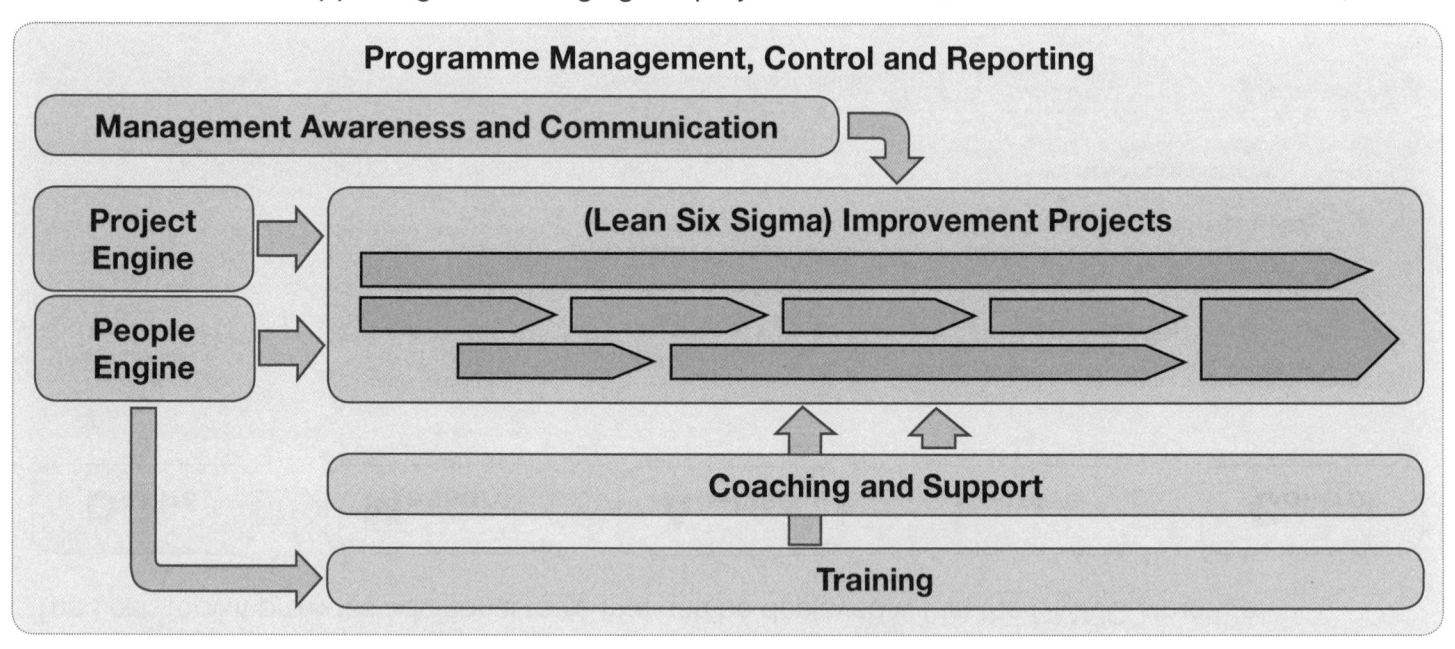

Some organisations adopt the entire Lean Six Sigma approach as their improvement programme, while others integrate the relevant tools and techniques into their existing programme structure – sometimes without the Six Sigma terminology and branding. In either case, most improvement programmes will contain the generic components shown above, which are described in more detail on the next page.

Building a Lean Six Sigma Programme (cont.)

Management Awareness and Communication:
All improvement initiatives require senior management support combined with an effective communication plan. Successful Lean Six Sigma initiatives can be thought of as a combination of pull and push. While there may be a significant amount of 'push' created by newly trained Green and Black Belts, it is important to create a 'pull' for Six Sigma, led by the senior management. Six Sigma awareness sessions can be useful in demonstrating to senior management their role in generating this 'pull' for data driven decision making – "show me the data!".

Programme Management, Control and Reporting:
As the size of a Six Sigma programme increases, a clear management structure is critical for monitoring and reporting on the many projects in progress. This function also includes the tracking of financial benefits accrued by the initiative.

Coaching and Support: The coaching and support provided to newly trained Six Sigma practitioners is the most important factor for driving successful projects forward with pace. Not coincidentally, a lack of coaching and support during their first projects after training is alsothe most common negative feedback from Black Belts. Support can be provided in a range of formats to cater for the different demands of Green and Black Belts, including:

- Project coaching surgeries to provide detailed one to one support.
- Six Sigma Helpdesks (by phone or e-mail) to resolve statistical or Minitab questions that could otherwise cause project delays.
- Community events and websites to provide the opportunity for the exchange of ideas and continued learning.
- Books (such as this one) and training manuals to provide a reference text for use after training.

Six Sigma Projects: The value of Six Sigma initiatives is delivered through a broad spectrum of improvement projects. These projects range from small 'one Black Belt' projects to larger team efforts (see next page), but they all share common features in terms of being clearly scoped, problem orientated and data driven.

The Project Engine: The 'Project Engine' refers to the process of developing a prioritised list of potential improvement projects, that are then taken forward by Black Belt teams. This process starts with a high level analysis of the business, its customers and strategy, in order to develop clear objectives for the Six Sigma programme.

The People Engine: While a large effort is usually devoted to finding the right projects for a Six Sigma programme, far less attention is sometimes paid to finding the right people! Lean Six Sigma training is a significant investment and therefore requires careful selection of delegates to ensure that they have the relevant change agent skills.

Training: Six Sigma inevitably involves an amount of training. It is important however to remember that Six Sigma is about delivering real process improvement through structured projects that are supported by training where required, not the other way round! Organisations that focus the majority of their Six Sigma effort solely on training often achieve a large throughput of Green and Black Belts, who then tend to dissolve back into the organisation without generating financial returns through successful projects.
Like all training, effective Six Sigma training requires a mixture of theory and practice, based on relevant case studies. Six Sigma trainers should be selected carefully based on their ability to explain and transfer statistics into a range of practical tools, rather than blinding their trainees with complex statistical formulae!

Different types of Lean Six Sigma projects

Lean Six Sigma provides a generic approach to problem solving, but its application will involve a wide spectrum of projects, from smaller local improvements through to larger more advanced projects.

Lean Six Sigma projects:
There is no clear distinction between Lean and Six Sigma when it comes to real life projects. You might hear people saying that they are working on a 'lean project' or a 'DFSS project' (Design for Six Sigma), but in reality they are all trying to improve processes and products. Instead, every project tends to be unique in terms of the types of tools that are found to be useful, and the diagram below demonstrates the two extremes of the spectrum.

It's not all about size!
Local improvement projects are not necessarily smaller projects (but they do tend to be). Some local projects have produced significant savings when rolled out across an organisation.

A more important aspect of a project is the **type** of problem involved and the most appropriate tools for solving it. The following page shows the different types of tools and techniques that might be applied for local improvement projects versus those that are useful in advanced projects.

The Lean Six Sigma project spectrum.

Local improvement projects ← From Leaner projects.... ...to the more Six Sigma orientated → **Advanced improvement projects**

- Many rapid incremental improvements.
- A 'just do it' approach.
- Smaller teams.
- Local scope.
- Lower projects savings (but not always!).
- Local deployment and locally led.
- Practical, cheaper solutions.

- Fewer, more substantial, step-change improvements.
- In-depth analysis, requiring longer timeframes.
- Larger teams with senior sponsorship.
- Broader scope, often part of larger initiative.
- Higher project savings or strategically critical.
- Local and company wide deployment.
- Mixture of practical and sophisticated solutions.

Different types of Lean Six Sigma projects (cont.)

Local improvement projects

Advanced improvement projects

Local improvement projects		Advanced improvement projects
Loose framework, with strong focus on Improve.	**DMAIC Framework**	Rigorously applied with strong focus on D,M & A to ensure successful Improve and Control phases.
Rarely required for local improvement projects.	**Advanced Statistical Tools**	GR&R, Capability Analysis, DOE, Regression, Hypothesis testing, Process Modelling.
Basic Process Mapping, Cause and Effect, 5 Whys, Paretos, Time Series plots, Histograms etc.	**Quality and Graphical Tools**	Basic techniques plus advanced tools such as QFD, KPI trees, Run charts, Scatter plots, Probability plots, FMEA etc.
Basic lean techniques (Value Stream Mapping, Spaghetti Diagrams, Seven Wastes etc.).	**Lean Tools**	Basic Lean tools plus advanced principles such as One Piece Flow, complexity reduction and Just in Time.
Small project teams led by process owners, therefore requiring less engagement skills.	**Project and Team Management Skills**	Strong leadership and stakeholder management skills are critical to success of larger projects.

Where do Lean Six Sigma projects come from?

Improvement projects usually come from a range of different sources within an organisation.

At any given point in time, world class organisations will have a range of different improvement projects taking place, but the question is where do they come from? The model on the right shows a simplified but typical scenario in which some improvement projects are part of 'top down' initiatives and others have been driven from 'bottom up' sources.

While not exhaustive, this model is a useful starting point to help organisations develop an overall improvement strategy. It is also worth noting that there is typically a spectrum of different types of improvement projects as described on the previous two pages.

Top down, centrally driven projects:

- **External VOC feedback** is often collated centrally and used to set up projects that focus on improving product/service quality.

- **Strategic goals** can produce specific projects, or act as criteria for assessing proposed projects (i.e. do they align with strategy?).

- **Major Change Programmes** are routinely broken down into sub-projects, some of which will be ideal DMAIC projects.

Bottom up, localised projects:

- **Internal VOC feedback** (from the next step in the process for example) is useful in prioritising local improvement projects.

- **Localised initiatives** can often be best delivered through DMAIC, to ensure they solve real problems and deliver benefits.

- **Employee suggestions** are an example of 'bottom up' projects, although they may be screened and monitored centrally.

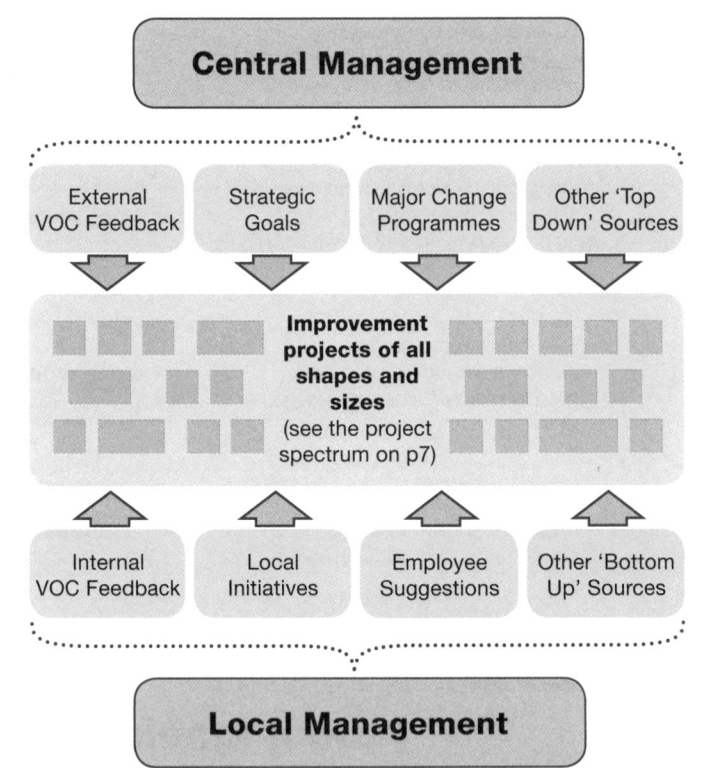

Managing Lean Six Sigma Projects

Like all projects, Lean Six Sigma projects require effective project management to succeed.

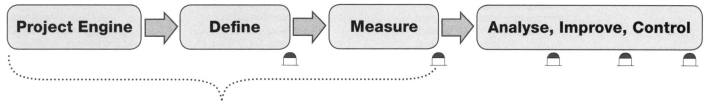

The screening process:

The 'Project Engine' (introduced on pages 5 and 6) is a screening process that takes a broad range of project ideas and reduces them down to a prioritised list of potential Six Sigma projects. However the screening process doesn't stop there. Project reviews at the end of the Define and Measure phases should also be considered as screening points, at which Six Sigma projects can be held or stopped if the conditions are not right for them to continue. The ability to stop projects that no longer have the right components for success is an important characteristic of a 'mature' improvement programme.

Why might projects get stopped?

Projects can be held or stopped at the Define phase review for a variety of reasons including lack of sponsorship, lack of resource, unclear problem and goal statements, an unclear business case, low potential returns, etc.

Although less likely, projects can also occasionally be stopped at the end of the Measure phase if, for example, the problem has been found to originate in the way the process is being measured rather than its actual performance.

Project Reviews / Milestones / Tollgates:

Good project management involves the development of clear project plans that include milestones and associated deliverables. It makes sense to align the project plan milestones with the DMAIC phases of Lean Six Sigma, as shown above. A checklist and list of review questions are provided at the end of each DMAIC phase throughout this guide.

Project Documentation:

An effective method of documenting a Six Sigma project is the use of a project working file that is updated (as a presentation) as the project progresses. Like a presentation, the project working file provides a summary of the project to date, which can then be used as the basis of project coaching and reviews.

The DMAIC phases of the project should be clearly demonstrated throughout the project working file (see page 29).

The value of maintaining a working file is that it promotes project clarity by encouraging a Black Belt to continuously summarise their progress within the DMAIC structure.

Minitab – Overview

What is Minitab?

Minitab is a statistical software package that is commonly used by improvement practitioners. Minitab is not the only software of this kind, but it has become the industry standard for Lean Six Sigma and operational excellence because of its specific functionality and ease of use.

For more information on Minitab statistical software, visit:

www.minitab.com

As the title of this book suggests, Minitab is tightly integrated into this guide, with detailed instructions on how to complete the tools and techniques using the software. Page 13 explains how you can download the Minitab data files for the examples throughout this guide.

The picture opposite shows a typical screen shot of the Minitab software. As shown, a Minitab project file (extension .MPJ) typically contains several standard types of windows, as described on the right.

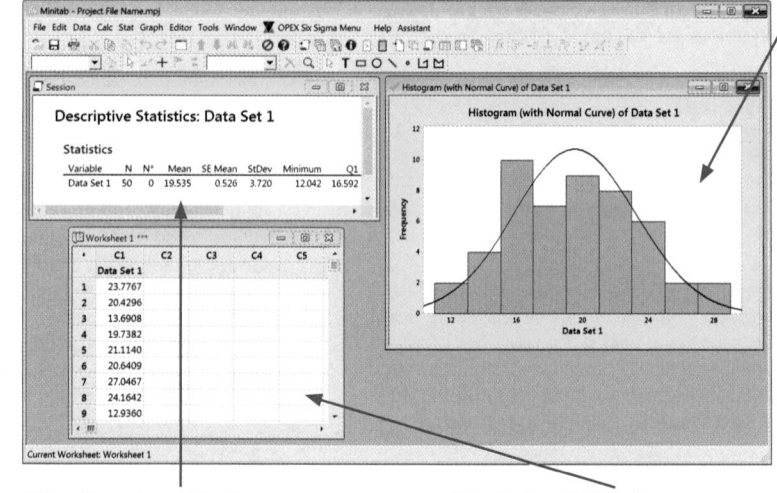

The Session Window:

A Minitab project **always** has a Session Window, where you will find all of the numerical output (as opposed to graphical output) that you create during your analysis work. The Session Window stores all of the numerical results in time order, so it can be a useful history of the analysis that you have completed.

Worksheet Windows:

Data is stored in Minitab Worksheets (which are similar to spreadsheets). Minitab works in columns, and each different type of data should be entered in its own column. This column format is very flexible and enables users to 'slice and dice' the data very rapidly during the analyse phase (see page 117 for more information on Minitab's data structure).

Graph Windows:

Every graph produced in Minitab is displayed in its own window, as shown with the histogram example on the left. Minitab graphs can be exported easily, and the link between a graph and the original data can be controlled (i.e. whether or not the graph updates when the data has been changed – see page 119).

Minitab graphs can also be 'explored' using the Brush function (see page 120) which is a powerful tool that helps look for clues within the data.

Companion by Minitab® – Overview

What is Companion by Minitab?

Companion by Minitab is software that helps organisations manage their continuous improvement programmes. As this book demonstrates, using Minitab to analyse data is only a small (but essential) part of a real life Lean Six Sigma project. Successful improvement projects also require careful management through a clear structure (e.g. DMAIC) and use a much broader range of tools than just graphs and hypothesis testing! Companion by Minitab supports this by enabling users to manage their improvement projects through a structured framework and by providing 'non-statistical' forms and tools such as Process Mapping, CTQ Trees, Fishbone Diagrams, Brainstorming etc.

Companion's full power comes from the seamless integration of project tools and dashboard reporting. As teams work through projects using tools in its desktop app, critical data automatically rolls up to a web app and dashboard, so executives and stakeholders can see the current status of their initiative on demand. Since the dashboard is automatically updated, reporting is literally effortless for teams, so they have more time to focus on project tasks. The Manage section of this book (p268) focuses specifically on Companion and provides instructions and screenshots for both the desktop and web apps.

1) The Companion Desktop App helps project teams manage and execute projects, by providing a:

- Structured, customisable routemap (the Roadmap).
- Central location for documenting a project.
- Range of process improvement tools.
- Selection of relevant project management tools.

The Project Today screen of the Companion desktop app (right) provides a homepage for an improvement project, and a summary of its key elements.

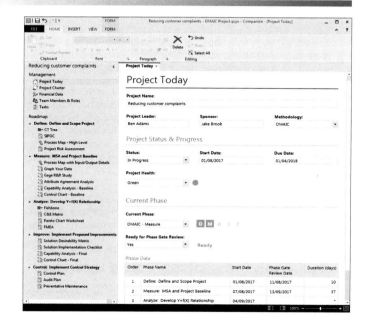

2) The Companion Web App helps executives, stakeholders, sponsors and programme managers gain instant insight into the status of their improvement programme overall, as well as individual projects. Dashboards and reports are easily customised for particular audiences. In addition, the web app's design centre (p285) enables centralised development of project templates and forms, providing standardisation across an organisation.

How to use this guide with Minitab

This book is designed to be a practical learning resource. You will get maximum learning value from it by working through the Minitab analysis examples yourself, as you go through the book.

To support that, the data files for all of the examples are available for free download from the OPEX Resources website, where you will also find other other useful resources.

This page explains how to follow the Minitab examples in more detail.

Download the data files and templates:
The following symbol, it indicates that a data file (of the name shown) is available for the example on that page:

Example Filename.mpj

Go to **www.opexresources.com** and download the data files from the **Resources** section (or the Quick Links menu).

All of the Minitab files and other templates will be downloaded in a single zipped folder. Just select the appropriate download for the for the version of Minitab that you have, and then download the zip file to your computer. Once saved, unzip the folder.

You can open the data files from within Minitab in the normal way (**File > Open Project** and then browse to the file) or double-click them directly.

Follow the Minitab menu commands:
Wherever a new tool or Minitab dialogue box is shown in this text, you will also find the accompanying Minitab menu command.

This will be written in blue as follows:

Minitab: Stat > Basic Statistics > etc.

NB: The > symbol refers to the next sub-menu.

The Minitab menu commands quoted are based on the standard menus of Minitab 18, with any differences with previous Minitab versions noted to ensure this text is 'backwards compatible'.

Use the OPEX Customised Minitab Menu:
Minitab provides an easy-to-use menu customisation tool, that makes it possible for you to modify and create your own menu structure. This enables you to group together your most frequently used tools and functions into a new menu, which can be saved as a profile and shared with other users.

And if don't want to prepare your own, we have created one for you! All of the Minitab tools discussed in this guide have been grouped together into the ready made 'OPEX Customised Minitab Menu', which can be downloaded for free from the OPEX website.

More information on this ready made profile can be found in Appendix C, along with detailed instructions on how to install it on your PC. The profile can be easily switched off or removed.

Define – Overview

The DMAIC process starts when you have identified a problem. The Define phase helps to clarify your understanding of **why** it is a problem, before investing time and money in commencing a project.

The flow through Define:

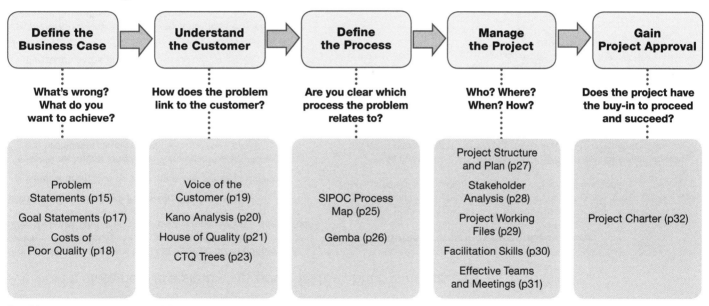

Define the Business Case	Understand the Customer	Define the Process	Manage the Project	Gain Project Approval
What's wrong? What do you want to achieve?	How does the problem link to the customer?	Are you clear which process the problem relates to?	Who? Where? When? How?	Does the project have the buy-in to proceed and succeed?
Problem Statements (p15) Goal Statements (p17) Costs of Poor Quality (p18)	Voice of the Customer (p19) Kano Analysis (p20) House of Quality (p21) CTQ Trees (p23)	SIPOC Process Map (p25) Gemba (p26)	Project Structure and Plan (p27) Stakeholder Analysis (p28) Project Working Files (p29) Facilitation Skills (p30) Effective Teams and Meetings (p31)	Project Charter (p32)

Six Sigma projects start with problems, not solutions:
The Define phase focuses only on the problem – root causes and solutions come later on. If the project already appears to have a proposed solution, or the project title infers one, it is the project leader's role to turn the project around to being 'problem oriented'.

Problem Statements

A problem statement is a simple yet powerful tool, but it is not as easy as it looks!

Problem statements are a brief but specific description of the problem. They should clearly explain what the problem is, how often it occurs, and what the impact is (cost) when it does occur.

What makes a good Problem Statement?

- **Keep it brief:** Two or three short sentences at the most.

- **Avoid technical language:** You should be able to explain the problem in simple terms.

- **Quantify the problem:** Use any data you have available.

- **Explain the cost of the problem:** You should refer to the key Costs of Poor Quality (p18) of the problem.

- **Define the scope:** Use terminology that helps to define the scope of the project.

Use the **SMART** checklist below to challenge how good your statement is. Is the problem statement:

Specific?

Measurable?

Achievable? (Goal statement)

Relevant?

Time Bound?

Some Problem Statement examples:

1) During 2016, 20% of overseas customer payments took longer than the agreed invoice terms. This resulted in an average outstanding debt of £357K, at a 5% cost of capital.

2) From Oct 2016 to March 2017, 5% of Product A manufactured on production line 1 failed the final test. This resulted in an extra inspection/rework process being implemented (at a cost of £25,000 per month), and a scrap rate of 2% costing £20K per month in lost revenue.

What is good about the examples above?

- Both of them provide dates and data that help baseline the problem.

- The scope of the problems are defined by phrases such as *product A, overseas* and *production line 1.*

- Both statements explain how the problem affects the organisation and provides an estimate of the cost.

- They do not refer to any solutions or root causes.

Problem Statements – How Low Should We Go?

A common difficulty in developing problem statements is deciding how detailed to make them and at what process level they should be pitched within the organisation.

The answer is to make sure your problem statement **does not** define a problem to which you **know** the answer.

Starting at the top...

"The business is not making enough profit!"

This is clearly too broad for a Lean Six Sigma project – you cannot solve all the problems at once! In addition it is not SMART enough to be a problem statement (see page above).
And! Realistically, you probably know why the business is not making enough profit.

So, try the next level down...

"During the last 12 months, our operating costs have been approximately 20% above the best in class (or target), leading to reduced profits."

This is getting more manageable because it is focusing on a lower level output within the business (operating expenditure) rather than a high level output (profit). However, it is still too widely scoped for a Lean Six Sigma project.

So, try the next level down again...

"Rework levels within the billing process of the Southern area office have been running at 70% for the last 12 months. This drives increased operating costs (labour, IT, office space), lost revenue and low customer satisfaction."

Finally, this problem statement appears to be at an appropriate level for a Six Sigma project. It's clearly scoped, it's SMART, and it focuses on a problem to which the root cause is not yet known (why are rework levels so high?). It also goes on to explain how the problem costs the business money.

Goal Statements

The Goal Statement responds to the Problem Statement and defines the target for the project.

Goal Statements should be as brief and specific as the Problem Statements to which they respond.

What makes a good Goal Statement?

- Keep it brief.
- Avoid technical language.
- Use the same metrics as the Problem Statement.
- Be as specific as possible about dates.
- Avoid defining the solution to the problem.

Some Goal Statement examples:

1) Reduce the percentage of overseas customer payments that take longer than the agreed invoice terms from 20% to 5%, by the end of quarter 4, 2017.

2) Reduce the Product A final test failure rate on production line 1 from 5% to X% by the end of October 2017.

How do you set a Goal during the Define phase?

At this point in the project, it is obviously difficult to quantify how much the process will be improved by. There are a couple of options available to cope with this:

- State your best estimate (to be revised later).
- Use an "X" (as in example 2, right), which means you will fill it in as soon as you can estimate it.

The Goal Statement is typically reviewed at the end of the Measure and Analyse phases to ensure it remains realistic.

What is good about the examples above?

- Both of them set a date for the improvement to be achieved by.
- Both of them are specific about the process measurement that will be improved.
- Neither of them contain a solution or root cause.
- They define success as improvement in a key measurement.
- They are brief.

Costs of Poor Quality (COPQ)

The Six Sigma phrase 'Cost of Poor Quality' refers to all the costs associated with the problem.

There are many Costs of Poor Quality (COPQs) that are easily recognised, such as rework, rejects, inspection, testing, customer returns and complaints etc. However, behind these, there is also usually a large range of COPQs that have become so common that we start to view them as 'normal', such as excess inventory, late payments, expediting costs, high employee turnover etc.

COPQ and the Problem Statement:

The Problem Statement should contain the **main** category of COPQ that impacts the business financially. For example, the financial impact of the problem may be lost revenue, material scrap costs, the labour costs of rework or the cost of capital tied up in excess inventory etc. However, there are usually many different COPQs for each problem, and it is worth expanding on these aside from the Problem Statement.

Hard versus Soft Benefits:

When a problem is solved, the COPQs help define a range of hard and soft benefits that will be created. This terminology is used to describe whether the benefit can be measured financially (hard) or non-financially (soft). While a project's business case will be based on the hard benefits, the softer benefits such as improved customer satisfaction should not be ignored, as it may be possible to convert them to hard benefits eventually.

It is important to involve the finance department in a review of a project's benefits during the Define phase, in order to agree how an improvement in process performance will be converted into financial savings at the end of the project.

Different types of Cost of Poor Quality

It may be useful to use the following categories for thinking about Costs of Poor Quality. However, it is only a framework to help ensure you don't miss anything in your COPQ assessment.

Appraisal:

This refers to any systems, processes or procedures that exist only to look for problems, such as inspection. How often do you do something and then immediately check it?

Prevention:

There are also lots of systems and procedures to prevent things going wrong. While beneficial, they are still actually Costs of Poor Quality.

Internal Failure:

Problems that occur within an organisation may not impact the customer directly but they should still be seen as Costs of Poor Quality. Eventually these COPQs will reach the customer in the form of higher prices or delays.

External Failure:

An external COPQ is the cost of any defect that reaches the customer. These costs of failure can become very significant.

Voice Of The Customer (VOC)

Even the smallest Six Sigma project must take the time to ensure it is customer focused. On a practical level this involves talking to and becoming a customer in order to understand their needs.

Different methods of researching the VOC:

- **Customer complaints –** A good place to start but be wary about possible bias.

- **Direct contact methods –** Phone calls, focus groups, interviews at the point of provision.

- **Less direct methods –** Surveys, feedback cards, market research and competitor analysis etc.

- **Become a customer of your organisation –** Phone your own call centre, order groceries from your own online store, buy one of your own brand washing machines, set up a new account with your own bank etc.

! There is no excuse not to consider the VOC!

Most Six Sigma projects are too small to have a budget for formal customer research, and they don't usually need it. The internet has huge quantities of market research made public by various organisations and many of the methods and suggestions on this page require nothing but time. No project is too small to do VOC.

Some practical examples of collecting the VOC:
Remember to think practical. VOC research cannot be done from the office, you have to get up and go and meet the customer!

Example 1:
For a project that aims to reduce the cost of collecting insurance premiums from residential customers, select a few random customers and ring them up and talk to them about the reasons behind their choice of payment method (credit card/direct debit/cheque/cash etc.)

Example 2:
For a project that aims to improve customer satisfaction of a home delivery service, go out with a delivery van for a day or two and talk to the customers directly at the point of delivery. What features are important? How would they prioritise them? What is acceptable? What is not acceptable?

Example 3:
For a project focusing on the production quality of an aeroplane component, go and talk to the customer's engineers and understand the thinking that went into their design of the component, its tolerances and materials etc.

Kano Analysis

Customers provide all sorts of feedback when collecting the VOC. The Kano model is a framework for categorising and prioritising the different performance features of a product or service.

The Kano model identifies three categories of performance features of a product or service.

Must haves fulfil a **basic** requirement of the customer and the customer assumes they will be present. You do not get any extra points for providing these features, but the customer will notice if they are missing, so they are known as **dissatisfiers**. Examples of **must have** features of a modern car are a reliable engine and a radio.

More is better fulfils a **performance** requirement. The more you provide of these features, the more the customer is satisfied, so they are also known as **satisfiers**. Examples of **more is better** features of a modern car are the efficiency of the engine, the range between refuelling and (for some customers) the number of cup holders!

Delighters fulfil an **excitement** requirement. These are the features of a product or service that provide a 'wow' factor, and really delight the customer – hence their name! The problem with identifying **delighters** is that even customers won't necessarily be able to express what features would delight them, because they haven't experienced them yet! Examples of **delighter** features of a new car delivery might be having the car delivered right to your home; ahead of schedule, freshly washed and with a free bottle of champagne!

Different ways of using the Kano model:

- You can map existing or proposed features of your products and services into the Kano categories, to better understand how your product or service fits customer needs.

- You can ask customers to do the same, in order to better understand the VOC.

- You can use the Kano model to categorise and structure general customer feedback.

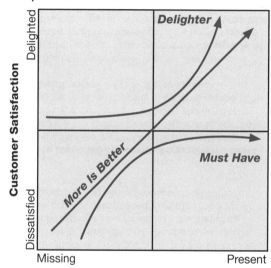

Required or actual feature of the product or service

! The Kano model often highlights how customer requirements are constantly changing. Today's **delighters** become tomorrow's **must haves**, requiring us to constantly develop new, differentiated customer offerings.

House of Quality

The House of Quality helps to correlate customer requirements with product (or service) capabilities, in order to ensure that a product (or service) delivers real value to the customer, not just compliance.

House of Quality is a structured methodology that:

- Captures the needs of the customers (the 'whats').

- Translates the customer's needs into general product (or service) features (the 'hows').

- Assesses the link between the product's features and the customer's requirements, and any interactions within the product features.

- Can then be used to develop specific requirements for how the product or service will be made (or delivered).

The component parts of a House of Quality are detailed on the next page. The approach itself is an integral part of the broader Quality Function Deployment approach described below.

What is Quality Function Deployment (QFD)?

The phrase Quality Function Deployment refers to an overall approach for understanding the needs of the customer and translating them into products/services that deliver real value. While the House of Quality is often seen as the lynchpin of QFD, a range of other tools (covered in this text) work alongside the House of Quality, such as:

- Kano Analysis, CTQ Trees and Affinity diagrams are useful for understanding, structuring and prioritising customer's requirements.

- The Pugh Matrix and Paired Comparisons are useful for comparing different options and weighting customer requirements.

A faster, team based approach to product development:
By involving all key stakeholders simultaneously, the House of Quality can play an important role in improving both the speed and quality of new product development. This contrasts with the traditional approach where a new product gets passed from marketing to design, and on to engineering and finally production, with little up front collaboration.

! A House of Quality can easily become an extensive task!
The House of Quality is a little like the FMEA technique (see page 114), in that it requires a team of people to work together to complete a detailed piece of work. Without careful facilitation and good team discipline, both techniques have the capacity to become cumbersome and bogged down in detail, negating much of their value.

One useful approach (for both techniques) is to ask the individual team members to complete specific tasks by themselves, outside of the main House of Quality (or FMEA) meetings. This speeds up the process by focusing the meetings on rapidly developing a consensus within the team (rather than starting from scratch).

So, for example, during an initial House of Quality meeting, the team can focus only on the Customer Requirements and Technical Features (the 'Whats' and 'Hows' – see next page). After the meeting, the team can individually complete the various matrices of the House of Quality, and then bring their results back to a second meeting, where the focus is on agreeing a consensus.

House of Quality (cont.)

There are lots of different versions of the House of Quality, depending on the specific application involved. This example is simple and generic, to demonstrate the key elements.

Customer Requirements (the 'Whats'):

The customer's requirements (grouped under sub-categories if useful) are listed on the left side of the House of Quality. This partially completed example is for a smartphone. Each customer requirement is rated in terms of relative importance.

Relationship Matrix:

The central area of the House of Quality is where the strength of relationship between each customer requirement and technical feature is rated.

Typically, a simple rating of either slight, medium, strong is used (although numerical scores are also suitable). In this example the key is:

△ Slight relationship
○ Medium relationship
◎ Strong relationship

Correlation Matrix (the 'Roof'):

Any interactions between technical features (both conflicting and competing) are recorded in the roof of the House of Quality. In this example, the interaction between screen size and the overall volume of the smartphone has been rated as negative, to reflect the design trade off that exists between a larger screen and overall phone size.

Technical Features (the 'Hows'):

The technical features that provide the customer's requirements are listed at the top of the house, under sub-categories if useful.

Planning Matrix:

The right side of the House of Quality supports strategic product planning. Using the Customer Importance ratings, the performance of the product (or service) is rated for each customer requirement. The performance of competing products (or services) can also be assessed. This information can then be used to plan strategic product (or service) changes that are focused on customer needs.

Technical Matrix:

The lower section of the House of Quality supports technical planning. The technical features are prioritised against each other and compared against competing products (or services). Target values are set for each technical feature, which can then prioritise future technical improvements.

House of Quality diagram showing:

Direction of improvement. Roof correlation matrix with + and − ratings.

Customer requirements		Customer importance	Touch screen	Network coverage	Replaceable cover	Screen size	Volume (size)	Battery type	Your product/service	Competitor A	Competitor B	Planned rating
User friendly	Easy to use	4	◎	△		○	○					
User friendly	Pocket sized	2			△	○	◎	○				
User friendly	Customisable	2			◎							
Performance	Fast data transfer	3		○								
Performance	Good Reception	5		◎								
Performance	Long battery life	3					△	◎				

Technical features (Physical)

Technical priority
Your product/service
Competitor A
Competitor B
Target values

Critical To Quality (CTQ) Trees

Having gained an insight into the Voice of the Customer, it can be useful to present the results as a CTQ Tree. This provides clarity and a structure for developing quantifiable specifications.

What are Critical to Quality Trees?

CTQ trees help to provide clarity and structure to the Voice of the Customer. VOC information can be quite wide ranging and it can often be difficult to identify the key requirements of the customer, and how they interrelate. CTQ Trees are useful because they provide a visual summary of the Voice of the Customer, in which the key customer requirements are clearly identified. They then drilldown to specific customer requirements and provide measurable specifications for those requirements.

CTQ Trees are an essential tool within the Define phase of an improvement project. They enable a project team to ensure they are working on something that is important to the end customer.

Where CTQ Trees fit with other VOC tools:

Voice of the Customer collection activities (such as those described on page 19) will usually provide lots of information on the customers' requirements and expectations. While Kano Analysis (p20) can help to better understand the customer's requirements and Affinity Diagrams (p112) can help to identify similar themes or groups within customer feedback comments, CTQ Trees can then be useful for providing a clear, hierarchical structure that summarises the customers' requirements.

The process for developing a Critical to Quality Tree:

Define the specific event:
At the top of the CTQ Tree is the specific event that is experienced by the customer. It's worth trying to define an event rather than a process, to avoid the CTQ Tree being too vague. So, the example on the next page focuses on *'fixing a fault on a residential broad service'* rather than just the *'fault repair process'*.

Identify the customer's broad requirements:
It's usually possible to summarise the customers expectations into three or four broad requirements, such as *'easy reporting'* or *'getting back on-line fast'*.

Break the broad requirements down into specific CTQs:
The next step is to break each broad requirement down into more specific requirements that provide more detail on the customer's expectations.

Develop CTQ Specifications:
Finally, each specific CTQ is translated into a measurable characteristic such as *'fix fault within 4 hours'*. These CTQ Specifications will be used later in the Measure phase, to develop customer driven KPIs (see page 35).

Critical To Quality (CTQ) Trees (cont.)

The CTQ Tree example below is for the process of fixing a fault on a residential broadband service. It provides a structured view of the customers' expectations and requirements when having a broadband fault fixed.

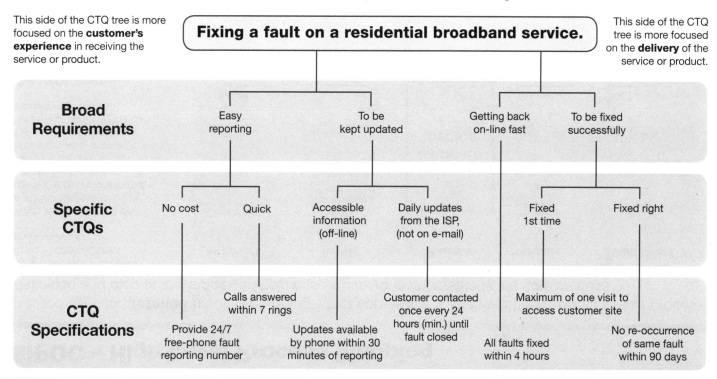

This side of the CTQ tree is more focused on the **customer's experience** in receiving the service or product.

This side of the CTQ tree is more focused on the **delivery** of the service or product.

Fixing a fault on a residential broadband service.

Broad Requirements

- Easy reporting
- To be kept updated
- Getting back on-line fast
- To be fixed successfully

Specific CTQs

- No cost
- Quick
- Accessible information (off-line)
- Daily updates from the ISP, (not on e-mail)
- Fixed 1st time
- Fixed right

CTQ Specifications

- Provide 24/7 free-phone fault reporting number
- Calls answered within 7 rings
- Updates available by phone within 30 minutes of reporting
- Customer contacted once every 24 hours (min.) until fault closed
- Maximum of one visit to access customer site
- All faults fixed within 4 hours
- No re-occurrence of same fault within 90 days

SIPOC – High Level Process Mapping

It is too early for **detailed** process mapping – that comes in the Analyse phase. But, a simple process definition and map at this stage can help ensure everyone understands the core process.

SIPOC stands for Supplier, Input, Process, Output and Customer.

What does a SIPOC do?
A SIPOC diagram helps to clarify the core process that a project is focused on. This can then be used in the Define phase review in order to check that all the stakeholders of the project agree on the core process involved.

The SIPOC Process:
1) A SIPOC starts with a simple definition of the process.

2) The 4-6 key steps of the process are then expanded at the bottom of the SIPOC.

3) The main inputs and outputs of the process are then listed.

4) The suppliers of each input and customers of each output are then identified.

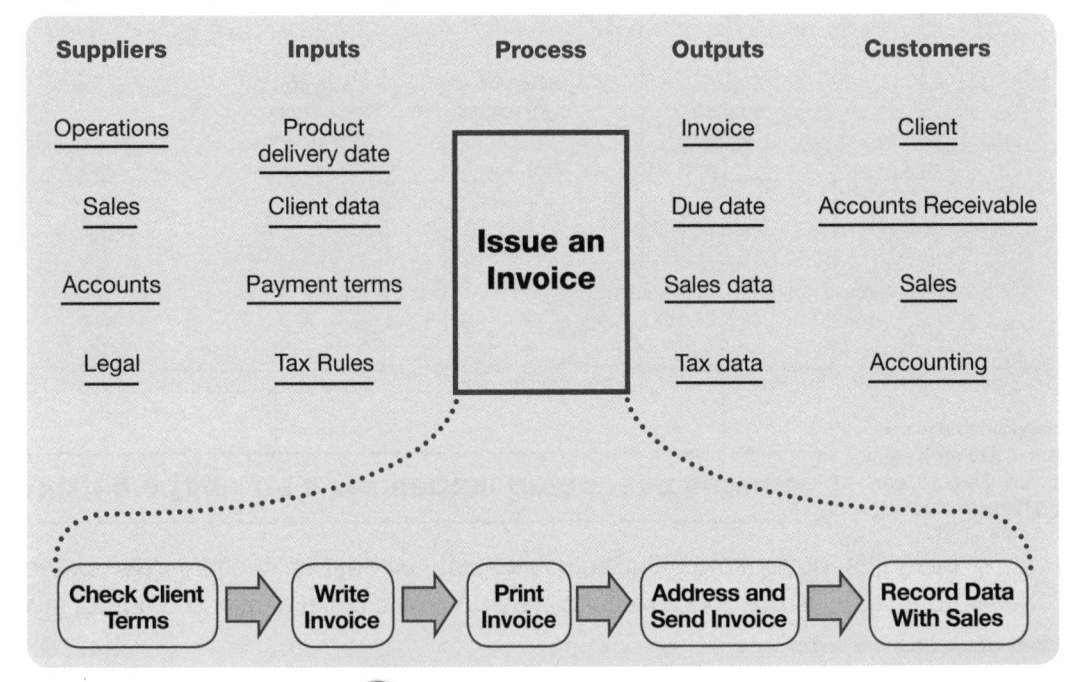

Suppliers	Inputs	Process	Outputs	Customers
Operations	Product delivery date		Invoice	Client
Sales	Client data	**Issue an Invoice**	Due date	Accounts Receivable
Accounts	Payment terms		Sales data	Sales
Legal	Tax Rules		Tax data	Accounting

Check Client Terms → Write Invoice → Print Invoice → Address and Send Invoice → Record Data With Sales

SIPOC Template.ppt

Gemba

Gemba is an approach that focuses on the *actual* place where key activities happen.

What is Gemba?

Literally translated, Gemba (a Japanese word) refers to the 'actual place'. So, in a manufacturing environment, Gemba can refer to the actual place where products are made – e.g. the shop floor. Similarly, in a service environment, Gemba can refer to the actual place where a service is created and delivered – e.g. a restaurant, a cinema, or a website.

How to apply the Gemba approach:

For business improvement, the Gemba approach reminds us that it is important to visit the Gemba, in order to understand how a process really works. In other words, only by spending time seeing a process actually happening, will you be able to observe things such as:

- How the process operates normally.
- How the process operates when things go wrong.
- What types of problems occur.
- How problems are resolved.
- How the process is managed and controlled.
- The differences between written instructions and reality.

The key outcome of Gemba, is a better overall understanding of a process, covering:

- What is **written** to be done (the intention).
- What is **thought** to be done (people's perceptions).
- What is **actually** done (the reality).

Key steps of Gemba:

Step 1 – Assemble a cross functional team: Make sure you include people who are new to the area/process and who can bring 'fresh eyes'.

Step 2 – Go and see: The team must visit the actual place (the 'Gemba') where the activity takes place (or the problems occur).

Step 3 – Observe and touch: The idea is to start by just observing and touching. Ideally, the team should spend at least 10-15 minutes silently observing the activity before starting to discuss and ask questions.

Step 4 – Ask open questions: The team will probably have lots of questions at this point, but it's important to keep them open. Questions that start with 'what, where, when, how many' can help bring informative answers about what actually happens.

Step 5 – Avoid assumptive questions: Questions that start with why or how can sometimes bring opinionated answers, that may only be one way of looking at things. Try to leave these types of questions to last.

Applying Gemba at the customer:

Gemba can also be applied to the customer. As discussed on page 19, in order to truly understand your customers viewpoint (and how they experience your products), it's important to visit the actual place that your customers use your product (or service).

Project Structure and Project Plans

As with any other project, a Six Sigma project needs a project team with a clear structure, roles and responsibilities, together with a preliminary project plan.

A typical Project Structure will include:

- **A Six Sigma Champion** – the project should have the support and awareness of the relevant Six Sigma Champion, whose role is to ensure that the project fits within the bigger picture of the Lean Six Sigma strategy.

- **The Project Sponsor** – who is responsible for the project. Be warned! Too many Project Sponsors will see their role as merely an adviser, with no responsibility for the success of the project.

- **The Project Leader** – usually a Black Belt, who leads the project on a day to day (and preferably full time) basis.

- **Team members** – often trained to Green Belt level and involved part time.

Who to involve in your team:

- Ensure all the relevant processes are represented in the team that you select.

- Pick the right people. Don't just end up with those available!

- Do not recruit too many people – you can always call in additional support at the right time. Four to six team members is about right.

Project Planning:

At the Define stage, it will only be possible to assign approximate dates for your project, but this is still important in order to communicate your expected rate of progress.

Milestone / Tollgate reviews are an essential part of a project, ensuring there are clear deliverables at every stage. The key points of a successful review are:

- The whole project team should be involved (before and during).

- Ensure the stakeholders are present (Champion, Sponsor etc.).

- Provide a summary to date, with key findings.

- Prepare and allow time for questions.

- Ensure any support requirements are made clear.

- Present clear next steps.

Checklists and Review Questions for each DMAIC phase:

It makes sense to structure project milestones around the DMAIC phases and so at the end of each phase, this book provides:

- A **Checklist** to help the project team develop milestone deliverables.

- A list of **Review Questions** for use by stakeholders and sponsors.

Stakeholder Analysis

Stakeholder analysis is something we do naturally every day without realising it. A structured approach provides a clear strategy for managing the stakeholders effectively and appropriately.

What is Stakeholder Analysis?
Stakeholder analysis is the process of considering those people that will be involved or affected by the project, or who have some level of control over the project and process.

Different formats for Stakeholder Analysis:
There are several formats for conducting an analysis, but they all tend to focus on two criteria (as shown in the stakeholder mapping tool opposite):

■ **Power –** the role of a stakeholder and their relationship to the project determines their ability to support the project, or to hinder its progress.

■ **Position –** the position of a stakeholder as a Blocker or Supporter and their level of interest will determine their response to a project.

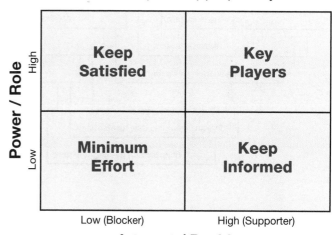

Communication Plans:
Stakeholder analysis is not something you just 'do' and then file away. Its purpose is to help create a strategy for the day to day management of key stakeholders, in order to minimise the potential project blockers. This strategy is often termed a communication plan but in reality its scope also covers the more subtle aspects of how a stakeholder should be involved in the project. A **communication plan** doesn't need to be a very formal affair, but for each key stakeholder it should detail:

■ The **format** that will be used to communicate with the stakeholder (e.g. e-mails, 1-2-1s, team meetings, weekly reviews etc.).

■ Who is going to be the **primary contact** responsible for managing the stakeholder.

■ **Key actions** for the stakeholder – an action plan that ensures the stakeholder is provided with the information that they need.

Project Working Files (Storyboards)

An effective method of documenting an improvement project is through the use of a project working file that is written as a presentation, kept updated as the project progresses, and structured clearly around the DMAIC phases.

The value of maintaining a project working file is that it promotes project clarity by encouraging a project leader to continuously summarise their progress within the DMAIC structure.

A typical group of core slides for Define, Measure and Analyse are shown below.

There are several additional advantages to maintaining an ongoing project working file including:

- The file can be used as the basis of project coaching sessions.
- Preparation time for tollgates (reviews) is minimised.
- Preparation of final project reports is quicker, with more detail available.
- Projects are reported in a consistent, recognisable format.

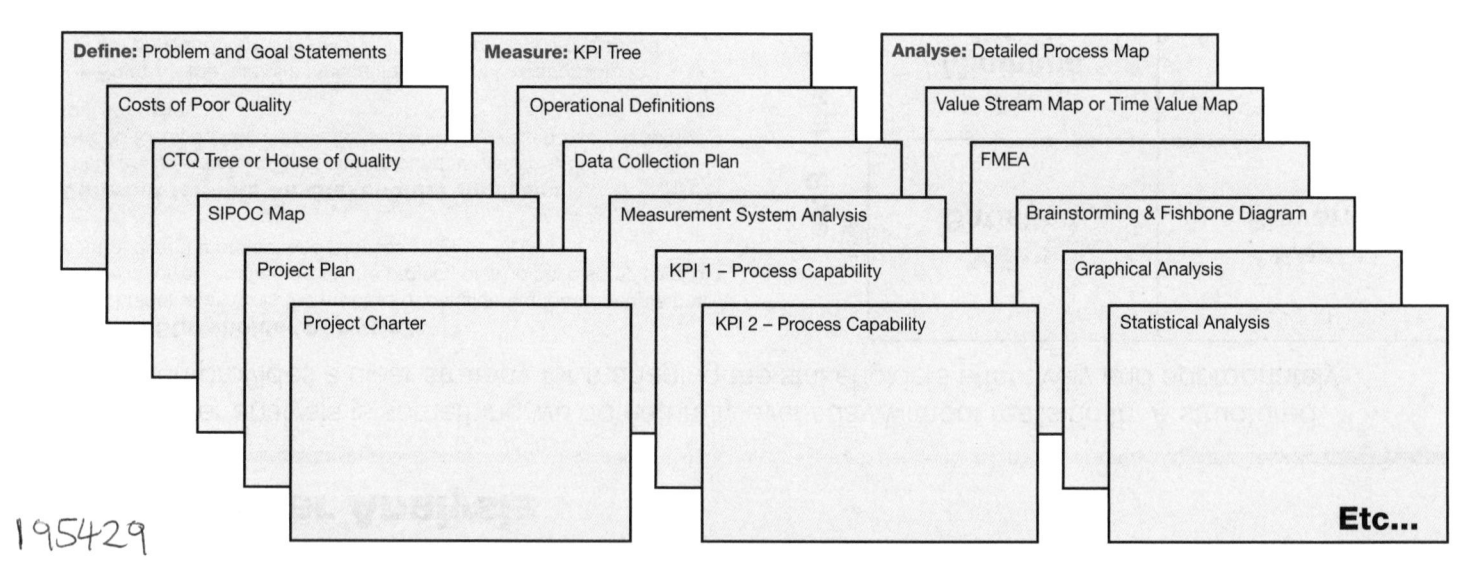

Define: Problem and Goal Statements
Costs of Poor Quality
CTQ Tree or House of Quality
SIPOC Map
Project Plan
Project Charter

Measure: KPI Tree
Operational Definitions
Data Collection Plan
Measurement System Analysis
KPI 1 – Process Capability
KPI 2 – Process Capability

Analyse: Detailed Process Map
Value Stream Map or Time Value Map
FMEA
Brainstorming & Fishbone Diagram
Graphical Analysis
Statistical Analysis
Etc...

195429

Facilitation Skills

Many Lean and Six Sigma techniques involve cross-functional teams where strong facilitation skills are critical to engaging all of the participants and getting maximum value from the event.

The role of a facilitator:
Whether it's a routine meeting, a process mapping event, a brainstorming session, or any other team activity, the facilitator's role is to ensure that the event delivers maximum value by:

- Preparing for the event.
- Getting the right people involved.
- Setting and communicating clear objectives, goals and scope.
- Maintaining a professional approach and leading by example.
- Keeping things focused.
- Establishing ground rules and ensuring they are respected.
- Ensuring participants feel able to engage with the process.
- Managing the physical environment (space, temperature, oxygen!).
- Keeping track of time.
- Managing the group dynamics (see Effective Teams on next page).
- Encouraging creativity.
- Managing the process (are the activities focused on the goals).
- Delegating where appropriate to ensure the group can stay focused.
- Having back up plans in place to cope with the unexpected.
- Steering the group towards decisions that have a consensus.

Facilitating versus doing:
Successful facilitators are those that are aware that they don't personally have to deliver the process map, figure out the root cause of a problem, or develop its solution. Instead, they understand that their role is to facilitate those outputs from their team.

The role of feedback: Developing facilitation skills takes time and lots of practice, and constructive feedback is an essential part of the development process. The opportunity for team members to give feedback to a facilitator should therefore be an integral and routine part of any group activity. So, at the end of a process mapping workshop for example, the group should not only review the process map and agree on next steps, but also provide feedback to the facilitator on what they did well (in terms of facilitation), and what they could focus on in the future. Routine, constructive feedback is a key part of cultural change.

The facilitators role is not easy! Of all the skills required by an improvement professional, being an effective facilitator is one of the most difficult to develop and yet will often make the difference between success and failure. Facilitation skills should therefore be a respected and core skill within any improvement programme.

! **Facilitation requires constant concentration and can therefore be very tiring!** So, be realistic in your goals. An all day event may be too much for both you and for your team. Perhaps a series of shorter events will enable everyone to be at the peak of their performance every time.

There's always room for improvement! So make sure that every time you facilitate an event, you choose an aspect of your facilitation skills that you are particularly going to focus on improving that day.

Effective Teams

An effective team doesn't happen by chance – it requires careful development and management:
All teams will include a variety of different characters, and team members inevitably need time to figure each other out and develop their own 'niche' within the team. Until that process is well progressed, the team will not be fully focused or delivering its full potential. Perhaps the most famous model for team development was developed by Bruce Tuckman, and is still relevant today. It proposes four stages:

Forming: Initially, team members will focus on being accepted within the group. Conflict is rare at this stage, while members assess each other and their new environment. Team leaders should be directive at this stage, facilitating introductions and setting clear agendas etc.

Storming: As the team leader starts to establish the group purpose and the way forward, differences of opinion, personal agendas and stronger characters will come to the fore. Team leaders should ensure they provide maximum clarity at this stage, and focus on managing key individuals that might be preventing the group moving forwards.

Norming: As the group settles into accepted methods of working, with established roles, behaviours and hierarchies, it develops a stronger identity and becomes more constructive. On an individual level, team members will generally feel more comfortable working within the team. Facilitation should focus on achieving agreed goals (through delegation where appropriate) and providing coaching to team members if needed.

Performing: A mature team is one whose team members work together constructively, and consistently deliver the teams objectives without significant support. The team leader can therefore focus on the progress of the team towards its goals, rather than day to day facilitation.

Effective Meetings

A culture of effective meetings can bring substantial efficiencies to most organisations:
Many people spend the majority of their working hours in meetings and often feel that they have little time for anything else! Effective meetings can therefore provide real benefits throughout an entire organisation, as well as within individual improvement projects.

Effective meetings require effective facilitation, and therefore many of the points on the previous page are applicable here too. In addition, the following points apply particularly to effective meetings:

- **Do you really need a meeting?** Could it be completed through several small discussions or emails?
- **Do you really need all of the invitees?** Inviting people that are not essential creates a larger group that is more difficult to manage.
- **The shorter the better!** Meetings are not workshops. They should move with more pace, and discussions should move quickly to decisions.
- **The chairman (i.e. the facilitator)** need not be the project leader. It's tempting to facilitate your own meetings, but it might also be best not too.
- **Set clear ground rules and follow them – lead by example!** Losing 5-10 minutes of a one hour meeting is a significant loss. Get their early, so that you always start on time, and manage interruptions rigorously.
- **Adhere to a clear routine:** If the meeting is regular, start with the actions from the last meeting, complete the meeting, and then review new actions from this meeting. This needs to happen consistently to work.
- **And most importantly:** A zero tolerance to phones and emails. If someone's mind is elsewhere, then they might as well be elsewhere!

Project Charter

A project charter is used to summarise the findings of the Define phase of the project.

The importance of pace in the Define phase:

Too many projects take too long to complete the Define stage, causing a lack of momentum before the project even gets started! In practice, the Define phase should be viewed as a screening process. The process generates a clear project scope, business case and project team, but it should also be possible for a project to be stopped at the Define phase review – the potential benefits might not be sufficient, the availability of resource might be an issue, or the solution may be pre-prescribed. A rapid pace through Define indicates that the project has the support and resource it needs to succeed.

A typical Project Charter contains:

- **Project Title** – this should state what the project is going to do.

- **Team Structure** – Project Sponsor, Project Leader, Team Members.

- **Problem Statement** and **Goal Statement.**

- **COPQ** – a summary of the cost of the problem to the business.

- **VOC** – the key customers and their Critical to Quality issues (CTQs).

- **Scope** – the scope of the project in terms of products, departments, locations, processes etc.

- **Stakeholders** – a list of the key stakeholders.

- **Project Plan** – planned dates for completion of the DMAIC phases.

Where does the Project Charter fit in?

To help the Define phase review, a Project Charter (also known as a summary/mandate/project description) is a **one page** document that enables all the stakeholders to review the project and commit to its support. A Project Charter is the Lean Six Sigma equivalent of the more traditional (and formal) project approval processes.

Project Charter			
Project Title:			

Project Team		Stakeholders	
Role	Name	Role	Name
Project Sponsor		Six Sigma Champion?	
Project Leader			
Team Members			

Problem Statement	Goal Statement

COPQ Summary	VOC - key customers

Scope	Project Plan	Plan	Actual
	Start of project		
	End of Define		
	End of Measure		
	End of Analyse		
	End of Improve		
	End of Control & Project		

 **Project Charter Template.xls**

Define – Checklist ☑

- ☐ Is the problem clear? And is there data / evidence to support the problem statement?
- ☐ Are the goals of the project clear (Goal Statement) and are they realistic at this stage?
- ☐ Does the project have a clear business case? (a problem linked to Costs of Poor Quality linked to business benefits).
- ☐ Has the potential business benefit been estimated in cash?
- ☐ Is the process involved clearly understood? (using SIPOC?)
- ☐ Are the internal and external customer(s) of the process clear?
- ☐ Are the customer's needs understood? And supported by evidence/data?
- ☐ Is the project focused on a customer requirement?
- ☐ Is the scope of the project clear?
- ☐ Are the key stakeholders in the project/process identified and a communication plan in place to manage them?

Project Management:
- ☐ Does the project have clear sponsorship?
- ☐ Is there a team in place with the time and resources to complete the project (within current scope)?
- ☐ Is there a structure in place for managing the team on a short term basis?
- ☐ Is a preliminary project plan in place (including planned finish date)? Does the plan have clear milestones and deliverables?

Define – Review Questions

- ■ Why this project?
- ■ How does it relate to the businesses needs? (strategic/operational)
- ■ In what ways does the problem impact the bottom line (cash)?
- ■ How much of the problem do you hope to eliminate?
- ■ Does the team have first hand experience of the process? If not, how do they intend to get it?
- ■ How does this project relate to the end customer? Who is it?
- ■ What has been done to really understand the customers requirements (VOC)?
- ■ What is the scope of the project? Are there any issues or overlaps with other projects to resolve?
- ■ Has this problem been looked at before? What happened?
- ■ Who are the key stakeholders in the project? Why?
- ■ How will the stakeholders be managed?

Project Management:
- ■ Who is accountable for this project's success? (The Sponsor?)
- ■ Is the project team in place? If so, who was selected? Why?
- ■ Does the project have enough time/resource?
- ■ Have the key team members freed up their time for this project?
- ■ How will the team be managed?
- ■ How will the project be documented?
- ■ What are the key milestones within the project plan?
- ■ What are the next steps right after this review?

Measure – Overview

The Measure phase aims to set a stake in the ground in terms of process performance (a baseline) through the development of clear and meaningful measurement systems.

The flow through Measure:

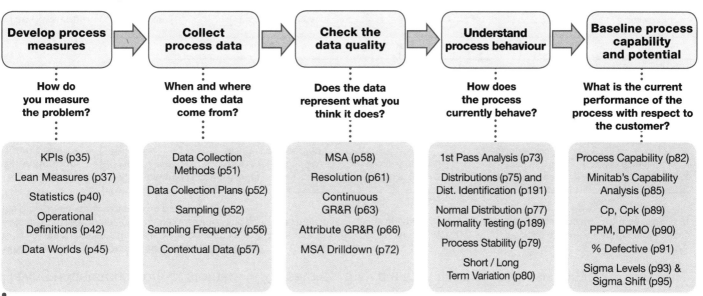

Develop process measures	Collect process data	Check the data quality	Understand process behaviour	Baseline process capability and potential
How do you measure the problem?	When and where does the data come from?	Does the data represent what you think it does?	How does the process currently behave?	What is the current performance of the process with respect to the customer?
KPIs (p35)	Data Collection Methods (p51)	MSA (p58)	1st Pass Analysis (p73)	Process Capability (p82)
Lean Measures (p37)	Data Collection Plans (p52)	Resolution (p61)	Distributions (p75) and Dist. Identification (p191)	Minitab's Capability Analysis (p85)
Statistics (p40)	Sampling (p52)	Continuous GR&R (p63)	Normal Distribution (p77) Normality Testing (p189)	Cp, Cpk (p89)
Operational Definitions (p42)	Sampling Frequency (p56)	Attribute GR&R (p66)	Process Stability (p79)	PPM, DPMO (p90)
Data Worlds (p45)	Contextual Data (p57)	MSA Drilldown (p72)	Short / Long Term Variation (p80)	% Defective (p91)
				Sigma Levels (p93) & Sigma Shift (p95)

❗ Don't be tempted to jump ahead to root causes (Analyse) or solutions (Improve) until the process can be measured effectively. The Measure phase builds upon the existing data available (introducing new data collection and measurements if necessary) in order to fully understand the historical behaviour of the process. Team members on their first Six Sigma project often find the Measure phase surprisingly detailed and rigorous but, with experience, realise that it is a worthwhile investment that always pays off later in the project.

Key Performance Indicators (KPIs)

Having understood your customers CTQ features, they are then used as the basis for your KPIs.

What are Key Performance Indicators (KPIs)?

KPIs are measurements that reflect the performance of the process. The acronym 'KPI' is widespread but they can also be called Primary Metrics. KPIs need to reflect the Voice of the Customer, and so the example below builds upon the Critical to Quality specifications that were developed in the broadband repair example on pages 23/24.

CTQ Specifications (from page 24)	Calls answered within 7 rings	Updates available by phone within 30 minutes of reporting	All faults fixed within 4 hours	Maximum of one visit to access the customer site	No re-occurrence of same fault within 90 days
Customer driven KPIs	% of calls answered within 7 rings	% of updates available within 30 mins	% of faults fixed within 4 hours	% of faults fixed with one (or less) visit to access customer site	% of faults with no re-occurrence within 90 days
The data you will need to collect	Time taken to answer each call	Time between fault reporting and update being available	Time to fix each fault	Number of visits to access customer site	Number of re-occurrences of fault within 90 days

Collecting the right data for KPIs:

Customer driven KPIs are usually percentages that classify the process output into pass or fail categories based upon the customer's CTQs.

However, in order to calculate these KPIs, you should aim to collect the raw data of the process (such as the **actual** time to answer each call).

Efficiency versus effectiveness:

The KPIs shown above focus on measuring the **effectiveness** of the process in the eyes of the customer. However, a project should also have some KPIs that reflect the **efficiency** of the process from the business perspective.

Efficiency KPIs are included in the KPI tree (next page).

Key Performance Indicator (KPI) Trees

A KPI Tree is a visual method of displaying a range of process measures that are relevant to your project or process. It's particularly useful for demonstrating the different categories of measures.

KPI Trees are a tool for bringing together a range of measures that are relevant to the situation (either a project or a process). Often, these measures will already exist within the organisation, and you can therefore 'source' them from other KPI trees. Alternatively, you might find that sometimes you have to develop some new measures.

Logical Categories:
It is useful to structure your KPI tree into logical categories (such as the blue shaded boxes in the example below), and to then check that you have found the right mixture of KPIs to represent each category.

A balanced approach:
A successful KPI Tree is one that contains a balance of measures covering both the **efficiency** and **effectiveness** of a process. So, for the example below where the project might be focused on improving the **speed** of repairing faults, the KPI tree also contains measures of customer satisfaction and the resource costs of repairing them. This is because it would be crazy to improve the speed of repair, only to find that your 'improvements' have made the customers more unhappy and that you have doubled the costs of repairing the fault!

So, you need a balance of measures covering quality, delivery and cost.

Fault Repair Project KPI Tree

Fixing the fault

% fixed within 4 hrs

% faults fixed in one or less visits

% faults with no re-occurrence within 90 days

Average # of visits / fault

Interacting with the customer

% customers satisfied with repair service

Helpdesk

% calls answered within 7 rings

% updates available within 30 minutes

Average answer time

Managing the business

Average resource hours per fault

faults repaired per week

repair department employees

Lean Measures

There are a number of Lean Measures that can be used to assess the lean performance of a process.

Processing Time (PT) – The lead time of an individual process step.

Queue Time (QT) – The queuing time between two process steps.

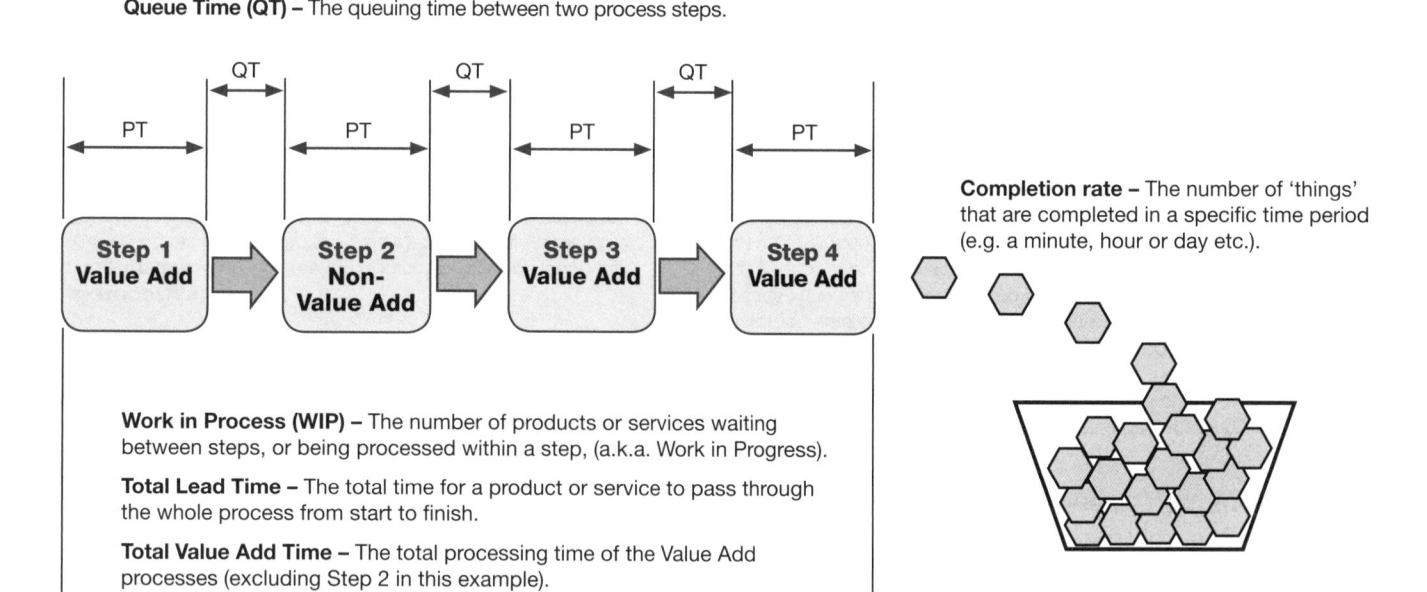

Completion rate – The number of 'things' that are completed in a specific time period (e.g. a minute, hour or day etc.).

Work in Process (WIP) – The number of products or services waiting between steps, or being processed within a step, (a.k.a. Work in Progress).

Total Lead Time – The total time for a product or service to pass through the whole process from start to finish.

Total Value Add Time – The total processing time of the Value Add processes (excluding Step 2 in this example).

Lean Measures: Process Cycle Efficiency, Lead and Takt Time

The Lean Measures can be combined to calculate several key Lean KPIs, as follows:

Process Cycle Efficiency (PCE) is the primary lean measure, combining elements of both speed (lead time) and value.

It represents the proportion of time spent in the process that a product or service is actually being worked on in a way that is adding value for the customer.

$$\text{PCE (\%)} = \frac{\text{Total Value Add Time}}{\text{Total Lead Time}}$$

So what PCE does a Lean process have?

As always, it depends on the type of process and environment, but here are some guidelines:

- Typical transactional and service type processes have a PCE of up to 10%, and a world class lean target would be 50% or more.

- Typical production processes have a PCE of up to 20%, and a world class Lean target would be 25%, or more for continuous processes.

Benchmarking PCE is difficult due to the different ways in which Value Add Time can be measured. However, the most important issue is that you measure it in a **consistent** way, and then improve on it.

Lead Time (the speed of a process) is an important Lean KPI. It can be calculated directly by measuring actual lead times from the process, or alternatively an average lead time can be calculated using Little's Law below.

This method is a useful reminder that WIP is a major cause of long lead times, and that reducing WIP is one of the best ways of achieving a faster process.

$$\text{Average Lead Time} = \frac{\text{WIP}}{\text{Completion Rate}}$$

Takt Time (the drumbeat of a process) is also an important Lean measure, but it is not strictly a KPI. Instead, it represents the rate of customer demand and is calculated by dividing the available work time in a day, by the number of products required by the customer in a day. Being aware of the Takt Time is critical when designing a Lean process, in order that it provides products at the rate the customers require them.

$$\text{Takt Time} = \frac{\text{Available Work Time}}{\text{Customer demand}}$$

Lean Measures: Overall Equipment Effectiveness (OEE)

As the name suggests, OEE is an overall measure that reflects performance from several perspectives.

The Overall Equipment Effectiveness (OEE) metric combines aspects of reliability, performance and quality into a single KPI (expressed as a percentage). Because it covers such broad inputs, OEE can be a useful metric when trying to improve the management and performance of a critical piece of equipment (particularly in terms of its maintenance, production scheduling, day to day operation and process capability).

OEE has links with many components of the Lean approach, particularly:

- **Total Productive Maintenance** – focusing on reducing unplanned stoppages through planned, predictive maintenance.

- **Rapid Changeovers** – which aims to reduce changeover times, enabling flexibility in scheduling, shorter batches and reduced WIP.

- **Reducing Waste** – defects are one of the seven wastes (p107).

Is the tail wagging the dog!?

OEE is intended to help drive improvement by highlighting which elements of your equipment (its availability, performance or quality) require the most focus. However, if an organisation becomes focused on improving OEE at all costs, then this can actually result in behaviours that are counter to the Lean approach.

For example, in a bid to improve OEE, a scheduling department may decide to run larger batches on a particular machine (in order to avoid the lost time and bad parts that result from a changeover). While this might improve the OEE measure, larger batches would result in higher inventory (WIP) and longer lead times – not very Lean at all!

Instead, the OEE measure should be used to highlight that improving changeover performance (faster with less scrap) would improve OEE and enable smaller batches and lower inventory – much Leaner!

OEE (%) **=** **Availability (%)**
Is the equipment available to run? **X** **Performance (%)**
Does it produce the level of output that it should do? **X** **Quality (%)**
Does it make good quality output?

! It's important to make sure that operational definitions (p42) are in place for each component of the OEE measure, to ensure that it is measured consistently.

Actual Availability
(after changeovers and *unplanned* losses such as breakdowns)
―――――――――――
Planned Availability
(excluding *planned* downtime such as breaks and *planned* maintenance)

Actual Output
(all parts, good and bad)
―――――――――――
Predicted Output
(based upon actual availability, and the machines cycle time)

Good parts produced
―――――――――――
Total parts produced
(including all bad parts and those made during changeovers)

Statistics for Summarising Process <u>Position</u>

It is more than likely that your chosen KPIs involve an 'average' of some kind. Despite the common use of the arithmetic average, it is worth remembering that there are alternatives!

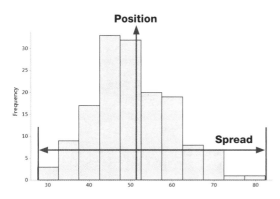

The two key features of a histogram are its central **Position** and its **Spread**:

The **Spread** of the histogram (how wide it is) is important because it gives an indication of the amount of variation in the process. This is explained further on the next page.

The **Position** of the histogram refers to where the process is centred. There are two common statistics that can be used to reflect Position:

1) The Average – commonly used because it is easy to understand and calculate. The average works well where the process is reasonably symmetrical and there are not any 'outliers' (unexpectedly small or large data points) which can significantly affect the calculation of the average.

2) The Median – less widely used, but a useful statistic due to its 'robustness'. The median is defined as the middle value of the data (the 50th percentile) and its calculation is not significantly affected by any outliers in the data.

Alternative terminology for the average:

- **Mean –** sometimes used instead of average.

- **$\bar{X}$ –** (pronounced 'X Bar') – used to represent the average of a sample.

- **μ –** (pronounced 'mu') – used to represent the average of the total population.

NB: In theory, X Bar and Mu are for use in the different situations described above. In reality, they're often used interchangeably (although this isn't very good statistical practice).

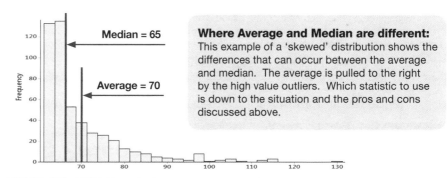

Where Average and Median are different:
This example of a 'skewed' distribution shows the differences that can occur between the average and median. The average is pulled to the right by the high value outliers. Which statistic to use is down to the situation and the pros and cons discussed above.

Statistics for Summarising Process <u>Spread</u>

Six Sigma focuses on reducing process variation and so a measurement for variation is essential.

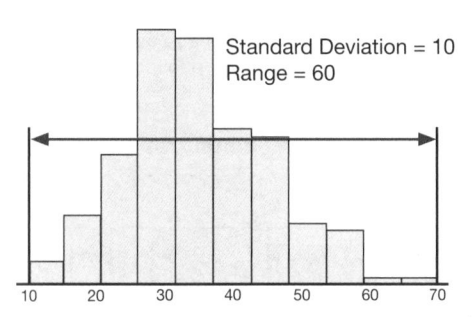

Standard Deviation = 10
Range = 60

Standard Deviation = 3
Range = 15

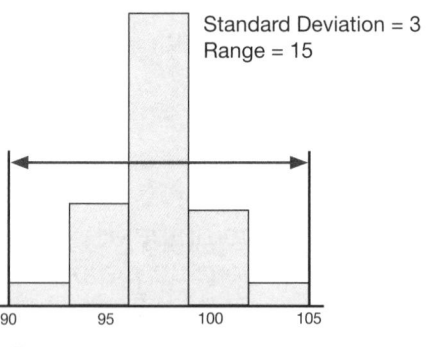

The **Spread** of the histogram indicates the amount of variation in the process. There are two alternative statistics that can be used to measure variation:

1) Range – commonly used because it is easy to understand. The range is the difference between the maximum and minimum results, and because of this 'simple' approach it is not very robust. Just one outlier in the process will increase the range dramatically.

2) Standard Deviation – is a more robust measure of variation, but it is perceived as difficult to understand because it is not easy to picture what it is. See below for an explanation.

What is Standard Deviation?

A **practical** definition of Standard Deviation is:

> *"The average distance of the data points from their own average".*

The distance of the data points from their own average is shown graphically here by the blue dotted lines on the Time Series plot.

The symbol used for standard deviation is the Greek symbol ' **σ** ' - pronounced Sigma!

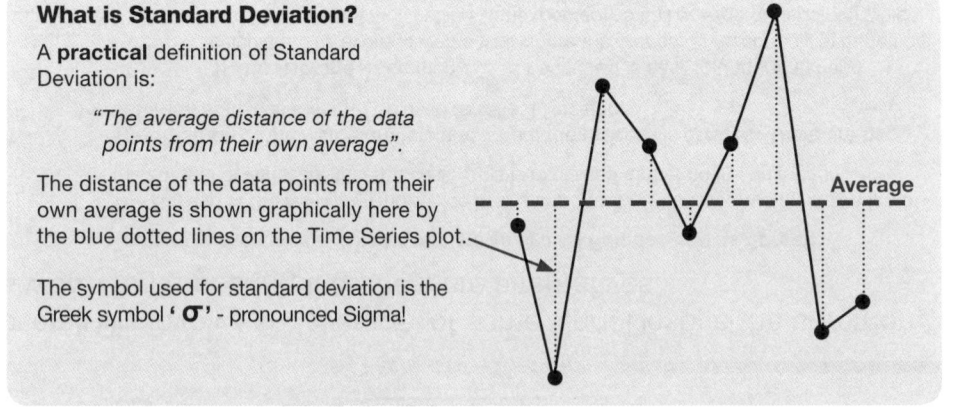

Average

⬇ **Distributions.mpj** This data file contains a selection of the different distributions shown over the last two pages.

Operational Definitions

Operational Definitions are developed to provide clear and unambiguous descriptions of each KPI.

Components of an Operational Definition:

- **KPI Name:** The terminology selected must be used consistently throughout the project. It is also useful to number the KPIs (for the duration of the project at least).

- **What is the KPI supposed to represent:** A down to earth description of the measurement (that someone who is not involved in the organisation or project could understand).

- **Process Diagram or Drawing:** (see next page).

- **Detailed definition:** Providing more detail aims to avoid any areas of ambiguity that might lead to the measurement being recorded differently by different people or systems.

- **Measurement Scope:** Although this is largely defined by the scope of your project, it might be that the some measurements cannot coincide entirely with the project scope.

What happens without an Operational Definition:

- Unreliable data will be collected in different ways.
- Different standards will be applied in different areas.

An Operation Definition example for the Fault Repair Time KPI (referenced on pages 35 and 36):

KPI Name: Fault Repair Time

What does the KPI represent: The time elapsed between the customer reporting the fault and the service provider informing the customer that the fault is fixed.

Process Diagram/Picture: see next page.

Detailed Definition:
Process start – the time (in days/hours/minutes/seconds) that the fault handling centre logs the call or e-mail as 'received'.

Process stop – the time that the phone call or e-mail (informing the customer the fault is fixed) is made/sent.

Customer Focused KPIs:
At this point, it is often found that **existing** measurements are not very customer focused. For example, the fault repair time (as defined above) is measured from the time at which the fault is **reported**, but would clearly be more customer focused if it were measured from the **actual** time of failure.

In reality this is usually more difficult to measure, and so a compromise is required. The benefit of developing an Operational Definition is that the project team are forced to consider these issues, where they might otherwise have been ignored.

Operational Definition Diagrams

A process diagram or picture is an essential part of an effective Operational Definition.

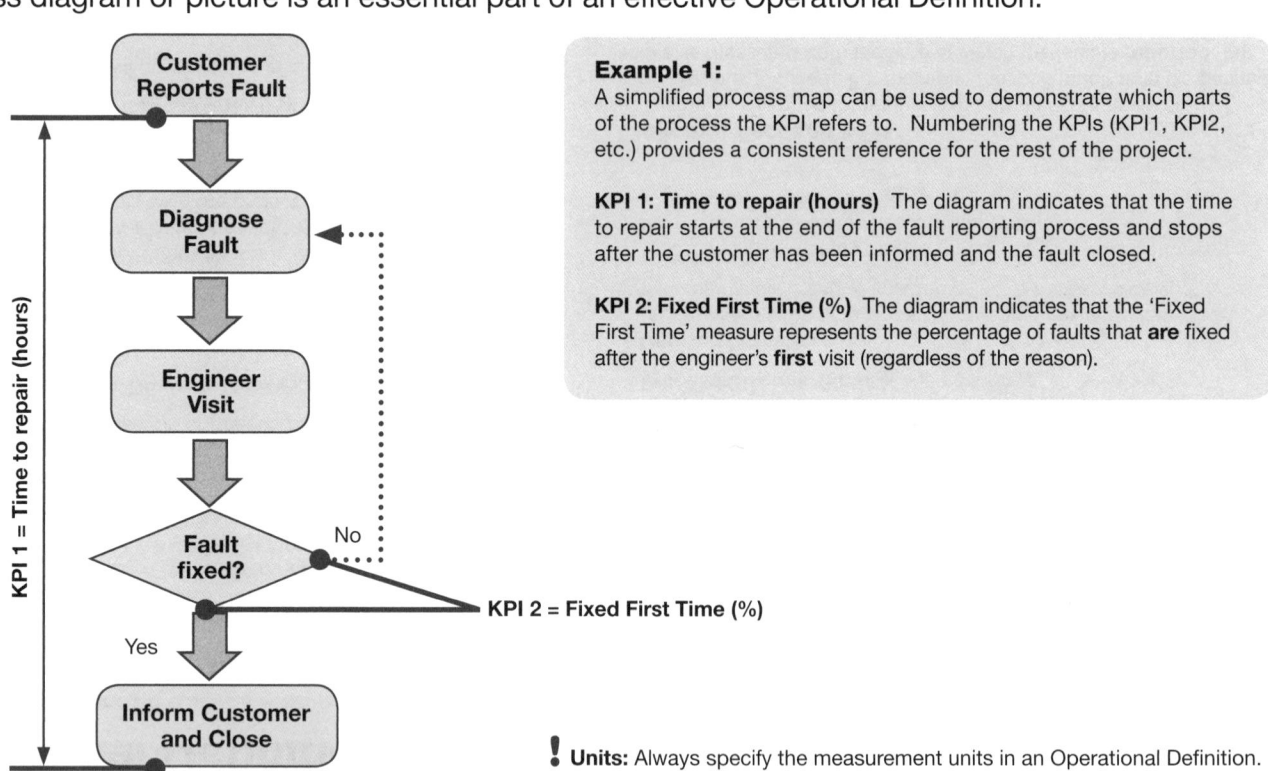

Example 1:
A simplified process map can be used to demonstrate which parts of the process the KPI refers to. Numbering the KPIs (KPI1, KPI2, etc.) provides a consistent reference for the rest of the project.

KPI 1: Time to repair (hours) The diagram indicates that the time to repair starts at the end of the fault reporting process and stops after the customer has been informed and the fault closed.

KPI 2: Fixed First Time (%) The diagram indicates that the 'Fixed First Time' measure represents the percentage of faults that **are** fixed after the engineer's **first** visit (regardless of the reason).

! Units: Always specify the measurement units in an Operational Definition.

Operational Definition Diagrams (cont.)

Example 2: The measurement (and units) of the width of this ring pull are indicated on a photograph.

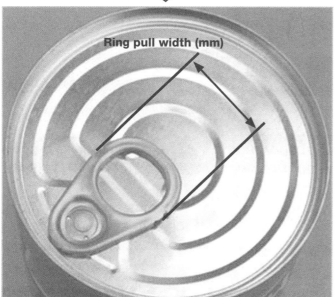

Ring pull width (mm)

Example 3: The acceptability of a defect on this weld is best demonstrated in a photo (or with a real sample part).

Unacceptable

Data Worlds – Overview

All numeric data can be placed into one of the three Six Sigma Data Worlds described below. Understanding the different data worlds is an important discipline because it has implications for the type of analysis, tools and techniques that will be used later on.

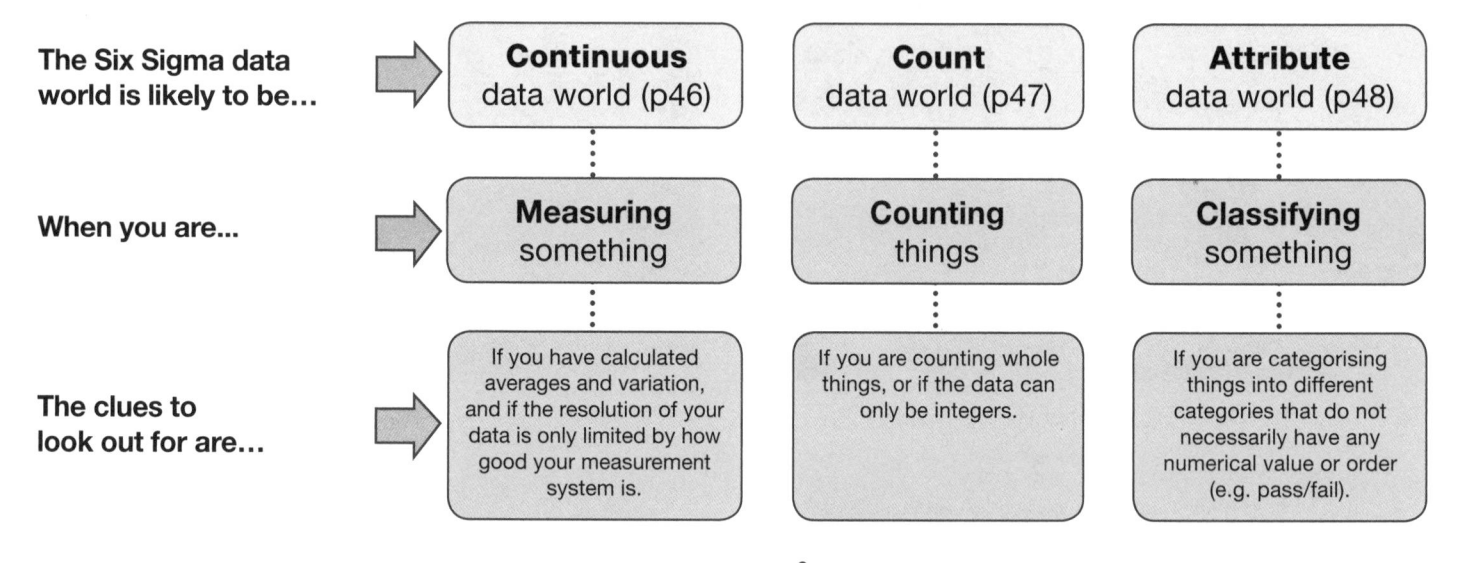

The Six Sigma data world is likely to be...

| **Continuous** data world (p46) | **Count** data world (p47) | **Attribute** data world (p48) |

When you are...

| **Measuring** something | **Counting** things | **Classifying** something |

The clues to look out for are...

| If you have calculated averages and variation, and if the resolution of your data is only limited by how good your measurement system is. | If you are counting whole things, or if the data can only be integers. | If you are categorising things into different categories that do not necessarily have any numerical value or order (e.g. pass/fail). |

Data Worlds – a forgotten principle:
Many training programs do not cover data worlds in enough detail. Understanding the different data worlds and their implications in detail is critical to ensuring that a Six Sigma analyst will be able to select the right tool or technique when back in their workplace.

! There are a variety of different terminologies used for the data worlds which can be very confusing. Appendix D compares and explains the different terminologies in more detail. The terms **Continuous**, **Count** and **Attribute** will be used consistently throughout this text.

The Continuous Data World

Continuous data results from **measuring** a product or service characteristic.

55.8
56.4
36.2
59.7
54.8
54.0
43.3
42.9
53.7
31.2
63.8
45.3
34.5
44.3

This data (left) is typical of **Continuous** data because it is clearly not limited to whole numbers.

This data could represent:

- Time to fill new job vacancies (days)
- The diameter of a metal shaft (millimetres)
- Oven temperatures (degrees)
- Letter weights (grams)
- Pressure (kg/cm²)
- Invoice processing time (days)

Note: Always state the units of Continuous data.

A **statistical model** that Continuous data sometimes follows (under certain conditions) is the Normal distribution (see page 77 for more details).

A **graphical tool** often used for analysing Continuous data is the histogram, as shown on the right.

Statistics: Continuous data is usually summarised by statistics such as **average** and **median** (which indicate the position of the data), and **range** and **standard deviation** (which indicate how wide the distribution is).

! A trap to avoid with Continuous data:

Sometimes the resolution of the measurement system can affect how the data appears. For example, data on the processing times of invoices might be rounded to the nearest day (so the data opposite would be recorded as 56, 56, 36, etc.). This can be misleading because it is still Continuous data, but the measurement system is rounding to the nearest whole number, making the data look 'discrete' (like Count data).

A histogram – A common tool for analysing Continuous data:

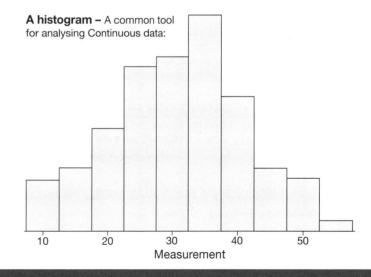

The Count Data World

As the name implies, Count data results from **counting** things. Sometimes you will be counting defects and sometimes counting volumes.

1
2
3
4
2
1
0
1

45
37
39
21
36
29
31
35

These data sets (left) are typical of **Count** data because they are all whole numbers.

This data could represent:

- Errors on invoices
- Applicants for vacant job positions
- Calls to an IT helpdesk during each hour
- Scrap parts in each production batch
- Scratches on sheets of glass
- Parcels delivered in a day

A **histogram** is often used for analysing Count data (see right).

The statistical model that Count data follows (when under statistical control) is the Poisson distribution, shown in the histogram opposite. When the average result is low, the Poisson distribution is skewed to the right, because it is impossible to count less than zero.

Statistics: Count data is usually summarised by calculating the **average** results. This is commonly known as the average 'Defects per unit' (DPU), and for the examples above might be 'average errors per invoice' or 'average number of applicants per job vacancy' etc.

How to spot Count data:

- **Half units are not possible** – half an error, half an applicant, half a call, or half a scratch just don't happen!
- **No physical upper limit** – in theory there is no upper limit to any of these Counts.
- **Zero is possible** - it should be possible to have a zero result.
- Count data is always recorded for a **specific area of opportunity** such as an invoice, a vacant position or an hour of IT helpdesk time.

Central position
Referred to as 'DPU'
(average Defects per unit)

Count Data.mpj Contains examples of several different ways in which Count data can be recorded in Minitab.

The Attribute Data World

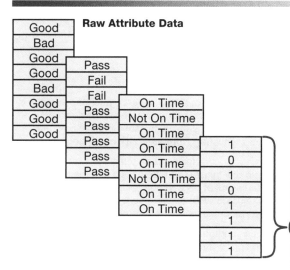

Raw Attribute Data

Good			
Bad			
Good	Pass		
Good	Fail		
Bad	Fail		
Good	Pass	On Time	
Good	Pass	Not On Time	
Good	Pass	On Time	1
	Pass	On Time	0
	Pass	On Time	1
		Not On Time	0
		On Time	1
		On Time	1
			1
			1

Attribute data results from **classifying** things.

All the data sets on the left are typical of Attribute data in its 'raw' state. The first thing you notice is that they are not all numerical data, but there are always only two categories, so Attribute data tends to look binary (as in the example containing 0s & 1s).

Depending on the industry sector involved, these data sets could represent:

- Computer inspection results
- Network availability
- Part availability
- On time delivery
- Helpdesk problem resolution
- Customer satisfaction

Summarised Attribute Data		
Number with Attribute	**Sample Size**	**%**
2	8	25.0
3	10	30.0
10	90	11.1
8	65	12.3
5	40	12.5
4	41	9.8
30	252	11.9

The statistical model that Attribute data follows (when under statistical control) is the Binomial distribution. Everyday examples that follow the Binomial distribution include tossing a coin, picking a playing card, or throwing a dice.

Statistics: Attribute data is usually summarised as a percentage. Percentages are one of the most common statistics in use, and in every case, a percentage implies that there were two categories of possible results, such as pass/fail.

Raw & Summarised Data:

The table on the left contains Attribute data in a **summarised** format. Each line represents a sample of **raw** Attribute data.

So, the first line (two out of eight) **summarises** the same information shown in the **raw** data samples from the top left of the page.

The third column is the same Attribute data converted into percentages.

⬇ **Attribute Data.mpj** Contains examples of several different ways in which Attribute data can be recorded in Minitab.

Comparing the Data Worlds

The performance of most processes is reported as a percentage (Attribute data). However, the Continuous and Count data worlds have more resolution and are therefore more valuable for analysis.

The graphs opposite show how Continuous or Count data can always be summarised as Attribute data.

The **performance** of a process is usually reported in % (Attribute data), because it is simpler to understand. However, **analysis** of the problem is far easier in the 'richer' data worlds of Continuous and Count data. Of course, it is also a compromise of:

- **Cost:** Continuous and Count data cost more because they take longer to collect and require more complex collection systems. It is far easier and quicker to implement an Attribute data system that just categorises results into groups of pass or fail (but the data is not as valuable).

- **Resolution and understanding:** Continuous and Count data provides more resolution. Instead of classifying a product or service into one of two categories (pass or fail), they provide more understanding of the extent to which something was good or bad.

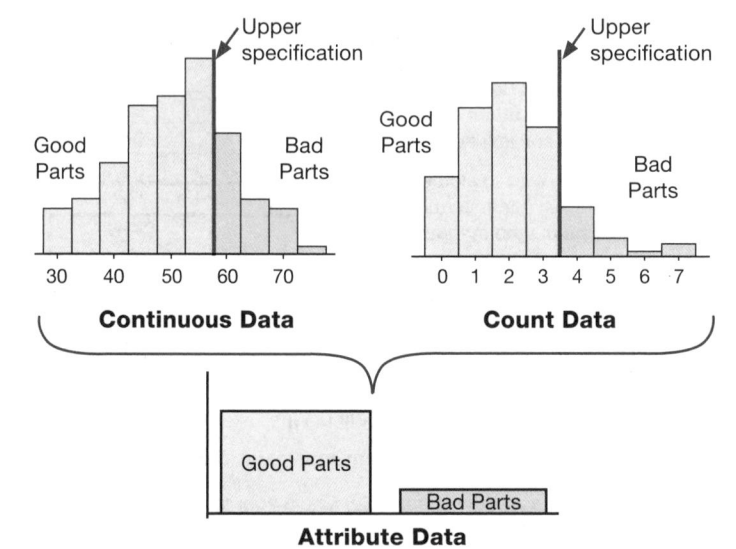

So...

...instead of asking a customer if they are satisfied or not (Attribute) – try and grade their satisfaction between 1 and 10 (Continuous).

...instead of recording if a delivery is on time or not (Attribute) – try and measure exactly how early or late it is (Continuous).

...instead of asking if a car is clean or not after being washed (Attribute) – record the number of bits of dirt that are still there (Count).

...instead of recording if the diameter of a football is within official specifications or not (Attribute) – measure exactly how big it is (Continuous).

Data Worlds – Summary

Building on the overview at the beginning of this Data Worlds section (p45), this summary incorporates the statistical models and statistics that have been introduced on pages 46 to 48.

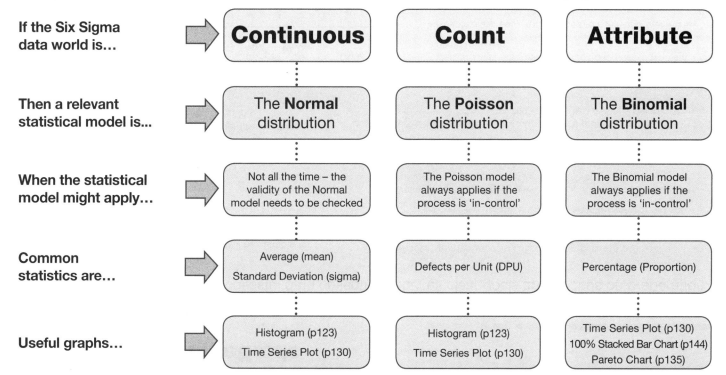

	Continuous	**Count**	**Attribute**
If the Six Sigma data world is...			
Then a relevant statistical model is...	The **Normal** distribution	The **Poisson** distribution	The **Binomial** distribution
When the statistical model might apply...	Not all the time – the validity of the Normal model needs to be checked	The Poisson model always applies if the process is 'in-control'	The Binomial model always applies if the process is 'in-control'
Common statistics are...	Average (mean) Standard Deviation (sigma)	Defects per Unit (DPU)	Percentage (Proportion)
Useful graphs...	Histogram (p123) Time Series Plot (p130)	Histogram (p123) Time Series Plot (p130)	Time Series Plot (p130) 100% Stacked Bar Chart (p144) Pareto Chart (p135)

Data Collection Methods

Data collection is an expensive process and yet most companies collect large amounts of poor quality data with high duplication. Successful data collection requires clear goals and a focus on preparation.

Existing or new data collection?

Be careful not to assume that existing data will be suitable for your project. Instead, you should compare any existing data against your Operational Definitions to decide if it is suitable for your needs.

Two key types of data collection:

- **In-Process** – where data collection is integrated into the process and therefore recorded automatically.

- **Manual** – where the data collection system is additional to the process and recorded by text or typing.

Checksheets are **manual** data collection forms which enable the information to be recorded by 'checking' a pro-forma sheet in the appropriate space. They are generally used to collect information on a temporary basis (i.e. for the duration of an improvement project).

- **Traveller Checksheets** – stay with a product or service throughout the process, collecting information at each stage.

- **Failure Checksheets** – collect information on the reasons for failure at specific process steps (see example on this page).

- **Visual Checksheets** – use pictures of the process or product to record where a failure occurred (e.g: car hire damage diagrams).

Invoice Number	Supplier	Reason For Failure				
		No PO	Wrong Value	Carriage Not Agreed	Tax Wrong	Other
454	Pro-Form	✔				
A633	Magna-Tech			✔		
A657	Magna-Tech					Not Received
LKS22	LKS	✔				
LKS25	LKS				✔	
476	Pro-Form					

Hints and Tips for Checksheets:

- Design the checksheet with a team of people who are going to use it.

- Keep it clear, easy and obvious to use – and trial it first.

- Communicate – if you don't let people know why they are being asked to fill in a checksheet, then they won't fill it in!

- Traceability – do not forget to record names, dates, serial numbers. This is useful contextual data – see page 57.

- Beware the 'other' column – if you end up with all your failures being classed under this column, then your reason columns are not the right ones.

Data Collection Plans and Sampling

Having decided what to measure and how to record it, a Data Collection Plan specifies how much data will be collected (the sample size), and how often (the sampling frequency).

Measure 100% or take a sample?

Too many organisations measure 100% of their output. This *'if in doubt, measure it'* approach is driven by a lack of confidence in the statistics.

In reality, most of the value of collected data is gained from the first few measurements taken – known as the Minimum Sample Size – and collecting more data than necessary provides ever decreasing returns in terms of statistical confidence and practical value.

Data collection from a Population or Process?

1) Collecting data from a static group is focused on a **Population**. Every day examples include taking a water sample from a swimming pool to estimate its chlorine content or market research with a focus group to estimate the population's view. In these situations, the main data collection decision is what **sample size** to use (how much data to collect).

2) Collecting data on an ongoing basis in order to detect changes over time, is focused on a **Process**. Everyday examples include tracking the fuel consumption of a car over its lifetime or monitoring a commute time to work. In these situations, the data collection decision is not only what **sample size** to use (how much), but also the **sampling frequency** (how often).

Sample Size (how much data) – (see next page), is based on the following considerations:

- The type of data (world) involved.
- The existing variation in the process.
- The precision required of the results.

Sampling Frequency (how often) – (p56), is based on the following factors:

- Any natural cycles that occur in the process.
- The precision required of the recorded data.
- The volume of products or service produced.

Minimum Sample Sizes – Continuous Data

The most common question concerning data collection is 'how much data should we collect?' Unfortunately the answer is often 'it depends'. But, there are some **minimum** guidelines:

For Continuous data, calculate the minimum sample size as follows:

How to calculate MSS for Continuous data

Estimate the standard deviation of the process (see right).

Decide on the precision that you require.

Calculate the minimum sample size (MSS) as follows:

((2 x Standard Deviation) / Precision)^2

NB: If the minimum sample size exceeds the parts available, measure them all (100%).

Example: Collecting data to assess the lead time of an invoice process. (Units are days)

Historically, invoices have taken anywhere from 10 – 30 days. So, estimate standard deviation at 4 days.

Required precision = +/- 2 days.

MSS = ((2 x 4) / 2)^2

= 16

So to estimate the mean invoice lead time to within +/- 2 days, you should collect at least 16 pieces of data.

Estimating standard deviation:
Knowing the variation in the process (standard deviation) helps to achieve a more realistic sample size. But how do you estimate standard deviation when you haven't even measured the process yet? The answer is that you estimate it.

A very basic approach for estimating standard deviation is to look at the historical range of a process (the difference between the highest and lowest results that you've seen) and to divide it by five.

Normally, there are around six standard deviations in the range, so this is a safe over-estimate.

Minimum Sample Sizes – Attribute (Discrete) Data

For Attribute data, calculate the minimum sample size as follows:

How to calculate MSS for Attribute data

Estimate the proportion of the process (p) – see opposite.

Decide on the precision that you require (d).

Calculate the minimum sample size (MSS) as follows:

$$MSS = (2 / d)^2 \times p \times (1-p)$$

If the minimum sample size exceeds the parts available, measure them all (100%).

Example: Collecting data to assess the proportion of furniture flat packs that are sold with parts missing. (Unit is one flat pack)

Historically you estimate the proportion is around 10% (expressed as 0.10).

Required precision = +/- 1.5% (expressed as 0.015).

$$MSS = (2 / 0.015)^2 \times 0.1 \times (1-0.1)$$

$$= 1600$$

So to estimate the proportion of flat packs sold with parts missing to within +/- 1.5%, you should collect at least 1600 pieces of data.

Estimating process proportion: Knowing the expected proportion in the process (p) helps to achieve a more realistic sample size.

But how do you know the expected proportion when you haven't even measured the process yet? The answer is that you estimate it.

Remember, it's just an estimate. If you later find it to be inaccurate, you can always recalculate your MSS.

This sample size example suggests a sample of 1600, which is **significantly** larger than the Continuous data example on the previous page (of just 16). This reflects the lower resolution and quality of the Attribute data world, as discussed on page 49.

Minimum Sample Sizes – Summary

Minimum sample sizes are just that – a **minimum** level that should be used as a sense check.

Where the minimum sample size can be used:
Minimum sample sizes are just a starting point for use in basic Six Sigma tools such as Histograms, Capability Studies and Sigma Levels. More advanced techniques such as SPC charts and Hypothesis Testing may require larger sample sizes.

The approaches explained in the previous pages can be used as a sense check when designing data collection plans during the Measure phase.

Firstly, calculate your minimum sample size then choose your data collection strategy, and then keep collecting data until you reach the minimum sample size **before** you make any calculations or decisions with the data.

Applying minimum sample sizes in reality:
In reality, the amount of data you have access to, and the time and resources you have available, can prevent you reaching the minimum sample size.

For example, if it takes one hour to collect one piece of Attribute data (pass/fail) for a specific product or service, then it could take several months to reach your minimum sample size.

Instead you could try and measure Continuous or Count data from the process since these are 'richer' data worlds and require smaller samples.

What if you cannot get enough data to meet the minimum sample size?

Use what you have got, but with the awareness that your confidence in any statistics or decisions generated from the data will be lower than you would like it to be.

Confidence Intervals can be used to assess the precision of any statistic that you do have – see page 151 for more details.

What if I have much _more_ data than my minimum sample size?

Don't complain! – but also check that you are not investing valuable resources in collecting unnecessarily large amounts of data.

It might be possible to reduce the amount of data being collected without compromising on the level of precision you require.

Sampling Frequency

Having decided to measure a process using a sampling approach, you will need to decide when and where to sample the process – **sampling frequency**.

Selecting the frequency with which to monitor your process:

Every process has some level of expected 'cycles' in its output. For example:

- For a process operating across 3 shifts, the duration of the expected cycles could be around eight hours.

- For a machining process, the tool wear might create an expected cycle duration of only a few hours.

- For an accounting process, the expected cycle duration might be around a week, to align with known procedures and systems that are in place.

Using this information, the sampling frequency should be set so that sampling occurs at least four times every cycle, in order that process changes *within* the expected cycles will be reflected in the data collected, as shown below.

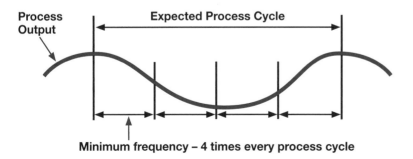

Process Output

Expected Process Cycle

Minimum frequency – 4 times every process cycle

Sampling from Populations:

A statistically sound approach to sampling is important when sampling a population, in order to ensure that the sample is representative.

A completely **random** approach gives the whole population an equal chance of being selected.

Alternatively, it may be important to ensure that specific categories within a population are represented in a sample. A **stratified** sampling approach involves randomly selecting data from specific categories **within** a population.

For example, a completely **random** approach to selecting a jury may not produce exactly six men and six women.

A **stratified** approach would be to deliberately select six women and six men in order to ensure that the male/female ratio of the population is reflected in the jury.

Contextual Data – The 4th Data World

Categorical data provides information on the context from which a particular piece of data was taken. This information is essential later on in the Analyse phase of an improvement project.

The spreadsheet shown here is typical of real data. It contains data on a fault repair process.

The first three columns demonstrate how the **output** of the process might be recorded in the three data worlds.

The remainder of the data columns contain **contextual** information about the fault repairs, and are mostly **categorical** in nature.

Why is contextual data important?
Contextual data is essential during the analyse phase of a project. Without it, you will have trouble looking for clues in the data. It is therefore important to record as much contextual information about process events as possible.

You can always decide not to use the data later on, but it is difficult to go back and find contextual data after the event.

Numerical Data
representing the process output.

Categorical / Contextual Data
Provides the background of each piece of data.

Continuous   Attribute   Count

A variety of categorical information – some numeric, some textual, and some mixed.

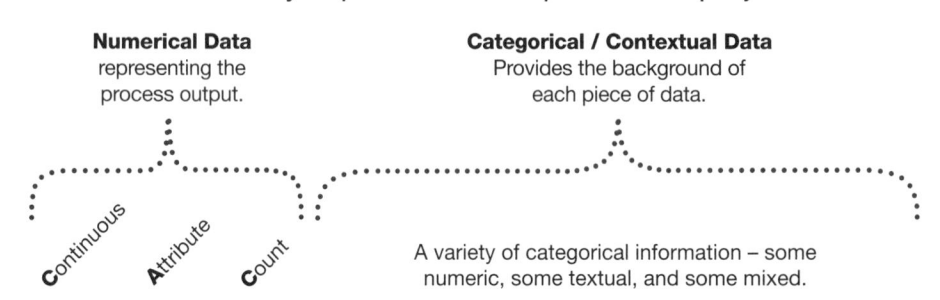

Time taken to complete	First result	Number of defects found	ID	Type	Technology	Location	Skills required	Priority
23.2	Pass	0	W182	Com	1	SW	Manual	Low
27.5	Pass	0	W183	Direct	1	N	Skilled-W	Med
28.3	Pass	0	W184	Com	2	SW	Skilled-D	Low
29.5	Fail	1	W185	Direct	3	S	Clerical	High
30.8	Pass	0	W186	Direct	1	N	Skilled-W	High
28.1	Fail	2	W187	Group	2	S	Manual	Med
29.9	Pass	0	W188	Group	2	SW	Skilled-D	Low
30.2	Fail	1	W189	Com				High

! Minitab is case sensitive, so contextual pieces of data may not be recognised as the same if they are not spelt in **exactly** the same way.

Measurement System Analysis (MSA)

Too many business problems are analysed with data that is known to be suspect. If the data is poor quality, there is no option but to stop and fix it during the Measure phase of a project.

What is a Measurement System?
A measurement system is not just a device, such as a ruler or timer, but it includes the people, standards, and procedures that surround the measurement process itself.

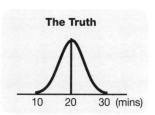

Example: Imagine a process that takes 20 minutes on average with a range from 10-30. The distribution curve on the right shows what we *should* see when we measure and plot the data. This is referred to as the **truth**.

The four plots below represent the range of actual results that might be provided by the measurement system. The top left picture is the only one that represents the 'truth'. The other three exhibit mixtures of errors that can be categorised into two themes - Precision and Bias (see p60).

```
People ──────▶
Devices ─────▶
Procedures ──▶    Measurement    Result
                     System      ──────▶
Standards ───▶                   (Data)
Training ────▶
```

Why is this relevant?
The data in our spreadsheets may not faithfully reflect the process data because it has been through a measurement system which could have introduced errors and bias to the data.

Measurement System Analysis refers to a range of techniques that can help to identify and measure the sources of error in our data.

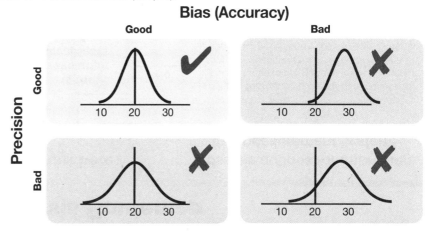

Measurement System Analysis Routemap

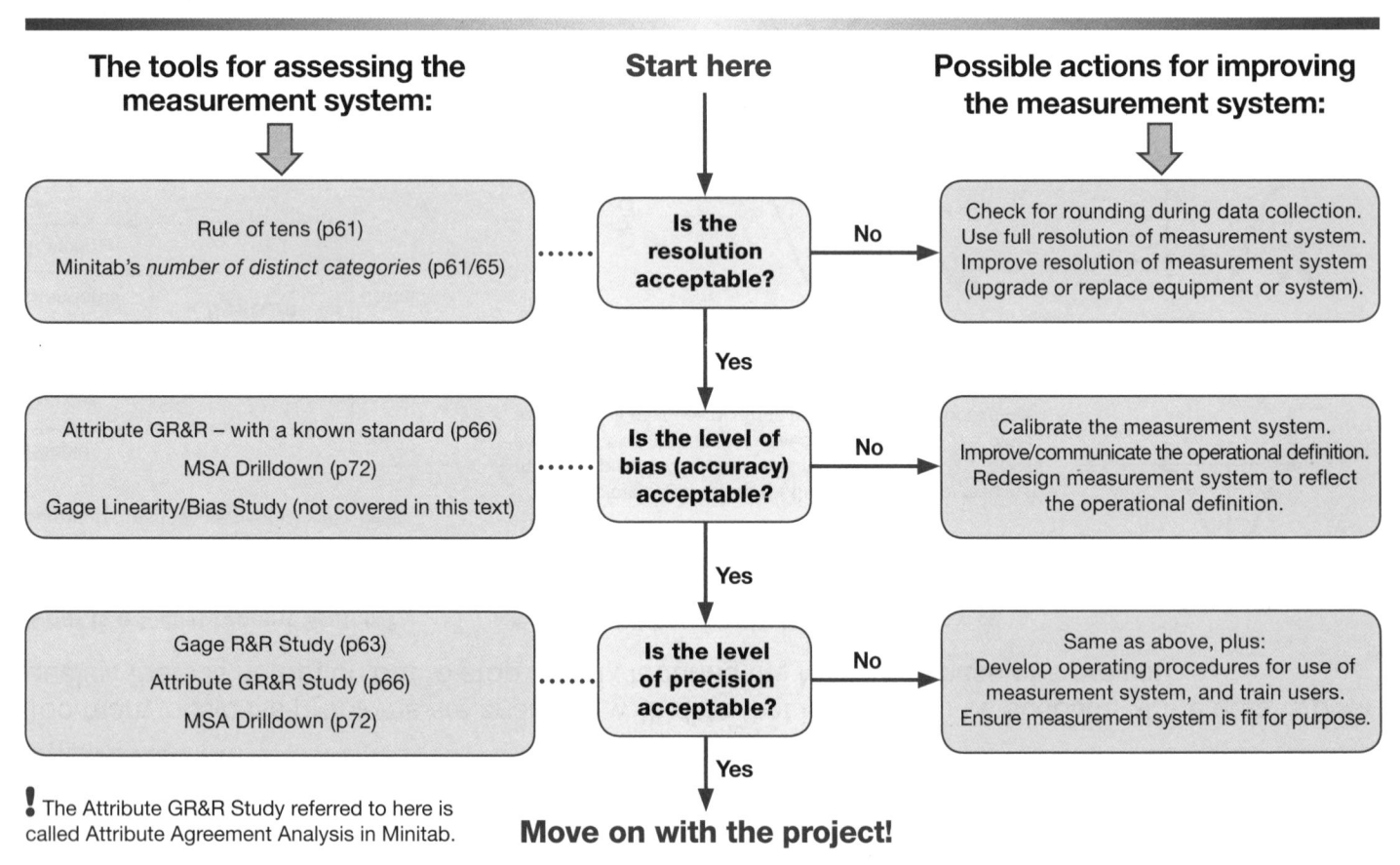

The tools for assessing the measurement system:

Start here

Possible actions for improving the measurement system:

Rule of tens (p61)

Minitab's *number of distinct categories* (p61/65)

.... **Is the resolution acceptable?** — No → Check for rounding during data collection. Use full resolution of measurement system. Improve resolution of measurement system (upgrade or replace equipment or system).

Yes

Attribute GR&R – with a known standard (p66)

MSA Drilldown (p72)

Gage Linearity/Bias Study (not covered in this text)

.... **Is the level of bias (accuracy) acceptable?** — No → Calibrate the measurement system. Improve/communicate the operational definition. Redesign measurement system to reflect the operational definition.

Yes

Gage R&R Study (p63)

Attribute GR&R Study (p66)

MSA Drilldown (p72)

.... **Is the level of precision acceptable?** — No → Same as above, plus: Develop operating procedures for use of measurement system, and train users. Ensure measurement system is fit for purpose.

Yes

! The Attribute GR&R Study referred to here is called Attribute Agreement Analysis in Minitab.

Move on with the project!

Sources of Measurement Error – Bias and Precision

As introduced on page 58, Measurement System errors fall into two categories – Bias and Precision.

Bias errors are consistent types of error that do not increase the variation you see in your results, but do shift the data so that results are consistently higher or lower than they should be. For example:

- A ruler has 20mm missing from the end, so it is *consistently* giving results 20mm too long.

- Your bathroom scales are not set up correctly and *consistently* over estimate your weight by three kilos.

- The start time for resolving a customer complaint is *consistently* recorded 20 minutes **after** the customer first called (i.e. too late!)

Assessing Bias errors can be done through Attribute Agreement Analysis (p66), MSA Drilldowns (p72) and Gauge Linearity and Bias Studies (see Minitab).

Fixing Bias errors is achieved through solutions such as routine calibration, limiting the allowable operating range of a gauge, training and using visual standards, etc.

Precision errors are those that do not happen in the same way all the time – in other words they add more variation into the data. This means that the variation in the data is more than is actually in the process. For example:

- Some people measure from the end of a ruler and others start from the point at which zero is marked.

- Your bathroom scales only have markings every five kilos, so that you have to (not very reliably) guess the last few kilos every time you weigh yourself.

- The start time for a customer complaint could be anything from 5-20 minutes after the customer first called, depending on operator training, workload, experience, breaks etc.

Precision errors can be further divided into two categories:

1) Repeatability: Differences caused by the gauge itself are called Repeatability errors, since they refer to the ability of a gauge to provide repeatable measurements if all other factors (such as the user) are held constant.

2) Reproducibility: Differences in the ways in which different people carry out a measurement are called Reproducibility errors, since they refer to the ability of people to reproduce the results of their colleagues (if all other factors are held constant).

Assessing Precision errors can be done through Gauge R&R Studies (p63), Attribute Agreement Analysis (p66) and MSA Drilldowns (p72).

Fixing Precision errors is achieved through solutions such as developing operational definitions and working standards, training, improving gauge resolution and sometimes changing the gauge in use.

Measurement System Resolution

If the resolution is too large to allow effective discrimination of the process variation then failing the GR&R test is inevitable. Checking resolution is a simple practical tool that is worth doing first.

Resolution:
The smallest units within the data represent the resolution of the measurement system. So, the resolution of data sets 1 and 2 below, is 0.05 and 1 respectively.

5.00	**Data Set 1**
4.95	**Resolution: 0.05**
4.90	Min: 4.80
5.05	Max: 5.15
5.15	Range: 0.35
4.95	
5.00	
4.80	**Data Set 2**
4.95	**Resolution: 1**
5.10	Min: 78
	Max: 94
	Range: 16

78
85
94
91
89
81
88
92
79
87

What causes poor resolution?

- Often it is because the system or gauge is not capable of any finer measurements. In this case, upgrading the system/gauge is inevitable.

- Sometimes however, you will find that data is being rounded at some point in the collection process. Stop the rounding and improve your data for free!

The '**Rule of Tens**' says that the resolution of your gauge should be able to fit at least ten times into the process variation you are measuring, as shown below:

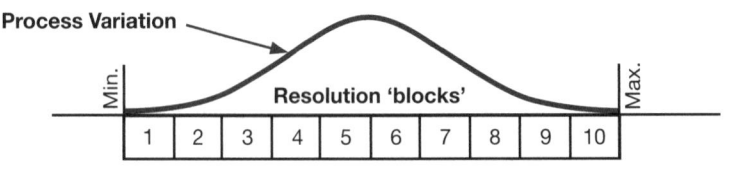

The **Rule of Tens** is a quick practical tool for assessing if the measurement system has any hope of passing the GR&R test. For example:

- Data set 1 (left) has a resolution of 0.05. The process variation can be estimated by the range of the data to be 0.35 (=5.15-4.80). The resolution (0.05) only divides into the process variation (0.35) seven times, and so the measurement system is unlikely to be acceptable because it fails the 'rule of tens'.

- The resolution of data set 2 (left) appears more acceptable. The resolution is 1, and the process range (variation) is 16, meaning that it comfortably passes the 'rule of tens'.

Minitab's equivalent measure of resolution is called the '*number of distinct categories*' (see page 65). The concept is the same but the calculations involved are slightly different, and so the criteria for acceptability is five or more (not 10 or more as described here).

GR&R – Gauge Repeatability and Reproducibility

GR&R studies quantify the Precision errors of a measurement system to determine its acceptability.

A GR&R Study measures precision error by taking one part and measuring it several times, with several different people.

Given that the part is not changing in size, any variation in the results must represent the Repeatability of the gauge and the Reproducibility of measurements by different people. This is abbreviated to GR&R.

A GR&R Study repeats this approach on several different parts to assess the results.

What is an acceptable level of GR&R variation?
It is not the **absolute** level of GR&R that is important, but the **relative** level. For example, the timer that is used for measuring the finish time of a marathon would not be acceptable for measuring the 100 metres sprint. Similarly the volt meter used to measure household electrics would not be acceptable for measuring voltages across electronic components. In other words, a measurement system must be fit for purpose.

So, the acceptability of GR&R variation is assessed on the **ratio** (expressed as a percentage) of the GR&R variation compared to the process (part to part) variation **and** the customer tolerance, as shown below:

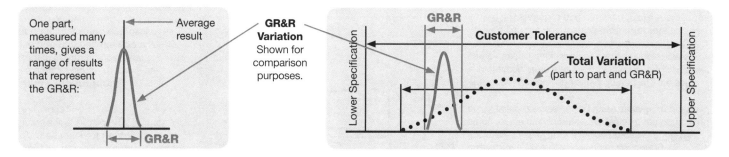

GR&R Acceptability Criteria	Unacceptable	Marginal	Good	Excellent
GR&R as a percentage of the Total Variation = GR&R / Total Variation x 100%	> 30%	< 30%	< 20%	< 10%
GR&R as a percentage of the Tolerance = GR&R / Tolerance x 100%	> 30%	< 30%	< 20%	< 10%

Continuous GR&R in Minitab – Overview

A common standard for a GR&R study is to use 10 parts, measured by three different people, three times each, providing a total of 90 results.

Data Preparation:
As usual, Minitab requires the data in columns; one each for the part number, the appraiser and the measurement results, as shown below:

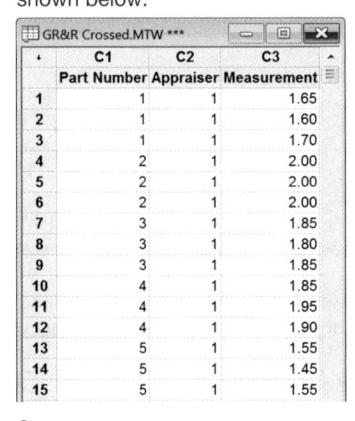

! The order of the rows doesn't matter, as long as the data is matched across the columns.

Minitab: Stat > Quality Tools > Gage Study > Gage R&R Study (Crossed)

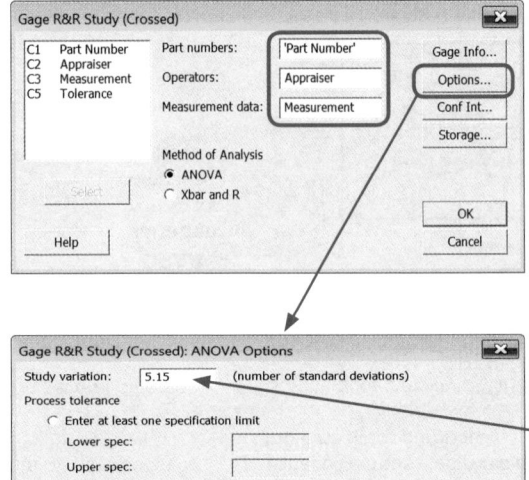

Example: A project is looking at controlling the thickness of steel from a rolling process. A GR&R study for the measurement gage has been completed on 10 pieces of steel, using three different appraisers.

The three key data inputs (highlighted left) are self explanatory. Note that the part number and appraiser can be textual data (such as names of appraisers).

Minitab can provide **Confidence Intervals** for the key GR&R statistics and can also **Store** them in the GR&R worksheet, although neither of these options are used in this example.

Options:
Study variation can be left at 6.0 (which is the Minitab default) or changed to 5.15 (as shown here), which is a common industrial standard for use in GR&R studies, particularly within the automotive industry.

The **Process tolerance** is optional but must be completed if you require GR&R as a percentage of tolerance. Minitab enables you to enter either the **actual** specifications or the difference between them (the **total** tolerance), which in this example is 1.0mm (because the specification is +/-0.5mm).

⬇ **GR&R-Crossed.mpj**

Continuous GR&R in Minitab – Graphical Output

The top left graph is the primary output for analysis.

The **Gage GR&R** group of columns should be small in comparison to the **Part-to-Part** group, which contains three columns, as follows:

- The first column in the GR&R group deals with **% Contribution** and is not a metric discussed here.
- The second column in the GR&R group shows the GR&R as a **% of Study Variation** (Total Variation).
- The third column in the GR&R group shows GR&R as a **% of Tolerance**. If you don't have this column it's because you didn't enter a tolerance under **Options**.

The middle two sets of columns represent the sub-components of the GR&R group (i.e. Repeatability and Reproducibility) separately.

This example shows that Reproducibility is the larger component of GR&R, indicating that improvements should focus on reducing the differences **between** appraisers first.

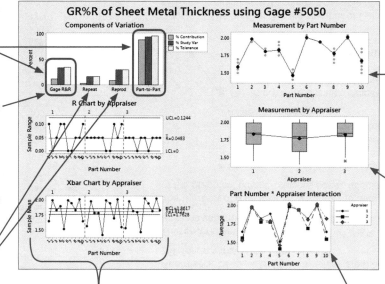

If the GR&R is too high, then the graphs on the right can be used to investigate why.

The top chart shows all the results for each part in order (1–10) to see if particular parts were difficult to measure. In this case, part 10 has the most variable results.

The second chart helps to show reproducibility by showing all the results for each appraiser. Minitab 16 onwards use a Box plot and previous versions show each data point. In this example, appraiser 2 has lower measurements (on average) than the others, which might be worth investigating.

The third chart is the same as the top chart, but separates out the results by appraiser.

The two lower left charts are effectively SPC charts (p249).

The middle chart is checking for unlikely results that might be a result of a special cause occurring during the GR&R exercise. If any of the points are outside of the red lines, check that there were no specific problems with that part and that there were no typing mistakes when entering the data.

In contrast, the bottom chart **should** have lots of points outside of the control lines, which indicates the GR&R % is low, so don't worry if your graph looks like this one.

Continuous GR&R in Minitab – Session Window Output

Gage R&R Study - ANOVA Method

Source	DF	SS	MS	F	P
Part Number	9	2.9232	0.324802	36.5530	0.000
Appraiser	2	0.0633	0.031694	3.5669	0.050
Part No. * Appraiser	18	0.1599	0.008886	8.8858	0.000
Repeatability	60	0.0600	0.001000		
Total	89	3.2065			

Variance Source	VarComp	%Contribution (of VarComp)
Total Gage R&R	0.0043889	11.11
Repeatability	0.0010000	2.53
Reproducibility	0.0033889	8.58
Appraiser	0.0007603	1.93
Appraiser*Part No.	0.0026286	6.66
Part-To-Part	0.0351019	88.89
Total Variation	0.0394907	100.00

Process tolerance = 1

Source	StdDev (SD)	Study Var (5.15 x SD)	%Study Var (%SV)	%Tolerance (SV/Toler)
Total Gage R&R	0.066249	0.34118	33.34	34.12
Repeatability	0.031623	0.16286	15.91	16.29
Reproducibility	0.058214	0.29980	29.29	29.98
Appraiser	0.027573	0.14200	13.88	14.20
Appraiser*Part No.	0.051270	0.26404	25.80	26.40
Part-To-Part	0.187355	0.96488	94.28	96.49
Total Variation	0.198723	1.02342	100.00	102.34

Number of Distinct Categories = 3

There is a lot of session window output from a GR&R study, but most of it just repeats the message contained within the graphs.

The ANOVA table is used to assess which sources of variation are statistically significant. In this case, the appraiser **does** have an affect on the result and there is an interaction between Part Number and Appraisers, because both the p-values are 0.05 or less (see pages 155/ 156 for an explanation of p-values).

This second set of data represents the GR&R in terms of its contribution towards variance and is not explored further in this text.

The third set of data (below) provides the detail behind the top left graph of the graphical output (previous page), as follows:

- Graphically the GR&R looked high (see previous page) and it is quantified here as being 33.34% of the Total Variation and 34.12% of the Tolerance. Both these results are above 30% and therefore indicate improvement is required in the measurement system.

- The graphical results also indicated that Reproducibility was a larger component of GR&R than Repeatability. The figures here support this, showing that Reproducibility factors (at approx 29%) are contributing twice the variation that Repeatability factors are (at approx 16%).

The number 3 is the Number of Distinct Categories that the measurement system is capable of discriminating within the process variation present. An acceptable target is more than 5, and so this result reinforces the conclusion that this measurement system needs improvement (see page 61) for more on gauge resolution).

Attribute GR&R – Overview

All the same principles of GR&R can be applied to the Attribute data world as well. The target for an Attribute MSA is for it to reach the correct decision, every time.

Attribute GR&Rs are conducted in almost identical fashion to those for Continuous data. Several different appraisers are asked to decide the acceptability of several different products (or services), each several different times. The results are used to assess the **reproducibility** (how well the appraisers agree with each other) as well as the **repeatability** (how consistently they agree with themselves).

The key differences of Attribute GR&R studies are:

- More data is required, because the Attribute data world has less resolution. At least 20 parts should be assessed at least 3 times by each appraiser.

- You should ensure your selection of parts includes some borderline products or services that will really challenge the capability of the measurement system.

Bias can also occur in an Attribute Measurement System. Even if all the appraisers reach a unanimous decision that a product/service is acceptable (in other words they have perfect GR&R), it might be that they are all making the wrong decision (i.e they are all biased).

The Attribute GR&R in Minitab allows bias to be assessed at the same time as GR&R. In order to do this, the correct decision for each part number must be known and entered in a separate column, as shown on the left.

Because of the often subjective nature of Attribute measurements, it is not always easy to determine what the correct decision is. One approach is to ask a group of experts (perhaps the process owner, engineer, or the customer) what their consensus decision is, and to define this as the truth (as shown here in the last column).

This selection of data (left) is taken from the example data file used in the following pages (and specified below). A first glance reveals that all the rows except 3 and 5 have perfect GR&R and no bias, because all the appraisers agreed with the expert decision all the time. Rows 3 and 5 (highlighted) show that Tom had problems repeating his own decisions on those parts. An in-depth analysis using Minitab will shed more light on these initial observations.

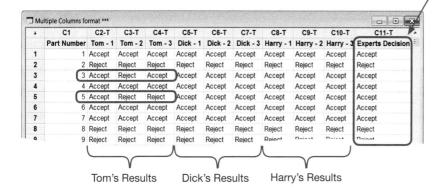

Tom's Results   Dick's Results   Harry's Results

GR&R-Attribute.mpj

Attribute GR&R – Data Input

Minitab: Stat > Quality Tools > Attribute Agreement Analysis

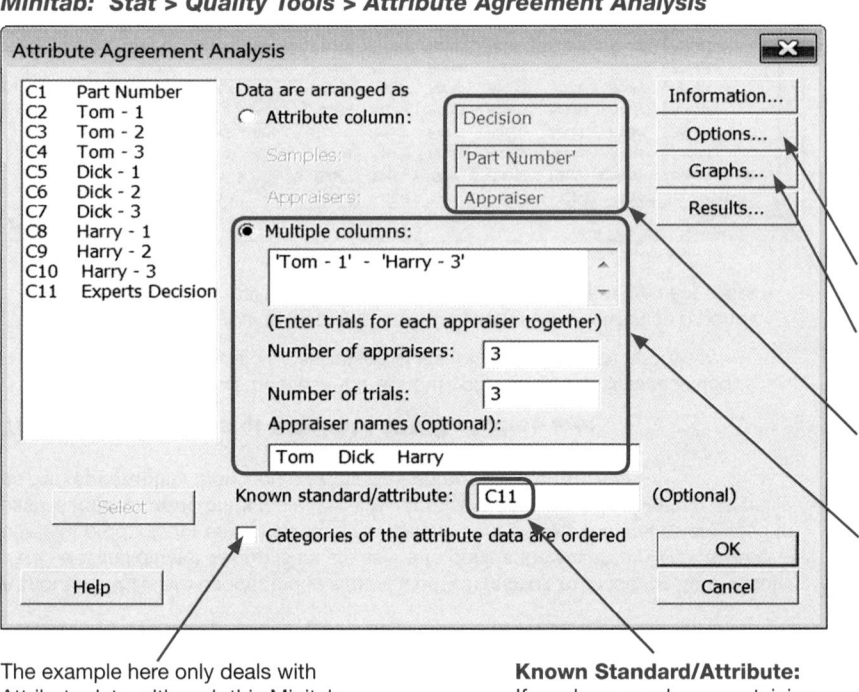

For most purposes within Lean Six Sigma projects, the Attribute Agreement Analysis described here is perfectly suitable, particularly in service and transactional environments. Minitab also has a similar technique called *Attribute Gage Study (Analytical Method)*, which is found under the Gage Study sub-menu. This technique is more complex and is beyond the scope of this book.

Options: Minitab provides an option for a Disagreement Table in the output, shown on page 70.

All **Graphs** should be selected by default, as well as the additional Kappa coefficients under **Results**.

Data formatting:
Use the Attribute Column option if all of your results (decisions) are in a single column, with two additional columns for the part number and appraiser.

Use the Multiple Columns option if your results are arranged across multiple columns (which is an easier format to view). When using this option, all the columns for one appraiser must be next to each other. Minitab then knows to take the first three (in this example) columns of your selection and assign them to the same appraiser (because the number of appraisers and trials is also entered).

The data file for this example includes two worksheets that contain each of the data formats described above.

The example here only deals with Attribute data, although this Minitab function can also deal with ordinal data (where the results have a natural ranking to them) by checking this box. See Minitab Help for more information.

Known Standard/Attribute: If you have a column containing the 'correct' decision, enter it here in order for Minitab to estimate the bias within the results.

Attribute GR&R – Graphical Output

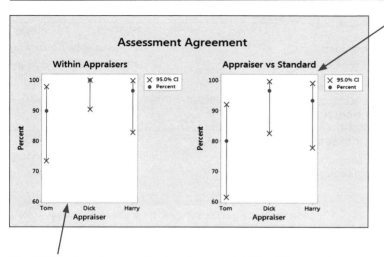

The Within Appraiser results show the **repeatability** of the appraisers as a percentage score. The dot indicates the actual calculation, while the lines extending in either direction indicate the (95%) confidence intervals for the result. Confidence intervals (p151) are used because a sample size of 20 or 30 parts is not very large when dealing with Attribute data (p48).

So, for this example:

- Tom reached the same decision on 90% of the parts, but the confidence interval indicates this could be anywhere from approx 73% to 97%.

- Dick reached the same decision on all of the parts (100%), but the confidence interval indicates his true performance could be between 90% and 100%.

Appraiser vs Standard:
Because there was an expert decision (a *known standard*) in the data for this example, the graphical output also shows the performance of the appraisers against that standard.

In this example:

- Tom only agreed with the expert decision on 80% of the parts.

- Dick (who had a perfect score in terms of repeating his own decisions), agreed with the expert for 97% of the parts.

- Harry only agreed with the expert for 28 of the 30 parts (93%).

If the appraiser did not agree with the standard then either the part was appraised as good but defined as bad by the expert, or vice versa. The results in the **session window** (see the following pages) provide more detail on this and all the exact calculations behind these graphs.

Where to focus improvement:

Low 'within appraiser' scores would indicate a need to help the appraisers reach consistent decisions, maybe through improved inspection conditions etc.

Low 'appraiser versus standard' scores would indicate the need to provide better operational definitions on the acceptability criteria of the product/service, supported by visual standards and training where necessary.

Attribute GR&R – Session Window Output

Each Appraiser vs Standard - Assessment Disagreement Table

Appraiser	# Reject / Accept	Percent	# Accept / Reject	Percent	# Mixed	Percent
Tom	3	14.29	0	0.00	3	10.00
Dick	1	4.76	0	0.00	0	0.00
Harry	1	4.76	0	0.00	1	3.33

 # Reject / Accept: Assessments across trials = Reject / standard = Accept.
 # Accept / Reject: Assessments across trials = Accept / standard = Reject.
 # Mixed: Assessments across trials are not identical.

Between Appraisers
Assessment Agreement

# Inspected	# Matched	Percent	95% CI
30	25	83.33	(65.28, 94.36)

 # Matched: All appraisers' assessments agree with each other.

All Appraisers vs Standard
Assessment Agreement

# Inspected	# Matched	Percent	95% CI
30	24	80.00	(61.43, 92.29)

 # Matched: All appraisers' assessments agree with the known standard.

Minitab's session window output for the Attribute Agreement Analysis function contains a substantial amount of data. The first two sections repeat the data shown in the graphical output (previous page) and are therefore **not** shown here.

The remainder of the output is shown here (except the Fleiss' Kappa Statistics, which are explained on the next page).

The Assessment Disagreement provides detail on **how** the appraisers disagreed with the expert decision (standard). For example:

1) None of the appraisers ever decided that a part was acceptable when the experts decision was that it was a reject.

2) Most of the disagreements with the standard occurred when the appraisers rejected the part, but the experts decision was that the part was acceptable. The two observations above indicate that appraisers are being cautious in their decisions and if in doubt, they are rejecting parts – a good, safe approach for consumers, but costly for the business!

This table summarises the results by showing that there was **complete** agreement (reproducibility) between the appraisers on only 25 of the 30 parts (83%).

This table summarises the results by showing that there was **complete** agreement between the appraisers **and** the standard on only 24 of the 30 parts (80%).

So, from the above, we can deduce that for one of the parts, **all** of the appraisers agreed with each other **and** disagreed with the standard at the same time! You will find that this was part number (and row number) 25 in the data file.

Attribute GR&R – Session Window Output (cont.)

Summary of Assessment Disagreement with Standard

Appraiser		Tom		Dick		Harry	
Sample	Standard	Count	%	Count	%	Count	%
1	Accept	0	0.00	0	0.00	0	0.00
2	Reject	0	0.00	0	0.00	0	0.00
3	Accept	1	33.33	0	0.00	0	0.00
4	Accept	0	0.00	0	0.00	0	0.00
5	Accept	2	66.67	0	0.00	0	0.00
6	Accept	0	0.00	0	0.00	0	0.00
7	Accept	0	0.00	0	0.00	0	0.00
8	Reject	0	0.00	0	0.00	0	0.00
9	Reject	0	0.00	0	0.00	0	0.00
10	Accept	0	0.00	0	0.00	0	0.00
11	Accept	0	0.00	0	0.00	0	0.00
12	Reject	0	0.00	0	0.00	0	0.00
13	Accept	3	100.00	0	0.00	0	0.00
14	Accept	0	0.00	0	0.00	0	0.00
15	Accept	0	0.00	0	0.00	0	0.00
16	Accept	0	0.00	0	0.00	0	0.00
17	Reject	0	0.00	0	0.00	0	0.00
18	Accept	0	0.00	0	0.00	0	0.00
19	Accept	0	0.00	0	0.00	0	0.00
20	Accept	0	0.00	0	0.00	0	0.00
21	Reject	0	0.00	0	0.00	0	0.00
22	Reject	0	0.00	0	0.00	0	0.00
23	Reject	0	0.00	0	0.00	0	0.00
24	Accept	0	0.00	0	0.00	0	0.00
25	Accept	3	100.00	3	100.00	3	100.00
26	Reject	0	0.00	0	0.00	0	0.00
27	Accept	0	0.00	0	0.00	0	0.00
28	Accept	0	0.00	0	0.00	0	0.00
29	Accept	3	100.00	0	0.00	2	66.67
30	Accept	2	66.67	0	0.00	0	0.00

Fleiss Kappa Statistics: These statistics reflect the level of agreement between results, and usually range from 0 to 1, where:

- 0 indicates no agreement (i.e. the results reflect random chance).
- 1 indicates perfect agreement between the results.

NB: Rarely, the statistic can be negative, where the level of agreement within the results is less than that expected by chance.

In Attribute GR&R, the Fleiss Kappa statistics reinforce the numerical output shown on the previous pages so, in this example:

- The agreement **Between Appraisers** of 25 out of 30 (83%) has a Fleiss Kappa Statistic of 0.854.
- Correspondingly, the agreement of the **Appraisers vs Standard** of 24 out of 30 (80%) has a slightly lower statistic of 0.822.

Disagreement Table (left): If you have an expert decision within your results, then Minitab can also provide a Disagreement Table that provides further detail on the errors that were made within the study. For example, in this study, we already know that:

- Tom only agreed with himself 90% of the time.
- Tom only agreed with himself **and** the expert 80% of the time.

The Disagreement Table provides further detail and shows that when Tom did not reach a consistent decision, it was **always** on parts that the experts decided were 'Acceptable' (highlighted). In fact, the whole table shows that none of the appraisers ever disagreed with a 'Reject' decision (even within the mixed results when appraisers did not agree with themselves, such as Toms).

So, **all** of the errors in this study occurred when assessing acceptable parts, which is useful to know in terms of making improvements.

GR&R Studies in Practice

GR&R studies are experiments that require careful control in order to ensure they provide valid results.

Conducting GR&R Studies:

A GR&R study is effectively an experiment in which components of the measurement system are adjusted in a controlled manner. As an experiment, careful planning is required to ensure the results are statistically valid:

- Select the sample parts at random and run the trial in a completely random order.

- Ensure the parts represent the full operating range of the process (i.e. its long term variation). This can be done by collecting the parts over an extended time period.

- Complete the study in standard operating conditions:
  - Use the same appraisers as usual.

  - Do not train the appraisers before hand – you want to measure the effectiveness of the **existing** system.

  - Conduct the experiment in the same location as normal.

- Ensure that the study is blind. This means that the appraisers should not be aware of the part number that they are measuring or be able to remember their last measurement. This is difficult if the parts have numbers written on them!

This is all a lot to ask! Make sure you have a facilitator for the study who controls the conditions and is aware of the statistical rigour required.

Within Part Variation:

All physical parts have levels of 'within part variation' in them. If you measured the diameter of a football in different places there would be some differences in the results because the ball would not be perfectly round.

Unfortunately, a GR&R exercise would wrongly attribute the variation within a part to that of GR&R error, since the GR&R process assumes the parts are perfectly consistent.

While it may be a **practical** problem if the football is not round, it is not an issue of measurement error and so needs to be removed from the experiment. The solution is to specify a point on the ball that the measurement must be taken from (for the purpose of the GR&R experiment).

GR&R with Destructive Testing or one-off events:

In certain situations, a measurement cannot be repeated. The tensile strength of a metal sample, for example, cannot be re-tested because it is destroyed the first time. The solution to this is the GR&R (Nested) function found in Minitab.

This advanced technique relies on the careful selection of parts so that small batches of parts that have been taken close together can be assumed to have identical properties. The batches are then selected at different times in order that the longer term process variation will be present between them. This technique is not detailed further in this text and requires expert support in its use.

MSA Drilldown

Even if GR&R studies cannot be applied in their purest form, you must be confident that your data represents what it is supposed to. MSA Drilldowns are a method for doing this.

What is an MSA Drilldown?
An MSA Drilldown is a structured approach to checking the quality of your data. Its principle is that you should not be using data if you do not know where it came from, and so an MSA Drilldown helps to challenge the 'pedigree' of the data. A tree diagram is the best way to structure the results, as shown on the right.

The key steps are:

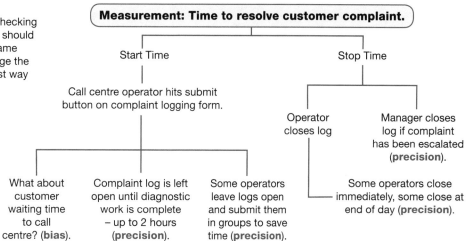

Drilldown through the data to find its source components.

Challenge each component in terms of possible errors (bias or precision).

For each potential source of error, decide if it's acceptable (within context).

If it is acceptable, then document your decision and move on with the project.

Measurement: Time to resolve customer complaint.

Start Time

Call centre operator hits submit button on complaint logging form.

What about customer waiting time to call centre? (**bias**).

Complaint log is left open until diagnostic work is complete – up to 2 hours (**precision**).

Some operators leave logs open and submit them in groups to save time (**precision**).

Stop Time

Operator closes log

Manager closes log if complaint has been escalated (**precision**).

Some operators close immediately, some close at end of day (**precision**).

Useful questions during an MSA Drilldown:

- Where does the data come from? ('a database' is not acceptable – how does it get there?).
- How is it collected and what triggers it to be collected? (the press of a button?, manual recording?, barcode scanning?).
- Are there different people or systems collecting the same data?

1st Pass Analysis – Time Series Plots and Histograms

Although this is not the Analyse phase yet, a '1st Pass Analysis' of the KPIs during the Measure phase provides a baseline, as well as an understanding of the current process behaviour.

The phrase '1st Pass Analysis' refers to the combined use of Histograms and Time Series plots to take a first look at your data. These two graphs are the primary graphical tools of Six Sigma and they work together to provide an understanding of how a process is behaving; both overall and over time.

A 1st Pass Analysis should be completed for each KPI within a project. Baseline figures quoted in the Problem Statement can be added to the graphs to aid understanding (blue dotted lines below).

The objective of a 1st Pass Analysis is to provide an initial, broad understanding of how stable a process is, and how it behaves. This is distinctly different from how the process performs against customer requirements, which is referred to as process capability, and dealt with later in the Measure phase.

At this stage, it is important not to read too much into the detail of the Histograms and Time Series plots, and instead to focus on high-level observations. Detailed analysis can be completed later on.

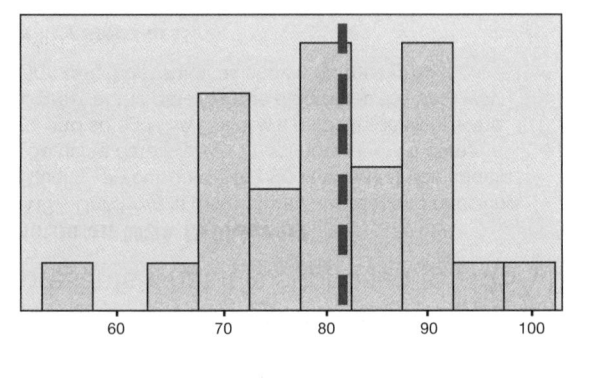  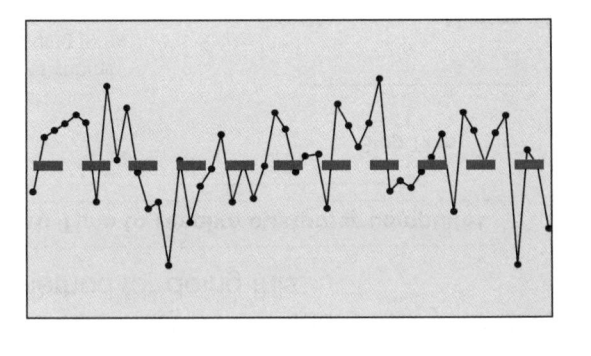

Histograms (above) summarise the data into bars based upon the frequency of results within each bar. They do not provide any indication of time - the order in which the results occured.

Time Series plots (above) show the data over time, by plotting each individual data point, connected by a line. This highlights trends and observations that would be missed using just a histogram.

1st Pass Analysis (cont.)

Histograms summarise the overall spread and distribution of a data set. They provide a visual indication of the range of the data (lowest to highest), where most of the data results fall (tallest bars), how the data is distributed (shape) and extreme results. Histograms help to:

Understand the shape of the distribution:

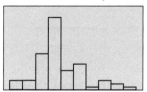

The shape of a distribution shows where most of the data results are, and whether a process is symmetrical, skewed or otherwise - see page 75.

Consider if the Normal distribution may apply:

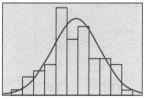

Some distributions follow the Normal distribution (indicated by the smooth curve left), which can help determine the most appropriate analysis techniques - see page 77.

Look for special events (including outliers):

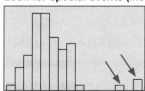

Exceptional, one off events that do not fit with the rest of the data can be seen clearly on histograms, and can then be investigated as required.

See page 123 for how to create a Histogram.

Time Series Plots show each individual result of data set, in time order. They provide a visual indication of how stable a process is and how it changes over time. This in turn can provide useful clues as to how it might be improved in the future. Time Series plots help to:

Understand the type of variation present:

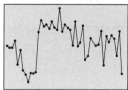

Understanding whether a process is under common cause or special cause variation has implications for the type of improvements that will be required - see page 79.

See the difference between short and long term variation:

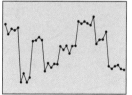

All processes 'shift and drift' over time, but some more than others. Measuring this shift helps to understand the potential for process improvement - see page 80.

Separate trends, seasonality and random noise:

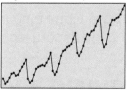

Most processes are a combination of trends, seasonality and noise. Identifying these parts can be useful in controlling and improving a process - see page 81.

See page 130 for how to create a Time Series Plot.

Distribution Shapes and the Normal Distribution

The Normal distribution is a common and useful statistical model, but it is not the end of the world! Continuous data that is **not** Normal (big N) is still useful data and it is still normal (little n!).

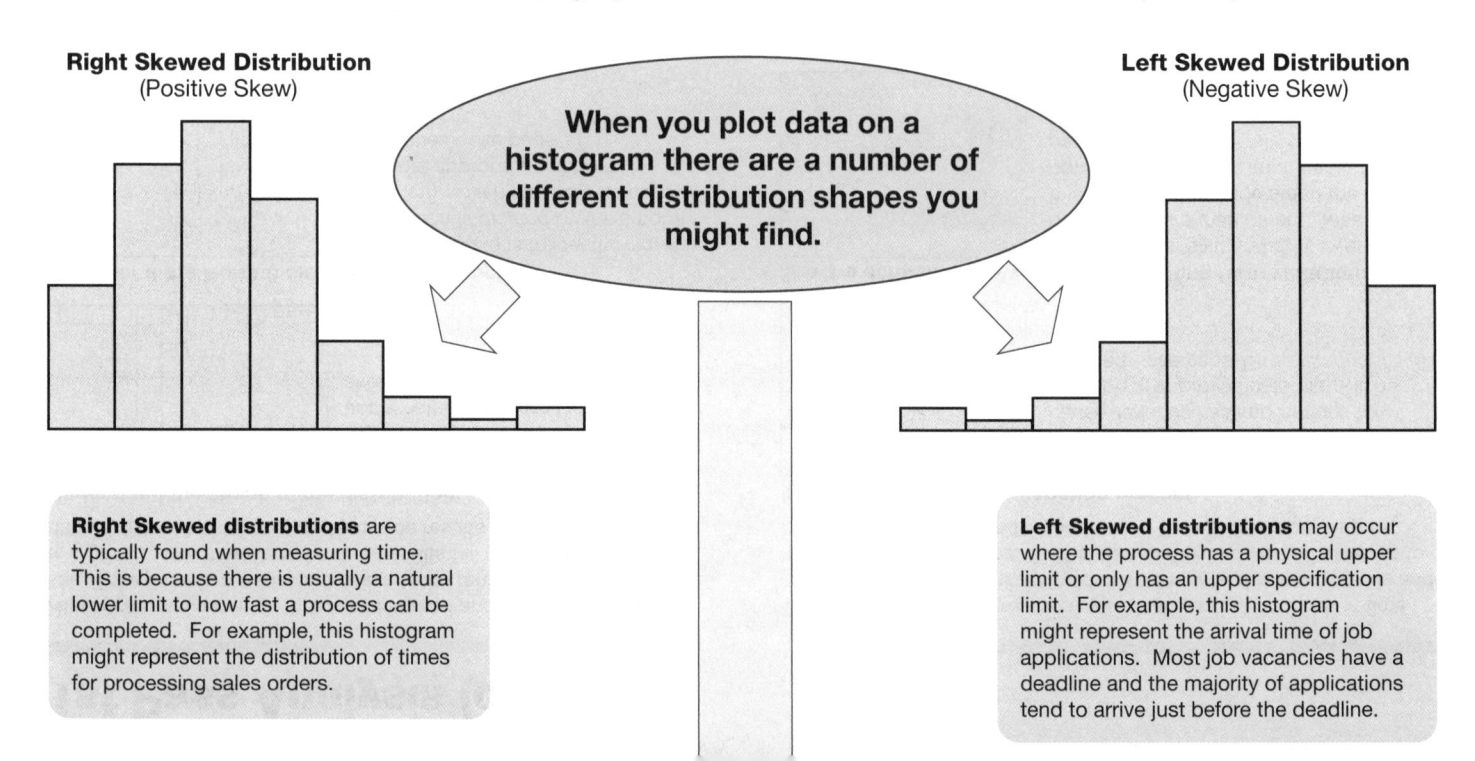

Right Skewed Distribution
(Positive Skew)

Left Skewed Distribution
(Negative Skew)

When you plot data on a histogram there are a number of different distribution shapes you might find.

Right Skewed distributions are typically found when measuring time. This is because there is usually a natural lower limit to how fast a process can be completed. For example, this histogram might represent the distribution of times for processing sales orders.

Left Skewed distributions may occur where the process has a physical upper limit or only has an upper specification limit. For example, this histogram might represent the arrival time of job applications. Most job vacancies have a deadline and the majority of applications tend to arrive just before the deadline.

A Normal curve is defined by its **Average** and **Standard Deviation**.

- The peak of the curve represents the **Average**.

- The spread (width) of the curve is equivalent to six times the **Standard Deviation** of the process (see next page for more detail).

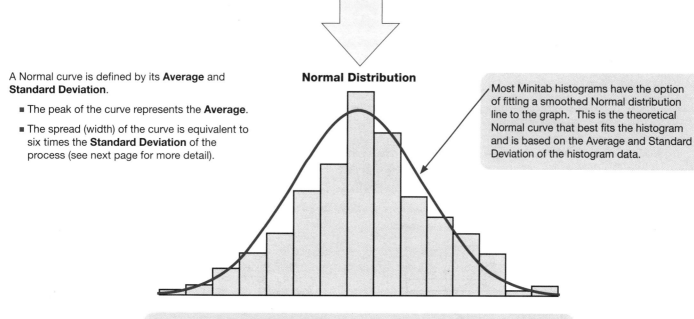

Normal Distribution

Most Minitab histograms have the option of fitting a smoothed Normal distribution line to the graph. This is the theoretical Normal curve that best fits the histogram and is based on the Average and Standard Deviation of the histogram data.

The Normal distribution is a commonly occurring distribution that is symmetrical, with most of the results in the middle and fewer towards the extremes. It is also sometimes called a bell shaped curve, or Gaussian curve. Remember that 'Normal' is a name, so it has a capital N.

- See the next page to find out more about the Normal distribution.

- See page 189 to find out how to decide if your data follows the Normal distribution.

- See Appendices H and I to find out more about why Normality is sometimes important, and other times when it is not so important.

The Normal Distribution in Theory

In theory the Normal distribution never ends but in practice, most results fall within +/- 3 Sigmas.

Standard Deviations and the Normal distribution:
A wider-flatter histogram demonstrates more variation in the process and therefore a higher standard deviation (vice versa for a narrower-taller histogram).

In theory, the Normal curve actually carries on forever, making it possible (but very unlikely) to have extreme results from time to time. However, for all intents and purposes, 100% of the results are contained within three Standard Deviations either side of the average – a total of Six Sigmas.

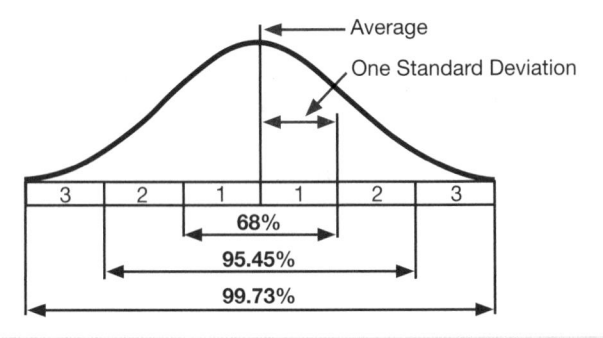

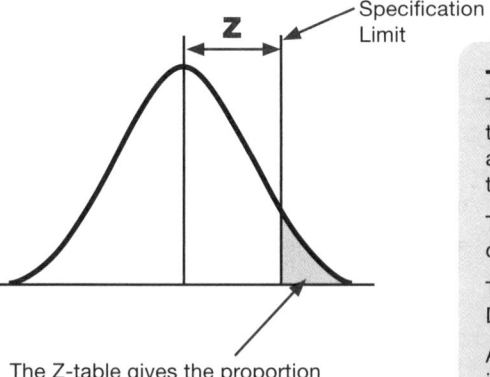

The Z-table gives the proportion of results that will be outside the limit, based on the distance 'Z' between the average and the limit, *in Standard Deviations*.

The Z-Table:
The shape of the Normal curve dictates that most of the results will be towards the centre of the distribution. In fact, as shown above, 68% of the results will be within +/- 1 Sigma of the average. The complex shape of the Normal curve has been converted into a mathematical table called the Z-table.

The Z-table provides the proportion of results that will fall outside of a specific limit, as shown on the left. All that is required is the distance 'Z' between the average and the limit in question.

The important point is that the distance 'Z' must be defined in terms of how many Standard Deviations it represents.

An abbreviated Z-table can be found inside the back cover of this guide. Alternatively, a full interactive Z-table is contained in the data file:

⬇ Z-Table & Sigma Levels.xls

The Normal Distribution in Practice

If the Normal distribution fits the data, it can be used to estimate future process performance.

1) A CD manufacturer has had problems producing CDs within the maximum thickness specification of 1.5mm. They are testing a new production machine that they hope will produce better CD products. A test run of 100 CDs has been made and the thickness results look like this:

2) None of the 100 test CDs were above the upper spec limit of 1.5mm so it appears that the machine will not make any oversize CDs. However, the Normal curve on the histogram still extends beyond the 1.5mm limit, which suggests that over the longer term some of the CDs will be oversize.

3) Since the histogram appears to fit the Normal curve, the Normal distribution can be used to make a better prediction of the number of failures that will occur in the long term. The Z-table (inside back cover) provides the area under the Normal curve outside of an upper specification limit. But, it requires the distance between the average and the specification limit **in standard deviations (not mm)**, as shown below:

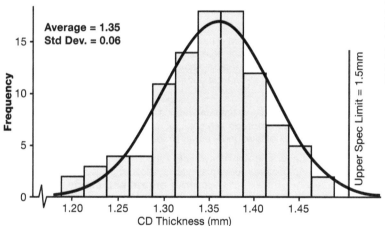

Average = 1.35
Std Dev. = 0.06

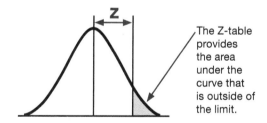

The Z-table provides the area under the curve that is outside of the limit.

4: So for this example: $Z = \dfrac{\text{(Upper Spec. Limit – Average)}}{\text{Standard Deviation}} = \dfrac{(1.5 - 1.35)}{0.06} = 2.5$

Capability-CD.mpj

The Z-table predicts the area under the curve to be 0.6% for a Z-value of 2.5. This is different, and a better prediction than, the 0% predicted by looking at the **actual** test run of 100.

Process Stability: Common and Special Cause Variation

A common phrase in terms of summarising the behaviour of a process is 'stability'. Understanding whether a process is stable or not has implications for the ways in which it might be controlled.

A stable process has stable inputs:

The key concept behind process stability is that the variation of a process output is dependant on the type of variation in its inputs.

- A stable process is one where all of the inputs are varying in a random way. Combining together, these **common cause** variations create a similarly random variation in the output, that is predictable within certain limits.

- An unstable process is one where one or more of the inputs are behaving in an extremely unpredictable way. The resulting output variation can therefore be assigned to **special cause** variation, and cannot be predicted.

A common example of special cause variation is the weather. A lightning strike might create a special cause surge of several thousand volts in mains voltage that normally varies in a relatively stable manner.

How to assess process stability:

In order to help detect signs of instability in a process that might not be easily spotted by the human eye, SPC charts can be used in the Measure phase to analyse historical process data. SPC charts are an advanced form of Time Series plot, and are introduced in detail on page 249.

A Stable Process... is in-control and **predictable**, and its output varies due to **common cause** variation in all of its inputs.

An Unstable Process... is out of control and **unpredictable**, and its output varies due to **special cause** variation in just one or two of its inputs, that tend to dominate the process.

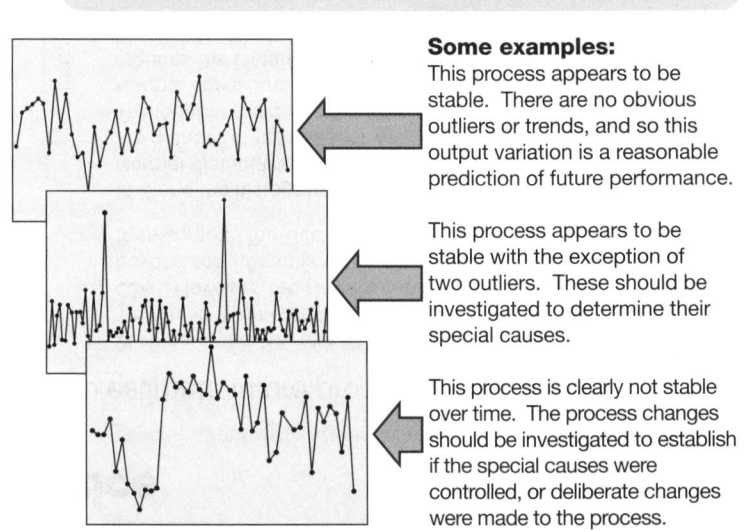

Some examples:
This process appears to be stable. There are no obvious outliers or trends, and so this output variation is a reasonable prediction of future performance.

This process appears to be stable with the exception of two outliers. These should be investigated to determine their special causes.

This process is clearly not stable over time. The process changes should be investigated to establish if the special causes were controlled, or deliberate changes were made to the process.

Process Stability: Short and Long Term Variation

The difference between short term and long term process stability can provide useful clues.

The difference between the short and long term variation of a process can provide clues as to the type of process improvements that may be required:

- **A large difference** indicates that the process performance could be improved through **better control**. The process **can** perform well but it is just not maintaining that performance. In this case, the process can be said to have **potential** if the control of it can be improved.

- **A small difference** indicates the process is already being controlled well over the longer term. So, if you still need better performance, it is unlikely to be available through improved control. In this case, the process can be said to be at the **limit of its potential** – the **technology** of the process can provide no more. This might suggest the project will involve re-designing the product or process.

So what is short and long term in real life?
Unfortunately the answer is once again 'it depends'. What may count as special cause variation when analysing short term data, might become viewed as common cause variation in light of the longer term data. It might be that your process has several levels of timescales; short term being just a few minutes, medium term being shift to shift, and long term might be month to month.

❗ Next time you are considering a major investment, make sure you are getting the most out of the existing one! A new machine or IT system can be an expensive solution to poor process control.

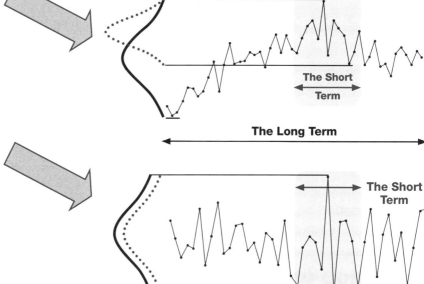

Process Stability: Trends, seasonality and random noise

The output of processes can be broken down into a combination of trends, seasonality and random variation. Being aware of these components can help in the interpretation of a Time Series plot.

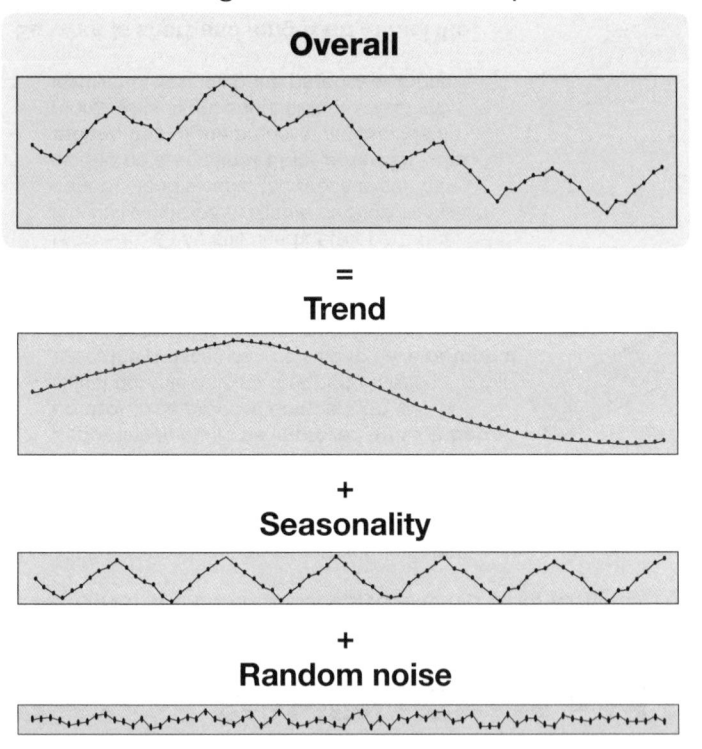

Overall

=

Trend

+

Seasonality

+

Random noise

The Overall chart (left) shows the output of a process as a Time Series plot. Processes are complex, and their output is generally the result of several different components, as follows:

Trends: Most processes are changing slowly over time, and these general changes are commonly referred to as trends. The trend chart on the left shows the trend component that is occuring within the overall results (top). Trends are more prevalent and easier to see when you look at the process over the longer term. If the trend is part of a repetitive increase or decrease that has no consistent duration, then it is referred to as a cycle. For example, many economic indicators are cyclic because they follow the inconsistent cycle of an economy. If you are making improvements to a process, then you are hoping to create an improvement trend as a result! Minitab's Trend Analysis tool can be used to identify and forecast these trends - see page 134.

Seasonality: Many processes have some consistent, time-based patterns that we refer to as seasonality. The seasonality chart (left) shows the season component from within the overall results (top). It is important to note that 'seasonality' does not mean these patterns are due to the climates' seasons. Instead, it refers to any cyclic patterns in the results that have a consistent duration, which may be hourly, daily, weekly or monthly. Minitab's Decomposition tool can help identify trends and seasons, although it is not dealt with in this text.

Random noise: All processes contain some level of random variation. If this variation is comparably low, then it is often masked by the trends and seasonality within a process. If it is relatively high, then reducing this variation will often be the first focus for improvement.

Process Capability – Overview

Process capability is the assessment of how well the process delivers what the customer wants.

What is Process Capability?

Process Capability refers to a range of KPIs (metrics) that measure the ability of a process to deliver the customer's requirements. There are many alternative metrics explored on the next few pages and Six Sigma introduces a new Process Capability measure – the Sigma Level – described on page 93.

Example: The histogram opposite shows the delivery times of a home delivery service. The actual time of delivery is measured from the target delivery time (agreed with the customer), and so delivering perfectly on time would be measured as zero.

The range between the lower and upper specification limits is referred to as the **Voice of the Customer** (VOC). In this example the VOC is two hours – one hour either side of the target delivery time.

The total variation in the process (affecting the width of the histogram) is referred to as the **Voice of the Process** (VOP) which, in a Normally distributed process such as the one shown here, is equivalent to six Standard Deviations.

> **❗ Specifications are not always the VOC!**
> Be careful not to assume that internal targets, specifications or manufacturing tolerances will reflect the customer's requirements.

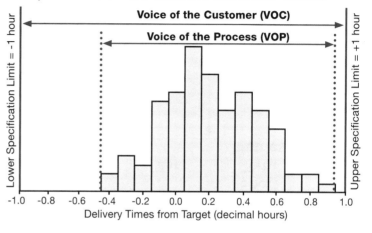

How do you _do_ process capability?

Process capability is the comparison of the VOP to the VOC (process versus customer). In this case, since the width of the histogram (VOP) is smaller than the gap between the specification limits (VOC), it appears that this process should be capable of delivering within specifications. However, the histogram is not positioned centrally between the specification limits, meaning that deliveries tend to get delivered after the target time, and therefore there is a risk that some deliveries will be made outside of the upper specification limit.

Both the **width** and **position** of the histogram define the capability of the process, and these characteristics are explored further on page 89.

Process Capability Routemap

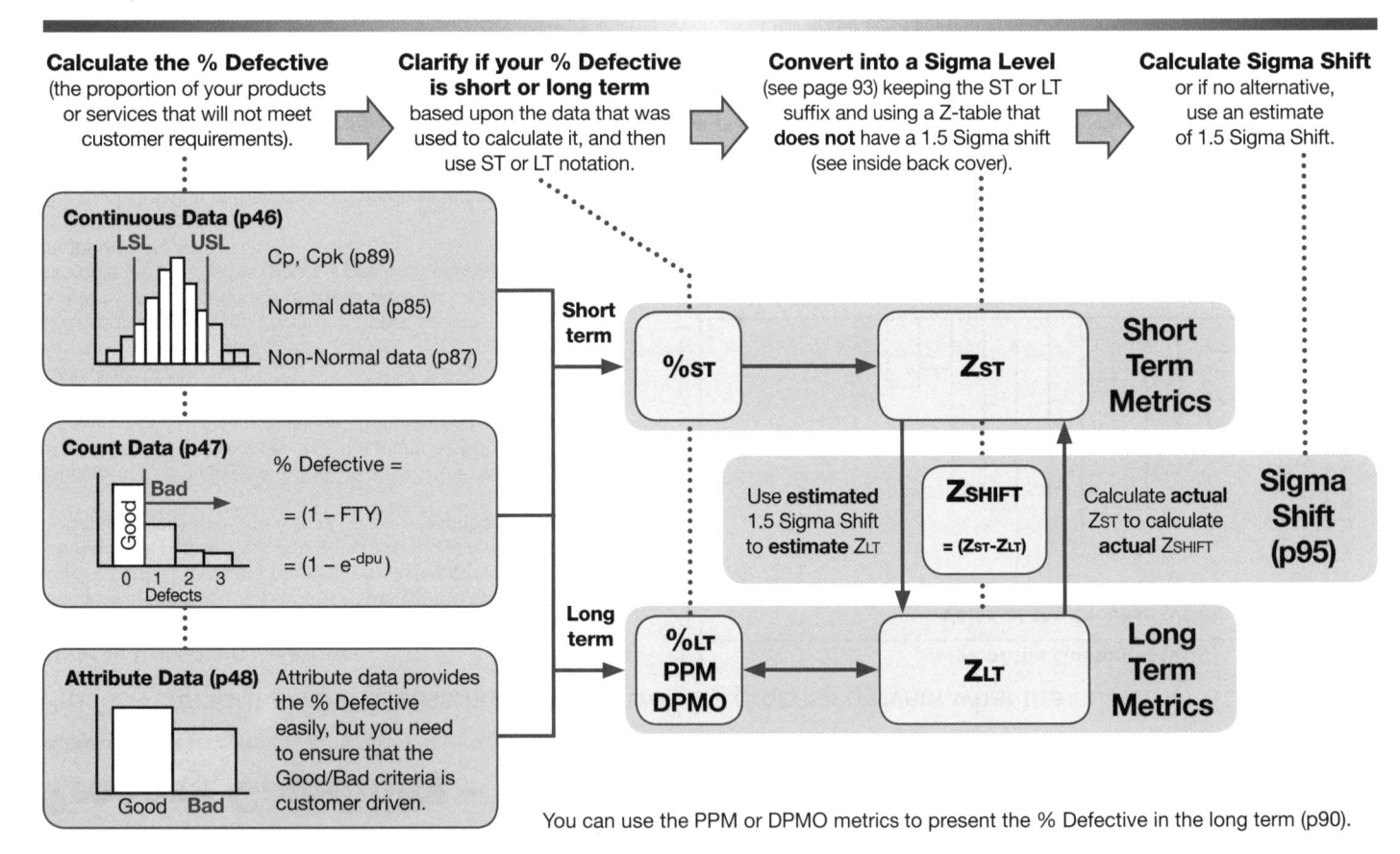

Calculate the % Defective (the proportion of your products or services that will not meet customer requirements).

Clarify if your % Defective is short or long term based upon the data that was used to calculate it, and then use ST or LT notation.

Convert into a Sigma Level (see page 93) keeping the ST or LT suffix and using a Z-table that **does not** have a 1.5 Sigma shift (see inside back cover).

Calculate Sigma Shift or if no alternative, use an estimate of 1.5 Sigma Shift.

Continuous Data (p46)

LSL USL

Cp, Cpk (p89)

Normal data (p85)

Non-Normal data (p87)

Count Data (p47)

Good / Bad

0 1 2 3
Defects

% Defective =

= (1 − FTY)

= (1 − e^{-dpu})

Attribute Data (p48) Attribute data provides the % Defective easily, but you need to ensure that the Good/Bad criteria is customer driven.

Good Bad

Short term → %ST → Z$_{ST}$ → **Short Term Metrics**

Use **estimated** 1.5 Sigma Shift to **estimate** Z$_{LT}$

Z$_{SHIFT}$ = (Z$_{ST}$−Z$_{LT}$)

Calculate **actual** Z$_{ST}$ to calculate actual Z$_{SHIFT}$

Sigma Shift (p95)

Long term → %LT PPM DPMO ↔ Z$_{LT}$ → **Long Term Metrics**

You can use the PPM or DPMO metrics to present the % Defective in the long term (p90).

Minitab's Capability Analysis Functions

Minitab's capability analysis functions bring together many of the concepts introduced during the Measure phase, such as histograms, distribution curves, short and long term variation.

The top three functions in Minitab's Capability Analysis menu are for use with Continuous data.

The **Normal** method (p85) is obviously for data that is Normally distributed. It allows for natural subgroups within the data if necessary, but can also cope with a subgroup size of 1 (i.e. no natural subgroups).

The **Between / Within** method is very similar to the Normal method. It is used for data that was collected in very specific subgroups, but you will not make a mistake by opting for the 'Normal' method (above) if you are in doubt.

The **Non-Normal** method (p87) should be used when your data is **clearly** skewed or Non-Normal in any way. However, it is more complex, and should only be used once you are familiar with 'Normal' capability analysis.

Minitab: Stat > Quality Tools > Capability Analysis

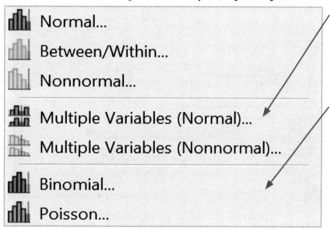

The middle two functions provide capability analysis for multiple variables at the same time, for comparison purposes. They are not explored further in this text.

The lower two functions are for use with Count data (Poisson function) and Attribute data (Binomial function). They are advanced techniques and are not dealt with in detail in this text.

Instead, see page 92 for an approach to process capability for Count data and Attribute data.

Conducting Capability Studies:

Capability studies can be conducted on historical data, or data that was collected specifically for the purpose. In either case, it is important to ensure that the data is recorded in time order, since Minitab will make this assumption. In addition, and if possible, both the short and long term performance of the process should be reflected in the data you collect. A common approach is to collect small samples (subgroups) of say five or so measurements to reflect the short term, and to repeat this sampling at specific intervals to capture the longer term variation in the process.

Capability Analysis with Normal data – Data Input

Example: A project is looking at the time it takes field teams to repair faults in air conditioning systems on customer sites. Five (consecutive) repair tasks were sampled randomly every day for 20 days (so the data clearly has natural subgroups within it).

Use this first option if your data is stacked in one column.

If the subgroup numbers are recorded in a separate column, then enter that column here.

Note that the subgroup sizes do not need to be equal. However, if the subgroups sizes **are** equal, then you can type the subgroup size directly instead of a column.
If there are no subgroups, enter '1'.

Use this second option if your data is across several columns, with a row for each subgroup, (enter all the columns that contain the data.)

The data file for this example (below) contains two different versions of the same data to show the alternative methods of recording sub-grouped data in Minitab.

Minitab: Stat > Quality Tools
> Capability Analysis > Normal

Capability Analysis (Normal Distribution)

C1 Time to fix fault
C2 Sub Group No

Data are arranged as
◉ Single column: 'Time to fix fault ('
Subgroup size: 'Sub Group No'
(use a constant or an ID column)

○ Subgroups across rows of:
'1st result' - '5th result'

Lower spec: 3   ☐ Boundary
Upper spec: 6   ☐ Boundary
Historical mean: (optional)
Historical standard deviation: (optional)

Transform...
Estimate...
Options...
Storage...

Select

Help   OK
            Cancel

If your data is not Normal, but can be transformed into Normal data using the Box-Cox or Johnson transformation methods (see Appendix G), then use this option.

The **Estimate** options define how the short term variation (within the subgroups) will be calculated. *Pooled standard deviation* and *Average moving range* are selected as default.

The **Options** allow you to select the type of metrics that will be calculated. Choose between:

- Parts per million (PPM) or Percent (see page 90)

- Cp/Cpks or Sigma Levels (see pages 89/93)

Use **Storage** if you want the outputs to be stored in your worksheet in addition to the graphical output.

Enter the **customer's specifications** here. If the process only has one specification, leave the other blank. Tick the Boundary boxes if a specification represents a natural or physical limit that it is impossible for the process to go beyond.

For this example, six hours is the maximum allowable by the customer, and three hours is an internal lower specification that indicates the process might be over-resourced (additional cost).

Capability-RepairTimes.mpj

Capability Analysis with Normal data – Output

The specifications and statistics of the capability are summarised here.

Standard Deviations:

- The **overall** value represents the long term.

- The **within** value represents the short term variation of the process.

Observed performance is based on the actual results used for the analysis. In this case no repairs took less than three hours, but 11 (out of 100) took longer than 6 hours. This 11% is equivalent to 110,000 parts per million.

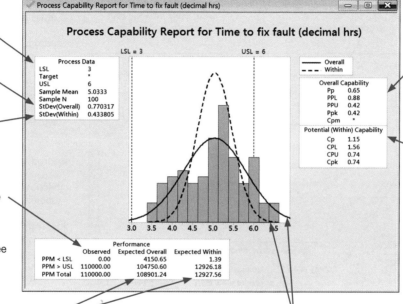

Process Capability Report for Time to fix fault (decimal hrs)

Process Capability Report for Time to fix fault (decimal hrs)

LSL = 3   USL = 6

Process Data	
LSL	3
Target	*
USL	6
Sample Mean	5.0333
Sample N	100
StDev(Overall)	0.770317
StDev(Within)	0.433805

Overall
Within

Overall Capability	
Pp	0.65
PPL	0.88
PPU	0.42
Ppk	0.42
Cpm	*

Potential (Within) Capability	
Cp	1.15
CPL	1.56
CPU	0.74
Cpk	0.74

3.0 3.5 4.0 4.5 5.0 5.5 6.0 .5

Performance			
	Observed	Expected Overall	Expected Within
PPM < LSL	0.00	4150.65	1.39
PPM > USL	110000.00	104750.60	12926.18
PPM Total	110000.00	108901.24	12927.56

The capability metrics given may be in Cp/Cpk (p89) or Sigma Level (p93) format depending on the Options selected.

The **Overall Capability** metrics are based on all the variation seen in the analysis (the long term) and reflect the current performance of the process.

The **Potential Capability** metrics are based on the short term variation. These reflect how good the process **could** be.

The long term metrics are called 'Pp' etc. to differentiate from their short term equivalents (Cp etc.).

Expected Performance statistics are **predictions** of the proportions that will fail the specification limits. They are based on the areas under the Normal curves, rather than the actual data in the histogram.

Two different sets are produced, one based on the short term performance (within) and one on the long term (overall).

Normal curves: In this example, the analysis found a large difference between the short term variation (Standard Deviation = 0.43) and the long term variation (Standard Deviation = 0.77).

The two Normal curves reflect this difference – the solid line represents the long term, and the dashed line represents the short term (it is much narrower/taller).

Capability Analysis with Non-Normal data – Data Input

A project is looking at the amount of time that mortgage applications spend queuing between two critical steps in the application process.

The queue times of 100 mortgage applications are sampled from the process over a two month period (so both long and short term data can be assumed to be reasonably represented).

For operational reasons, the maximum acceptable queue time is five (working) hours, and the project leader wants to understand the capability of the process to meet this specification.

A histogram of the data indicates that the process distribution is skewed, and a Normality Test also indicates that the data is **not** Normally distributed.

Minitab's **Non-Normal** Capability analysis function is therefore appropriate, but it requires you to select an appropriate distribution for your data.

The Individual Distribution Identification function (see example on page 191) indicates that this data fits a Weibull distribution.

Minitab: Stat > Quality Tools
*   > Capability Analysis > Nonnormal*

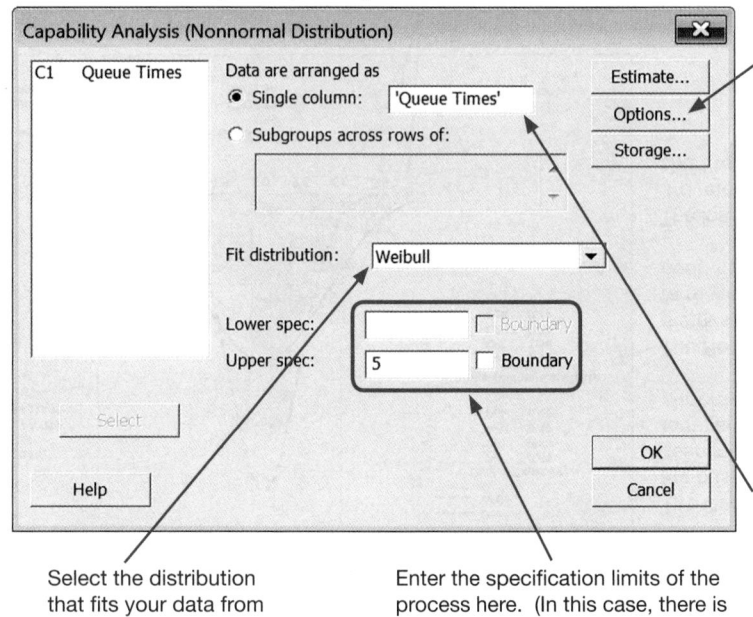

Select the distribution that fits your data from the drop down list.

Enter the specification limits of the process here. (In this case, there is only an upper specification).

For this example, leave the **Estimate** options as their default values.

The **Options** allow you to select the type of metrics that will be calculated. Choose between:

- Parts per million or Percents (see p90)

- Cp/Cpks or Sigma Levels (see p89/93)

Use **Storage** if you want the outputs to be stored in your worksheet in addition to the graphical output.

Enter the column containing your sampled process data here.

Capability-QueueTimes.mpj

Capability Analysis with Non-Normal data – Output

The specifications and statistics of the process are summarised here.

Observed performance statistics are based on the **actual** results within the data sample used for the analysis.

So, in this case, 2 of the 100 mortgage applications queued for more than five working hours and so the observed performance that exceeds the upper specification limit (USL) is 20,000 PPM (2%).

Because there was no lower specification limit (LSL), Minitab provides just an asterisk for **PPM < LSL.**

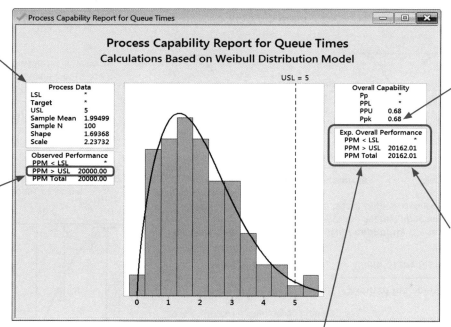

Process Capability Report for Queue Times

Process Capability Report for Queue Times
Calculations Based on Weibull Distribution Model

USL = 5

Process Data	
LSL	*
Target	*
USL	5
Sample Mean	1.99499
Sample N	100
Shape	1.69368
Scale	2.23732

Observed Performance	
PPM < LSL	*
PPM > USL	20000.00
PPM Total	20000.00

Overall Capability	
Pp	*
PPL	*
PPU	0.68
Ppk	0.68

Exp. Overall Performance	
PPM < LSL	*
PPM > USL	20162.01
PPM Total	20162.01

The Pp and PPL statistics are blank because there is no lower specification limit in this example.

Ppk is similar to the Cpk statistic described on the next page, and a value of 0.68 (0.64 in V17 due to different calculation method) indicates that this process is **not** capable for the longer term.

In this case, the expected performance figures predict that 20,162 parts per million will be above the USL, if the process continues as it is. 20,162 PPM is the same as 2.01%.

Weibull Curve:
In this example, we specified that Minitab should fit a Weibull distribution to the data (see previous page). The Weibull curve shown here appears to fit the shape of the histogram reasonably well (as predicted by the Individual Distribution Identification function on page 191) and so we can assume that the expected performance figures (described opposite) will be reasonably reliable.

Expected Performance statistics are **predictions** of the proportions that will fail the specification limits. They are based on the areas under the fitted curves (in this case the Weibull distribution), rather than the actual data in the histogram, and so can be a more reliable prediction (if the fitted model is suitable).

Process Capability – Cp and Cpk measures

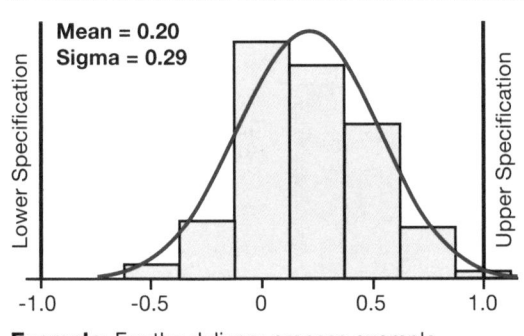

Mean = 0.20
Sigma = 0.29

Lower Specification

Upper Specification

-1.0   -0.5   0   0.5   1.0

Example: For the delivery process example introduced on page 82 and re-shown above, the Cp and Cpk measures can be calculated as follows:

Cp = (1 - (-1)) / (6 x 0.29) = 1.15

Cpk = (1 - 0.2) / (3 x 0.29) = 0.92

Cp values of 1.33 or above are considered acceptable, and a Cp above 2 is excellent (since it indicates that the specification window is twice as wide as the process variation).

So, in this example the Cp of 1.15 indicates the delivery process is **potentially** almost capable (1.33 is acceptable), but the lower Cpk of 0.92 indicates that its **actual** capability is poor. The Cpk is lower than the Cp because the process average is not positioned centrally between the specification limits.

The Cp metric reflects the *potential* capability of the process assuming that the histogram is positioned centrally within the specification limits (VOC).

Cp is therefore a ratio, and is defined as:

$$Cp = \frac{\text{Voice of the Customer}}{\text{Voice of the Process}} = \frac{\text{Width of the specification}}{\text{Width of the histogram}} = \frac{\text{(USL - LSL)}}{6 \times Sigma}$$

The Cpk metric reflects the *actual* capability of the process by measuring the same ratio as the Cp, but only to the nearest specification limit (since this is the limit which is most likely to be failed). Cpk is defined as:

$$Cpk = \frac{\text{Nearest Voice of the Customer}}{\text{Half of Voice of the Process}} = \frac{\text{(Nearest spec. – Average)}}{3 \times Sigma}$$

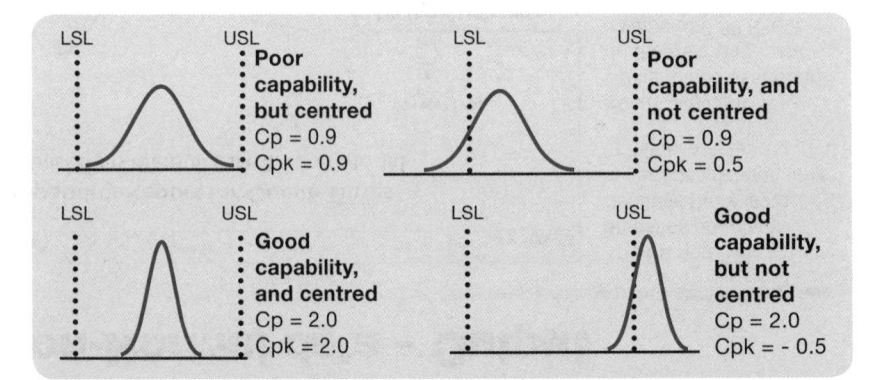

LSL   USL
Poor capability, but centred
Cp = 0.9
Cpk = 0.9

LSL   USL
Poor capability, and not centred
Cp = 0.9
Cpk = 0.5

LSL   USL
Good capability, and centred
Cp = 2.0
Cpk = 2.0

LSL   USL
Good capability, but not centred
Cp = 2.0
Cpk = - 0.5

Process Capability – PPM and DPMO measures

Per Opportunity: Process capability metrics that contain the phrase 'per opportunity' are used to account for the level of complexity in a process, when assessing its capability. They work by dividing the number of failures in a process by the number of opportunities for things to go wrong (complexity).

So, a highly complex process that is producing 5% scrap would have a better (lower) failure rate 'per opportunity' than a less complex process running at the same 5% scrap.

This seems reasonable but in reality the use of 'per opportunity' measures has proven to be far from practical, because of the difficulty in measuring complexity.

So how do you measure complexity?

Most approaches to measuring complexity do so by counting the number of **opportunities for defects** (OFDs) in a product or process. The counting of OFDs usually involves counting factors such as the number of process steps, parts, connections or handovers in a process, but this is not dealt with in any more depth within this text.

Whichever approach is used, the key success factor is that it must be applied **consistently**. There is little value in comparing *per opportunity* metrics, if the basis for counting OFDs is inconsistent!

While the use of complexity measures can be difficult for process capability purposes, it does have an important role in the (re)design of processes and products, i.e: Design for Six Sigma (DFSS). A focus on reducing complexity should be a corner stone of every Business Process Re-engineering (BPR) project or new product design. For this reason, measuring complexity is often more relevant within the Improve phase of a project.

Per Million: Process capability metrics that contain the phrase 'per million' are used to expand the scale so that smaller differences become more measurable. This may not seem relevant to your processes at this stage, but as process capability improves, so will the resolution required to measure it. With this approach, a 0.2% scrap rate becomes expressed as 2000 scrap parts **per million** – a much more challenging target to reduce!

An everyday example of this type of metric is chemical dilution rates (such as the amount of chlorine in a swimming pool). Because these rates are very low, they are sometimes quoted as 'parts per million'.

PPM – Parts per million: As discussed, this metric can be used to amplify a percentage and is often used to convey how many defective products or services will be delivered over the longer term.

DPMO – Defects per million opportunities: This metric incorporates both the *per million* and *per opportunity* concepts and is often proposed as a key Six Sigma metric. In reality, we would recommend avoiding DPMO unless the pitfalls of complexity measurement can be reliably overcome.

❗Only use long term data to calculate PPM and DPMO rates! PPM and DPMO are both aimed at describing the defect rate over the longer term (several million). For this reason, you should not take a % defective rate that is based upon short term data and magnify it into a PPM or DPMO metric. Your long term prediction would inevitably be over optimistic, since actual performance over the longer term is almost always worse than the short term.

Calculating the % Defective for Continuous Data

Calculating the overall % Defective is the key output from a Capability Analysis.

Calculating the total % Defective:
As shown in the graph opposite, the total % Defective is calculated by adding the % Defectives falling outside of each specification limit together.

The % Defectives that fall outside each specification limit are calculated using the Z-table as described below, or using Minitab (below right).

Example: Continuing the CD thickness example from page 78, suppose a lower specification limit (LSL) of 1.25mm was required by the customer, in addition to the existing upper limit of 1.5mm. The histogram opposite shows clearly that some CDs will fail the LSL, and we already know a small number (0.6%) will fail the USL (p78).

We also know that: Average CD thickness = 1.35mm (rounded)
Standard Deviation of CD thickness = 0.06mm

- The USL is 2.5 Sigma away from the average ((1.5 - 1.35) / 0.06), and the Z-table predicts that 0.6% of CDs will be too thick (above USL).

- The LSL is ≈ 1.65 Sigma away from the average ((1.35 - 1.25) / 0.06), and the Z-table predicts that 4.95% of CDs will be too thin (below LSL).

So, the total % Defective CDs will be (0.6%+ 4.95%) = 5.55%

Short term or Long term?
Don't forget to add a short term or long term code to this % Defective. From page 78, we can find that the data is based upon a small sample of just 100 CDs, and so we should add the code 'ST' (short term) to this % Defective figure (to remind us that it may not represent how the process will perform in the longer term).

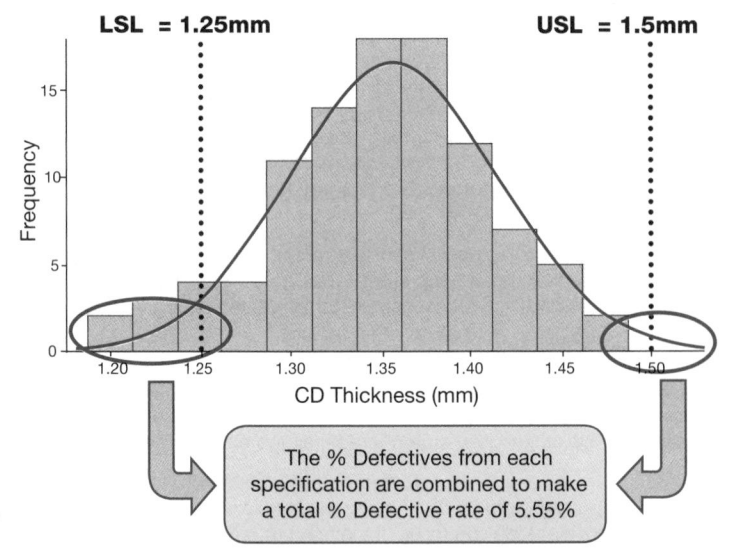

LSL = 1.25mm   USL = 1.5mm

CD Thickness (mm)

The % Defectives from each specification are combined to make a total % Defective rate of 5.55%

Using Minitab to calculate the total % Defective:
The *Expected Overall Performance* figures in either the Normal or Non-Normal versions of Minitab's capability analysis function will provide the total % Defective figure discussed here. The figure will be quoted as *PPM Total* or % *Total*, depending on the options selected.

Exp. Overall Performance	
PPM < LSL	50786.71
PPM > USL	6221.17
PPM Total	57007.88

Calculating the % Defective for Count and Attribute Data

% Defective in the Count data world:

If you are counting **defects**, then by definition, the products or services which are 'good' are those that have **no** defects. For example, the histogram below shows the number of scratches found on 100 mobile phone screens when they reached customers. The majority (58) of the phones had **no** scratches, but some had one or more scratches. So, the % Defective is the proportion of phones that had **one or more** scratches, as follows:

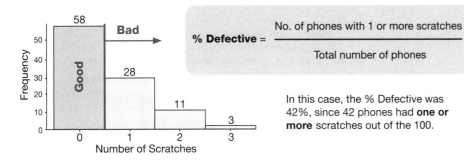

$$\text{\% Defective} = \frac{\text{No. of phones with 1 or more scratches}}{\text{Total number of phones}}$$

In this case, the % Defective was 42%, since 42 phones had **one or more** scratches out of the 100.

Alternative approach to calculating the % Defective with Count data:

Defects per unit (DPU) is the key statistic of the Count data world (page 47) and it represents the average number of defects found on each unit. It would seem rational that there is a relationship between DPU and the % Defective, since a **high DPU** (lots of defects) would mean a **high % Defective rate**. The mathematical relationships shown below can be used to calculate the % Defective from the average DPU. This approach provides a better estimate of the % Defective, since it utilises the Poisson model that lies behind Count data.

$$\text{FTY} = e^{\text{-DPU}} \times 100\% \quad \textbf{OR} \quad \text{\% Defective} = (1 - e^{\text{-DPU}}) \times 100\%$$

% Defective for Attribute data:

Attribute data is already divided into *good* and *bad* results, and therefore the % Defective is simply just the % of *bad* results from the sample.

For example, out of a sample of 100 computers, 79 passed and 21 failed the final test before shipment, and so the % Defective is 21%. As always, this should be quoted with a short term or long term code (since only 100 computers were tested, this example would be likely to be short term).

So, for the mobile phone example:

The DPU is 0.59 (average scratches/phone) which is calculated as follows:
28 phones had one scratch, 11 phones had two scratches, three phones had three scratches – making a total of 59 scratches on 100 phones (0.59 per phone).

With a DPU of 0.59, the equation shown on the left provides a % Defective of 44.6%. This is slightly higher, and more reliable, than the 42% produced directly from the raw data.

Process Capability – Sigma Levels

With so many different process capability metrics available, Six Sigma aimed to create one common metric that would apply to all data worlds and environments – the Sigma Level (or Sigma Value).

Sigma Levels in Theory:

As can be seen on the previous pages, there are numerous metrics used for quantifying Process Capability, and many more that are company or industry specific. Six Sigma aims to bring them all together through a common Sigma Level metric.

Two key advantages of Sigma Levels are:

- They are a common capability measure that allow processes to be benchmarked against each other across different industries, technologies, data worlds etc.

- Their scale is not linear. Sigma levels have increasing resolution at low defect levels, allowing the difference between 99.8% and 99.9% (for example) to be reflected in a more significant way.

Sigma Levels in Practice:

It's a nice idea, but unfortunately there is already a universal measure of process capability – the percentage! The percentage is something that is so common place and well understood that it is difficult to envisage a complete transition to Sigma Levels.

However, having said that, this book would not be complete without providing an understanding of how Sigma Levels work, so that the reader can converse in either format!

What is a Sigma level?

The Sigma level is the same as the Z value in the Z-table.

Imagine a Normally distributed process that only has an upper specification limit (USL), as shown below. Its Sigma level is defined as the distance between the average and the USL, in units of standard deviations (i.e its Z value).

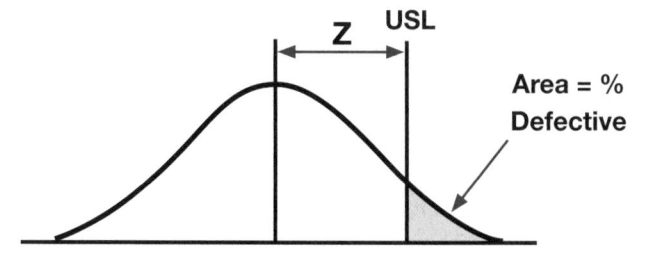

To work out the Sigma level for any process, you must equate it to this Normally distributed process, with just an upper specification limit.

It can be seen from the diagram above, that as the process moves further away from the specification limit (to the left), the Sigma Level (Z) will increase, and the proportion of products falling outside the USL (the % Defective) will reduce. So, a higher Sigma Level equates to higher performance and vice versa.

Process Capability – Sigma Levels (cont.)

Regardless of the environment or the data world, Sigma Levels are calculated by equating every process to the 'imaginary' (one sided) process defined in the Z-table.

As explained on the previous page, the Z-table is also a table of Sigma Levels, and can be used to translate the % Defective of a process into a Sigma Level, and vice versa. So;

- If you know the % Defective of your process (either as a proportion, percentage, PPM or DPMO), then you can use the Z-table to convert this into a Sigma Level.

- Alternatively, if someone tells you that a process is running at a Sigma Level of 2 Sigma, then you can use the Z-table to convert this into a % Defective of 2.3%.

The Z-table is therefore really a conversion table between two different scales – % Defective and Sigma Level. The (very) abbreviated table below shows some key Sigma Levels to remember, and a fuller version can be found inside the back cover of this guide.

% Defective	Sigma Level
50 %	0.0
31 %	0.5
16 %	1.0
7 %	1.5
2.3 %	2.0
0.6 %	2.5
0.13 %	3.0

Sigma Level examples from previous pages:

Continuous Data World example on page 91:

For the CD thickness example, the total % Defective was calculated to be 5.55% (or thereabouts allowing for rounding).

So, from the Z-table, this equates to a Sigma Level of 1.60 Sigma.

Count Data World example on page 92:

For the example about scratches on mobile phone screens, the total % Defective was calculated to be 44.6% (from the alternative method using DPU).

So, from the Z-table, this equates to a Sigma Level of 0.15 Sigma.

Attribute Data World example on page 92:

For the example on the final testing of computers, the total % Defective at final test was 21%.

So, from the Z-table, this equates to a Sigma Level of 0.8 Sigma.

❗ Note that some of the above Sigma Levels have been rounded slightly from the Z-table.

Process Capability – Sigma Shift

The difference between short and long term performance needs to be reflected in Sigma Levels

Page 80 describes the significant differences in performance that can occur between the short and long terms. This is shown graphically in the time series plot opposite, but has not been considered so far during the range of process capability measures described over the last few pages. When summarising process performance, it is important to be aware of whether the data being used represents the process over the short or long term.

Minitab's Capability Analysis uses a statistical approach to identify short term and longer term variation within a data set. It separates the capability of the process in the short term (for which it uses Cp and Cpk) from that of the long term (using Pp and Ppk metrics). A detailed example can be found on page 85.

Sigma Shift in Theory:
Sigma Levels based on long term data are generally lower than those calculated from short term data. The difference between them is called **Sigma Shift**.

Based on empirical evidence, a typical Sigma Shift between the short and long term is around 1.5. This means that the difference between short and long term performance is caused by the process average 'wandering' by up to +/- 1.5 Sigma.

Sigma Levels were originally intended only to be used to represent the capability of a process in the short term.

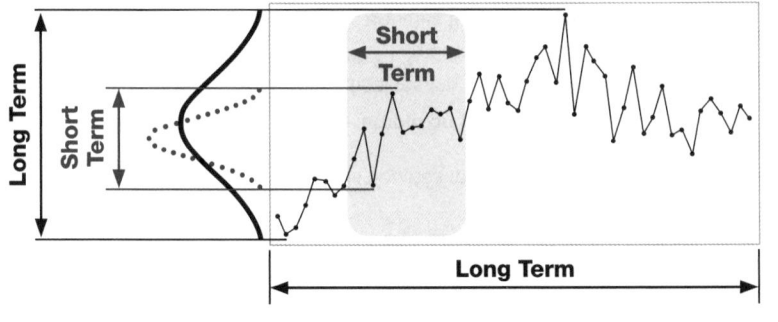

Sigma Shift in Practice:
In reality, Sigma Shift is different for every process and its measurement is important to understanding how the process might be improved. So, the generic application of 1.5 Sigma Shift should be only be used as a last resort, to estimate the difference between the short and long terms.

In addition, Sigma Levels tend to be used for Long and Short term data, with no distinction between them, causing significant confusion!

A practical approach to using Sigma Levels:

- If at all possible, collect long term data from your process, and calculate the actual Sigma Shift of your process (see next page).

- Always add a suffix code to your capability metrics (including Sigma Levels), to indicate whether they represent the short term (Z_{ST}) or the long term (Z_{LT}).

Process Capability – Sigma Shift (cont.)

The use of a generic 1.5 Sigma Shift causes a significant amount of confusion, and it is fair to say that this situation is perpetuated by 'experts' who continue to confuse and baffle their trainees with it during Six Sigma training! For example:

- You will hear people refer to a Six Sigma process as delivering 3.4 DPMO, when what they actually mean is that a process that is Six Sigma **in the short term**, will be 4.5 Sigma **in the long term**, and **that** is equivalent to 3.4 DPMO.

- In addition, some Z-tables and Sigma Level tables have been pre-adjusted to include the 1.5 Sigma Shift, whether you like it or not! This is why some Z-tables look different from others.

How confusing! So, how to get around this problem:

1) Avoid Z-tables that have the 1.5 Sigma Shift built into them. It is easy to make the wrong prediction with these tables.

2) Use the routemap through Sigma Shift described opposite, and always keep your Sigma Levels labelled as either short or long term.

3) Do not estimate Sigma Shift to be 1.5! Using the generic 1.5 Sigma Shift misses the whole point (and as many statisticians will tell you, is highly dubious in its validity). Instead, you should always try and collect **real** data from your process that represents the **real** Sigma Shift of your process. Sigma Shift represents the difference between the short and long term variation of your process - see p80.

 **Z-Table & Sigma Levels.xls**

If you have collected long term data...

- You can work out the long term Sigma Level and label it Z_{LT}.

- You can also convert your long term data into PPM or DPMO metrics, since these are for use with long term data.

...and now you want to work out the short term performance of the process, to see how good the process could be:

- You can find the short term performance of your process from **within** your long term data (Minitab process capability can do this).

- You can then convert the short term performance into a Sigma Level, and work out your Sigma Shift ($Z_{ST} – Z_{LT}$).

If you have collected only short term data...

- You can work out your short term Sigma Level, but make sure you label it Z_{ST}, so that people know it represents the short term only.

- **Do not** multiply your short term proportions into PPM or DPMO figures, since these are for long term data only.

...and now you want to work out what the long term performance of your process will be:

- Unless you can continue collecting real data over the long term (the ideal option), you can only estimate what Z_{LT} will be!

- If you really have to estimate it, then you can subtract 1.5 from your short term Sigma Level to estimate a long term Sigma Level (Z_{LT}). Be careful with this long term estimate! Make sure you keep it clearly labeled as an **estimate**. Your process might actually turn out to be better or worse in the long term – time will tell!

Measure – Checklist ☑️

- ☐ Have relevant Key Performance Indicators (KPIs) been selected and/or developed?
- ☐ Have the KPIs been defined clearly using process maps or diagrams and operational definitions?
- ☐ Is there a data collection plan in place for the KPIs, including sampling where appropriate?
- ☐ Is relevant contextual information being collected alongside the KPIs (for stratification of the data during Analyse)?
- ☐ Has the quality of the data been checked/challenged using Measurement System Analysis (GR&R etc.) techniques?
- ☐ Has a '1st Pass Analysis' (Histograms and Time Series plots) of the KPIs been completed using the historical data?
- ☐ Has the type of variation in the process (common cause or special cause) been considered?
- ☐ Has the difference between the short and long term performance of the process been considered?
- ☐ Have valid KPI baselines been set based on the historical data?
- ☐ Have defect definitions and specification limits been developed that are relevant to the Voice of the Customer?
- ☐ Has the process capability been analysed, and the problem and goal statement updated if necessary?
- ☐ Has a Sigma Level been calculated? (if your organisation uses this capability measure).

Measure – Review Questions

- ■ What KPIs have been selected for the problem? Why?
- ■ What data worlds do the KPIs come from (continuous/count/attribute)?
- ■ Where is the data for the KPIs coming from?
- ■ Was the data already available, or did you have to introduce more data collection?
- ■ If so, is it temporary for the project, or permanent?
- ■ Is 100% of the process being measured, or is it being sampled?
- ■ If sampling – what is the sampling strategy and why?
- ■ What other contextual information is being collected with the KPIs?
- ■ How was the quality of the data checked (does it represent what it is supposed to represent)?
- ■ What has been learnt about the historical behaviour of the process?
- ■ Does the process look stable (statistically in control) or unstable?
- ■ What is the best the process has ever performed? And worst?
- ■ Over what time period was the baseline performance of the process established?
- ■ How was the Voice of the Customer reflected when establishing the capability of the process?
- ■ Has the process capability been converted into a Sigma Level?

Analyse – Overview

The Analyse phase aims to identify critical factors of a 'good' product or service, and the root causes of 'defects'. It has less of a logical flow, but provides more of a toolbox of tools and techniques.

The flow through Analyse:

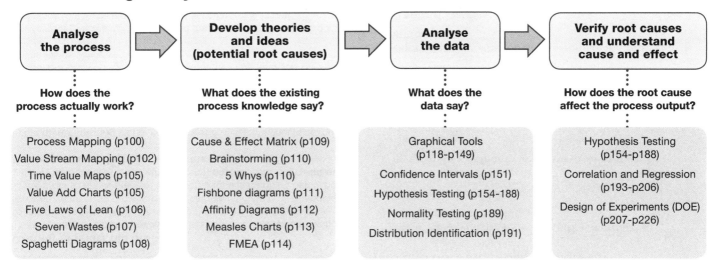

Analyse the process

How does the process actually work?

Process Mapping (p100)
Value Stream Mapping (p102)
Time Value Maps (p105)
Value Add Charts (p105)
Five Laws of Lean (p106)
Seven Wastes (p107)
Spaghetti Diagrams (p108)

Develop theories and ideas (potential root causes)

What does the existing process knowledge say?

Cause & Effect Matrix (p109)
Brainstorming (p110)
5 Whys (p110)
Fishbone diagrams (p111)
Affinity Diagrams (p112)
Measles Charts (p113)
FMEA (p114)

Analyse the data

What does the data say?

Graphical Tools (p118-p149)
Confidence Intervals (p151)
Hypothesis Testing (p154-188)
Normality Testing (p189)
Distribution Identification (p191)

Verify root causes and understand cause and effect

How does the root cause affect the process output?

Hypothesis Testing (p154-p188)
Correlation and Regression (p193-p206)
Design of Experiments (DOE) (p207-p226)

The Process Door Routemap (page 99):
The first two steps of Analyse are also referred to as the 'Process Door' because they aim to understand and gain clues directly from the process itself. The tools focus on gaining an in-depth understanding of how the process really works, and so most of them involve the people who know the process best – those who make it happen.

The Data Door Routemap (page 116):
The last two steps of Analyse are also referred to as the 'Data Door' because they focus on gaining clues and understanding from the data itself. These tools include a range of graphical and statistical tools that help to analyse the data.

The Process Door Routemap – Finding The Right Tool

Mapping the real process is a common starting point within the Process Door. The remainder of the Process Door tools then focus on analysing when, where and how the process might fail.

Getting to know the process:

The first stage of Analyse involves getting out of the office and going to see the process. Regardless of the type of product or service involved, there is no substitute for gaining an intimate understanding of the process at this stage of a project. Process mapping helps, but before that it should be something even more practical… **go and do the process, provide the service or make the product!**

In the **manufacturing** world, engineers and designers should spend time operating the machines and products that they design. The same principles apply to the **transactional** environment, where team members could spend a shift or two answering phone calls or filling out purchase requisitions, go out with a service technician for a day, or spend a week on the reception desk of the hotel, and you will soon notice things you never knew before.

The following boxes will help you find the appropriate Process Door technique to use, based upon what it is you need to know.

Getting to know the process as it actually happens…

- Process Mapping (p100) and Value Stream Mapping (p102)
- Time Value Maps (p105) and Value Add Charts (p105)
- Seven Wastes (p107) and Spaghetti Diagrams (p108)

Understand which process inputs are critical to customer requirements…

- Cause and Effect Matrix (p109)

Investigate a defect to understand its root cause…

- 5 Whys (p110)

Assessing what <u>could</u> go wrong and where…

- Failure Mode and Effects Analysis (FMEA) (p114)

Understanding what <u>does</u> go wrong in the process, and where…

- Affinity Diagrams (p112)
- Measles Charts (p113)

Identifying possible root causes…

- Brainstorming (p110)

Structure possible root causes in a logical manner…

- Fishbone (Cause and Effect) Diagrams (p111)

Process Mapping

The flowcharts contained in procedures and quality manuals show how a process **should** work. Process mapping helps to show how a process **really** works.

What is process mapping?

Process mapping is a way of visually representing a process. It helps in understanding how the process actually works, and is a foundation for further process analysis.

Among other benefits, process maps help bring clarity to complex processes and can be used to highlight particular aspects of the process that are relevant to your improvement project, such as:

- Value add / non-value add steps
- Decision points
- Hand-offs
- Rework loops (see below)
- Redundant or repeated processes etc.

Rework loops:

One of the most common purposes of process mapping is to help identify the rework loops in a process. Most processes have some formal, documented rework loops for recognised problems. This might be evident by finding complaint forms, stock adjustment forms, RMA (Return Merchandise Authorisation) forms etc. However, most processes also have an abundance of informal rework loops that can only be identified by asking 'what can go wrong?' at every stage of the detailed process mapping.

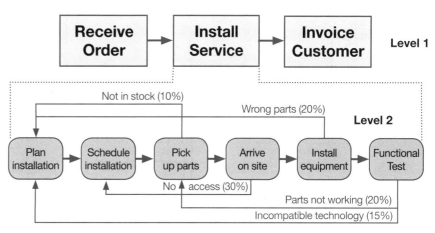

Example: The process map above looks at a generic **Service Installation** process and is organised by different process levels. This hierarchical layout shows clearly that it is the middle **Install Service** Level 1 step that is then broken down further into Level 2 sub-steps. The map then focuses on the rework loops, failure modes and failure rates that occur at Level 2, but information of interest for other projects might include lead times, process ownership (geographical, organisational or contractual etc.), data collection points, yields, inventory levels, optional processes etc.

Process Mapping (cont.)

How process mapping supports process improvement:

Process mapping is a fundamental tool within process improvement. By documenting how a process actually works, process mapping stimulates questions and provides useful insights. This enables a project team to start thinking about potential improvements.

Process mapping links with other elements of process improvement, by helping to:

- Identify the value stream within a process.
- Document standardised work.
- Focus on eliminating Non-Value Add activities.

Standard symbols help to ensure process maps are written in a consistent manner. There are a number of different standards but process steps are usually contained in squares and formal decision points (such as inspection or testing) in diamonds. Page 104 shows a selection of common Process Mapping symbols, although it is worth checking whether your organisation has any standard symbols that you should comply with first.

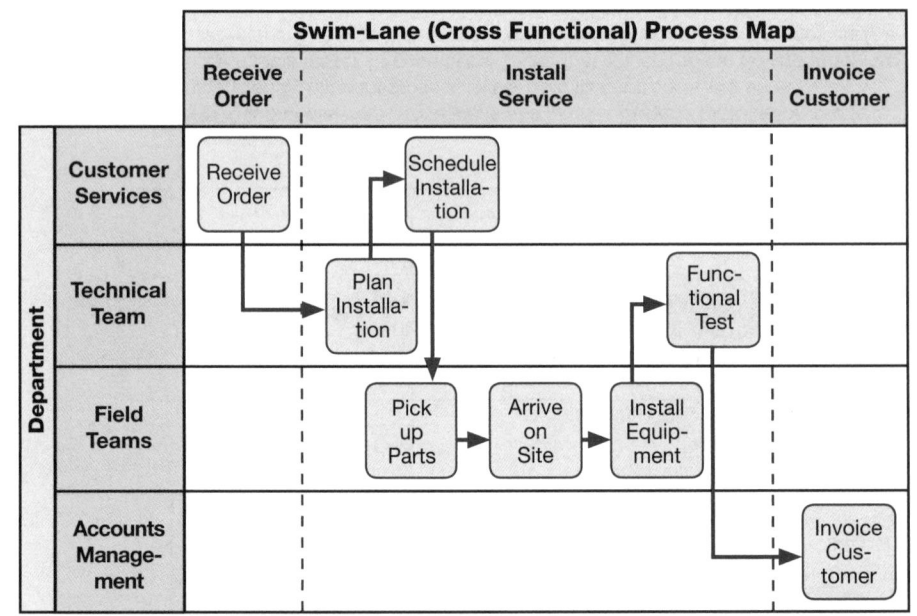

Example: The process map above looks at the same **Service Installation** process shown on the previous page, but in this case organised into 'swim-lanes' for different departments within the organisation.

Process maps can become complex very quickly, and you will soon find you have to re-write a process map for clarity. This 'swim-lane' layout (also known as a Cross Functional Process Map) is useful for structuring your process map and detailing which departments own which processes, as well as identifying key handover points.

Value Stream Mapping

For projects that are focusing on improving flow and efficiency and reducing waste, it can be useful to develop the process map further into a Value Stream Map.

What is Value Stream Mapping:

Value Stream Mapping (VSM) is an advanced form of process mapping that focuses on a process using the principles of Lean and from the perspective of value.

A Value Stream Map helps to understand the flow of products (or services) through a process, and identifies key material and information flows. A VSM also captures key process data such as processing times, inventory levels and data sources etc.

When to use Value Stream Mapping:

VSM mapping is typically used in two key ways;

- **Current state** mapping for analysing existing processes is typically completed in the Analyse phase of an improvement project (although some practitioners might apply it slightly earlier as part of the Measure phase).

- **Future state** mapping for designing improved processes is typically completed in the Improve phase, to design processes that will meet future needs and solve key problems.

The Value Stream Mapping Process:

1) Gain clear scope for the VSM.
2) Document the process flow (current or future), focusing on material and data flows.
3) Collect additional data, as required by your project focus – see information on Data Boxes, right.
4) Gain consensus from the process owners and your project team.

Data Boxes:

Once the process flow has been identified, data that is relevant to the focus of the project is collected and recorded in Data Boxes alongside each process step, as shown in the example below:

Data Box	
Set up Time	10 minutes
Process Time	22 minutes
Queue Time	2hrs 35 mins
Queue Quantity	65 units
Operators	2
Batch Size	4

Lean focused data that is useful to collect:

- Times (cycle, queue, set-up, changeover, transport).
- Inventory locations and levels, and existence of Kanbans.
- Number of people or machines.
- Batch (lot) sizes and pack sizes.
- Defect rates (both scrap and rework).
- Planning information (shipping schedules, production plans etc.).
- Customer shipments and demand rates (Takt time).
- Changeover frequency and product variations.
- Sources of data.

Value Stream Mapping (cont.)

Example: A project is looking at improving the speed of a telecom equipment installation process, and the **current state** Value Stream Map shown below has been developed by the project team. The map helps to present clearly where inventory exists within the process, the flow of parts and information as well as process metrics for key process steps. VSM introduces lots of new symbols, some of which are shown on the next page.

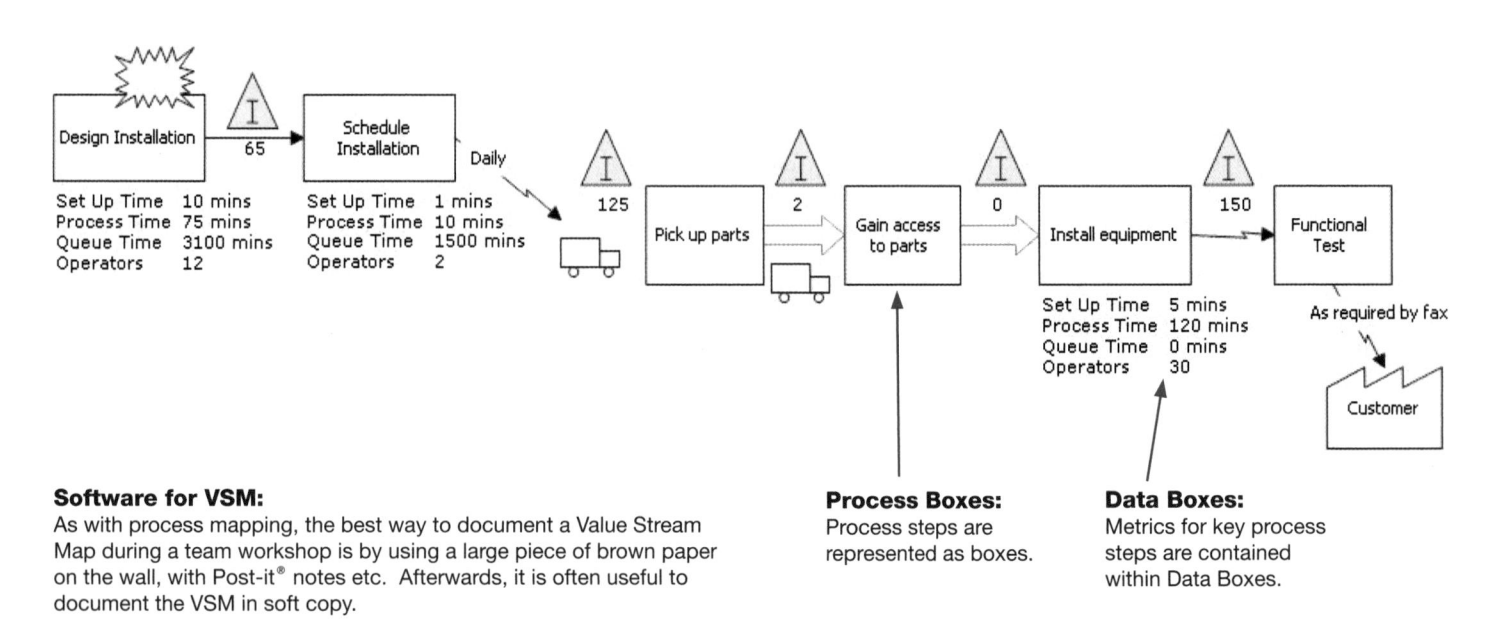

Software for VSM:
As with process mapping, the best way to document a Value Stream Map during a team workshop is by using a large piece of brown paper on the wall, with Post-it® notes etc. Afterwards, it is often useful to document the VSM in soft copy.

Process Boxes:
Process steps are represented as boxes.

Data Boxes:
Metrics for key process steps are contained within Data Boxes.

Process Mapping and Value Stream Mapping Symbols

A selection of useful Process Mapping symbols:

Process Step

Decision / Inspection Point

Direction of Flow

Start / End

Connector

Document

Delay

Storage

A selection of useful VSM symbols:

Customer or Supplier

A queue of 125 units of inventory

Physical flow of parts

Flow of manual information (e.g. forms)

Flow of electronic information (e.g. EDI)

A potential improvement project

An electronic database

Number of employees

Transport

Time Value Map

A Time Value Map demonstrates graphically the proportion of time that is spent adding value.

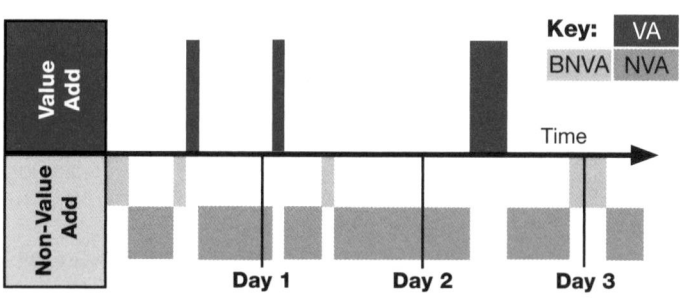

A Time Value Map is constructed using the queue and process times recorded during Value Stream Mapping. In addition, each process step is classified into one of the following three categories:

- **Value Add Activities** (VA - blue) increase the value of the product (or service) from the customer's perspective.

- **Business Non-Value Add Activities** (BNVA – light grey) are necessary for the business, but the customer would not be willing to pay extra for them (e.g. regulatory, data entry, invoicing, purchasing, research and development).

- **Non-Value Add Activities** (NVA – dark grey) add no value and are not required for business operational reasons either. This includes all of the seven wastes (see page 107).

Value Add Chart

A Value Add Chart helps to compare the balance of time across process steps.

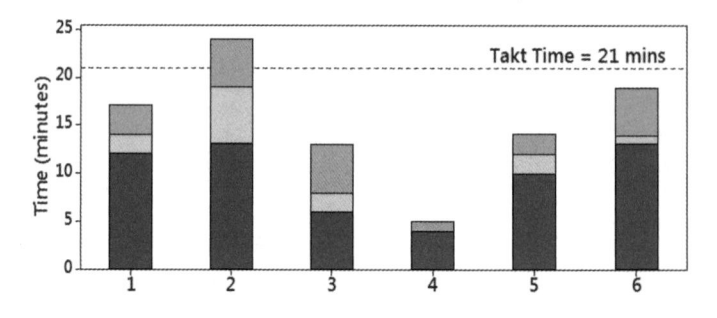

The Value Add Chart above shows the process time for each process step, in order that they can be compared against the Takt Time of the process (see page 38) and against one another. The process times are also then broken down into the three value categories described on the left. The main objectives of the chart are to establish:
- If the process step times are balanced (similar).
- If any process steps take longer than the calculated Takt Time.

The Value Add Chart also then helps to identify which process steps contain opportunities for improvement through the removal of NVA.

! The key difference between the charts on this page is that Time Value Maps show the entire processing time (including waiting time **between** steps) while Value Add Charts only show specific process step times (including only waiting time that occurs **within** steps).

The Five Laws of Lean

The Five Laws of Lean encapsulate the Lean approach and provide key principles for improvements.

1) The Law of the Market effectively says that the customer is king. Critical to Quality characteristics can only be defined by the customer, and should be our highest priority for defining value and making improvements. Everything else (such as sustained market growth and returns on our investments) are reliant on our focus on the customer.

2) The Law of Flexibility says that the speed and flexibility of a process are linked. An inflexible process will hinder the flow (and therefore speed of delivery) of a product or service, and vice versa for a flexible one. Expanding on this idea further:

- If a production line is inflexible (so that it's very difficult to change between products), then this encourages the company to run larger production batches and schedule each product less frequently, both of which will increase Work in Progress (WIP) and lead times of all products.

- If a loan company has lots of different types of loan, but it takes its employees a long time to switch between using different forms, processes and IT systems, then again, the employees will be encouraged to batch and queue the loan applications, and it will take longer to get your loan!

3) The Law of Focus says that 80% of the delays in a process will be caused by just 20% of the activities, and so you should find and focus on these 'time traps' in order to create a leaner process.

A similar observation is made when solving quality problems using DMAIC, where you will often find that most of the problems (about 80%) are caused by a few key root causes (about 20%).

4) The Law of Velocity (a.k.a. Little's Law) says that the more WIP there is in a process, the longer its lead time will be. This makes sense, since high WIP means more queues and more waiting between each process step. Little's law can be expressed as an equation, which enables us to calculate the average lead time of a process by knowing how much WIP there is, and the production rate of the overall process – see page 38 for more detail.

5) The Law of Complexity and Cost says that products and services that are more complex require significantly more cost to produce and deliver. This may seem in conflict with the first law, in which customers are king and often want highly customised products, but lots of companies have found ways to provide 'mass customisation'. Dell, for example, are well known for rapidly delivering custom made computers.

To summarise, the Five Laws of Lean say that:

1) Priority should be placed on providing the customers needs.

2) Processes should be flexible in order to provide products and services faster.

3) Focusing on key 'time traps' will also create significantly faster processes.

4) Work in Progress (WIP) is a key enemy, since it slows down processes, costs money and hides quality problems.

5) Unnecessary product complexity should be challenged, but we still need to develop flexible processes that can deliver complex products and services that are customised to individual customers.

The Seven Wastes, plus some new ones

The Seven Wastes are a useful structure for identifying, eliminating and preventing waste. Several new wastes have recently been added, along with wastes specific to service industries.

The Seven Wastes:

Overproduction: Making more products than the customer requires. This waste increases WIP and lead times, hides poor quality rates, requires extra storage and promotes a 'batch and queue' type approach.

Waiting: Any time that products are waiting, lead times are increasing, and no value (the only thing a customer pays for) is being added.

Transporting: Moving things unnecessarily costs money, time and usually requires a return loop – all without adding value for the customer!

Over processing: Refers to adding more value (i.e. features and specifications) to the product or service than the customer is willing to pay for. Inappropriate processing is slightly different, and refers to the use of inappropriate equipment that is over engineered for the purpose, and therefore adds more cost than value.

Unnecessary inventory: Holding and creating excessive inventory costs money and increases lead times. Some inventory is necessary, but most processes can be managed differently to minimise inventory.

Unnecessary motion: Needless movements at an ergonomic level have a significant effect on overall efficiency, and are increasingly the source of health and safety issues.

Defects (or errors): The clearest waste of all, defects and mistakes require fixing or replacing and have a direct impact on the bottom line.

Some New Wastes:

Wasted human potential: Traditional hierarchical cultures waste significant skills and expertise in the workforce.

Wasted energy: The finite aspect of fossil fuels has raised awareness of wasting energy and increased its effect on the bottom line. This will increase further as climate change takes hold.

Pollution: Historically a hidden shared cost to us all, the producer is increasingly being made to pay for pollution, thus raising its importance.

Wasted space: The premium on space in certain environments is at an all time high, and its waste is something the customer will not pay for.

Wastes from the Service Perspective:

Delay in provision: Time is an important element of the value of a service, and therefore can have a significant cost impact.

Incorrect inventory: The wrong inventory (or being out of stock) is a significant waste in the service sector, where customers tend not to wait, and instead move on to another provider.

Duplication: Service processes rely heavily on the handling and processing of data, and frequently involve duplicated data entry or the unnecessary transfers of data.

Spaghetti Diagrams

Spaghetti diagrams are a simple tool that can help to highlight process waste (particularly excessive transportation) by mapping the actual route of a particular resource through a physical environment.

Like many Process Door tools (page 99), spaghetti diagrams are a practical tool that are very easy to use and provide valuable information.

They are very similar to process mapping, in that they focus on what **really** happens (rather than what **should** happen) in a process. However, while process maps focus on steps, spaghetti diagrams focus on the actual physical journey of a resource (e.g. a part or piece of paper) through an organisation (e.g. an office, warehouse or production plant).

Spaghetti diagrams usually demonstrate that resources have a surprisingly long and wasteful journey, with poor organisational layouts hiding inefficiencies and causing excessive transportation and WIP.

Completing a spaghetti diagram:

- You will need a layout diagram of the facility (to scale if possible).

- Select an item (part or paper) at random, and follow its journey.

- Ensure that you track the path taken, not just start and finish points.

- You may need to attach a tracking sheet or be available whenever a part is moved.

- Follow several items through the process. Different items will take different routes, and this will enable you to build up an overall picture.

- Look out for rework loops and unofficial storage locations or queues.

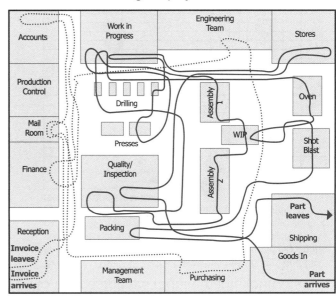

Example: The spaghetti diagram above shows the route of a part through a production process (the solid blue line) and an invoice through a payment process (the dotted line). Both examples demonstrate the significant distances travelled in order to complete just a few process steps.

Cause and Effect (C&E) Matrix

Having identified inputs and outputs during process mapping, a C&E Matrix can be used to identify which of the process inputs are most important in relation to the customers requirements (outputs).

What is a C&E Matrix?

A C&E Matrix helps to identify the most important process inputs, in relation to the customers requirements. Like many of the tools in the Process Door of the Analyse phase, a C&E Matrix is a team effort – you will need to assemble a cross-functional team that understand both the customers and the process itself.

It's important to note that a C&E Matrix is distinctly different from a C&E Diagram (Fishbone). A C&E Matrix prioritises process inputs against process outputs (from the customer perspective), while a C&E Diagram focuses on root causes to a particular problem or defect.

A C&E Matrix links with several other Lean Six Sigma tools. The Process Capability of the key process outputs should be assessed and the key process inputs should be used within FMEA and Control Plans.

How to complete a C&E Matrix:

1) Identify the process outputs.

2) Rate each process output in terms of its importance to the customer.

3) Identify the process steps, and the inputs for each process step, using the process map.

4) Rate the correlation between each process input and output (a low score means that the input has little effect on the output, and vice versa).

5) Multiply each correlation value by the same outputs importance and add up the results for each row (i.e. for each process input).

And finally, act on the results! You should focus on controlling (or improving) the few process inputs that have the highest total scores.

Example: The C&E Matrix below has been completed for an online order process. It demonstrates that the highlighted process inputs (correct product codes/quantity, correct picking lists, adequate inventory, suitable boxes and correct printed invoices) are the most important input factors in relation to customer satisfaction.

		Rating of Importance to Customer	10	8	5	7		
		Process Outputs	Correct products	Effective packaging	On time delivery	Correct invoice		Total
	Process Step	Process Input						
1	Receive Order	Product codes	10	1	4	7		177
2		Product quantities	8	1	4	7		157
3		Delivery address	1	1	9	3		84
4		Invoice address	1	1	1	8		79
5		Payment details	1	1	5	5		78
6	Pick order	Operator	6	1				80
7		Picking list	8	1	4	1		115
8		Inventory	5	1	8	1		105
9	Package	Operator	1	7	2	1		83
10		Boxes	1	9	4	1		109
11		Bubble wrap	1	6	2	1		75
12		Filler	1	8	1	1		86
13	Ship	Courier	1	1	10	1		75
14		Delivery address	1	1	9	1		70
15		Weight / dimensions	1	1	7	2		67
16		Agreed delivery	1	1	9	3		84
17		Printed invoice	1	1	6	9		111
Total			490	344	430	371		

Brainstorming

Brainstorming can be used to consider a whole range of possible root causes to a **type of failure**.

Brainstorming is a valuable technique that can be used in many environments, and for many purposes. In Lean Six Sigma projects, brainstorming is often used at the beginning of the Analyse phase. While the 5 Whys technique (right) can be used to investigate **specific** failures, brainstorming can be used to identify a range of potential root causes for a generic **type** of failure.

Brainstorming in practice:
A brainstorming session needs careful facilitation (see page 30). If ideas are slow, then the facilitator can use prompting questions to help the group focus on a specific area for a while. If someone is feeling unable to participate, the facilitator needs to help them to do so. The brainstorming team should include people from a variety of levels within the organisation, since this helps to capture the different impressions people may have of the problem.

Different approaches to brainstorming:
When running a brainstorming event, participants can either be asked to give an idea each in turn (better for ensuring everyone feels able to participate, but can also be intimidating) or can be given a 'free-for all' (which requires more careful facilitation).

Alternatively, brainstorming can be done over time by placing a Fishbone diagram (see next page) on the wall for a week or two and inviting everyone to write their ideas on it.

5 Whys

The 5 Whys can be used to investigate a **specific failure** to find a problem's real root cause.

If a problem is going to be fixed, the real root cause needs to be understood. Sometimes it is useful to randomly select two to three real failures in the process and to investigate them in much more detail using 5 Whys, a simple but effective technique.

5 Whys is a bit like being an inquisitive four year old who keeps asking why? You take a real failure and investigate by asking why, why, why?

Example: Parcel got lost in post...
Why? Because it got stolen from the customer's front door.

Why? Because the customer was not in to sign for it.

Why? Because the customer had gone out during the agreed delivery period.

Why? Because the customer had forgotten the delivery was due.

Why? Because the delivery was arranged several weeks in advance, and the customer was not reminded.

Once the real root cause is understood, the chance of an effective solution is greatly improved. In this example, the lead time between arrangement and delivery could be reduced or reminders could be sent out (by e-mail/text/post) just prior to delivery.

Be careful not to let your answers get too broad. If you always end up concluding that the root cause is 'poor management' or 'terrible suppliers' (even though they might be true!) then it is not going to be specific enough to help solve the problem.

Fishbone (Cause and Effect) Diagrams

Fishbone diagrams are usually used during brainstorming, to identify root causes. However, they can be also be used throughout the Analyse phase as a great tool for structuring a team's thoughts.

Fishbone diagrams are an effective tool to help facilitate brainstorming sessions. The example shown here is the output of a brainstorming session on the causes of low fuel efficiency in a car.

Categories on Fishbone diagrams:

There are many different versions of Fishbone diagrams – with different branch names (people, methods etc). This is because there are no right or wrong ones; just use those that are appropriate to your project, or create your own.

Other uses of Fishbone diagrams:

As projects move into the Analyse phase, they usually start to have several specific areas of investigation. Although not technically being used for 'root cause analysis', a Fishbone diagram can provide clarity by being used to document the structure of the project, with each area of investigation represented by a different branch.

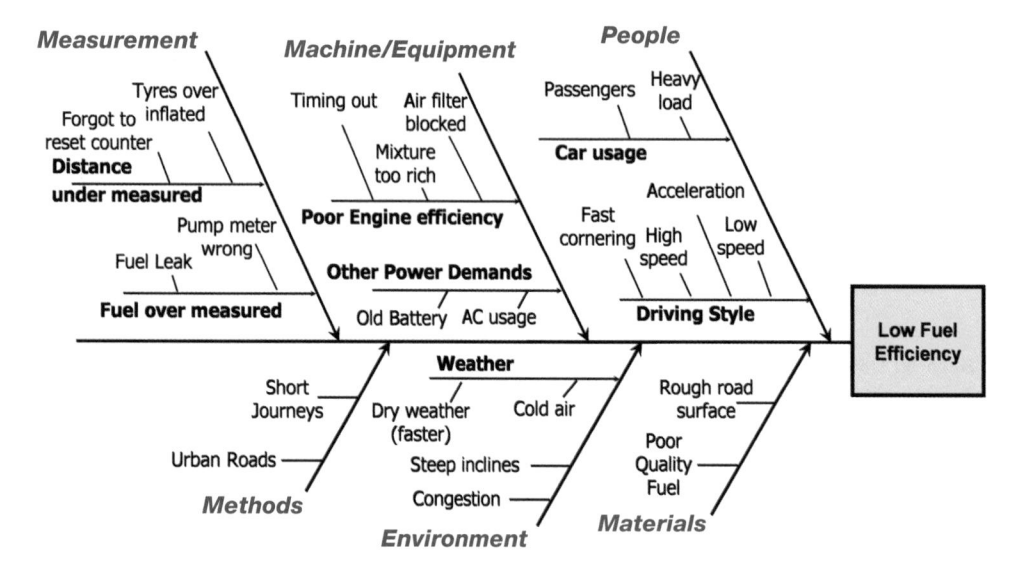

How to document a Fishbone diagram:

The best way to start a Fishbone diagram is with a large piece of paper on the wall or a white board (a pretty Fishbone diagram is not your first objective!). Companion by Minitab can also be used to document your results and has a brainstorming function too, which works alongside the Fishbone tool – see the Manage section of this guide for more detail.

Affinity Diagrams

Affinity Diagrams help to identify key categories within textual data, such as the key types of failure in a product or service or the key issues contained within customer feedback forms.

During the Measure phase, you may have implemented data collection forms that ask for the details of a failure to be written down. During the Analyse phase, you will probably find lots of anecdotal evidence of failures within the process, particularly during process mapping. Affinity diagrams are a useful technique for finding similar groups within these types of textual (non-numeric) sources of data.

How to construct an affinity diagram:

- Write each bit of textual data on a separate paper note and lay them out on a table or stick them on a wall.

- Ask the project team to start moving the notes around so that ones that are similar are placed together. They should do this in silence, and not look to explain their thinking for moving a note – just do it! Other participants are allowed to move notes back again if they disagree.

- Once natural clusters have emerged in the notes, discuss them within the group and give each cluster a name. Some clusters may have only one or two notes.

What can be done with the output of affinity diagrams:

- Reason codes (for data collection forms) can be designed with more relevance.

- The largest clusters can be focused on when problem solving during the Analyse phase.

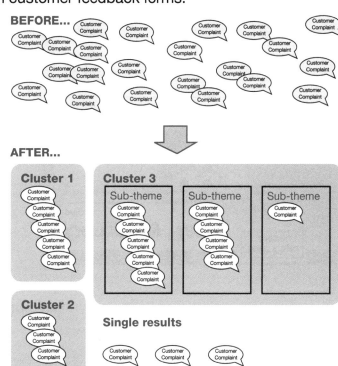

Measles Charts

Measles charts are a practical tool for collecting data that helps when analysing the location of failures in a product or process.

Although you may be measuring the failure rate or First Time Yield of a process, these will not necessarily tell you where most of the problems occur. Measles charts are a very visual and practical method of plotting the location and density of failures onto a symbolic drawing or picture of a product or process.

When to use Measles Charts:
They can be done alongside process mapping during Analyse, or used as part of a data collection plan during Measure.

Example: A project is looking at reducing the number of invoices that get returned from clients because they have mistakes on them. A standard invoice (right) is printed out as a poster and placed on the wall of the office. For every returned invoice, a dot is placed on the invoice poster to indicate the area of the mistake. This quickly highlights that the delivery address and the calculation of tax are the two most common problems areas.

Example: A production process for cans has excessive downtime due to parts jamming in the pressing machine. A picture of the press is set up on the shop floor and every time a can jams, the location of the jam is marked on the picture (Measles chart) with a red dot.
After a short period of time, a clear cluster of red dots emerges, which helps to confirm that the biggest cause of jams is the lip of the can catching a specific part of the ejection mechanism.

Example: Car hire companies use Measles Charts to record car damage. When you deliver back a hire car, you are asked to note any damage to the car on a simple picture of the car.

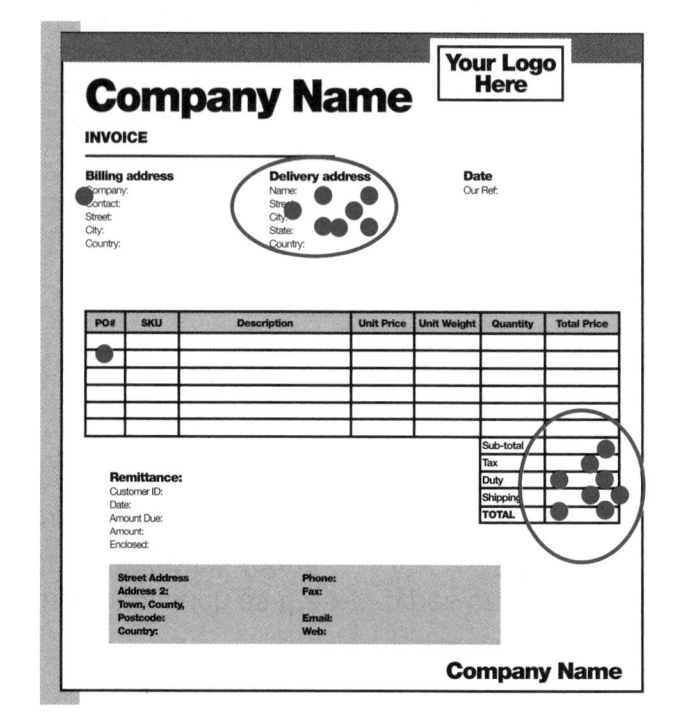

Failure Mode and Effect Analysis (FMEA)

FMEA can be used during Analyse, Improve or Control, to highlight the aspects of a product or process that should be targeted for improvement (without any failures having actually occurred).

Process Step or Product Part	Potential Failure Mode	Potential Failure Effects	S E V	Potential Causes	O C C	Current Controls	D E T	R P N	Actions Recommended	Who?	Actions Taken	S E V	O C C	D E T	R P N
Accept order	Wrong customer address	Missed delivery	5	Typo on postal code	3	Check street name with customer	4	60							0

What is an FMEA?

An FMEA is essentially a risk analysis tool that can be useful in environments where you have to prevent an event ever happening (e.g. safety) or where the failure rate for a process is so low that there is little opportunity to learn from past failures. There are two key types used within Six Sigma, as follows:

1) Product FMEAs analyse the function, design and potential failure of each component of a product.

2) Process FMEAs analyse the key outputs and potential failures of each step of a process, and consider the effect of process failure on the product or service concerned.

The FMEA process:

- Identify the process steps or components of the product.

- For each process step (or component), list the different failure modes that might occur, and rate their severity (SEV).

- For each failure mode, consider the different potential causes that might cause the failure and rate their occurrence (OCC).

- For each potential cause, consider the controls that are in place to prevent it happening and/or to detect the failure if the cause does occur. Then rate the likelihood of detection (DET).

- Calculate a Risk Priority Number (RPN) for each potential failure by multiplying the severity by occurrence by detection.

- Act on the results! Assign actions to tackle the highest RPNs, and set a date to review progress.

The **FMEA structure** above shows a typical format.

The left hand side (first nine columns) are completed during the first draft of the FMEA, and the right hand side (remaining seven columns) are used to track subsequent actions and document reduced RPNs.

FMEAs should be seen as living documents, not something that you do and store away in a filing cabinet somewhere. Having identified a risk, you must do something about it!

Failure Mode and Effect Analysis (cont.)

Rating Severity, Occurrence and Detection:

The ratings for severity, occurrence and detection are usually on a scale of 1 to 10. There are several versions of tables that help to define the different ratings, as shown opposite. These are available in the FMEA template data file:

⬇ FMEA Template & Ratings.xls

Applying ratings can create much discussion and debate. Be careful not to let your FMEA team waste time on deciding whether something should be rated a 2 instead of a 3! The most important thing is that you apply your rating scales **consistently**.

It is often worth customising your rating tables to your organisation's environment. Using plain language helps people to relate to the definitions and to apply more consistent ratings.

FMEAs in practice:

As with many of the other tools in the Process Door, you need to assemble a team from across the process. Make sure you involve the people who operate, manage and design the process.

FMEAs rapidly expand in size, as each process step (or part) can have several failure modes, which in turn have several potential causes, which can have several relevant controls. For this reason, they require careful facilitation in order to keep them on course and completed in time. You will need to plan for several sessions!

SEVERITY of Effects of Failure Mode

Effect	Criteria	Ranking
Hazardous- without warning	Very high severity ranking when a potential fail... and... gov...	10
Hazardous- with warning	Ver... fail... and... gov...	
Very High	Pro... prin...	
High	Pro... leve... Cus...	
Moderate	Pro... con... Cus...	
Low	Pro... con... leve... Cus...	
Very Low	Fit & finish / squeak & rattle... not conform. Defect noticed by most cus...	
Minor	Fit & finish / squeak & rattle... not conform. Defect noticed by average c...	
Very Minor	Fit & finish / squeak & rattle... not conform. Defect noticed by discrimina...	
None	No effect.	

OCCURRENCE of Failure Mode

Probability of Failure	Possible Failure Rates	Ranking
Very High: Failure is almost inevit...		
High: Repeated failure...		
Moderate: Occasional...		
Low: Relatively few fai...		
Remote: Failure is unli...		

Likelihood of DETECTION of the Failure Mode

Detection	Criteria	Ranking
Absolute Uncertainty	Design Control will not and / or can not detect a potential cause mechanism and subsequent failure mode; or there is no design control.	10
Very Remote	Very remote chance the design control will detect a potential cause / mechanism and subsequent failure mode.	9
Remote	Remote chance the design control will detect a potential cause / mechanism and subsequent failure mode.	8
Very Low	Very low chance the design control will detect a potential cause / mechanism and subsequent failure mode.	7
Low	Low chance the design control will detect a potential cause / mechanism and subsequent failure mode.	6
Moderate	Moderate chance the design control will detect a potential cause / mechanism and subsequent failure mode.	5
Moderately High	Moderately high chance the design control will detect a potential cause / mechanism and subsequent failure mode.	4
High	High chance the design control will detect a potential cause / mechanism and subsequent failure mode.	3
Very High	Very high chance the design control will detect a potential cause / mechanism and subsequent failure mode.	2
Almost Certain	Design control will almost certainly detect a potential cause / mechanism and subsequent failure mode.	1

The Data Door Routemap – Finding The Right Tool

Graphical tools are the starting point for the 'data door'. Theories and ideas that are gained from the graphical analysis (left) can then be investigated with more advanced statistical techniques (right).

For graphical analysis:

Looking at distributions...
- Histogram (p123), Dot Plot (p125)
- Minitab's Graphical Summary (p126)
- Probability Plot (p127)

Looking for changes over time...
- Time Series Plot (p130), Trend Analysis (p134)

Comparing distributions or groups of data...
- Box Plot (p140), Individual Value Plot (p143)
- Multi-Vari Chart (p139)

Comparing proportions and percentages...
- 100% Stacked Bar Chart (p144)

Looking for relationships between data sets...
- Scatter Plot (p145), Matrix Plot (p149)
- Bubble Plot (p147)

Looking at different categories of data...
- Pareto Chart (p135)

For statistical analysis:

Deciding if data fits a particular model (e.g. Normal)...
- Normality Test (Anderson Darling) (p189)
- Individual Distribution Identification (p191)

Deciding if changes over time are significant...
- Statistical Process Control (SPC) (p249)
- Run Chart (p132)

Deciding if groups of data are different and quantifying the difference...
- Confidence Intervals (p151), Hypothesis testing (p154)

Quantifying the relationships between process inputs and outputs...
- Correlation & Regression (p193)
- Simple Regression (p197), Fitted Line Plot (p198)
- Multiple Regression (p201), Binary Logistic Regression (p203)

Adjusting the process to look for relationships between its inputs and outputs...
- Design of Experiments (DOE) (p207)

Minitab – Data Types and Data Manipulation

Traditionally, we are used to arranging data in spreadsheets in a way that is easily readable to the human eye. A feature of Minitab however, is that it **always** requires data to be stored in columns.

	Jan	Feb	March	April
Location 1	289	295	300	301
Location 2	70	73	75	76
Location 3	168	174	180	189

A typical spreadsheet file may look like this (left).

But, in Minitab, the same data must be arranged in columns like this (below):

The raw data in the spreadsheet above (the numbers, locations and months) must all be given their own columns in Minitab. This is because many of the functions in Minitab work on a whole column of data at once.

Minitab also assumes that data in the same row is linked, so the data can be arranged in several different ways (including the two alternatives shown on the right) as long as the rows still correspond with each other.

OR

Ordered by Month ***

	C1 Data	C2 Location	C3-D Month
1	289	1	Jan
2	70	2	Jan
3	168	3	Jan
4	295	1	Feb
5	73	2	Feb
6	174	3	Feb
7	300	1	Mar
8	75	2	Mar
9	180	3	Mar
10	301	1	Apr
11	76	2	Apr
12	189	3	Apr

Ordered by Location ***

	C1 Data	C2 Location	C3-D Month
1	289	1	Jan
2	295	1	Feb
3	300	1	Mar
4	301	1	Apr
5	70	2	Jan
6	73	2	Feb
7	75	2	Mar
8	76	2	Apr
9	168	3	Jan
10	174	3	Feb
11	180	3	Mar
12	189	3	Apr

Different types of data in Minitab:
Minitab recognises three types of data (Numeric, Text, Date/time) and adds a 'T' (text) or a 'D' (date/time) to the column number as required. It does this automatically by looking at the first piece of data that is typed, or the content of data that is pasted.

! Be careful when pasting data into Minitab. If there is a mixture of data types in your data selection, then Minitab may identify some of the data as missing, or incorrectly identify the data type of the whole column. If this happens, you can change the data type of a column using the function:

Minitab: Data > Change Data Type

This function enables you to change between several different Numeric, Text and Date/Time formats.

! **Missing/deleted text data** is marked as '*Missing*' and missing Numeric or Date/time data marked as an '*'. These are inserted automatically.

Minitab – Graphs

Minitab offers a wide range of graphs and often provides suggestions as to the most appropriate one for the analysis tool you are using (through the **Graph** option).

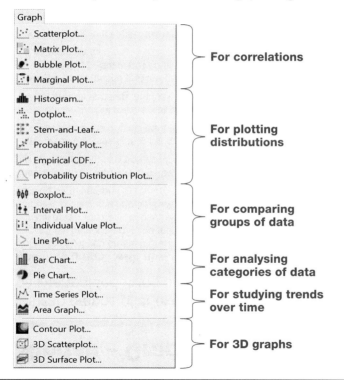

Graph

- Scatterplot...
- Matrix Plot...
- Bubble Plot...
- Marginal Plot...

For correlations

- Histogram...
- Dotplot...
- Stem-and-Leaf...
- Probability Plot...
- Empirical CDF...
- Probability Distribution Plot...

For plotting distributions

- Boxplot...
- Interval Plot...
- Individual Value Plot...
- Line Plot...

For comparing groups of data

- Bar Chart...
- Pie Chart...

For analysing categories of data

- Time Series Plot...
- Area Graph...

For studying trends over time

- Contour Plot...
- 3D Scatterplot...
- 3D Surface Plot...

For 3D graphs

How to find graphs in Minitab:
Minitab provides access to graphs in two ways.

- The Minitab **Graph** menu (shown left) offers a range of common graphs.
- Alternatively, when you are using a statistical function, Minitab usually offers a number of graphs that are appropriate to the analysis that you are doing.

Graph management:
You'll soon find that Minitab gets very full with numerous graphs. The key is to remain in control, which can be done by being disciplined about:

- (re) naming your graphs, so the title reflects what the graph is showing.
- closing down any unwanted graphs, and minimising those you want to keep.
- saving graphs you want to keep for a long time as separate files (File extension: .mgf).

! Graph discipline:
Don't forget the basics when you create a graph. Make sure that each graph has a **title**, axis **labels**, a note of the **sample size** and a record of the **units** used.

Minitab – Graphs (cont.)

Minitab graphs offer excellent functionality. Their link with the original data can be controlled, they can be interrogated using brushing (see next page) and their format can be easily customised.

Updating graphs with new data:
Unlike Excel, if you create a graph in Minitab it will not necessarily be updated if you then subsequently change the original data. You can choose between updating a graph manually or having it update itself automatically, by right clicking on the graph.

The status of a graph is indicated by the symbol in the top left corner of the graph window, as follows:

- A green tick means that the graph is up to date, and still reflects the original data that it was based upon.

- A yellow symbol means that the graph is not up to date, but **can** be updated (manually or by automatic updating).

- A red cross means that the graph is set to update automatically but is **not** up to date because of an issue with the data.

- A red cross in a circle means that the graph is not up to date, and **cannot** be updated (this can happen for a variety of reasons – you will have to create the graph again).

How do you update a graph in Minitab?

1) Right click the graph, and select **Update Graph Now** or **Update Graph Automatically**, or

2) Go to **Minitab: Window > Update All Graphs Now**

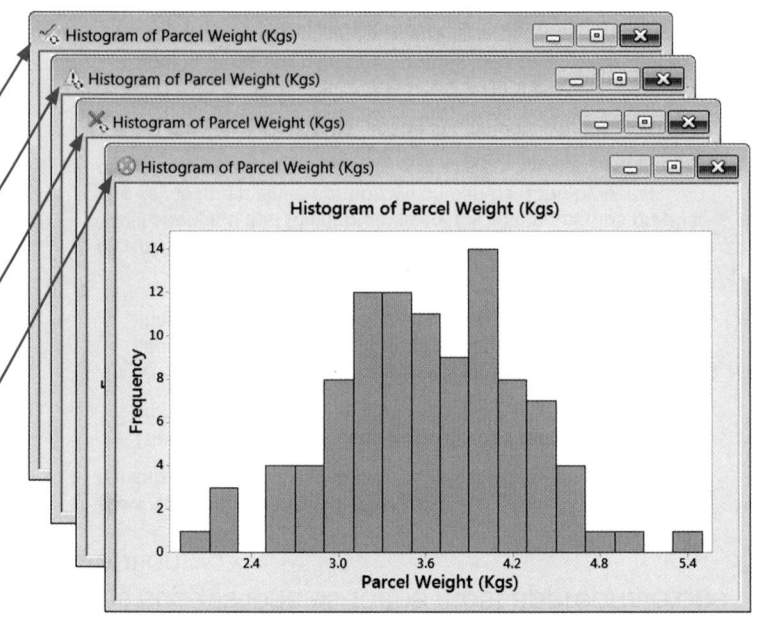

Customising a graph: Most aspects of a graph can be customised and amended after you have created the graph, by double clicking on the feature that you are interested in. Additional features (e.g.reference lines, subtitles, distribution fits) can also be added by going to: **Minitab: Editor > Add**

Minitab – Graphs (cont.)

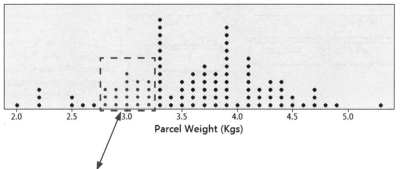

Dotplot of Parcel Weight (Kgs)

Brushing

Row	Location	Business Type
6	France	Residential
7	England	Residential
9	France	Residential
12	France	Commercial
18	England	Residential
26	France	Residential
29	England	Residential
32	England	Commercial
36	England	Residential
46	France	Residential
47	France	Residential
53	France	Commercial
54	England	Commercial
56	France	Residential

Graph Brushing:

Minitab has a brush tool that enables graphs to be dynamically interrogated, in order to identify which row numbers specific data points come from.

Once a specific subset of data has been selected (indicated by the dashed square in this example), the relevant row numbers appear in a small brushing window (shown bottom left).

At the same time, a black dot is placed by each relevant row number in the associated worksheet, and the same data points are also highlighted in any other active graphs. A very useful function!

Minitab: Editor > Brush

Advanced Graph Brushing Techniques:

1) Setting ID Variables:
In addition to showing the row numbers of the brushed area on the graph, the brushing window can also be used to show information from other columns in the worksheet. In this example (left), the location and business type of the brushed dots are also being shown in the brushing window, alongside the row numbers.

This is done using *Minitab: Editor > Set ID Variables* (when in brush mode).

2) Creating an Indicator Variable:
Minitab can also create a column of data that is based upon the data points that have been brushed on the graph. The default output is that brushed points will be recorded as **1**, and others as **0**.

This is done using *Minitab: Editor > Create Indicator Variable* (when in brush mode).

Minitab's Display Descriptive Statistics

The first Minitab command used on most data is *Display Descriptive Statistics*. It provides a range of statistics that summarise your data and also offers a basic range of graphs.

Minitab: Stat > Basic Statistics > Display Descriptive Statistics

The left hand area lists the columns that have data in them.

Only the columns that have the right type of data for the analysis that you are currently doing are displayed here, so you may see the list changing.

Data columns are entered into the data entry areas by double clicking them directly, or using **Select**.

The right hand areas of Minitab functions are usually the data entry areas. Place the data columns that you want to analyse in here.

❗ To enter data, you must first click the relevant box once so that your cursor is inside it.

In this example, C1 (parcel weight) has been entered as the column for analysis.

Later on, when you want to stratify data (divide it up into different subgroups – see page 138) you can enter the subgroup code in the second (optional) box.

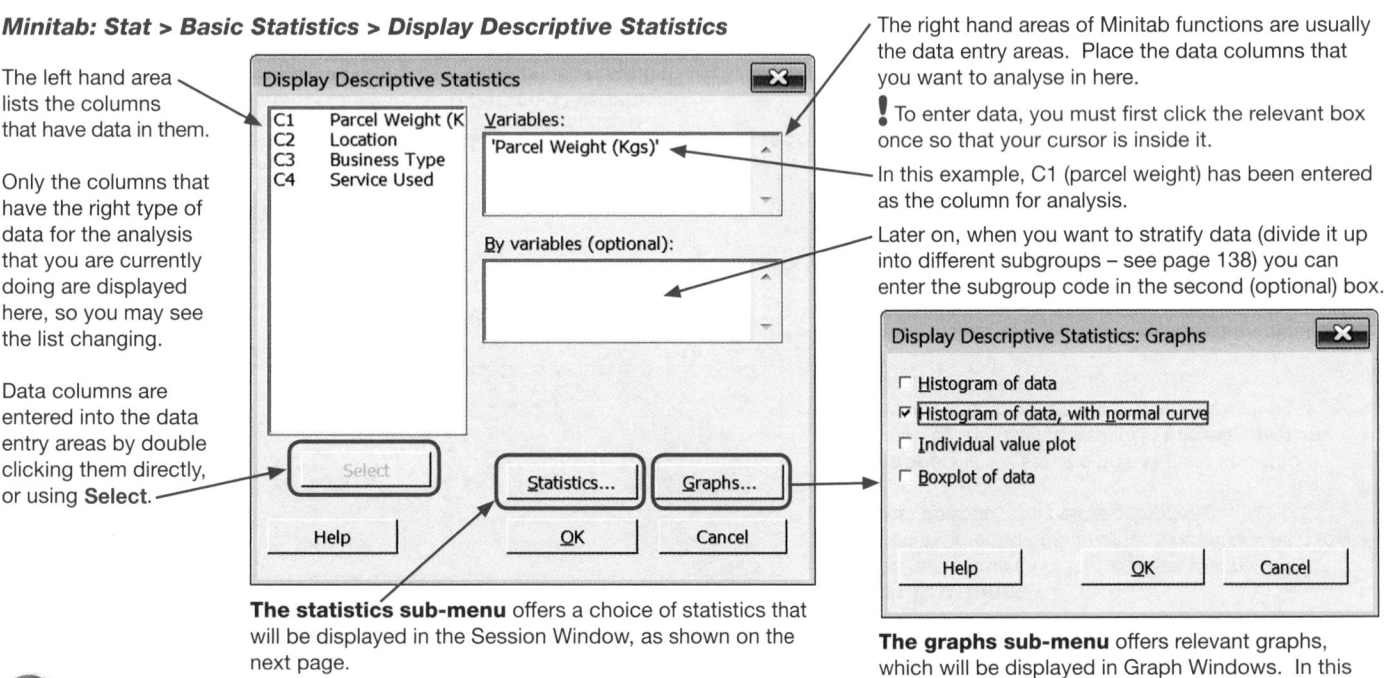

The statistics sub-menu offers a choice of statistics that will be displayed in the Session Window, as shown on the next page.

The graphs sub-menu offers relevant graphs, which will be displayed in Graph Windows. In this example the **Histogram of data, with Normal curve** is selected, which is analysed on page 124.

⬇ **Courier Process.mpj**

Minitab's Display Descriptive Statistics (cont.)

The statistics sub-menu (right) for the **Display Descriptive Statistics** function introduced on the previous page provides a wide range of statistics that can be calculated for your selected data.

The top left group provides basic statistics including Mean, Standard Deviation and Range etc.

The bottom left group provides percentile information including First Quartile (25th percentile), Median (50th percentile) etc. as well as some advanced statistics for distribution shapes (Skewness, Kurtosis etc.).

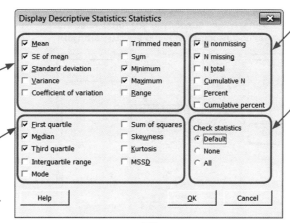

The top right group provides information about your sample including the sample size (N nonmissing) and the amount of missing data (N missing).

Any of the statistics shown can be selected individually, but the bottom right options provide a default list (shown here) or enable you to select **None** or **All**.

The selected statistics will be calculated and the results displayed in the Session Window within Minitab, as shown on the right.

For the parcel weight example introduced on the previous page, these show that there was 100 parcels in the sample (N), with an average weight of 3.61kgs (Mean) and a range from 1.98kgs (Minimum) to 5.33kgs (Maximum).

Descriptive Statistics: Parcel Weight (Kgs)
Statistics

Variable	N	N*	Mean	SE Mean	StDev	Minimum	Q1	Median
Parcel Weight (Kgs)	100	0	3.6121	0.0644	0.6441	1.9800	3.1875	3.6500

Variable	Q3	Maximum
Parcel Weight (Kgs)	4.0825	5.3300

Histograms (sometimes called Frequency Plots)

Histograms are one of the most common Six Sigma tools. They show the shape of the distribution and form an essential part of the '1st Pass Analysis' of any data (see page 73).

Minitab: Graph > Histogram

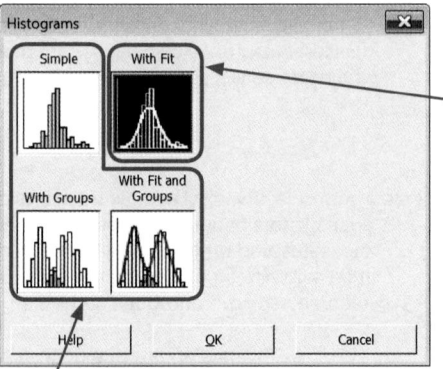

Other options:

- **Simple;** provides a histogram for a column of data, with no distribution curves fitted. This is the best place to start in many cases.
- **With groups;** allows you to stratify a single column of data into several subgroups, and produces a histogram for each subgroup.
- **With fit and groups;** provides the same as above, but also fits a distribution curve to each histogram.

 **Courier Process.mpj**

Example: A project team at a courier company is analysing the weights of a sample of 100 parcels. They have calculated some basic statistics for the data (see previous page) and now want to understand how the parcel weights are distributed using a histogram. They also want to have a Normal distribution fitted to the histogram, in order to help them decide if the process is Normally distributed. The team therefore select the **With Fit** histogram option and enter the *Parcel Weight* (C1) column as shown below.

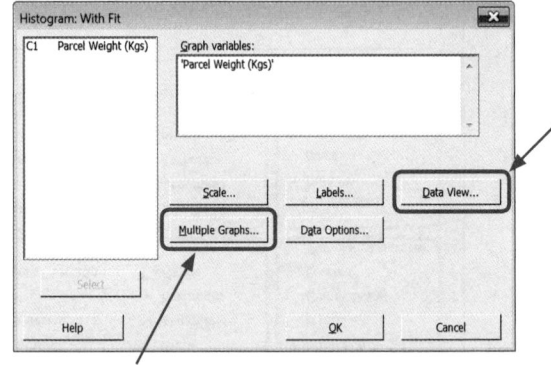

Data View: The **Distribution** tab within **Data View** provides different distributions that can be fitted to the data. The Normal distribution is selected by default, and used in this example.

Multiple Graphs provides options if you are creating several different histograms at the same time. The histograms can be either:

- **Overlaid on the same graph;** useful for comparing a 2-3 histograms.
- **In separate panels of the same graph;** useful for comparing lots of histograms at the same time.
- **On separate graphs;** a rapid way of producing multiple histograms that you do not want to compare.

Histograms (cont.)

The histogram below is the same output from both the Histogram function (previous page) **and** the Display Descriptive Statistics function (page 121). Both functions will produce exactly the same histogram – showing that there is often more than one way to produce the same chart in Minitab. Minitab scales the axes automatically, but if you want a certain range to be displayed, you can set them yourself by double clicking the relevant axis.

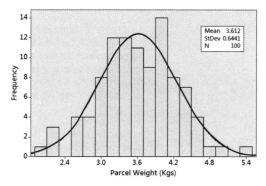

Interpreting Histograms:

The golden rule when analysing histograms is not to read too much into them. Instead, the results should be summarised using day to day language. So, for this example, we could say:

"This histogram shows that the parcel weights range from about 2kgs up to 5.5kgs, with most of the parcels being between 3 and 4.5" or

"the distribution looks symmetric around the average parcel weight of 3.6kgs, and appears to fit the Normal distribution curve".

Things to watch out for with histograms:

Sample size: Histograms often get used without any indication of the amount of data that they are based upon. This is not only bad practice, but leads to observations being made on very little data. The recommended minimum sample size for a histogram is 25. Watch out for histograms that have very few columns like the one below, since this can be an indication that the sample size was small.

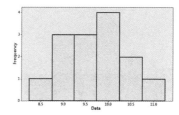

Rounding: Another problem that histograms can show up clearly is rounding or a lack of resolution within the measurement system (see page 61). The histogram below shows several thin columns of data, with no results occurring between them. Normally, the columns of the histogram would be adjoining each other, indicating that data occurs across the whole range of the histogram.

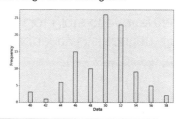

Dot Plots

Dot Plots are an alternative to histograms and are also a type of Frequency Distribution diagram. Histograms are widely used and suitable for most applications, but Dot Plots offer alternative features.

The Dot Plot on the right shows the same parcel weight data contained in the histogram on the previous page. Usually, every dot represents a piece of data, but when there is lots of data, each dot may represent four or five results.

The Dot Plot will use a different number of columns from the histogram and so the **exact** shapes are not the same. However, the **overall** shape is the same as the histogram (it is the same data after all!).

Minitab: Graph > Dotplot

Brushed area

Dot Plot or Histogram?
They are both frequency distributions and so the overall shape of the distribution will be the same. Which graph to use depends on your application and preference:

- Histograms summarise the data well and can be useful for presentations.
- Dot Plots usually show one dot for every data point which allows Minitab's graph brushing function (see right and p120) to be used.

The brushing function in Minitab allows you to investigate graphs such as the Dot Plot and to identify specific data points. In this example, with brushing 'on', a rectangle has been dragged over the last few points on this Dot Plot. At the same time, a small window appears with the row numbers of the 'brushed' data, and the relevant rows are also highlighted in the worksheet. See page 120 for more information on graph brushing.

Minitab: Editor > Brush

⬇ **Courier Process.mpj**

Brus...
Row
4
15
22
24
45
65

Minitab's Graphical Summary

Minitab's Graphical Summary provides a range of useful outputs for analysing a column of data.

Minitab: Stat > Basic Statistics > Graphical Summary

This Graphical Summary shows an analysis of the time it takes an online retailer to ship orders.

The **histogram** shows that the *Time to ship* ranges from about 1.5 hours to 6 hours and the process **does not** appear to fit the Normal curve very well; appearing slightly skewed to the right.

The **Box plot** (see page 140) summarises the distribution of the data, and uses the same scale as the histogram directly above it.

The **Confidence Intervals** for the Mean and Median are displayed, but it is important to note that this diagram has its own scale, and so cannot be compared directly with the histogram or Box plot above.

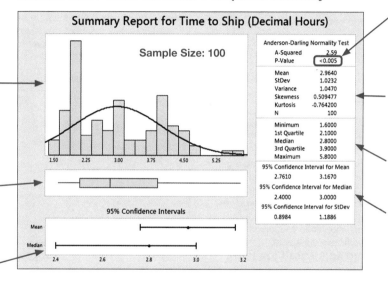

The Anderson Darling Normality Test is explained on page 189. In this example, a p-value of 0.005 (very low) indicates the process is definitely **not** Normally distributed.

The mean, standard deviation and sample size are summarised here. Skewness and Kurtosis are not dealt with in this text.

This information on quartiles is used to generate the Box plot (see page 140).

The limits of the Confidence Intervals for the Mean, Median and Standard Deviation are summarised here.

Confidence Intervals (CI) are explained in detail on page 151, but for now, a practical definition of a confidence interval for the mean (average) is:

*'You can be 95% confident that the **mean time to ship** for this process lies within the limits of the confidence interval shown here'.*

Probability Plots

So far in this guide, histograms with Normal curves have been the primary method for deciding if a sample of data fits the Normal distribution. Probability plots can provide a more decisive approach.

Minitab: Graph > Probability Plot

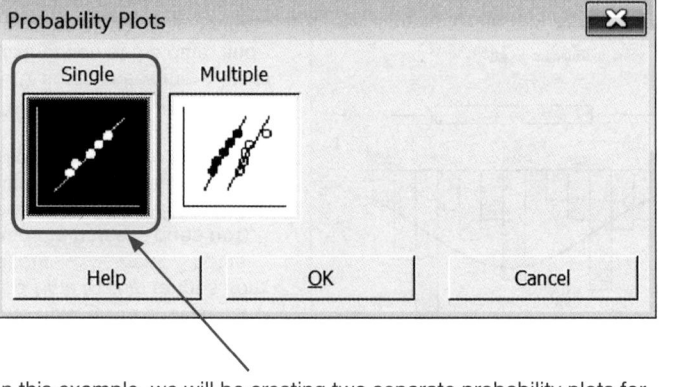

What are probability plots?
Trying to decide if a histogram fits the Normal distribution can be a very subjective decision. Probability plots help answer the question more decisively by plotting the data in a different format.
A probability plot is constructed in such a way that the points will fall in a straight line if they fit the distribution in question (e.g. Normal). This is a useful technique, since the human eye is better at assessing if a pattern fits a straight line, or not.

In this example, we will be creating two separate probability plots for two **Single** columns of data. If you want to stratify a single column of data into separate plots (overlaid on the same graph or not) then choose **Multiple.**

Enter the columns that you want to create probability plots for here.

Select the distribution that you want to compare your data against here. The default setting is the Normal distribution.

 **Distributions.mpj**

Probability Plots (cont.)

Interpreting the probability plot:

Each data point is plotted on the probability plot, which has the actual data units on the horizontal axis.

The vertical axis represents the estimated cumulative probability. The key point to note is that the scale of this axis is not linear (it is more like a logarithmic scale), and in this case it is symmetrical around 50% (much like the Normal curve) because the Normal distribution was selected by default on the previous page. It is this non-linear scale that creates a straight line **if** the data is Normally distributed.

So, in short, if the distribution is Normally distributed, the data points will form a straight line on the probability plot.

So how straight should the line be?

Just as histograms are never perfectly smooth, the line of data points on a probability plot will never be perfectly straight, even if the data is Normal. So, Minitab places 95% Confidence Interval (CI) limits on the diagram and if all the points fall within the lines, you can assume the data is Normally distributed. This is similar to the more informal (and subjective) 'fat pencil test', in which you imagine a fat pencil laying on top of your data points, and if it can cover all of the points, then the data is probably Normal.

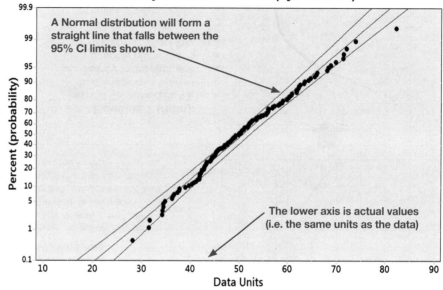

Probability Plot for Column C2 (Symmetric 1)

A Normal distribution will form a straight line that falls between the 95% CI limits shown.

The lower axis is actual values (i.e. the same units as the data)

Probability plots in practice:

Even probability plots do not provide a clear cut answer all the time, but they are an improvement. Points at the extremes of the data are more likely to be outside of the 95% CI limits, so do not decide your data does not fit the distribution just because one or two points fall outside of the CI lines. The next page contains two further examples to help you decide.

Probability Plots – Examples

Example 1

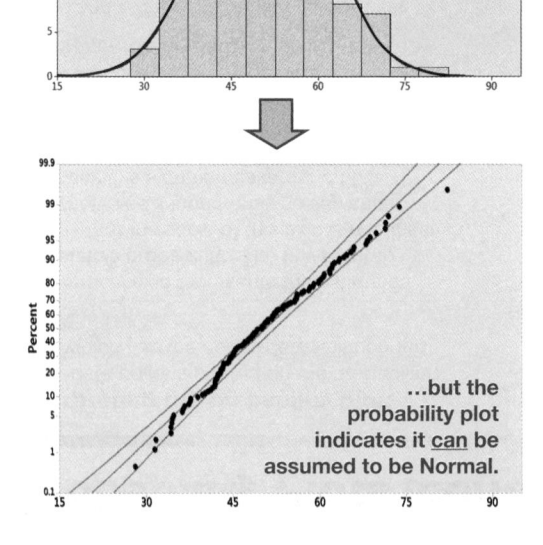

> Histogram looks possibly Normal, or maybe a little skewed to the right?...

> ...but the probability plot indicates it <u>can</u> be assumed to be Normal.

Example 2

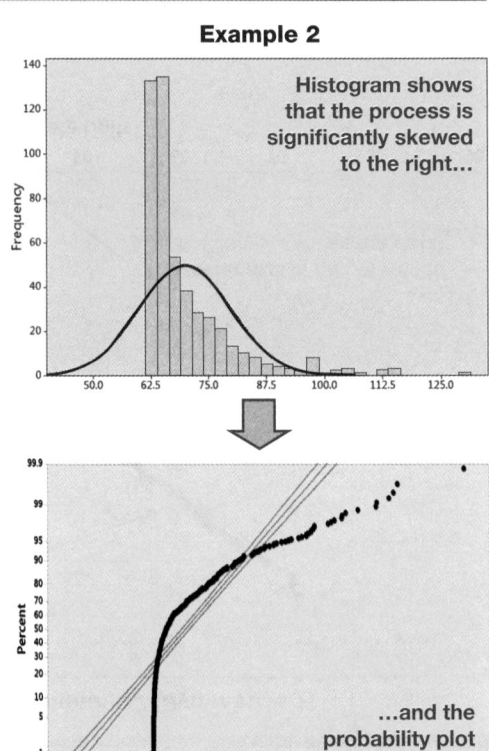

> Histogram shows that the process is significantly skewed to the right...

> ...and the probability plot confirms this.

Example 1 (left):
(column C2 in the data file) This data is actually from a Normal distribution, but on a histogram it **appears** to be very slightly skewed.

However, the probability plot helps to correctly conclude that the data **is** Normally distributed, because it shows a straight line that falls mainly between the limits.

Example 2 (right):
(column C5 in the data file) The histogram is skewed significantly to the right, and the probability plot wanders radically to reflect this.

Notice however, that the line of points is very smooth, indicating that the data follows a very specific distribution in a controlled manner (but not the Normal distribution!).

Time Series Plots

Time Series plots, combined with Histograms, are the two most important graphical tools in Six Sigma.

Minitab: Graph > Time Series Plot

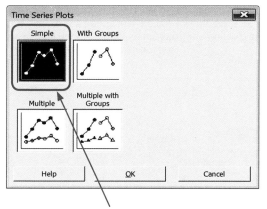

In this example, we will be creating a single Time Series plot from a single column of data, so select **Simple**. If you want to create Time Series plots for several different columns of data, and overlay them on the same chart, then choose **Multiple**.

Enter the columns that you want to create Time Series plots for here.

Courier Process.mpj

What are Time Series plots?
Time Series plots are line charts where the data is plotted in time order (the order in which it occurred). Time Series plots can help you spot time-based changes and trends that histograms just cannot see, such as:

- Upwards or downwards trends.
- Changes in the amount of variation.
- Differences between the short and long term.
- Repeating patterns or cycles.
- Anything that doesn't appear to be random.

Time Series plots are introduced in detail on pages 73 & 79-81 in the Measure phase and Minitab instructions for them are provided here.

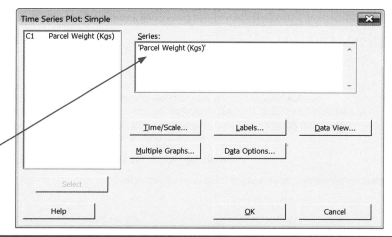

Time Series Plots (cont.)

The Time Series plot below shows the parcel weights (over time) from the courier process example. In this case, the process appears to be reasonably random (there are no obvious patterns) and stable (there are no obvious trends up or down).

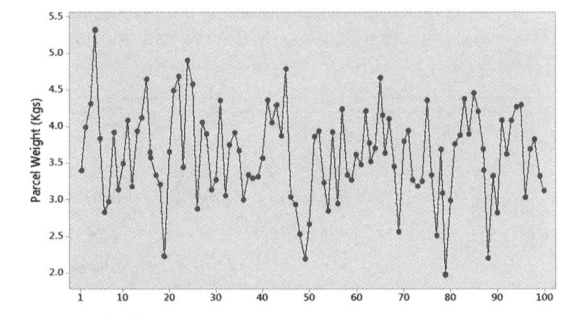

Time Series plots in practice:

Be careful not to read too much into Time Series plots. It is easy to see trends that are not actually there, or to draw conclusions on only a few data points. If there is something worth finding it will usually be obvious.

If you decide that you need a more advanced technique for assessing the stability of a process over time, you could try a Run Chart (next page) or an SPC chart (page 249), both of which are essentially more advanced Time Series plots.

Things to watch out for with histograms:

1) Make sure your data is time ordered:

Time Series plots require data that is in the order that it actually happened, so that time-based trends can be detected. This may sound obvious but it is often forgotten (or ignored!), making a Time Series plot meaningless. **Do not complete a Time Series plot if your data is not time ordered!**

2) Mixed processes:

This Time Series plot (right) appears to have two different levels, which might indicate two different processes have been mixed together. If this is the case, these should be separated and analysed individually.

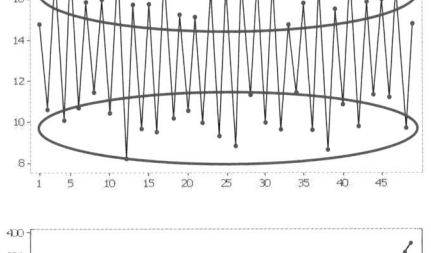

3) Mixed trends and patterns:

As discussed on page 81, very often there might be several different types of changes happening within a process over time. For example, this Time Series plot (right) appears to have a repeated pattern **and** an overall upward trend. Trend Analysis (p134) can be used to help

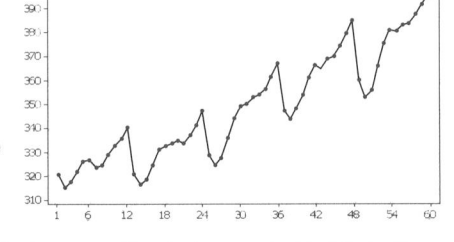

identify overall trends and Minitab's decomposition (not presented in this text) can be used to seperate seasonality, trends and random variation.

Run Charts – Overview

Run charts provide a more sophisticated method of deciding if your process is stable.

Sometimes it can be difficult to decide if your process is stable just by looking at a Time Series plot. Conversely, it can be easy to read too much into Time Series plots and start seeing trends that are not actually there!

Run charts are a quick and easy tool that help you to decide if your process is statistically stable.

Example:

A kitchen equipment manufacturer is finding that some of their saucepan lids don't fit the saucepans. One theory is that the diameter of the saucepans is varying because the production process is unstable. To investigate the problem, the diameter of the saucepans is monitored and recorded in Minitab.

25 saucepans are measured (you need at least 20 or more data points for a Run Chart) and Minitab's Run Chart function is used to analyse the results.

If your data is in a single column, then check the **Single column** box and enter the column here.

If your data was collected in subgroups (groups of measurements taken at the same time) then enter the column that contains the subgroup number in **Subgroup size**. If in doubt, or if your data was not collected in subgroups, enter a subgroup size of 1 as shown.

Minitab: Stat > Quality Tools > Run Chart

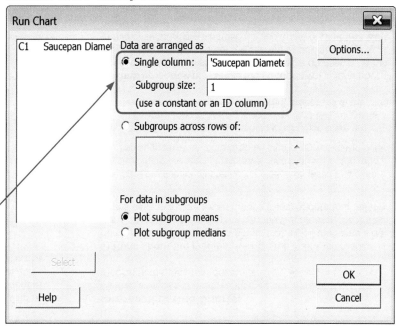

Run Chart-Diameters.mpj

Run Charts – Interpreting the Results

Run Charts work by analysing the **actual** number of runs in your data points and comparing them to the **expected** number of runs (for the amount of data that you have). If there is a big difference between the actual and expected runs, then it is likely that your process has some special cause variation, and you should investigate further.

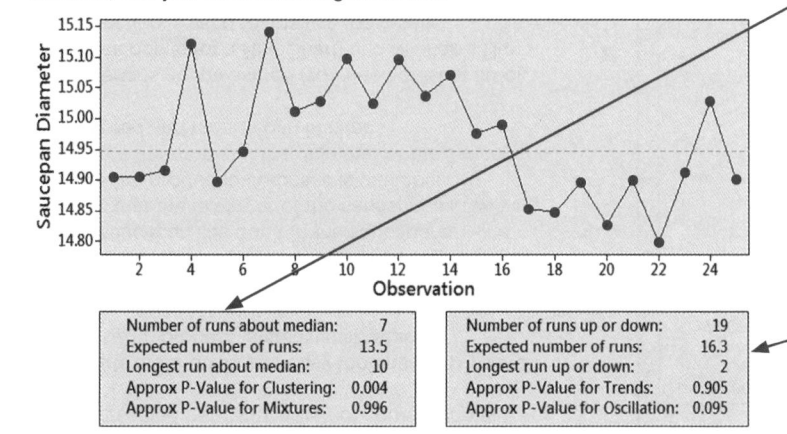

Number of runs about median:	7
Expected number of runs:	13.5
Longest run about median:	10
Approx P-Value for Clustering:	0.004
Approx P-Value for Mixtures:	0.996

Number of runs up or down:	19
Expected number of runs:	16.3
Longest run up or down:	2
Approx P-Value for Trends:	0.905
Approx P-Value for Oscillation:	0.095

Interpreting this example:

In this example, the only p-value that is below 0.05 is the p-value for clustering (0.004). This suggests that there is unexpectedly high clustering within the data. This observation requires investigation, but the key conclusion is that the process is not completely random and **does** have some level of special cause variation. The clustering suggests the process output is drifting over time, and this **might** be linked to why the saucepan lids don't always fit!

Interpreting Run Charts:

Minitab analyses two different types of run; runs about the median, and runs up or down.

1) Runs about the median: A single run about the median is a number of consecutive data points that all fall the same side of the median line. A run stops when the line crosses the median. In this case there are seven groups (runs) of data that fall the same side of the median.

- If the p-value for clustering is below 0.05 (as in this case) then there are statistically fewer runs than expected, and this suggests that there is some clustering within the data.

- If the p-value for mixtures is below 0.05 then there are statistically too many runs in the data, and this suggests that there is some mixing of different processes in the data.

2) Runs up or down: A single run up (or down) is a number of consecutive data points that all increase (or decrease). A run stops when the direction of the line (up or down) changes. In this case there are nineteen groups (runs) of data that either go up or down.

- If the p-value for trends is below 0.05 then there are statistically fewer runs than expected, and this suggests that there are some trends within the data.

- If the p-value for oscillation is below 0.05 then there are statistically too many runs in the data. This suggests that the process is not stable because it varies up and down too much.

Trend Analysis

As discussed on page p81, real life processes often contain a combination of trends and cycles, as well as seasonal and random variation. If a Times Series plot suggests that an overall trend exists, Minitab's Trend Analysis tool can help to identify, model and even forecast that trend.

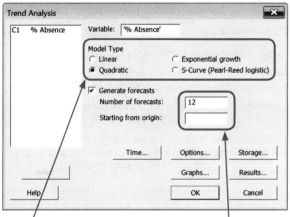

Repeat the Trend Analysis with a number of different models until you find one that best fits the data both graphically and through its accuracy measures (right).

If you want a forecast of how the fitted trend will behave in the future, select **Generate forecasts** and enter the number of points required.

 **Trend Analysis.mpj**

Example: A school district improvement project has been working on reducing absence due to gastroenteritis by implementing infection control measures. The % of school days lost to gastroenteritis has been recorded monthly over the last 5 years and the Trend Analysis plot below indicates an overall improvement, alongside both a seasonal effect and random variation.

In this example, the Trend Analysis fits a downward sloping curve that indicates absence rates **have** improved over the last five years and are now levelling out.

The analysis also provides the exact mathematical equation of the fitted model, which in this case is a quadratic equation.

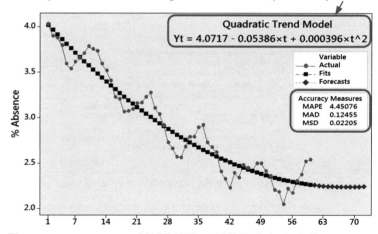

The accuracy measures (MAPE, MAD and MSD) all aim to do the same thing; provide a measure of how accurate the fitted model is. Lower values indicate a better fit, and while the values don't mean much by themselves, they can be used to compare and decide which model best fits your data.

Pareto Analysis – Data Input

Pareto charts are used to help identify the most common categories in a column of textual data.

Example: A project looking at reducing postage delays took a sample of 240 delayed postage items and recorded the reason for the delay of each item. In addition, it was recorded if the items had originated in a rural or urban location. There are two options for recording this data in order to construct a Pareto chart, as follows:

Minitab: Stat > Quality Tools > Pareto Chart

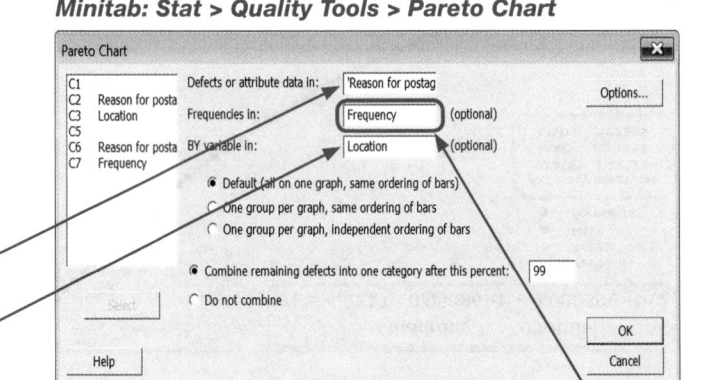

Option 1: Raw Data format (preferred):
In this format, a single column contains all of the results, with one row for each of the delayed items (the first seven rows of which are shown below).

To create a single Pareto chart of the postage delays, enter the column containing the raw data in **Defects or attribute data in** here:

To stratify (divide) the data, and create two Pareto charts (one each for Rural and Urban results), enter the *Location* (C3) in **By variable in**:

With this data format, you must leave **Frequencies in** blank.

C2-T	C3-T
Reason for postage delay	**Location**
Not franked	urban
No Postcode	urban
No Stamp	rural
No Stamp	urban
Postcode unreadable	rural
No Postcode	urban
Not franked	urban

Option 2: Table Format:
Use this option if your data is already summarised as a table, as shown on the right.

For this example, enter the *Reason for postage delay* (C6) in **Defects or attribute data in** and the *Frequency* (C7) in **Frequencies in.**

It is possible to stratify your data by urban/rural locations using this format, but the table would need to be adjusted first, as shown in the example data file below.

⬇ **Pareto-Postage.mpj**

C6-T	C7
Reason for postage delay.	**Frequency**
Not franked	42
No Stamp	76
No Postcode	98
Postcode unreadable	14
No address	6
Wrong postage	4

Pareto Analysis – Graphical Output

What are Pareto charts?

A Pareto chart is essentially a bar chart for categorical/contextual data (see page 57), where the most frequent results are placed in order from the left hand side of the chart.

The **Cumulative Frequency** is also plotted (as a line) and shows the total (cumulative) count of all the reason codes combined from the left of the chart. The table at the bottom gives the exact numerical results.

Interpreting this example:

For this example, *No Postcode* is the most frequent reason for delay with 98 found (40.8%), and *No Stamp* is the second most frequent with 76 found (31.7%). **Together** (cumulatively) they represent 72.5% of the failures found – shown by the cumulative frequency curve.

The 80/20 Principle:

Reasons for failure are often found to conform to the 80/20 principle which says that 80% of the failures are generally caused by around 20% of the root causes.

This 80/20 effect can be seen to some extent in this example, since the first two reasons for postal delay (out of 6) account for 72.5% of the delayed items.

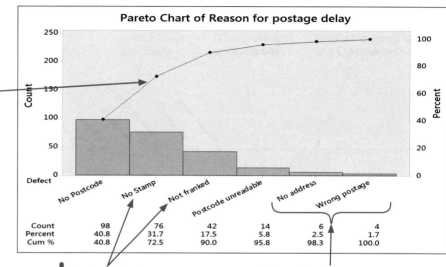

Pareto Chart of Reason for postage delay

	No Postcode	No Stamp	Not franked	Postcode unreadable	No address	Wrong postage
Count	98	76	42	14	6	4
Percent	40.8	31.7	17.5	5.8	2.5	1.7
Cum %	40.8	72.5	90.0	95.8	98.3	100.0

❗ Watch out for similar reason codes. In this example, the reasons *No Stamp* and *Not Franked* could have been combined into a *No Payment* category, which would have been more frequent than *No Postcode* and changed the Pareto chart completely. However, only reason codes that have the same root cause should be combined.

The 'Other' category:

You may find that you have lots of very small categories that are not of interest. The Pareto chart can be set to combine all categories after a certain point into one. This Pareto chart was constructed with this option set at 99% (see previous pages). Using the default of 95% would have combined the last two categories into one, called 'other'.

Pareto Analysis – Graphical Output (cont.)

As explained on page 135, the **By variable in** box can be used when constructing a Pareto chart in order to produce separate charts for different categories. This can be useful if you want to compare the frequency of different failure types across several different locations, machines or departments etc.

In the example output shown on the right, the data has been separated out by the two different locations (rural and urban), as described on page 135.

Why aren't the biggest bars on the left anymore?

Because Minitab's default display option was selected in this example, which places the charts on the same page, with the same ordering of the bars. The *No Postcode* category has been placed furthest to the left on both charts because it is the largest category **overall**.

Pareto Chart of 'Reason for Postage Delay' by Location

No Stamp is the biggest problem in rural areas, (and also occurs in urban areas).

No Postcode is the biggest problem in urban areas (and also occurs in rural areas).

Not Franked only appears to be a significant problem in urban areas, but perhaps this is due to there being more businesses with franking machines in urban areas... to be investigated.

❗ Watch out for reduced sample sizes:

Be careful when separating your data out into subgroups. If you had six different locations, (not just urban/rural) then you would have ended up with 6 different Pareto charts. This may sound more detailed, but at the same time the amount of data in each Pareto chart will reduce very quickly, and you have to make sure that each Pareto chart still contains enough data to be meaningful.

Data Stratification

Analysing the differences between subgroups of data can provide clues and insights into how the process behaves. The process of dividing a data set into subgroups is called stratification.

Databases often contain lots of categorical data about the environment from which the data was taken. This is very useful in the Analyse phase because it enables you to investigate many of the theories and root cause ideas that you will have developed.

Example:

The data below is a sample of parcel weights from a courier process. Categorical information on the Location, Business and Service was collected along with the weight of each parcel, and this can now be used to further understand the process.

Categorical data that provides information on the different subgroups within the data.

Parcel Weight	Location	Business Type	Service Used
3.40	England	Commercial	Normal
3.99	England	Commercial	Express
4.31	England	Commercial	Normal
5.33	France	Commercial	Overnight

Why divide up the data?

The differences between subgroups may be a substantial cause of the variation in a process. Identifying subgroups that are different can lead onto an analysis of **why** they are different. For example:

- The best performing subgroups can be investigated for benchmarking opportunities.
- The root causes of the worst performing subgroups can be investigated using 5 Whys, Fishbone diagrams etc.

Questions that might be answered by stratifying the data:

- Is there a difference in parcel weights between countries?
- Do commercial customers send heavier parcels?
- Do residential customers send a bigger variety of parcel weights?
- Does the weight of the parcel influence the service used?

Graphical tools for analysing and comparing subgroups:

- Box Plots (page 140) – useful for comparing subgroups that have at least 25 data points in them.
- Individual Value Plots (page 143) – similar to Box plots, but used with smaller subgroups (less than 25).
- Multi-Vari Charts (page 139) – useful for comparing the averages of lots of different subgroups.
- 100% Stacked Bar Charts (page 144) – useful for comparing different proportions within Attribute or categorical data.

Multi-Vari Charts

Multi-Vari Charts are useful for an initial look at data that has been stratified by several different factors. Box Plots and Individual Value Plots can then focus on specific factors in more detail.

Minitab: Stat > Quality Tools > Multi-Vari Chart

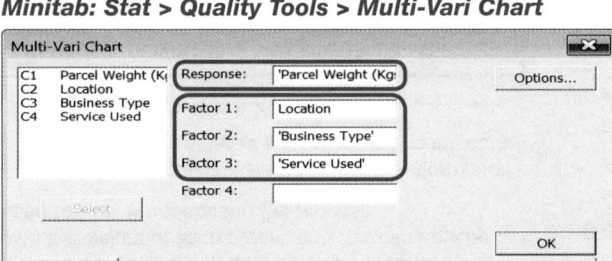

What are Multi-Vari Charts?

Multi-Vari Charts stratify a data set by several factors at the same time and display the averages of the resulting subgroups. They can be used at the start of data analysis in order to look for differences between subgroups that can then be investigated in more detail.

Things to look out for with Multi-Vari Charts:

- **Sample Sizes;** The more you stratify a data set, the smaller the resulting subgroups will be <u>behind</u> the averages displayed.

- **Averages, not variation;** Multi-Vari Charts display subgroup averages but do not provide any indication of the variation <u>within</u> each subgroup.

Example: The parcel weight example introduced on the previous page can be stratified by all three categorical data columns at the same time. Enter the *Parcel Weight* as the **Response**, and the categorical data columns as **Factors**. The resulting Multi-Vari Chart (right) suggests that, on average:

- *Residential* parcel weights are lower than for *Commercial*.
- *Express* parcel weights are lowest, and *Normal* highest.
- *French* parcel weights are higher than *English* for *Commercial* parcels, but lower for *Residential* parcels.

All of these observations are statistically unproven at this point, but can now be investigated and tested in more detail.

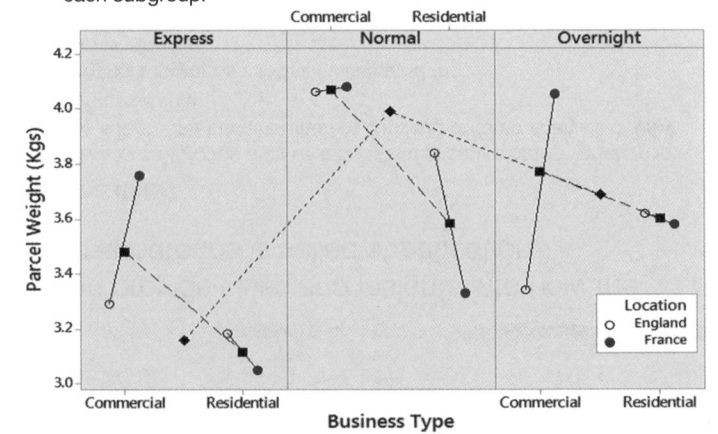

Courier Process.mpj

Box Plots – Overview

Whenever you are comparing samples of data against each other – think Box plots!!

How Box plots work:
Box plots take key statistics from the data and summarise them in a box and whiskers format, as shown here:

The box represents 50% of the data, starting at Quartile 1 (Q1) and finishing at Q3.

The whiskers represent the range of the data (minimum to maximum).

Outliers: The length of the whiskers is limited (they can only be as long as 1.5 times the length of the box). Any data results beyond that point are considered to be 'outliers' and are represented with an asterisk: **✱**

! Don't use Box plots if you're looking at just **one** data set – histograms are much better. Box plots should be used when comparing **several** sets of data against each other.

The middle line of the box is the median, **not** the average.

Some of the Box plots in Minitab can also place a dot on the Box plot to represent the average.

Different Box plot formats:
Box plots can be drawn horizontally or vertically. Sometimes the height of the box (or the width if drawn vertically) represents the sample size, but usually it has no significance.

Box plots in Minitab:

Box plots can be found in many Minitab functions, including:

- *Graph > Boxplot*
- Display Descriptive Statistics (p121)
- 2 Sample t-test (p160).

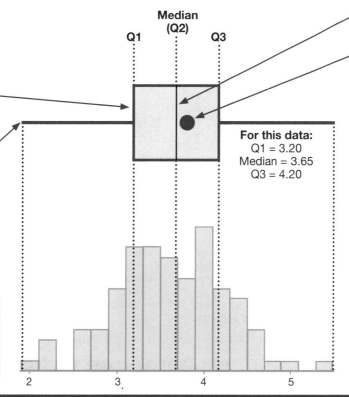

Median (Q2) · Q1 · Q3

For this data:
Q1 = 3.20
Median = 3.65
Q3 = 4.20

Box Plots – Data Input and Analysis

Minitab: Graph > Boxplot

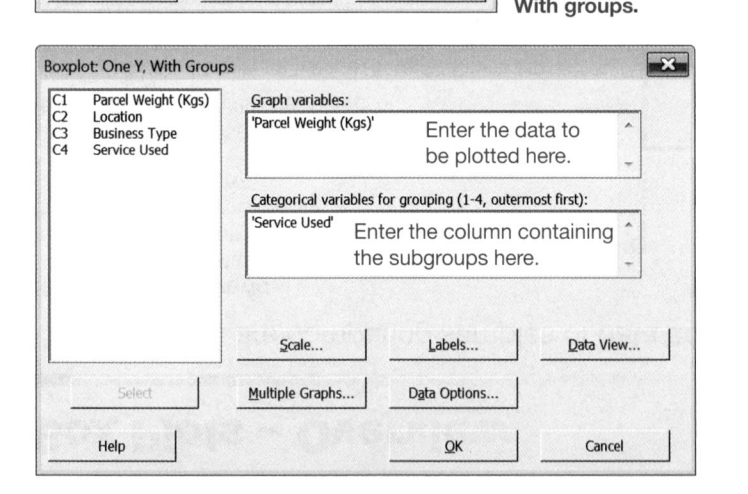

In this example, we want to compare several subgroups of data against each other on the same graph.

The data is in one column and needs to be divided into subgroups, so select **One Y, With groups.**

Sample sizes:

Box plots should not be used for subgroups that have less than 25 data points because the size of the box and whiskers can vary significantly. In this example, the *Overnight* subgroup (shown below) has a sample size of just 10, which makes the calculation of quartiles very variable and unreliable.

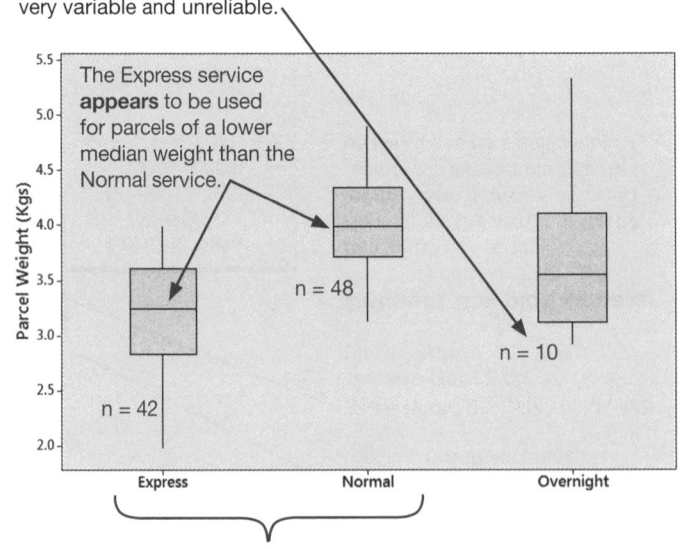

The variation (range) of parcel weights **appears** to be roughly the same for the *Express* and *Normal* services.

Courier-Process.mpj

Box Plots – Data Input and Analysis (cont.)

Minitab: Graph > Boxplot

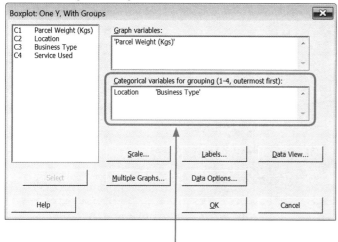

Entering two columns into the Categorical variables box will stratify the data by both variables.

The order in which they are entered is important. In this case, the location was entered first, and so the Box plot (right) shows the data stratified by location first, then by the business type.

Once again, be careful of sample sizes (shown on the right). This technique can create a lot of subgroups, but each one may contain very little data. It might be worthwhile trying an Individual Value Plot instead (next page) if your sample sizes are less than 25.

Observations of interest from this Box plot:

- Parcels from Residential customers **appear** to have lower (median) weights than those from Commercial customers.

- This difference **appears** in both France and England. In fact the results for France and England are very similar overall.

- All the subgroups **appear** to have similar levels of variation in parcel weight (the height of the Box plots is similar).

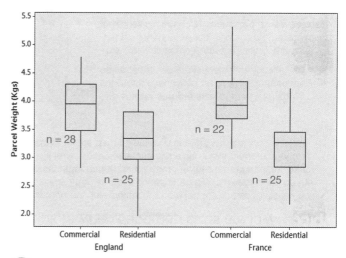

Courier-Process.mpj

Individual Value Plots

Individual Value Plots should be used in preference to Box plots when subgroup sizes are low (<25).

The Individual Value Plot below represents the same data as the Box plot of parcel weights shown earlier on page 141. For smaller subgroups, Individual Value Plots provide more 'feel' on the distribution of the data, and can be useful for spotting outliers.

Jitter: Minitab can spread the data points out from left to right so that they do not overlap. This is called 'Jitter' and can be adjusted by double clicking on the data points and selecting Jitter under the **Identical Points** tab. With Jitter, every Individual Value Plot will look slightly different, since Jitter is a random effect. Turning off Jitter will place all the data points on a straight vertical line.

Minitab: Graph > Individual Value Plot

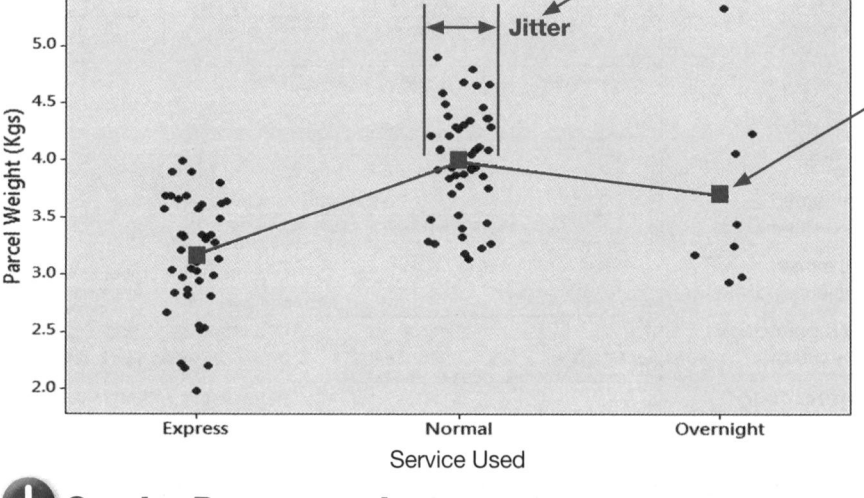

The smaller **sample size** of the Overnight subgroup (discussed on p141) is immediately obvious with an Individual Value Plot.

This plot was actually created using Minitab's ANOVA function, which also shows the subgroup averages (as squares) connected by a blue line.

Minitab's Brush function (p120) can be used on Individual Value Plots since each point represents an individual piece of data.

Minitab: Like most graphs, Individual Value Plots (IVPs) can be found in several different menu locations in Minitab, including:

- *Graph > Individual Value Plot*
- Display Descriptive Statistics (p121)
- 2 Sample t-test (p160)

Courier-Process.mpj

100% Stacked Bar Charts

Box plot and Individual Value plots are useful for Continuous data, but the 100% Stacked Bar Chart should be used for comparing **proportions** of categorical or Attribute data.

If you have just **one sample** of categorical data, then a Pareto chart is useful for analysing the different proportions within that sample. However, a 100% Stacked bar chart is more useful when investigating the differences in proportions between **two or more samples**.

Using data from the example on postage delays (see page 135), the frequency in each category has been recorded and used with Excel's 100% Stacked Column Chart function, to create the graph shown on the right.

Like Pareto charts, the **sample size** is not automatically shown on this chart. It is therefore good practice to make a note of the relevant samples sizes when analysing or presenting this type of graph, as shown here:

Excel Graph Function: 100% Stacked Column Chart

Legend:
- Other
- Postcode Unreadable
- Not Franked
- No Stamp
- No Postcode

Rural Sample size (n) = 104

Urban Sample size (n) = 136

Pareto-Postage.mpj

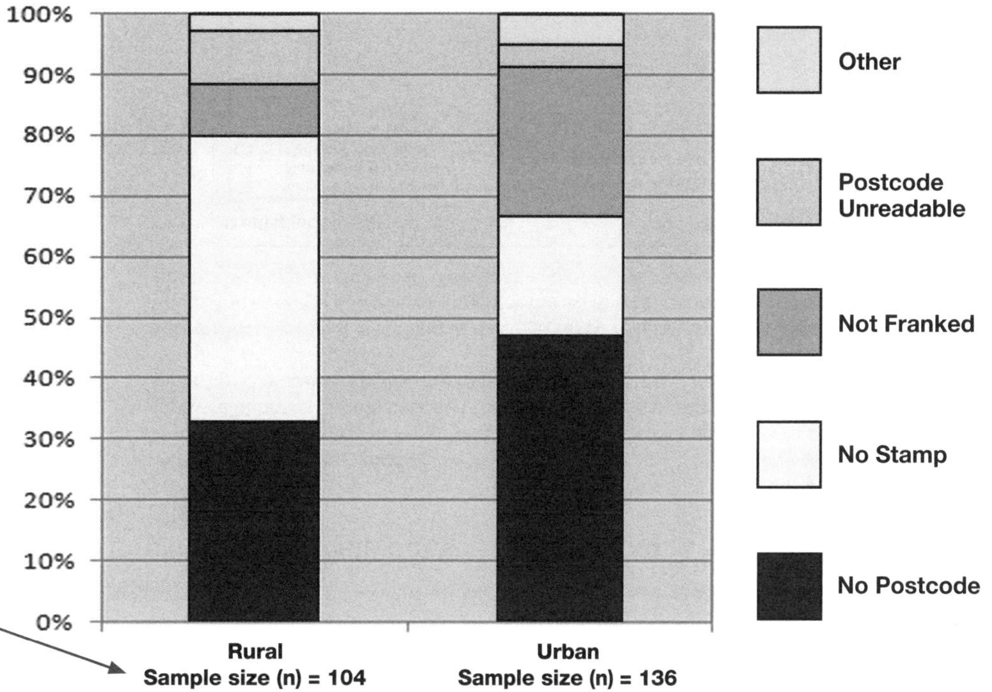

Scatter Plots – Overview

When you are investigating whether a relationship exists between two factors, a Scatter plot is the best first step for analysing the data graphically.

Minitab: Graph > Scatterplot

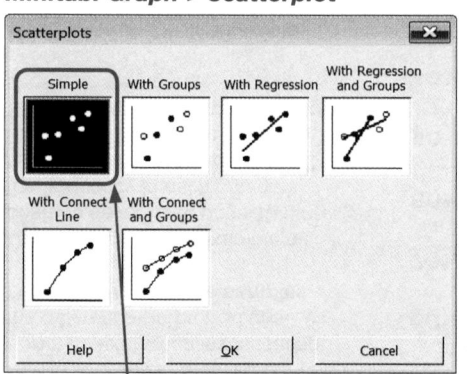

What are Scatter plots?

Scatter plots are a tool for graphing two factors against each other in order to help identify if any relationship exists between them. A relationship between two factors will look like a clear trend or pattern within the data points, rather than just random variation.

Example: A project is looking at the time taken to answer calls at a call centre. Over 80 shifts, the average call answer time (for the shift) was recorded alongside the number of people working on that shift. The Scatter plot of the results is shown on the next page.

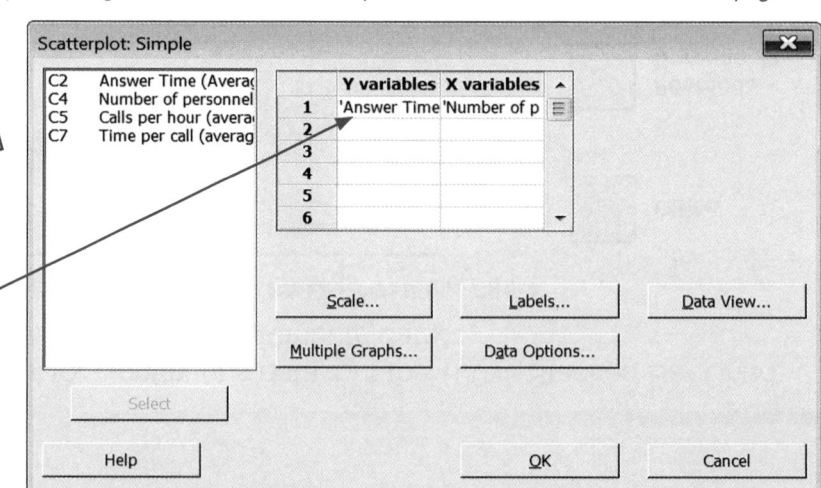

In this example, we will be creating a single Scatter plot for two factors of data, so select **Simple**. Alternatively, Scatter plots with stratified groups and regression or connect lines can also be created. Enter the two columns that you want to graph against each other on the Scatter plot here:

The **axis protocol** for Scatter plots is that the input to the process should be placed on the X (horizontal) axis and the output from the process on the Y (vertical) axis.

Scatter Plots – Interpreting the Results

Example (cont.): The Scatter plot for the call centre example introduced on the previous page is shown on the right. It graphs the average *Answer Time* against the *Number of Personnel* for 80 shifts, and appears to show that a relationship exists where the higher the number of personnel available, the lower the average answer time.

Cause and Effect:

Be careful before concluding that a direct 'cause and effect' relationship exists. In this example, it seems rational that more personnel will directly enable calls to be answered more quickly. However, there are many other situations where a mathematical correlation might exist between two data sets, without a direct cause and effect. For example, the sales of ice cream and incidents of sunburn might well be mathematically correlated, but there is no direct cause and effect relationship between them.

Data Types:

Scatter plots work with both Continuous and Count data. In this example, *Answer Time* is Continuous data and *Number of Personnel* is Count data.

 **Correlation.mpj**

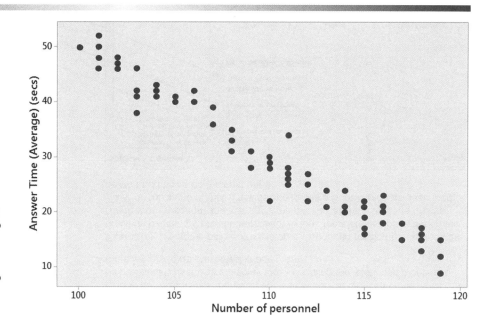

Next steps after a Scatter plot:

A Scatter plot is the first step in defining the relationship or correlation between two factors. In cases where the relationship is not clear cut, **correlation** (see page 195) can be used to help decide if a relationship exists. **Regression** techniques (see page 197) go a step further and are used to define a relationship (correlation) in a mathematical format. The simplest of the regression techniques is the Fitted Line Plot, shown on page 198.

Bubble plots – Overview

While Scatter Plots only allow two factors to be mapped against each, Bubble Plots allow a third variable to be added to the picture - enabling more complex relationships to be visualised.

Graph > Bubble Plot

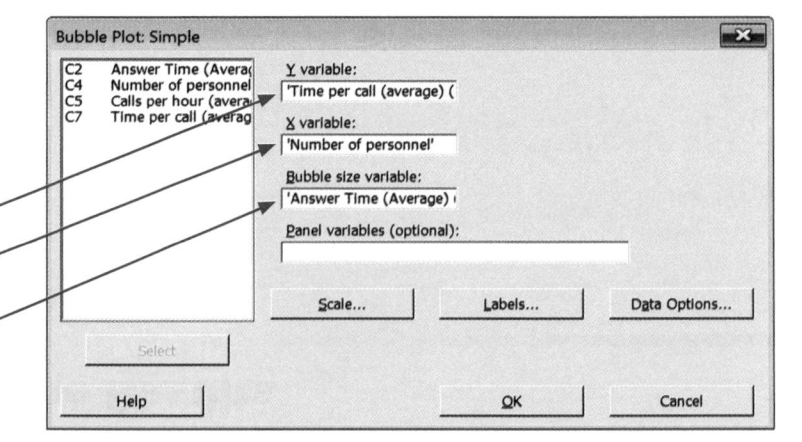

In this example, we are creating a **Simple** Bubble plot for three factors. If we had a fourth, categorical factor then that too could be added to the Bubble plot using the **With Groups** option. This would use different colour bubbles for different sub-groups within the data.

Enter a process output as the **Y variable** here:

Enter a process input as the **X variable** here:

Enter a third variable, which will be represented by different bubble sizes, here:

What are Bubble Plots?

Bubble plots are a tool for graphing three factors against each other, in order to look for relationships between all three factors at the same time. They can be particularly useful as a display tool – enabling the relationship between three factors to be presented in one graph.

Example: Using the call centre example introduced for Scatter plots on the previous pages, the project team want to look for relationships between the *Number of Personnel,* the average *Time per Call* **and** the average *Answer Time,* on the same graph. They decide to use a Bubble plot, as described below and shown on the next page.

Correlation.mpj

Bubble plots – Interpreting the Results

Example (cont.): The Bubble plot for the example on the previous page is shown on the right. Initially, the relationship between the *Number of Personnel* and *Time per Call* can be assessed by considering the **position** of the bubbles, as you would with a normal Scatter plot. In this example, there appears to be a relationship between the two factors, where the average *Time per Call* increases as the *Number of Personnel* increases.

Secondly, the average *Answer Time* can also be considered by looking at the **size** of the bubbles. In this example, it is apparent that the bubbles get smaller towards the right hand side of the plot. In other words, it appears that the average *Answer Time* decreases as the *Number of Personnel* increases (and therefore as the *Time per Call* increases too).

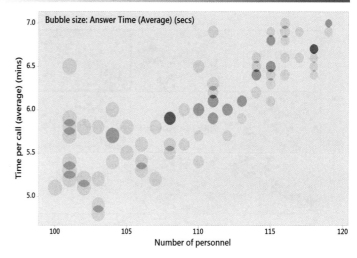

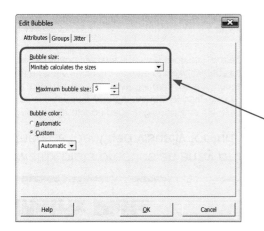

Setting the right Bubble Size: Because the size of the bubbles is significant, it is important to ensure they are sized in the most effective way. The **Edit Bubbles** function (left) can be opened by double-clicking any of the bubbles on a plot.

The default setting for bubble size is that **Minitab calculates the sizes**. This means that Minitab sets the size of the bubbles so that their **area** is proportional to the value of the factor they represent. Using this option, the size of all the bubbles can be adjusted using the **Maximum bubble size**, which was adjusted to 5 for the Bubble plot example shown above.

The alternative setting in Minitab is that the **Bubble size variable contains the sizes**. This means that the **radius** of the bubbles is proportional to the value of the factor that they represent. This can provide more differentiation between bubbles, but there is no option to limit their absolute size in Minitab, so they can tend to be too large.

Matrix Plots

Matrix plots produce an array of Scatter plots for several columns of data. Potential correlations can then be identified visually for further investigation.

The Scatter plot on page 146 correlates the average call answer time with the number of people working at a call centre. However the data file also contains data on the incoming volume of calls (average calls per hour) and the time spent on each call (average time per call).

A Matrix plot is a quick way of producing a Scatter plot for every combination of these four data columns, allowing a rapid visual assessment of which ones might be related in some way.

So, as we know from page 146, *Answer Time* and the *Number of Personnel* are correlated and this stands out clearly here.

The volume of incoming *Calls per Hour* does not **appear** to be correlated either with *Answer Time*, the *Number of Personnel*, or with the *Time per Call*, because all of the plots on this row show no obvious trends.

However, there does **appear** to be some relationship between the *Time per Call* and both *Answer Time* and *Number of Personnel,* shown in the first two plots on this row.

Minitab creates mirror images of the plots, which means that the bottom left plot is the same (but reversed) as the top right plot.

Minitab: Graph > Matrix Plot

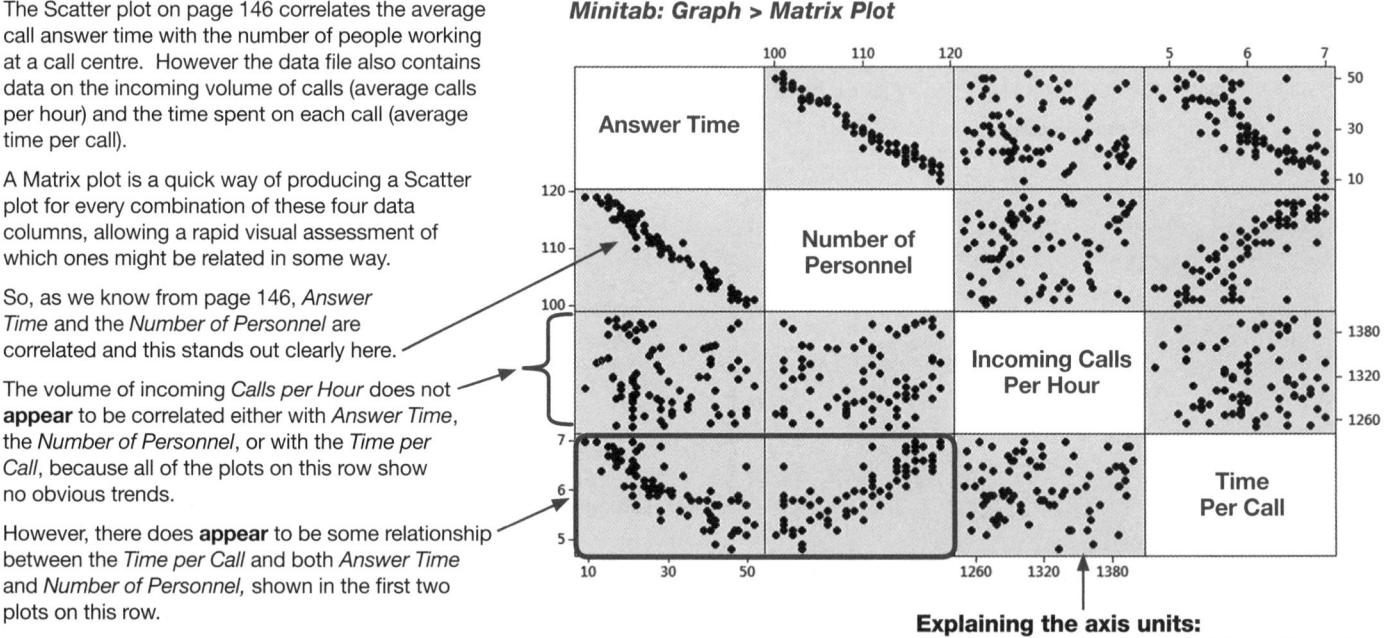

⊘ **Correlation.mpj**

Explaining the axis units:
For this graph, the lower units (1260-1380) refer to the *Calls per Hour*, and the *Time per Call* units are located at the far left of the matrix (5-7 minutes).

From Graphical Results to Statistical Significance

Looking back over the last few pages of Box plots and Individual Value Plots, you will notice that every time an observation has been made from a graph, the word '**appears**' has been used. **Why?** Because we cannot actually be sure that observations are true until we have checked them statistically.

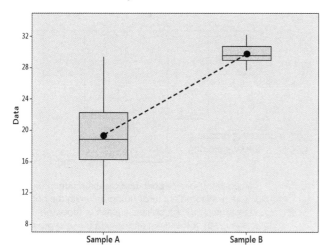

What would give you more confidence that your observations are true?

If you collected more data and still got the same results, your confidence that processes A and B are different would probably be increased. Increased sample size is a major contributor to gaining statistical confidence. The more data you have, the more confident you are.

The graphical results:

The Box plot on the left shows two samples that were taken from two processes A and B. It **appears** that:

- Process A has a lower average than process B.
- Process A has more variation than process B.

The statistical significance:

- How confident are you that the observations you have made are true?
- Would you stake your life on it?!
- How do you know that these differences didn't happen just by chance?
- What if processes A and B actually have the same average and variation, but you just happened to get a few high results when collecting sample B, and more varied results when collecting sample A?

The answer is that, at this point, we have to treat the observations that we have made from the graphical results as theories – to be proven one way or the other using more advanced statistical tests for significance.

Hypothesis Testing (page 154) covers a range of statistical tests for significance that can be used to help you reach decisions on your data.

Confidence Intervals (CIs)

Instead of assuming a statistic is absolutely accurate, Confidence Intervals can be used to provide a range within which the true process statistic will fall (with a specific level of confidence).

Example:
A saw mill is trying to estimate the average thickness of its 25mm plywood, to see if it really is 25mm! Nine sheets of plywood are taken randomly from the process, their thickness measured, and the histogram plotted, as shown below:

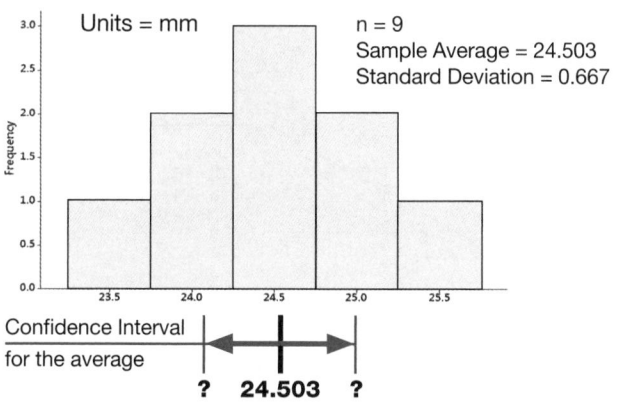

Units = mm

n = 9
Sample Average = 24.503
Standard Deviation = 0.667

Confidence Interval for the average

? 　24.503　 ?

The average thickness of the sample turns out to be 24.503mm, not 25mm, and so it **appears** that the plywood sheets are too thin. But does this mean that the whole process is too thin, or that we just happened to select a sample of nine sheets that were on the thin side?

Confidence Intervals can be used to help decide (right).

(Simplified) mathematical equation for a Confidence Interval:

$$\text{95\% Confidence Interval for the average of the Population} = \text{Sample Average} \;+/-\; \text{'t'} \left(\frac{\text{Sample Sigma}}{\sqrt{n}} \right)$$

The equation above says that a confidence interval is dependant on:

■ **The sample average:** This is a good starting point!

■ **The sample size (n):** As sample size decreases, the confidence interval gets bigger (exponentially) to cope with the fact that less data was collected.

■ **The Process variation (Sample Sigma):** The higher the process variation (estimated from the sample) the bigger the confidence interval.

■ **The Confidence level required (t):** The value of 't' is taken from statistical tables similar to the Z-table. If a 99% Confidence Interval were required, then the value of 't' would be larger, to increase the interval.

Using the equation above, and a 't' constant of 2.306 (tables not provided), the 95% CI for the average plywood thickness can be calculated as follows:

95% CI = 24.503 +/- (2.306 x (0.667 / √9)) = 24.503 +/- 0.5127
= **23.99mm to 25.02mm**

So, we can be 95% confident that the average thickness of the process is between 23.99 and 25.02mm. Since this includes the target of 25mm, there is a **chance** that the process is producing an average thickness of 25mm after all.

Confidence Intervals within Minitab's Graphical Summary

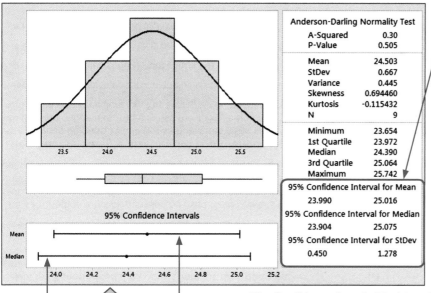

Anderson-Darling Normality Test	
A-Squared	0.30
P-Value	0.505
Mean	24.503
StDev	0.667
Variance	0.445
Skewness	0.694460
Kurtosis	-0.115432
N	9
Minimum	23.654
1st Quartile	23.972
Median	24.390
3rd Quartile	25.064
Maximum	25.742

95% Confidence Interval for Mean
23.990   25.016
95% Confidence Interval for Median
23.904   25.075
95% Confidence Interval for StDev
0.450   1.278

Median C.I.   **Average C.I.**

The Confidence Intervals for the Median and Average are also shown graphically here.
(NB: The scale is not shared with the histogram).

 Wood Thickness.mpj

Minitab's Graphical Summary function (see page 126) provides Confidence Intervals for the average, median and standard deviation of the process, as shown here for the plywood thickness example introduced on the previous page.

Converting statistics into 'real' language is an important skill for a Six Sigma analyst. The Confidence Intervals shown here can be interpreted into everyday language as follows:

We can be 95% confident that:

- The **average** thickness of the plywood is somewhere between 23.99 and 25.016 (or 25.02mm rounded).

- The **median** thickness of the plywood is somewhere between 23.904 and 25.075.

- The **standard deviation** of the plywood thickness is somewhere between 0.45 and 1.278.

The Confidence Level of the intervals (in this case 95%) can be adjusted in Minitab's Graphical Summary function. As the confidence level is increased, the size of the Confidence Intervals increases, because you are demanding **more** confidence that the value is within the interval (this can seem a little counter intuitive). So, for the plywood thickness example:

The 90% CI for the average =   24.1 to 24.9   90%
The 95% CI for the average =   24.0 to 25.0   95%
The 99% CI for the average =   23.7 to 25.2   99%

24.503

Confidence Intervals for Proportions

Minitab's 1 Proportion function can be used to calculate confidence intervals for percentages (Attribute data). You do not need a data file to use this function since Minitab enables you to directly enter summarised data, as follows:

Select the **Summarised data** option from the drop down list, enter the total sample size (in the **Number of trials**) and the **Number of events**. The definition of an event is up to you. So, if you are looking at a product failure rate, you enter the number of failures (events) in your sample and the total sample size.

The 1 Proportion function can also be used to complete a hypothesis test (see page p183). However, in this case we only require a confidence interval, and so the **Perform hypothesis test** box should be left unchecked, as shown.

The effect of sample size on the confidence interval:

As explained on page 151, larger sample sizes allow us to be more confident in our results. You can use the 1 Proportion function to demonstrate this relationship. For example, try the following:

Keeping 20% as your proportion and using different sample sizes…

- For a sample size of 50 (10 out of 50), the CI is 10% to 33.7%.
- For a sample size of 500 (100 out of 500), the CI is 16.5% to 23.7%.
- For a sample size of 1000 (200 out of 1000), the CI is 17.5% to 22.6%.

Minitab: Stat > Basic Statistics > 1 Proportion

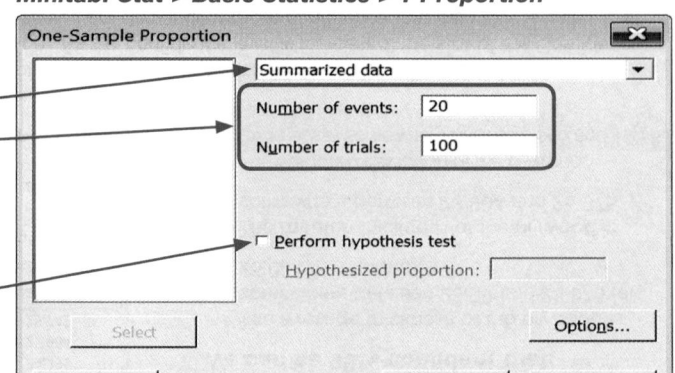

Example:

A political polling company is interested to find out the percentage of voters that are intending to vote for a Liberal party in an upcoming election. A random selection of 100 voters are polled and 20 of them indicate that they intend to vote Liberal (20%).

However, 100 is not a very large sample (particularly for Attribute data), and so Minitab's 1 Proportion function is used to calculate a confidence interval for the 20% result. The session window results (left) provide a 95% confidence interval of between 12.7% and 29.2%.

This is quite a large interval, and confirms that a poll of just 100 voters does not provide a very precise prediction of the actual result of an election. In reality, political pollsters tend to use a minimum sample size of 1000 people, which provides around +/- 3% precision.

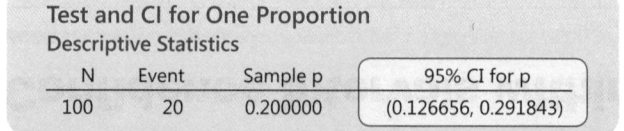

Test and CI for One Proportion
Descriptive Statistics

N	Event	Sample p	95% CI for p
100	20	0.200000	(0.126656, 0.291843)

Hypothesis Testing – Overview

So if Confidence Intervals mean that you can never take a statistic at face value anymore (because there is always some potential for error), how are you going to prove (or disprove) anything?

The short answer is you're not!
We can be very certain, even 99.9% certain, but never 100% certain anymore. Hypothesis testing refers to a set of tools that can tell us how certain we can be in making a specific decision or statement. So, we can now place a level of certainty on the observations that we make from graphs.

This may all sound a bit strange, but it is actually a step in the right direction. By telling us how certain (confident) we can be in our decisions, hypothesis testing also tells us our risk of being wrong – something that has rarely been quantified before in business organisations. In reality, we have always known there was a chance of being wrong but, because we have not had a way of measuring this risk, it has generally been ignored. Because Six Sigma is data driven, we cannot take this blinkered approach anymore.

Hypothesis testing has its own flow and terminology, shown opposite and explained on subsequent pages.

If you are having trouble interpreting hypothesis testing results on the following pages, come back to the basics within the flow chart shown here.

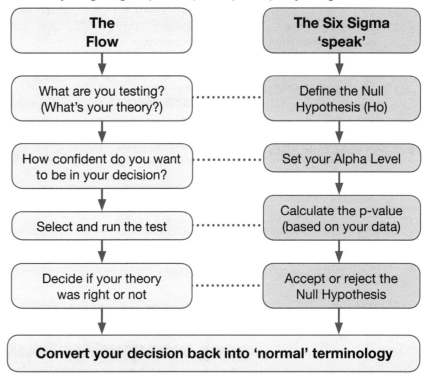

The Flow

What are you testing? (What's your theory?)

How confident do you want to be in your decision?

Select and run the test

Decide if your theory was right or not

The Six Sigma 'speak'

Define the Null Hypothesis (Ho)

Set your Alpha Level

Calculate the p-value (based on your data)

Accept or reject the Null Hypothesis

Convert your decision back into 'normal' terminology

Tossing a Coin – An Everyday Hypothesis Test

This everyday example of tossing a coin demonstrates that hypothesis testing is actually something we do quite naturally, without realising it.

Imagine that a friend of yours says he has a coin that lands on heads more often than it lands on tails. You don't believe him, because we all know that coins are 50/50 in the way they fall, and so you ask him to toss the coin a few times, and you'll make up your own mind based on the results (**show me the data!**).

	Results (in time order)	Probability (p-values)
After five throws, it is Heads 80%, Tails 20%. He says that proves it, but you're not so sure.	Heads Tails Heads Heads Heads	*Not* unlikely (37.5%)
After 10 throws, it is still Heads 80%, Tails 20%. Now you don't know what to think – the data is starting to look like he could be right!	Heads Heads Tails Heads Heads	Quite unlikely (10.9%)
After fifteen throws, it is still Heads 80%, Tails 20%! Now you're convinced, and you agree with him that the coin is not 50/50 because of the results you've seen.	Heads Heads Heads Tails Heads	Very unlikely (3.5%)

What happened?

After every five throws, you reviewed the results, and the percentage of heads and tails was always the same – 80/20. So why did it take you so long to decide that the coin was **not** 50/50?

Probably because you were waiting to be more confident in your decision?

From a hypothesis testing point of view:

After every five throws, you worked out the probability (the p-value) of getting the results you had, if the coin were 50/50 (your Null Hypothesis).

- **First hypothesis test:**
  After five throws, 80/20 didn't seem unlikely if the coin was 50/50. The p-value was 0.375.

- **Second hypothesis test:**
  After ten throws, 80/20 was quite unlikely if the coin was truly 50/50. The p-value at this point was 0.109.

- **Third hypothesis test:**
  After fifteen throws, 80/20 was very unlikely if the coin was 50/50, so you decided it couldn't be a 50/50 coin, and agreed with your friend. The p-value at this point was 0.035.

When the p-value reached 0.035, we say that it had dropped below your 'alpha level' (p157) – the point at which you decided the Null Hypothesis (a 50/50 coin) was not very likely, and so you **rejected** the Null hypothesis.

Interpreting p-values (also see Appendix B, p291)

Understanding p-values is critical to interpreting hypothesis results. The best way is to find and learn a definition that works for you, and repeat it back every time you need to interpret a p-value.

A statistical definition of the p-value is:
'The probability of getting the same results (data) that you have got (or worse) if the Null hypothesis were true.'

The definition above sounds a little abstract by itself, but take a few minutes to look back at the coin example. Every time you got another five results, you looked at **all** the results so far and estimated the probability of those results occurring if it were a 50/50 coin. You were estimating p-values.

A practical definition of the p-value is:
The p-value is your confidence in the Null Hypothesis...

*...so, when it's low, you **reject the Null** and when it's **not** low, you **keep the Null***

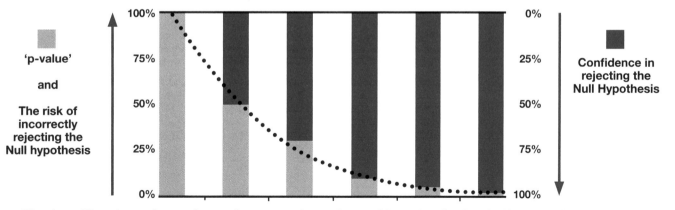

'p-value'

and

The risk of incorrectly rejecting the Null hypothesis

Confidence in rejecting the Null Hypothesis

The dotted line shows that as the p-value comes down, the confidence in rejecting the Null Hypothesis goes up.

Confidence Levels and Alpha Levels (a.k.a Alpha Risk)

Before you perform a hypothesis test you must set your Alpha Level, which is the level that the p-value must drop below if you are to reject the Null Hypothesis and decide there is a difference.

As explained on the previous page, the p-value is related to your confidence in deciding that a difference exists between samples of data. So, you must also decide on how much confidence you want (in saying that a difference exists between samples of data) in order to set your Alpha Level.

How do you decide on your required confidence?

You need to consider the risks of making the wrong decision in order to establish your required confidence. This will often depend on the environment in which you are working and the particular decision you are trying to make. Working in a safety critical environment such as an oil platform at sea or in a hospital, you would probably look for higher confidence in your decisions. The key point is that you must decide on your Alpha Level **before** you carry out the Hypothesis test, **not** once you have seen the results!

Example: Your company makes machined components for the aerospace industry and you are currently considering a major investment in new machinery that will (hopefully) resolve some current quality issues. You have two sets of data – one from the current machine and one from the new machine – and they appear to suggest that the new machine provides an improvement.

Because of the high investment involved, you decide you need a confidence level of 95% if you are to purchase the new machinery. So, you will need a p-value of less than 0.05 when comparing the results of the old and new machines (if you are to decide they are different).

Example: Your project on call centre customer service is piloting a change to the process flow that appears to improve performance. The proposed change has very little cost and possibly better performance, and so you decide that you only require 90% confidence in your decision. Consequently a p-value less than 0.10 will be acceptable.

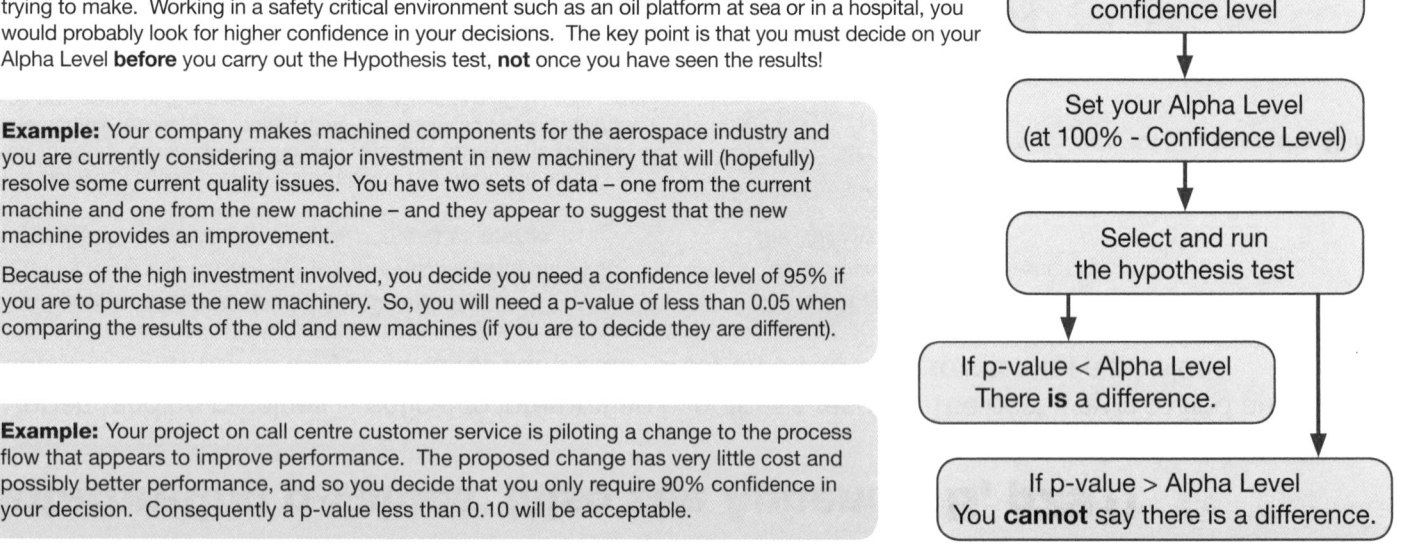

Setting The Right Null Hypothesis (Ho)

The Null and Alternative Hypotheses (Ho & Ha) are always set up in a very similar fashion, regardless of whether you think you are going to prove or disprove the Null Hypothesis.

What you are looking at?	The Null Hypothesis (Ho)	The Alternative Hypothesis (Ha)
Average call answer times between call centres or operators	There is **no** difference in average call answer time between centres/operators	There **is** a difference in average call answer time between centres/operators
Customer satisfaction levels for different cars	There is **no** difference in customer satisfaction levels between the cars	There **is** a difference in customer satisfaction levels between the cars
The variation in a product dimension between different production machines	There is **no** difference in the variation of the dimension from the different machines	There **is** a difference in the variation of the dimension from the different machines
Process waiting times across different regions	There is **no** difference in the waiting times across the different regions	There **is** a difference in waiting times across the different regions

Hypotheses are always the same:
The Null Hypothesis always starts with 'there is **no** difference' and is therefore very specific.

In reverse, the Alternative always starts with 'there **is** a difference' which is not so specific, but that is a distinctive characteristic of hypothesis testing.

Proving or disproving?
Because of the way they are set up, if you decide that there **is** a difference between two sets of data (rejecting the Null), a hypothesis test does not tell you how big that difference is, only that it is there.

This is because you are not **proving** the Alternative Hypothesis, but just finding enough evidence to **disprove** the Null Hypothesis.

Hypothesis Tests for Averages – Routemap

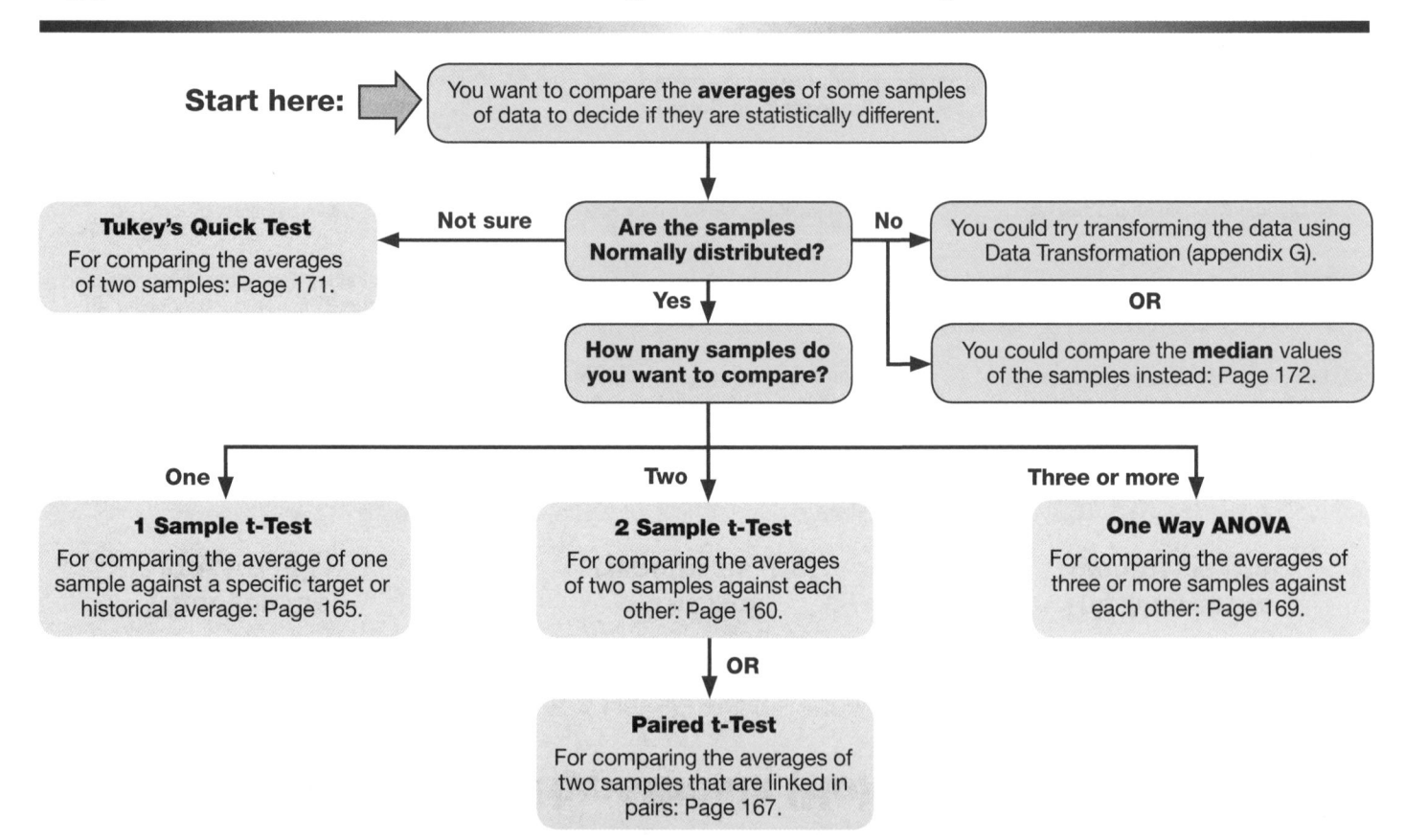

2 Sample t-Test – Overview

A 2 sample t-test looks at differences in the averages of two different samples. Many of the issues described here for this test also apply to the other hypothesis tests on subsequent pages.

What does 'two different samples' mean?
This could mean you have samples of data from two different machines, time periods, geographies, departments, processes or methods etc.

❗ Be careful not to get confused with terminology. The number of samples (in this case two) is different from the samples' sizes. For example:

- The first sample may have a sample size of 30 'pieces' of data.
- The second sample may have a sample size of 150.

Does the data need to be Normally distributed for a t-test?
In theory, the data should be Normally distributed for a 2 sample t-test. This means that each separate sample of data that you have should be Normally distributed.

In reality, if your sample distributions are smooth and 'roughly' Normal, then go ahead and try a t-test. Of course, if you are using a 2 sample t-test on data that is not Normal, and you plan to spend large sums of money based on the results, then it might be a little dangerous (and you should worry about your approach to reaching decisions – Six Sigma or not!).

In the end, it is all about taking a logical and practical approach.

Alternatively, you could test for a difference in the medians of the samples using the tests introduced on page 172, since these tests do not require the data samples to be Normally distributed.

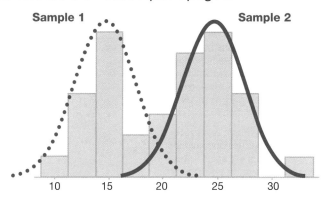

Do the two samples have to be the same size?
No. The two sample t-test takes account of the different sample sizes involved and adjusts the result accordingly.

What if my data is not reliable, and I don't think I'll see a difference even if there is one?
You shouldn't be here! If your data is not reliable, you shouldn't be trying to analyse it. Instead, go back to the Measure phase and look at Measurement System Analysis (page 58). You should only be making decisions with your data if it reliably represents the process that it measures.

2 Sample t-Test – Data Input

As with many Hypothesis tests, the Minitab input screen for the 2 sample t-test has several different options depending on how your raw data is laid out.

If all of your data (from both samples) has been placed together into one column, then use the first option on the drop down list: **Both samples are in one column.**

Using this option, you will need a second column that contains **Sample IDs** (*Subscripts* in V16), which is coded data that indicates which sample each row of data came from.

Example: The data for this t-test was taken from a project at a shipping company, looking at the number of days it takes for its ships to travel its most lucrative route to Japan.

A new route has been trialed over the last few months to see if it reduces the average number of days for each trip. The data can be found in:

Minitab: Stat > Basic Statistics > 2-Sample t

Two-Sample t for the Mean

C1	
C2	Time (days)
C3	Route
C4	
C6	New
C7	Old
C8	
C9	Summarised data
C10	
C11	

Both samples are in one column ▼

Samples: 'Time (days)'

Sample IDs: Route

Select   Options...   Graphs...

Help   OK   Cancel

If your two samples are in different columns, then use the second option on the drop down list: **Each sample is in its own column.**

Using this option, the columns do not need to be the same length, since the amount of data in each sample won't necessarily be the same.

The third option on the drop down list is **Summarised data**. This enables you to manually enter just the key statistics of each sample (the sample size, mean and standard deviation), which is enough information for Minitab to complete the t-test.

The data file for this example contains the data in three different formats, for each of the data input options described on this page.

Two-Sample-T-Shipping.mpj

The trial route data is labelled 'new'.
The historical route data is labelled 'old'.

2 Sample t-Test – Data Input (cont.)

Most of Minitab's hypothesis tests have similar graphs and options, as follows:

Minitab: Stat > Basic Stat > 2-Sample t > Graphs

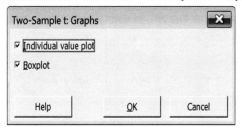

Minitab: Stat > Basic Stat > 2-Sample t > Options

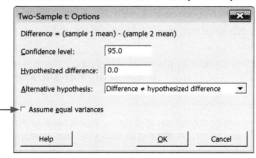

Graphs: For a 2 sample t-test, Minitab offers two relevant graphs.

- Individual Value Plot (p143).
- Box plot (p140).

The most important thing about graphs is that you **use** them! Without them, it is very difficult to translate your statistical output into a practical decision. **So, always use at least one graph!**

The **Assume equal variances** option will be discussed in more detail later. It is used when your two samples have similar levels of variation in them, since it can then improve the power of the test slightly. However, it is not wrong if you don't select it, so if in doubt, leave it blank.

Options: Hypothesis test options enable you to adjust the test, as follows:

- **The Confidence Level** is the confidence you require in your decision.
- **The Hypothesized Difference** (*Test Difference* in V16) is effectively your Null hypothesis and should be zero if your Null hypothesis is that there is no difference (which it normally is).
- **The Alternative Hypothesis** (Ha) is normally that there **is** a difference (i.e. the difference does not equal zero). So, this option is generally left at its default setting of **Difference ≠ hypothesized difference** (*Not Equal* in V16).

Minitab enables you to specify if you expect one of the sample means to be less than or greater than the other, by using an Alternative Hypothesis of **Difference > Hypothesized Difference** or **Difference < Hypothesized Difference**. This can make your test slightly more precise but it is also very easy to get wrong, so if in doubt, the best advice is to always leave this option at its default setting.

2 Sample t-Test – Session Window Output

The trick with interpreting hypothesis tests is to convert them back into day-to-day language. Not everyone wants to hear about your p-values! They just want to know what you have decided, and why.

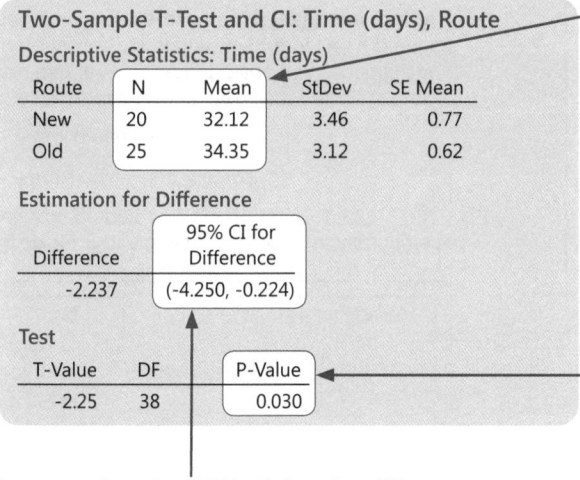

The first section of the Session Window output is just a summary of the statistics of the samples used in the test.

It can be noted that the sample sizes are different (although this is not a concern for the function of the t-test). The new shipping route has only been completed 20 times, to compare with 25 data points for the old route.

These statistics suggest that the average (mean) time for the new route is lower than the old route, by over 2 days (34.35 down to 32.12).

Whether this difference in average is 'real' or not (i.e. statistically significant), is determined by the hypothesis test results below.

Interpreting the p-value:
Assuming a confidence level of 95% is required in the decision (an Alpha Level of 0.05):

- The p-value of 0.03 is very low (and more importantly lower than 0.05).

- This means that there **is** a difference between the average shipping time of the two routes – so we have **rejected** the Null hypothesis.

- To be more specific, our confidence in saying this is actually 97% (=1-0.03).

Interpreting the 95% CI for the difference:
So, we know from the p-value (see right) that there **is** a difference between the averages. Minitab actually provides more information on how big the difference is, as the **95% CI for Difference**.

For this example, the results indicate that we can be 95% confident that the reduction in average shipping time with the new route is somewhere between 0.22 and 4.25 days. As always, with more data, we could be more specific.

2 Sample t-Test – Graphical Output

The graphical results help to show what the statistical difference really is.

The Box plots and Individual Value Plots from the 2 Sample t-test are shown here on the right. The best way to present the findings of a hypothesis test (depending on your audience) is to use graphs like these, combined with a statement that presents the hypothesis test conclusion in day-to-day language, such as:

"We can be over 95% confident (in fact 97%) that using the new route will reduce our shipping times".

or

"The data gives us a high degree of confidence that the new route will provide a reduction in average shipping times of between 0.2 and 4.25 days".

Practical versus Statistical Significance:
Both of the charts show that although we have proved a real difference in average, there is still quite a lot of overlap in the results because of the large (natural) variation in the process.

In fact, the reduction of two days becomes of less **practical** significance when you consider that the total range of the shipping times is about 10-15 days for both routes.

So, although we found an improvement, the data suggests there might be bigger, more important process inputs that we need to find in order to reduce shipping times with more practical significance.

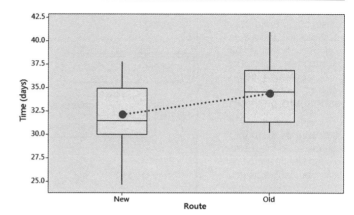

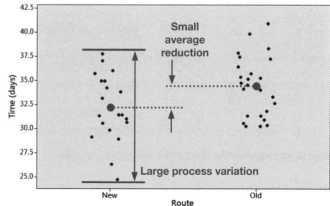

1 Sample t-Test – Overview

1 sample t-tests allow you to compare the average of just one sample against a known average value, such as an industry benchmark or well established historical average.

Example: Over the last few years (the long term), the time taken to process an invoice has always averaged 16.5 days.

Following a number of minor process improvements you have measured a small sample of 15 invoices, and found their average time for processing was 14.98 days.

It therefore **appears** that there has been an improvement (reduction) in the average, but the process has lots of variation anyway, and so it is difficult to be sure. The 1 Sample t-test helps answer the question:

'Can you say for sure that your process average is different from the historical average?'

For this example, check the **Perform hypothesis test** box, and enter 16.5 as your **Hypothesized mean** (this is the average value that you are comparing your sample against).

The data file for this example can be found in:

One-Sample-T.mpj

Minitab: Stat > Basic Statistics > 1-Sample t

One-Sample t for the Mean

C1   New Process
C4

One or more samples, each in a column ▼

'New Process'

☑ Perform hypothesis test

Hypothesized mean: 16.5

Select   Options...   Graphs...

Help   OK   Cancel

If your sample data is in a single column, select **One or more samples, each in a column** from the drop down list and enter the column that contains your *New Process* data here.

Alternatively, you can enter just the summarised statistics of your data, by selecting **Summarized data** from the drop down list.

Graphs & Options are similar to the 2 Sample t-test. Remember to select at least one graph (in this example, a histogram) in order to help interpret the results.

❗ Be careful to use the **1 sample t** function, **not** the **1 sample Z**. T-tests work with small sample sizes because they compensate for the lower confidence of small samples. The Z-test is very similar but doesn't compensate, so you should usually avoid it.

1 Sample t-Test – Interpreting the Results

Before you interpret any hypothesis test results, remind yourself what the Null and Alternative hypotheses are for your test. This will help avoid confusion later on when interpreting the p-value.

The Null hypothesis for this example is:
*'There is **no** difference between the new process average and the historical average of 16.5'.*

And the Alternative hypothesis is:
*'There **is** a difference between the new process average and the historical average of 16.5'.*

For this example, the required confidence has been set at 95% and so the Alpha Level is 0.05.

One-Sample T: New Process

N	Mean	StDev	SE Mean	95% CI for μ
15	14.982	3.122	0.806	(13.253, 16.711)

Test

T-Value	P-Value
-1.88	0.081

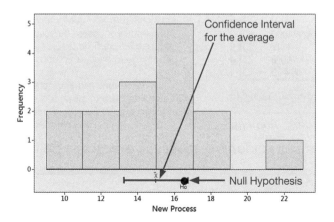

Confidence Interval for the average

Null Hypothesis

Session Window Results (above): The p-value is 0.081, which is **not** lower than the Alpha Level of 0.05, and so you **cannot** reject the Null. In other words, you **cannot** say there is a difference. The Session Window output also contains the 95% CI for the average of the sample, which is from 13.25 to 16.71. This interval includes the test mean of 16.5, which is why the test has not been able to prove a difference.

The resulting histogram (left) also indicates why the reduction in average is unproven by the hypothesis test result. The confidence interval for the average of the sample is marked at the bottom of the histogram, and the test mean (16.5) is marked with a large dot. They are clearly overlapping, so they could be the same.

What if we still think there is a difference?
We cannot say that the new process has reduced the average, **but**, be careful how this is interpreted. The hypothesis test is indicating that **with the data available** (just 15 data points), we cannot say the process has improved. It might be that with more data we find a different result, but that will take more time to collect.

Paired t-Test – Overview

Paired t-tests are similar to 2 sample t-tests, but are used where the data samples are linked in **pairs**.

Example:
A bank is looking at how long it takes their operators to process customer calls at their call centre.

Five operators have been through a new training programme and their processing times for a variety of standard customer requests were recorded before and after the training.

A Paired t-test is relevant because it ignores the differences between the operators, and just tests the difference between the pairs of results – before and after training – for each operator.

The Paired t-test helps answer the question…

'Can you say for sure that there is a difference in processing time between the 'before' and 'after' training results? (Ignoring the difference between operators)'

↓ **Paired T-Test-Training.mpj**

Minitab: Stat > Basic Statistics > Paired t

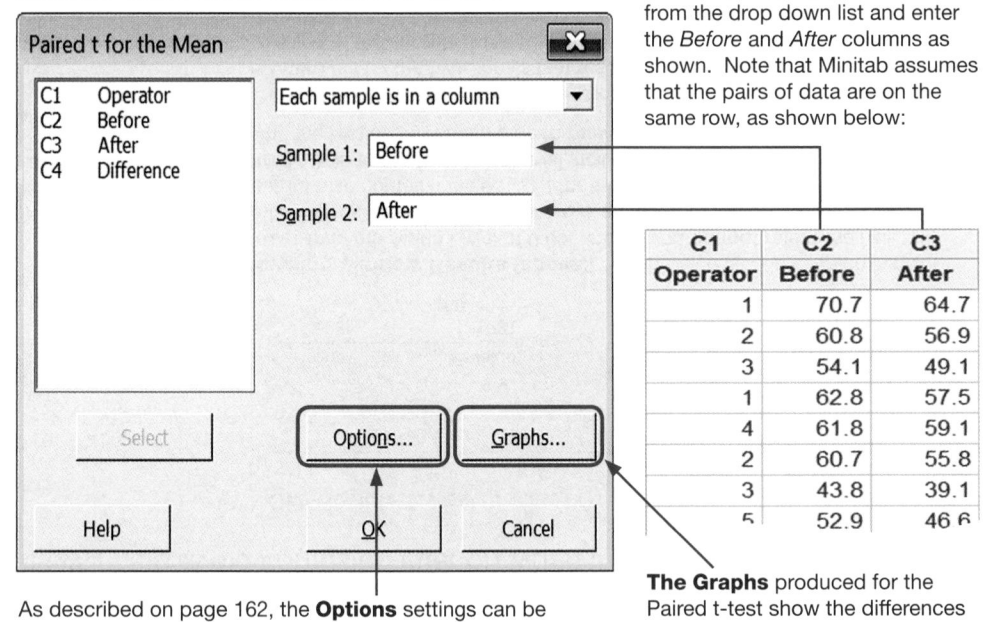

Select **Each sample is in a column** from the drop down list and enter the *Before* and *After* columns as shown. Note that Minitab assumes that the pairs of data are on the same row, as shown below:

C1	C2	C3
Operator	Before	After
1	70.7	64.7
2	60.8	56.9
3	54.1	49.1
1	62.8	57.5
4	61.8	59.1
2	60.7	55.8
3	43.8	39.1
5	52.9	46.6

As described on page 162, the **Options** settings can be altered if you want to refine your test, in particular the Alternative Hypothesis. However, these are generally advanced techniques, and if in doubt, the options should be left at their default settings.

The Graphs produced for the Paired t-test show the differences between the pairs of data, not the absolute values. For this example, the **Histogram of differences** is shown on the next page.

Paired t-Test – Interpreting the Results

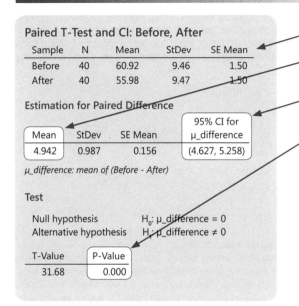

Paired T-Test and CI: Before, After

Sample	N	Mean	StDev	SE Mean
Before	40	60.92	9.46	1.50
After	40	55.98	9.47	1.50

Estimation for Paired Difference

Mean	StDev	SE Mean	95% CI for μ_difference
4.942	0.987	0.156	(4.627, 5.258)

μ_difference: mean of (Before - After)

Test

Null hypothesis H_0: μ_difference = 0
Alternative hypothesis H_1: μ_difference ≠ 0

T-Value	P-Value
31.68	0.000

Statistical results:
The first table in the session window provides the two samples' statistics.

The average difference between processing times before and after training is a reduction of 4.9 seconds.

More precisely the 95% confidence interval for this difference says that the reduction is at least 4.6 seconds and may be as high as 5.2 seconds.

The p-value is very low (0.000) which means that the Null Hypothesis can be rejected and we can be (very) confident that the reduction of 4.9 seconds is statistically significant.

Graphical Results:
The Paired t-test histogram shown on the right plots the **differences** between the pairs of data.

It shows clearly the average reduction of 4.9 seconds and the 95% Confidence Interval for this difference (discussed top right).

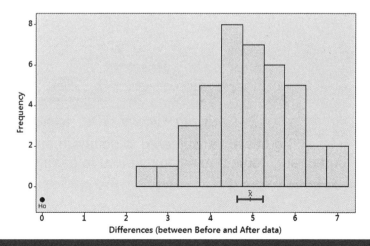

Differences (between Before and After data)

One Way ANOVA – Overview

ANOVA techniques allow the analysis of averages with three or more samples at a time. The maths behind the scenes is different, but the approach and interpretation of p-values is the same.

Example: A project is looking at the average transaction value across three different sales centres. The Box plot below shows the results of a one month survey at each sales centre, and it looks like there are differences in the average values (the connected dots). However, the Box plot only has a sample size of 20 for each sales centre, and so it is not clear if the differences between the average transaction values are statistically significant.

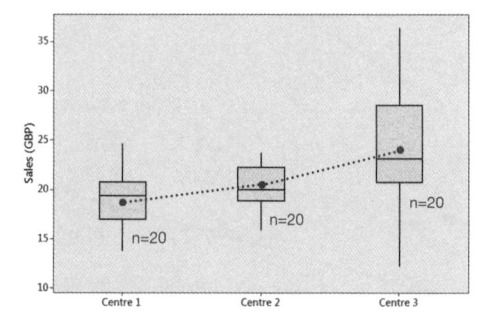

The Analysis of Variance (ANOVA) method uses a different mathematical approach (see appendix F) to compare the averages of three or more samples, but we must still be clear of the hypotheses before applying the technique, as follows:

- The Null hypothesis is: There is **no** difference in the average transaction value between the sales centres.

- The Alternative is therefore: There **is** a difference - at least one of the sales centres average transaction values is different.

Minitab: Stat > ANOVA > One-Way

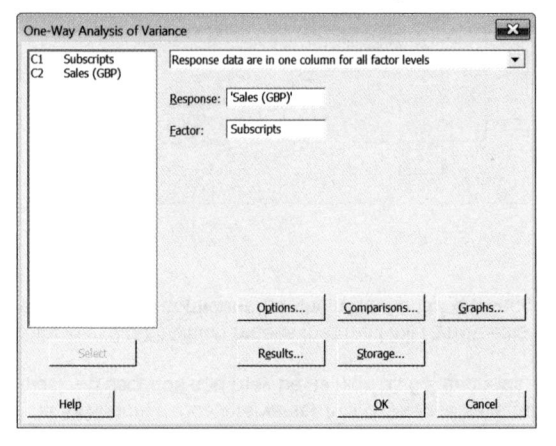

If all of the data is stacked in a single column, with the subgroup names in a separate column, then choose **Response data are in one column for all factor levels** from the drop down list, as shown above.

Alternatively, if your samples are in separate columns, then select **Response data are in a separate column for each factor level**.

The data file for this example contains the data in both the formats described above.

ANOVA-Sales.mpj

One Way ANOVA – Interpreting the Results

One-way ANOVA: Sales (GBP) versus Subscripts

Analysis of Variance

Source	DF	Adj SS	Adj MS	F-Value	P-Value
Subscripts	2	285.8	142.90	10.25	0.000
Error	57	794.8	13.94		
Total	59	1080.6			

Model Summary

S	R-sq	R-sq(adj)	R-sq(pred)
3.73409	26.45%	23.87%	18.50%

Means

Subscripts	N	Mean	StDev	95% CI
Centre 1	20	18.775	2.870	(17.103, 20.447)
Centre 2	20	20.300	2.151	(18.628, 21.972)
Centre 3	20	23.98	5.38	(22.30, 25.65)

Pooled StDev = 3.73409

So, to summarise the results in day to day language:

We are very confident that there are some differences between the average transaction values of the call centres.

Centre 3 appears to be most different from the others, and it has the highest average transaction value, of £23.98 pounds (GBP).

Session window results:

The p-value on the ANOVA table output is the result for the hypothesis test.

The p-value for this example is 0.000, which means that we can say (with effectively 100% confidence) that there **is** a difference in the average transaction value between the call centres. However, we should be careful how we phrase any conclusions, because the Alternative hypothesis was that '*there is a difference*' not '*they are all different*'.

Minitab also summarises the key statistics of each subgroup in the session window, and provides 95% Confidence Intervals for the **average** of each subgroup. These Confidence Intervals can be useful in understanding which (if any) of the subgroup averages are different, and are shown graphically in the Interval Plot below (which is selected by default in the Graphs submenu). The Interval Plot shows that the sample for Centre 3 has the average value that is most different from the others, and so it is likely to be this centre's results that have caused the p-value of the whole test to be 0.000.

To be more specific and decide if Centres 1 & 2 are different, a two sample t-test could be carried out on just these two centres.

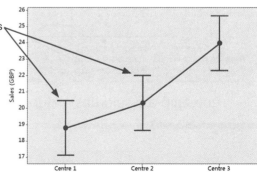

Tukey's Quick Test – Overview

Tukey's Quick Test is a simple technique for deciding if the averages of two samples are different.

Tukey's Quick Test is a hypothesis test that is simple to calculate and does not require any software. It is used to test if the averages of two samples are statistically different.

It works by counting the number of data points that fall above and below the overlapping region (as shown on the right). This is called the Total End Count, and if it is seven or more, then there is over 95% confidence that the sample averages are different. It's that simple!

Remember, the higher the Total End Count, the higher the confidence in deciding that the averages of the samples **are** different, as follows:

Total End Count	% Confidence in deciding averages are different
6 or more	90%
7 or more	95%
10 or more	99%

NB: If two values at the edge of the overlapping region are **exactly** the same, then this counts as 0.5, as in the example on the right.

Statistical conditions for Tukey's Quick Test:

- The sample sizes must be roughly the same (ratio < 4:3).
- The samples must be independent (i.e. not linked in pairs).
- Both sample sizes should be at least 5.
- The sample distributions do not need to be Normal.
- One sample must not contain the lowest **and** highest values.

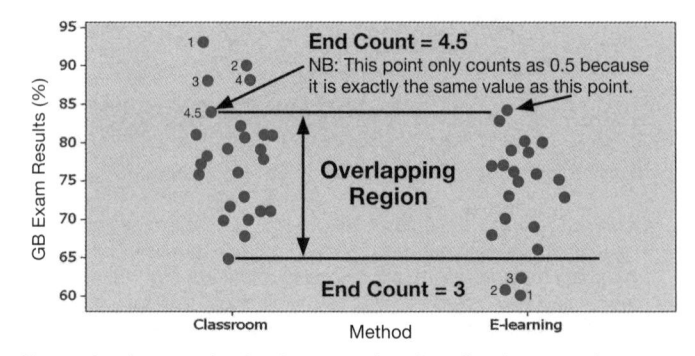

Example: An organisation is comparing the effectiveness of two methods of training delivery. Two groups of Green Belts are asked to sit an exam; the first group contains 24 delegates who have received classroom training and the second group 20 who have received e-learning. The results are shown above, and it **appears** that the classroom trained Green Belts score higher in the exam than those who received e-learning. This is supported by the Total End Count of 7.5, which gives over 95% confidence that the averages results are different.

The Total End Count of 7.5 is calculated by adding 3 from the lowest e-learning scores and 4.5 from the highest classroom scores (NB: the 5th highest classroom score is exactly the same as the highest e-learning score and is therefore counted as 0.5).

See the data file for more detail: ⬇ **Learning.mpj**

Hypothesis Tests for Medians – Routemap

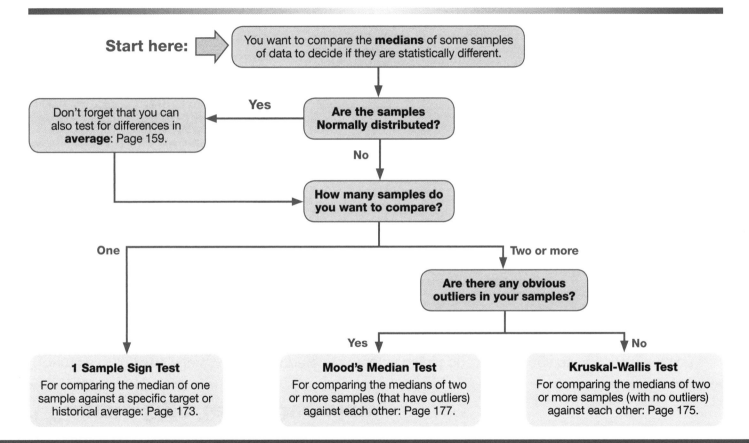

1 Sample Sign Test – Overview

1 Sample Sign Tests allow you to compare the median of just one sample against a known median value, such as an industry benchmark or well established historical median.

Example: A recruitment consultancy has recently implemented a new salary negotiation process and a project team is trying to verify that it has improved (increased) the salaries that are being achieved.

The salaries of the first 20 placements made using the new negotiation process have been recorded, and the project team want to compare these results against a historical salary benchmark.

Because the sample of salaries is **not** Normally distributed and there is only one sample (to compare against the benchmark), the team select a 1 Sample Sign test.

The median salary of the sample is €60K (the units are thousand of Euros) and the historical salary median was €48K, and so it *appears* that there has been an increase in the median of €12K. However, it's quite a small sample (n=20) and there is lots of variation within the sample (from €30K to €144K) and so it is difficult to be sure.

The 1 Sample Sign test helps answer the question:

'Can you say for sure that the new process median is more than the historical median?'

The data file for this example can be found in:

 **Salaries.mpj**

Minitab: Stat > Nonparametrics
> 1-Sample Sign

1-Sample Sign

C3   New Salaries (€K   Variables:
'New Salaries (€K)'

○ Confidence interval
   Level: 95.0

● Test median: 48
   Alternative: greater than ▼

Select   OK   Cancel

Help

Enter the column that contains the sample here (in this case, this is the sample of *New Salaries*).

This function can also be used to calculate a **Confidence Interval** for the median (not explained further in this text).

In this example, the sample median is being tested against a historical benchmark (the *Test median*). So:

- Select **Test median**.
- Enter 48 (the historical benchmark level).

Alternative Hypotheses:

The default Alternative hypothesis in Minitab is **Not Equal**. However, Minitab also offers additional Alternative hypotheses that are more specific (**Less than** and **Greater than**), which can be used to improve the power of a test. In this example, because it appears that the sample median is greater than the Test Median, the Alternative **Greater than** has been selected.

❗ If you're in any doubt however, always use Minitab's default alternative hypotheses, as selected in most examples in this guide. While not perfect, this approach minimises the risk of mistakes.

1 Sample Sign Test – Interpreting the Results

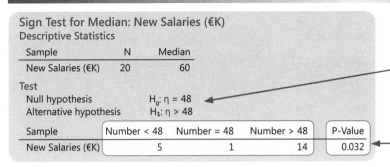

Sign Test for Median: New Salaries (€K)
Descriptive Statistics

Sample	N	Median
New Salaries (€K)	20	60

Test
Null hypothesis $H_0: \eta = 48$
Alternative hypothesis $H_1: \eta > 48$

Sample	Number < 48	Number = 48	Number > 48	P-Value
New Salaries (€K)	5	1	14	0.032

Session Window Results:
The first section provides a reminder of the key statistics. The sample size is 20 and the sample median is 60.

The Null and Alternative Hypotheses are then summarised in a technical shorthand, which says that the test is for the sample median being equal to 48 (the Null) versus it being greater than 48 (the Alternative). Remember, on the previous page, the Alternative Hypothesis was selected as **Greater than.**

The p-value is 0.032 (which is lower than an Alpha Level of 0.05), and so you **can** reject the Null, and conclude (with over 95% confidence) that the median salary in the sample is greater than the historical median of 48. So, the new negotiation process **does** increase placement salaries!

How the Sign Test works:
While the Sign Test produces a p-value that can be interpreted in a similar way to other hypothesis tests, the mathematics behind the Sign Test are quite different.

The Sign Test works by classifying each result within the sample as either above, below or equal to the Test Median. If the Null Hypothesis were true, we would expect to see approximately half the results above, and half below, the Test Median (allowing for a little random variation).

However, in this case, the majority of the results (14 out of 20) were **above** the Test Median, and this was high enough for the test to indicate (with statistical confidence) that the sample median (60) is greater than the Test Median (48). It is interesting to note that one of the results was **exactly equal** to the Test Median, as summarised in the session window output above. This was row 7 in the example data file:

The 1 Sample Sign test in Minitab does not offer any additional graphs. However, using a Dot plot from the Graph menu (shown below), the sample results can be visually compared to the historical benchmark of €48K (marked on the Dot plot below). As can be seen, while some of the results are below 48, most of them are above, and this is enough to conclude, statistically, that the median New Salary is higher than €48K.

Salaries.mpj

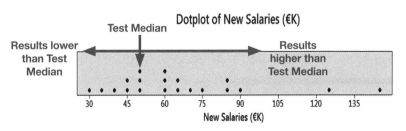

Dotplot of New Salaries (€K)

Test Median

Results lower than Test Median

Results higher than Test Median

New Salaries (€K)

Kruskal-Wallis Test – Overview

The Kruskal-Wallis test compares the medians of different samples of data, and can be used where the data samples are not Normally distributed and do not have any obvious outliers.

Example:
A project is looking at the time to deliver different home internet products (ISDN and ADSL). The Box plot below shows that the ISDN product appears to be delivered quicker than ADSL, and the team are keen to validate this conclusion before other tools (such as detailed process mapping) are used to find out why.

Because the ISDN results do not appear to be Normally distributed (a histogram and Box plot both indicate a skewed distribution), a Kruskal-Wallis test is being used to compare the **median** values of the two samples.

Minitab: Stat > Nonparametrics > Kruskal-Wallis

(No graph options are available with this function).

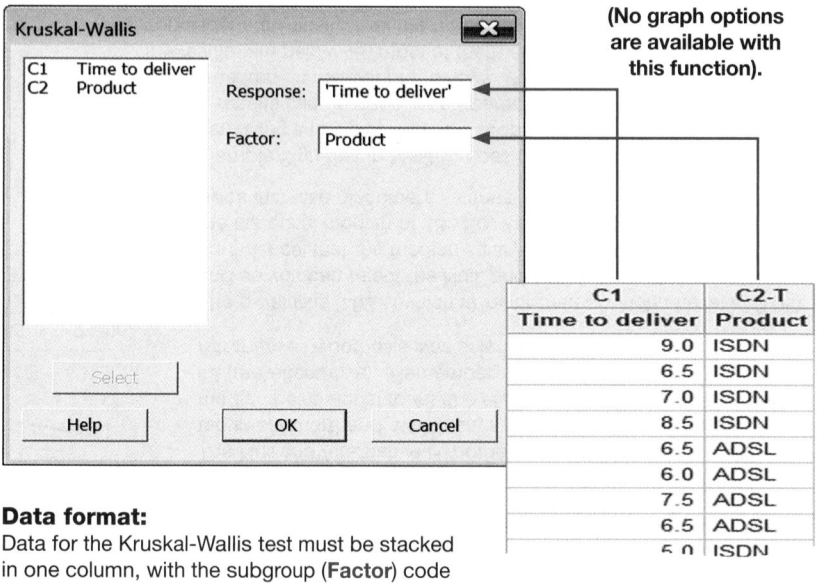

C1	C2-T
Time to deliver	**Product**
9.0	ISDN
6.5	ISDN
7.0	ISDN
8.5	ISDN
6.5	ADSL
6.0	ADSL
7.5	ADSL
6.5	ADSL
5.0	ISDN

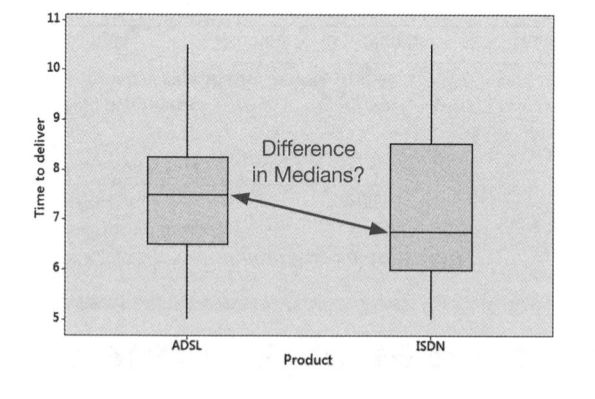

Data format:
Data for the Kruskal-Wallis test must be stacked in one column, with the subgroup (**Factor**) code alongside, as shown on the right.

⬇ **Time to Deliver.mpj**

Kruskal-Wallis Test – Interpreting the Results

Kruskal-Wallis Test on Time to deliver versus Product

Product	N	Median	Mean Rank	Z-Value
ADSL	25	7.50	29.7	0.73
ISDN	30	6.75	26.6	-0.73
Overall	55		28.0	

Test

Null hypothesis	H_0: All medians are equal
Alternative hypothesis	H_1: At least one median is different

Method	DF	H-Value	P-Value
Not adjusted for ties	1	0.53	0.467
Adjusted for ties	1	0.54	0.463

Analysing the p-value:
The p-value from this test is 0.463. Since this is (a lot) higher than 0.05, we **cannot** say with confidence that there is a difference in the medians of the two samples.

In other words, the median delivery times of the two internet products (that the two samples of data represent) **could** be the same as each other.

Note: The two p-values are usually very similar, but if not, use the value that is 'adjusted for ties'.

 **Time to Deliver.mpj**

Session window results:
Minitab produces only Session window results for this test (no graphical output), as follows:

Firstly, the sample sizes and medians of the samples (subgroups) are summarised. The difference in the median values is 0.75 days (7.5-6.75), but this should be considered in combination with the following:

- The size of the samples (25 for ADSL and 30 for ISDN) appears to be relatively low.
- The resolution of the data was to the nearest 0.5 days (see previous page).

For these reasons, a hypothesis test is essential in order to decide if the difference in medians is statistically significant, as described on the left.

So, to summarise the results in day to day language:
Based on the data we have collected, we **cannot** say with confidence that there is a difference between the medians.

The difference of 0.75 hours between the sample medians could easily have occurred just by chance.

If there **is** a difference, more data will have to be collected to prove it.

Mood's Median Test – Overview

Mood's Median test compares the medians (central position) of different samples of data, where the samples are **not** Normally distributed and where there **are** obvious outliers in the data samples.

Example:

A hospital project is looking at the time it takes to process Accident and Emergency (A&E) patients. The data has been stratified into two sub groups (weekdays and weekends) and the Box plot below shows that it appears to take longer to process patients at the weekend.

The team are keen to validate this before they set out to find and understand the root cause of this difference. Mood's Median test is being used because the weekend data appears to be skewed and also has some outliers (the asterisks on the boxplot below).

Minitab: Stat > Nonparametrics > Mood's Median Test

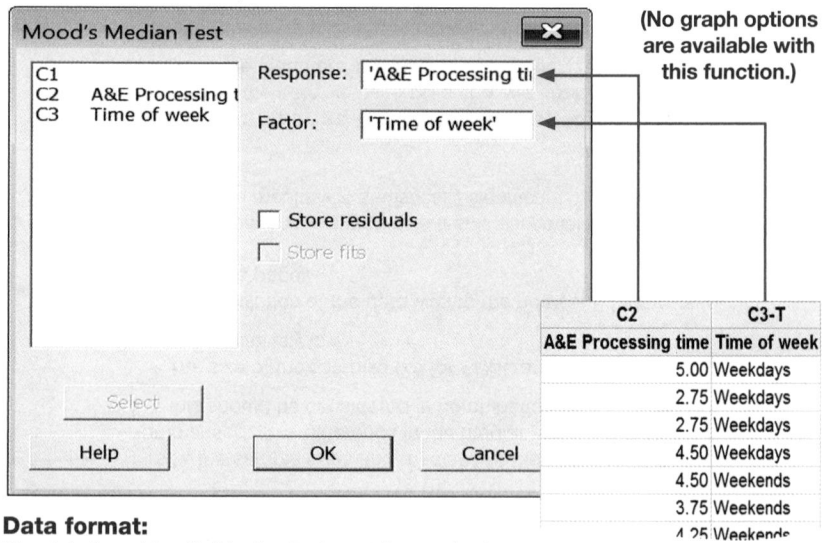

(No graph options are available with this function.)

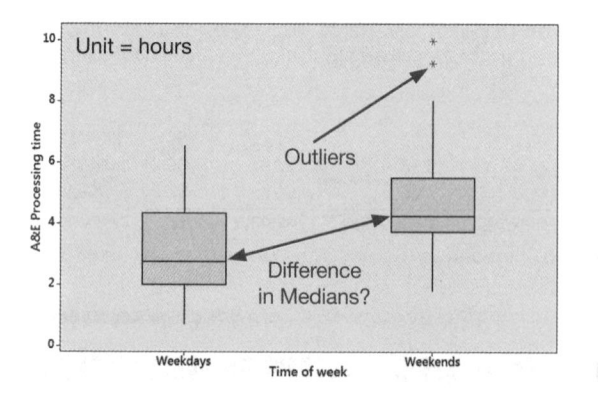

Data format:

The data for a Mood's Median test must be stacked in one column with the subgroup (**Factor**) code alongside, as shown on the right.

A&E Processing Times.mpj

Mood's Median Test – Interpreting the Results

Mood's Median Test: A&E Processing time versus Time of week
Descriptive Statistics

Time of week	Median	N <= Overall Median	N > Overall Median	Q3 – Q1	95% Median CI
Weekdays	2.75	20	10	2.3125	(2.5, 4.13564)
Weekends	4.25	10	15	1.7500	(3.75, 5)
Overall	3.75				

95.0% CI for median(Weekdays) - median(Weekends): (-2.27134, -0.228664)

Test

Null hypothesis	H₀: The population medians are all equal

Null hypothesis H_0: The population medians are all equal
Alternative hypothesis H_1: The population medians are not all equal

DF	Chi-Square	P-Value
1	3.91	0.048

Analysing the p-value:
The p-value for the test is 0.048. Since this is **less** than an Alpha Level of 0.05 we can say, with 95% confidence, that the medians of the subgroups **are** different.

Session window results:
Minitab produces only session window results for this test (no separate graphical outputs).

Based on the data in the subgroup samples, the difference between the subgroup medians is 1.5 hours (4.25-2.75, highlighted).

In fact, the confidence interval for the difference provides more detail and confirms (with 95% confidence), that the difference in medians is somewhere between 0.23 and 2.27 hours (or -0.23 and -2.27 depending on which way round it is calculated). Crucially, this interval does not include zero, and so the p-value analysis (left) concludes that the medians **are** different.

So, to summarise the results in day-to-day language:
We can be very confident that there is a difference in the median processing time for A&E patients that are treated during the week versus those that are treated at the weekend.

The weekday median processing time is at least 0.23 hours quicker than at the weekend, but could be as much as 2.27 hours quicker.

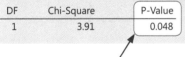 **A&E Processing Times.mpj**

Hypothesis Tests for Standard Deviation (Variation)

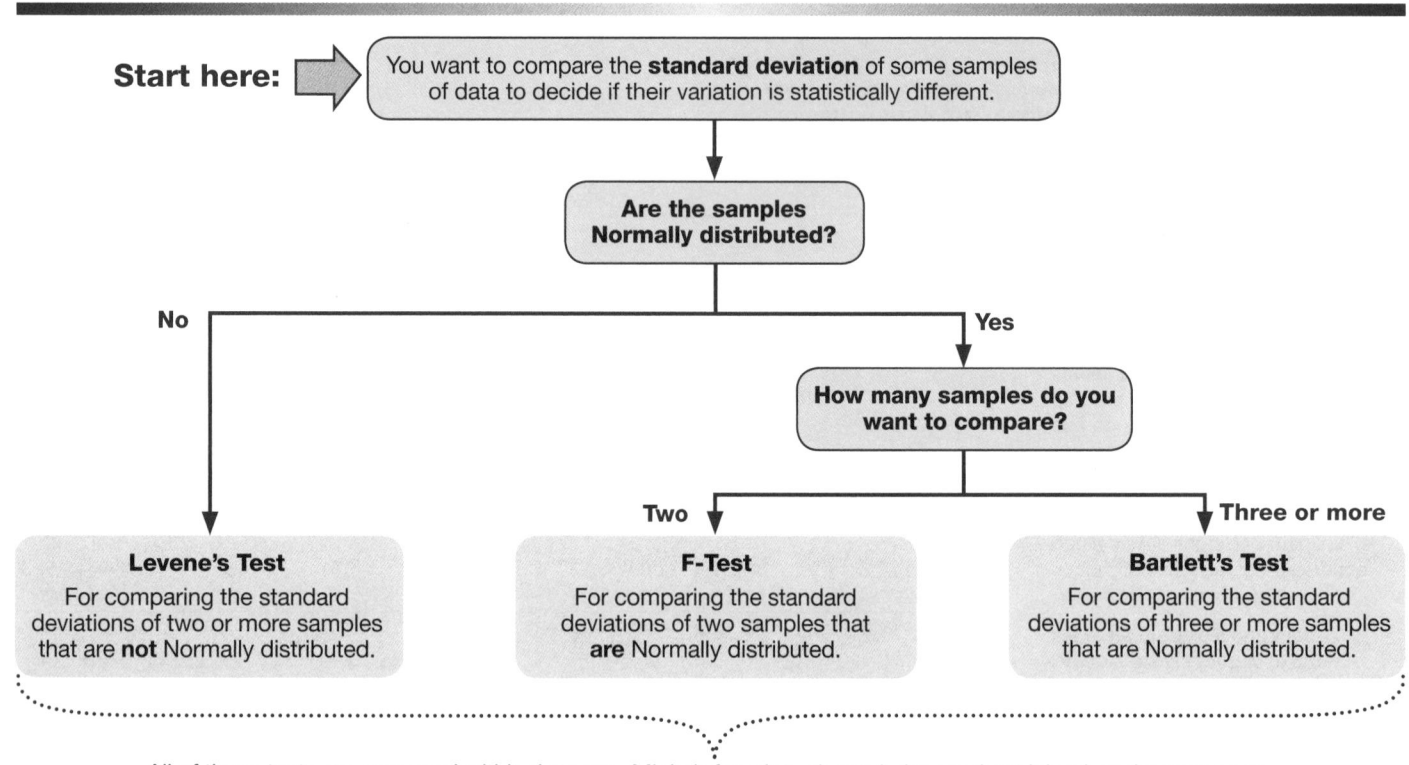

Start here: ➡ You want to compare the **standard deviation** of some samples of data to decide if their variation is statistically different.

Are the samples Normally distributed?

No → / Yes →

How many samples do you want to compare?

Two → / Three or more →

Levene's Test
For comparing the standard deviations of two or more samples that are **not** Normally distributed.

F-Test
For comparing the standard deviations of two samples that **are** Normally distributed.

Bartlett's Test
For comparing the standard deviations of three or more samples that are Normally distributed.

All of these tests are accessed within the same Minitab function, shown below and explained on the next page.

Minitab: Stat > ANOVA > Test for Equal Variances

Test for Equal Variance – Overview

Minitab's Test for Equal Variance function provides all three of the F-Test, Levene's and Bartlett's tests.

Example: A project is looking at the time it takes for three different IT Helpdesks to provide an e-mail response to their enquiries. The Box plot below shows that Helpdesk 3 appears to have a much lower level of **variation** than the other two Helpdesks, but a hypothesis test is required to find out if this is statistically significant.

Note that the Helpdesks also appear to have different averages, but a Test for Equal Variance only considers the **range** of the Box plots.

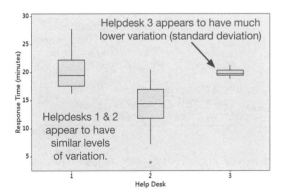

Test for Equal Variances.mpj

Minitab: Stat > ANOVA > Test for Equal Variances

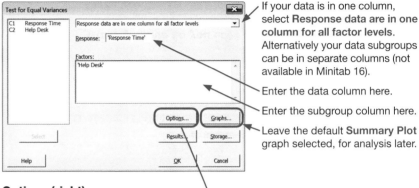

If your data is in one column, select **Response data are in one column for all factor levels**. Alternatively your data subgroups can be in separate columns (not available in Minitab 16).

Enter the data column here.

Enter the subgroup column here.

Leave the default **Summary Plot** graph selected, for analysis later.

Options (right):
For this example, the option to **Use test based on normal distribution** is checked, because all three subgroups can be assumed to be Normally distributed (verified by a Normality test). This option is new to Minitab 17 & 18 and enables you to specify at this point, if your data samples are Normally distributed. In version 16, Minitab provides test results relevant to both Normal **and** Nonnormal data, and the correct choice is then made by the user.

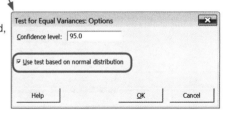

Test for Equal Variance – Interpreting the Results

Test for Equal Variances: Response Time vs Help Desk

Help Desk	N	StDev	CI
1	20	3.23049	(2.32031, 5.17197)
2	30	3.88025	(2.94560, 5.59623)
3	15	0.62091	(0.42614, 1.09567)

Tests

Method	Test Statistic	P-Value
Bartlett	34.09	0.000

Alternative test results if non-normal data:

Method	Test Statistic	P-Value
Multiple comparisons	—	0.000
Levene	8.85	0.000

Statistical Results: The Bartlett's test provides a p-value of zero indicating that at least one, if not all, of the Helpdesk samples has a (statistically) different standard deviation from the others. If the data samples were not Normally distributed (and the Normal distribution option not been checked on the previous page), then Minitab would have provided the Levene's test result instead (shown), which is also 0.00 for this example.

 **Test for Equal Variances.mpj**

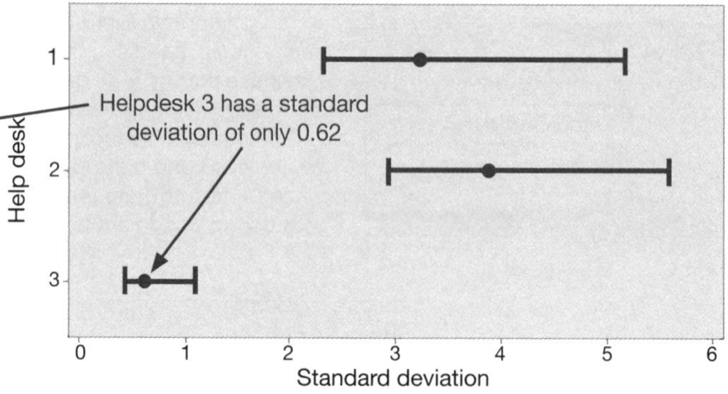

Helpdesk 3 has a standard deviation of only 0.62

Graphical Results: By default, Minitab produces the Summary Chart (above) that shows the Confidence Intervals for the standard deviation of each sample. The chart for this example clearly shows Helpdesk 3 is different (lower variation), and that Helpdesks 1 and 2 have very similar, higher levels of variation.

Which p-value do you use?

If the Normal distribution option (previous page) is **not** selected; Minitab provides a p-value for the Multiple Comparisons method and Levene's test. Although the Multiple Comparisons method can be more powerful, this text recommends using the Levene's test to avoid confusion and to cope with smaller, skewed samples.

If the Normally distribution option is selected; Minitab automatically provides a p-value for the F-Test if there are just two samples, or for the Bartlett's test if there are three or more samples.

Hypothesis Testing for Proportions and Percentages

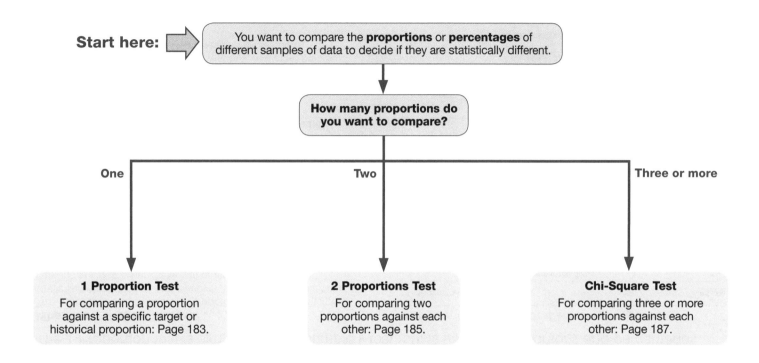

Start here: You want to compare the **proportions** or **percentages** of different samples of data to decide if they are statistically different.

How many proportions do you want to compare?

One

Two

Three or more

1 Proportion Test

For comparing a proportion against a specific target or historical proportion: Page 183.

2 Proportions Test

For comparing two proportions against each other: Page 185.

Chi-Square Test

For comparing three or more proportions against each other: Page 187.

1 Proportion Test – Overview

The 1 Proportion test is similar to the 1 Sample t-test, but is used for proportions and percentages.

What is a 1 Proportion Test?

This hypothesis test compares a proportion (or percentage) from a single sample of data against a known proportion such as a target, baseline or industry benchmark, in order to decide if they are (statistically) different.

Example: A new wine delivery service has accounted for a 2% breakage rate in its deliveries (the industry average).

However, when they start operating, four of the first 100 deliveries are broken when they arrive. Based on this, can they say that their breakage rate is higher than the industry standard? The **Summarized data** option from the drop down list (opposite) enables the data to be entered directly as follows:

- The number of breakages (in this case, four) is entered as the **Number of events.**

- The size of the sample (in this case, 100 deliveries) is entered as the **Number of trials**.

- Check the **Perform hypothesis test** box, and enter the 2% industry standard as the **Hypothesized proportion**.

Minitab: Stat > Basic Statistics > 1 Proportion

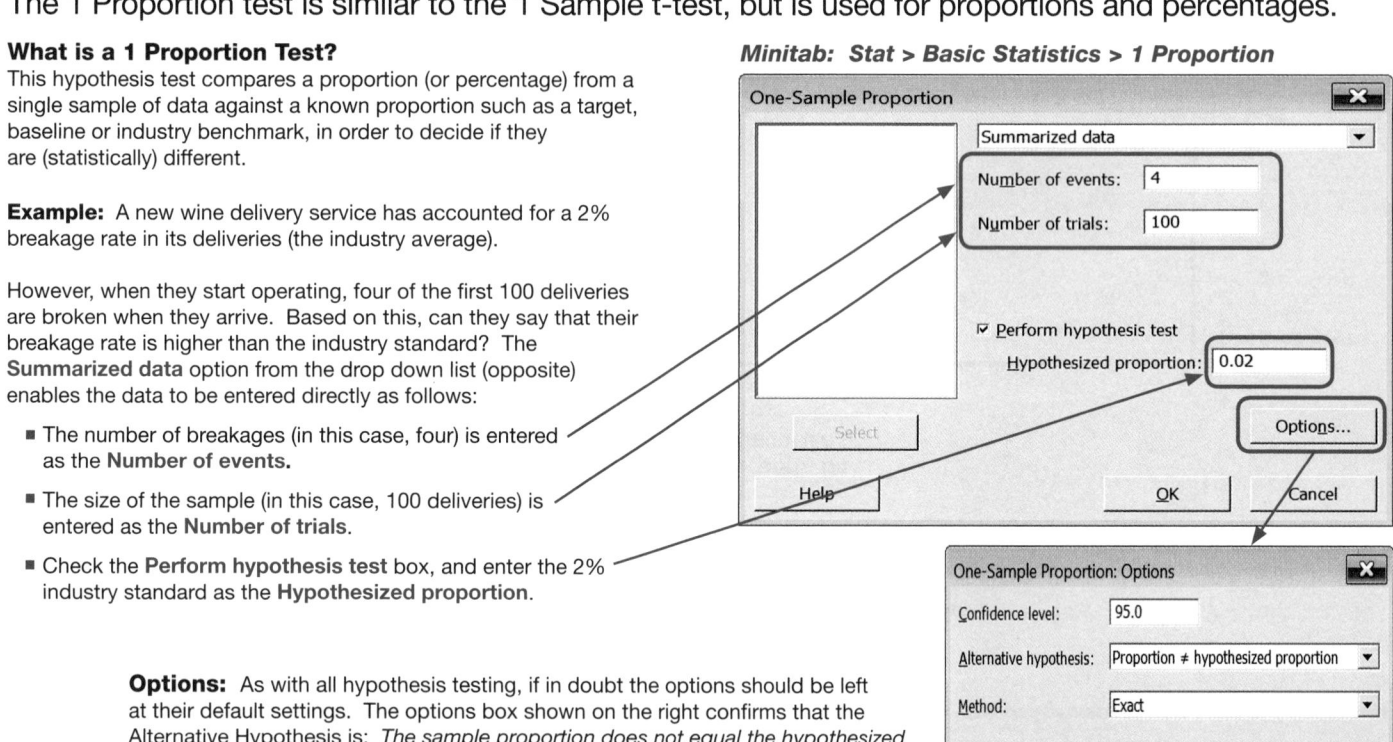

Options: As with all hypothesis testing, if in doubt the options should be left at their default settings. The options box shown on the right confirms that the Alternative Hypothesis is: *The sample proportion does not equal the hypothesized proportion (of 2%)*. In other words, the Alternative Hypothesis is that there **is** a difference between the sample and hypothesized proportions.

1 Proportion Test – Interpreting the Results

There is no graphical output for the 1 Proportion test, just numerical output in the Session Window.

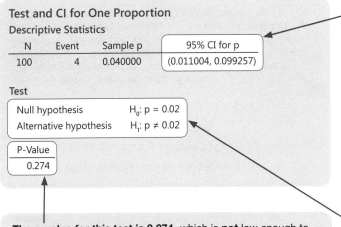

Test and CI for One Proportion

Descriptive Statistics

N	Event	Sample p	95% CI for p
100	4	0.040000	(0.011004, 0.099257)

Test

Null hypothesis	H_0: p = 0.02
Alternative hypothesis	H_1: p ≠ 0.02

P-Value
0.274

The p-value for this test is 0.274, which is **not** low enough to reject the Null Hypothesis.

This means that we cannot be (statistically) confident that the sample breakage rate of 4% is different from the industry standard of 2%.

This might seem surprising, particularly given the large sample size of 100. However, remember that because this is Attribute data (e.g. yes/no, pass/fail etc.) it has quite low resolution, and you therefore need larger sample sizes to gain statistical confidence.

95% Confidence Interval for the sample proportion:
A confidence interval for the sample proportion is also given. In this case, the confidence interval indicates that, based on the sample of four breakages out of 100, the actual proportion of breakages could be anywhere between 0.011 (1.1%) and 0.099 (9.9%).

Confidence intervals for percentages are discussed in more detail on page 153.

Hypotheses: Before interpreting the p-value (see left), its useful to remind yourself what the hypotheses are for the test. In this case:

- The Null Hypothesis is that there is **no** difference between the proportion from the sample, and the test proportion.

- The Alternative Hypothesis it that there **is** a difference.

The next section of the session window summarises the Null and Alternative hypotheses for this test in a technical shorthand, which says that the test is for the sample proportion being equal to 0.02 (the Null) versus it **not** being equal to 0.02 (the Alternative).

2 Proportion Test – Overview

The 2 Proportion test is similar to the 2 Sample t-test but is used for proportions and percentages.

What is a 2 Proportion Test?
This hypothesis test compares two proportions (or percentages) from two different samples against each other, in order to decide if they are (statistically) different.

Example: Two surveys of customer satisfaction have been conducted in two different areas (A and B). The results were:

- 72 out of 80 customers were satisfied in Area A (90%).
- 79 out of 100 customers were satisfied in Area B (79%).

It therefore **appears** that there is a difference and the 2 Proportion Test can be used to validate this statistically.

> **How to enter the data into Minitab:**
> The data for a 2 Proportion Test can be entered in several different ways. The first two options in the drop down list are used when you have the raw data in a Minitab file. The data file below contains the raw data for this example structured for both these options, if you would like to try these.
>
> The third **Summarized data** option allows the data to be entered directly into Minitab; as shown for this example.

Minitab: Stat > Basic Statistics > 2 Proportions

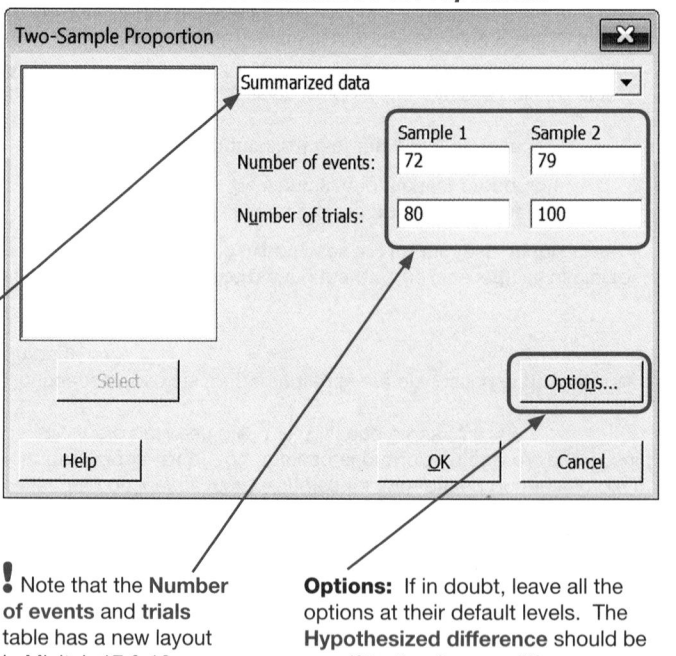

! Note that the **Number of events** and **trials** table has a new layout in Minitab 17 & 18.

Options: If in doubt, leave all the options at their default levels. The **Hypothesized difference** should be zero if testing for **any** difference.

2 Proportion Test mpj

2 Proportion Test – Interpreting the Results

There is no graphical output for the 2 Proportion test, just numerical output in the Session Window.

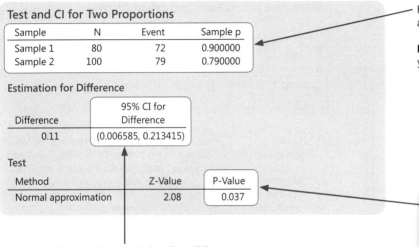

Test and CI for Two Proportions

Sample	N	Event	Sample p
Sample 1	80	72	0.900000
Sample 2	100	79	0.790000

Estimation for Difference

Difference	95% CI for Difference
0.11	(0.006585, 0.213415)

Test

Method	Z-Value	P-Value
Normal approximation	2.08	0.037

Firstly the results for each of the samples are summarised, along with their proportions.

Before interpreting the p-value, it's useful to remind yourself what the hypotheses are. So, in this example:

- The Null Hypothesis is that there is **no** difference between the two proportions.

- The Alternative Hypothesis it that there **is** a difference between the two proportions.

The p-value for this test is 0.037, which is very low (and below 0.05) and therefore the Null Hypothesis can be rejected.

In other words, we can be (statistically) confident that there **is** a difference in the customer satisfaction rates of the two samples.

To find out how big that difference might be, see the notes on the 95% Confidence Interval for the difference (left).

95% Confidence Interval for the difference:
The absolute difference between the two proportions is 0.11 (90% - 79% = 11%).

However, as with all statistics, we should place a confidence interval around this value, in order to reflect the amount of data in the samples.

The 95% Confidence Interval indicates that the difference between the proportions could be anywhere from 0.006 (0.6%) to 0.21 (21%).

This might seem surprisingly wide but remember that Attribute data (yes/no, pass/fail etc.) has less resolution and therefore requires larger samples to gain statistical confidence.

Chi-Square Test – Overview

The Chi-Square Test is similar to the One Way ANOVA, but is used for proportions and percentages.

The Chi-Square hypothesis test is used to compare three or more proportions (or percentages) against each other in order to decide if they are (statistically) different.

Example: Building upon the two customer surveys discussed in the 2 Proportion Test example on the previous pages, two further customer surveys are conducted (in areas C & D) and the results are shown in the table below. It appears that there might be different proportions of satisfied customers across the four areas surveyed, and a Chi-Square test can be used to validate this statistically.

↓	C1-T	C2	C3	C4	C5
		Area A	Area B	Area C	Area D
1	Satisfied	72	79	35	9
2	Not Satisfied	8	21	15	1

! A data table is the best format for a Chi-Square test and it is distinctly different from other hypothesis tests. All the data for the different categories of results should be recorded, but **not** the total sample size. Minitab will then calculate the total sample size for each area surveyed.

Minitab: Stat > Tables > Chi-Square Test for Association

Chi-Square Test for Association

C1
C2   Area A
C3   Area B
C4   Area C
C5   Area D

Summarized data in a two-way table

Columns containing the table:
'Area A' 'Area B' 'Area C' 'Area D'
Enter all columns containing data here

Labels for the table (optional)

Rows: C1   (column with row labels)

Columns: (name for column category)

Select   Statistics...   Options...

Help   OK   Cancel

If your data is contained in a table, as in this example, select the **Summarized data in a two-way table** option from the drop down list, and enter all the **Columns containing the table** (in this example, columns C2-C5 inclusive). If you have a column containing the **Labels for the table**, enter it as shown by C1 above.
Finally, if you want to record the chi-square values for each individual cell, then select **Each cell's contribution to chi-square** from the **Statistics** sub-menu.

Chi-Square.mpj

Chi-Square Test – Interpreting the Results

There is no graphical output for the Chi-Square test, just numerical output in the Session Window.

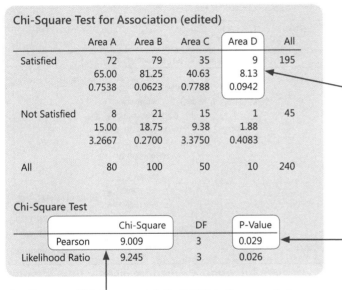

Chi-Square Test for Association (edited)

	Area A	Area B	Area C	Area D	All
Satisfied	72	79	35	9	195
	65.00	81.25	40.63	8.13	
	0.7538	0.0623	0.7788	0.0942	
Not Satisfied	8	21	15	1	45
	15.00	18.75	9.38	1.88	
	3.2667	0.2700	3.3750	0.4083	
All	80	100	50	10	240

Chi-Square Test

	Chi-Square	DF	P-Value
Pearson	9.009	3	0.029
Likelihood Ratio	9.245	3	0.026

The Pearson Chi-Square statistic (9.009) is the sum of all the Chi-Square values calculated in the table above.

If all the proportions were **exactly** the same in all the areas, then this Chi-Square statistic would be zero.

How the Chi-Square Test works:
The Chi-Square test uses a different mathematical approach, based upon the observed and expected results in each category, to decide if there is a statistical difference. However, it still produces a p-value which is analysed and interpreted in the normal way.

For each category of results, such as Area D highlighted here, the Session Window shows, in the following order:

- **The observed count** of results in that category.
- **The expected count** of results for that category (if all the areas had the same level of customer satisfaction).
- **A Contribution to Chi-Square** value which represents the relative difference between the observed and expected results.

The p-value for this test is 0.029, which is very low (and below 0.05) and therefore the Null hypothesis can be rejected.

In other words, we can be (statistically) confident that at least one, if not all, of the areas surveyed has a (statistically) different customer satisfaction rate from the others.

Anderson Darling Normality Test – Overview

Histograms with Normal curves (p123) and Probability Plots (p127) both provide **graphical** methods of assessing Normality. The Anderson Darling method provides a Hypothesis Test for assessing Normality.

Minitab: Stat > Basic Statistics > Normality Test

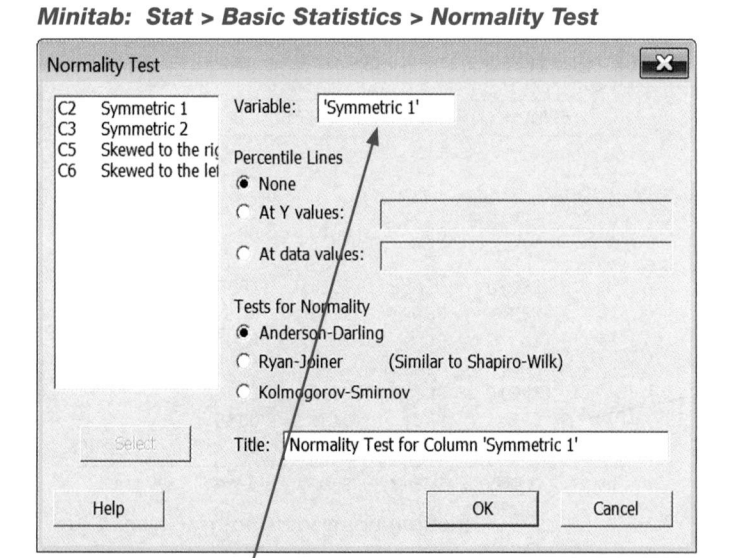

How to enter the data into Minitab:
The single column containing the data that you want to test is entered under **Variable**, and all other options should be left as standard.

Distributions.mpj

The Anderson Darling Normality Test is slightly different from other hypothesis tests and therefore requires careful interpretation. The hypotheses are as follows:

- The Null Hypothesis (Ho) is that the data **is** Normally distributed.
- The Alternative Hypothesis (Ha) is that the data **is not** Normally distributed.

Whereas often in hypothesis testing we are looking to **reject** the Null Hypothesis, in the case of Normality testing we are generally looking to **accept** it.

For this reason, the interpretation of the p-value is the reverse of what we are used to, as follows (for an Alpha Level of 0.05):

- If the p-value is less than 0.05, we can be confident that the data is **not** Normally distributed.
- If the p-value is greater than 0.05, there is a reasonable chance that it **could** be Normally distributed, and so we usually assume it is.

Where to find the Anderson Darling Normality test:

- Minitab's **Normality Test** function (shown on the left) produces a Probability Plot (p127) and a p-value (next page).
- Minitab's **Graphical Summary** (p126) also produces the p-value result of the Anderson Darling Normality test.

Anderson Darling Normality Test – Interpreting the Results

Minitab's Normality Test produces a probability plot with a summary of the data statistics and a p-value for the Anderson Darling Normality Test, as shown in the two examples below.

The two examples shown here are taken from the following data file:

 **Distributions.mpj**

Example 1:
The probability plot below shows a clearly curved line, which indicates that the data set is definitely **not** Normally distributed.

In addition, the Anderson Darling p-value is very low (<0.005) which fits with the probability plot, and means that we can be very confident that the data is **not** Normally distributed.

Example 2:
The probability plot below shows a (relatively) straight line, which indicates that the data **may** be Normally distributed.

The Anderson Darling p-value (of 0.098) fits the probability plot because it is **above 0.05**, which means that the data **can** be assumed to be Normally distributed.

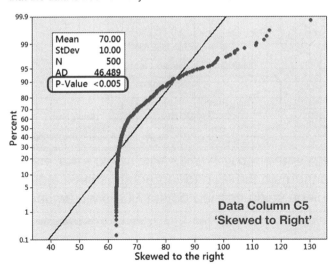

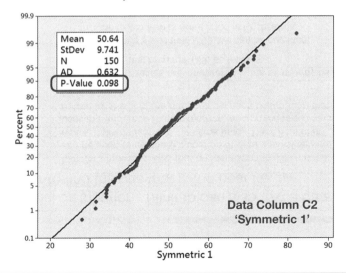

Individual Distribution Identification – Overview

So far we have only tested data samples against the Normal distribution. Minitab can also test a data sample against a number of different distributions, in order to find the one that is the best fit.

Minitab: Stat > Quality Tools > Individual Distribution Identification

Individual Distribution Identification

C1   Queue Times

Data are arranged as
- Single column: 'Queue Times'
- Subgroup size: 1

(use a constant or an ID column)

- Subgroups across rows of:

- Use all distributions and transformations
- Specify

☑ Distribution 1:	Normal
☑ Distribution 2:	Exponential
☑ Distribution 3:	Weibull
☑ Distribution 4:	Gamma

Box-Cox...
Johnson...
Options...
Results...

Select

Help   OK   Cancel

Minitab's Individual Distribution Identification (IDI) function can be used to compare a column of data against several different distributions at the same time. The IDI function uses the Anderson Darling method, and provides a p-value output for the fit of the data against each distribution that is being considered.

The resulting p-values are interpreted in the same way as the Normality Test on page 189, as follows:

- If the p-value is less than 0.05, we can be confident that the distribution **is not** a good fit for the data.

- If the p-value is greater than 0.05, then we can assume that the distribution **is** a good fit for the data.

If in doubt, leave all four option boxes with their standard default settings for this function.

Enter the **Single column** of data to be analysed here and enter a subgroup size of 1 if your data was not collected or sampled in rational subgroups.

For this example, select **Use all distributions and transformations**. This will compare the data sample against fourteen different distributions (and two transformations).

Alternatively, you can **Specify** the distribution that you want to compare against your data by selecting it from one of the drop down lists.

Capability–Queue Times.mpj

Only a portion of the session window output is shown here for interpretation.

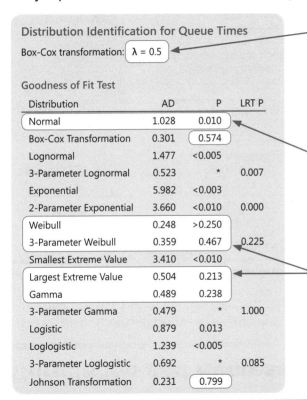

Distribution Identification for Queue Times

Box-Cox transformation: $\lambda = 0.5$

Goodness of Fit Test

Distribution	AD	P	LRT P
Normal	1.028	0.010	
Box-Cox Transformation	0.301	0.574	
Lognormal	1.477	<0.005	
3-Parameter Lognormal	0.523	*	0.007
Exponential	5.982	<0.003	
2-Parameter Exponential	3.660	<0.010	0.000
Weibull	0.248	>0.250	
3-Parameter Weibull	0.359	0.467	0.225
Smallest Extreme Value	3.410	<0.010	
Largest Extreme Value	0.504	0.213	
Gamma	0.489	0.238	
3-Parameter Gamma	0.479	*	1.000
Logistic	0.879	0.013	
Loglogistic	1.239	<0.005	
3-Parameter Loglogistic	0.692	*	0.085
Johnson Transformation	0.231	0.799	

Interpreting the Box-Cox Transformation result:
Minitab provides the optimal value of Lambda for use in the Box-Cox transformation of the data (see appendix G). In this case, the p-value for the Box-Cox transformed data is 0.574 (highlighted in the second row of the **Goodness of Fit Table**), which is above 0.05 and therefore indicates that the Box-Cox transformed data **can** be assumed to be Normally distributed.

There is also a p-value for the Johnson transformation (last line of table) which indicates that the Johnson transformed data could also be assumed to be Normal.

Selecting the distribution that best fits the data sample:
If the Normal distribution p-value is above 0.05 (and is not significantly lower than the p-values for other distributions) then select the Normal distribution as your model, since it provides access to a larger range of analysis tools. In this case, the p-value of 0.01 indicates that the data is **not** Normally distributed, and you should therefore find an alternative distribution with a higher p-value.

If a number of distributions have close p-values, then select one that you are familiar with, or that will enable you to complete the particular analysis that you require.

In this case, there are four distributions (excluding the transformations) that would provide a reasonable fit for the data (i.e. they have p-values well above 0.05). They are, the Weibull, 3-Parameter Weibull, Largest Extreme Value and Gamma distributions.

Graphical Outputs:
Minitab also produces a probability plot of the data against each distribution, which supports the numerical analysis completed here. As explained on page 127, a straight line on a probability plot indicates that the data fits the distribution in question.

Correlation and Regression – Overview

The phrase 'Correlation and Regression' refers to a number of similar tools, all of which can be used to quantify (mathematically) the relationship between process inputs and outputs.

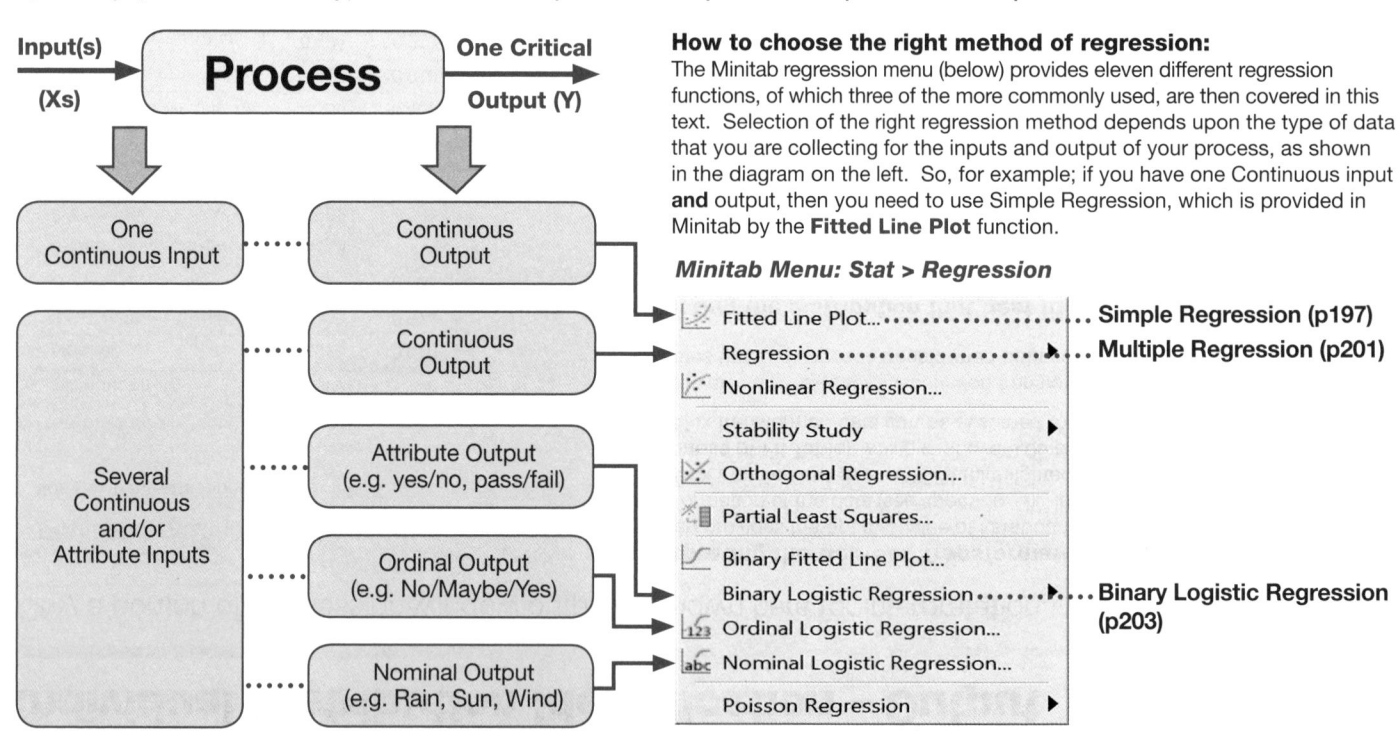

How to choose the right method of regression:
The Minitab regression menu (below) provides eleven different regression functions, of which three of the more commonly used, are then covered in this text. Selection of the right regression method depends upon the type of data that you are collecting for the inputs and output of your process, as shown in the diagram on the left. So, for example; if you have one Continuous input **and** output, then you need to use Simple Regression, which is provided in Minitab by the **Fitted Line Plot** function.

Minitab Menu: Stat > Regression

Fitted Line Plot.................... **Simple Regression (p197)**

Regression .... ▶ ... **Multiple Regression (p201)**

Nonlinear Regression...

Stability Study ▶

Orthogonal Regression...

Partial Least Squares...

Binary Fitted Line Plot...

Binary Logistic Regression ....▶ ... **Binary Logistic Regression (p203)**

Ordinal Logistic Regression...

Nominal Logistic Regression...

Poisson Regression ▶

Input(s) (Xs) → **Process** → One Critical Output (Y)

One Continuous Input .... Continuous Output

Several Continuous and/or Attribute Inputs

Continuous Output

Attribute Output (e.g. yes/no, pass/fail)

Ordinal Output (e.g. No/Maybe/Yes)

Nominal Output (e.g. Rain, Sun, Wind)

Correlation and Regression – Overview (cont.)

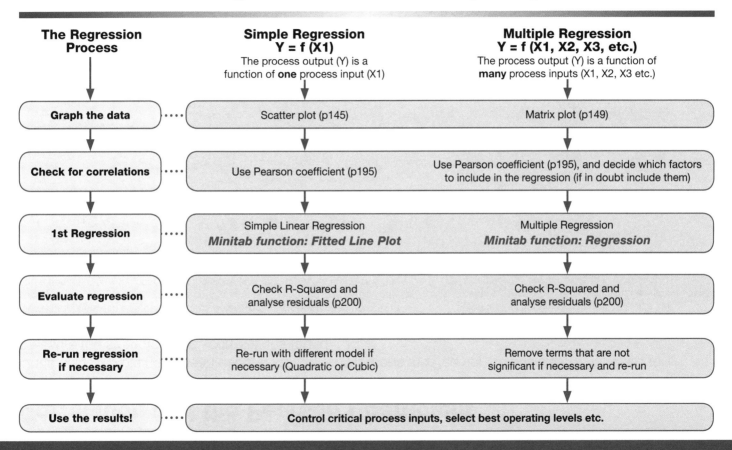

The Regression Process	Simple Regression Y = f (X1) The process output (Y) is a function of **one** process input (X1)	Multiple Regression Y = f (X1, X2, X3, etc.) The process output (Y) is a function of **many** process inputs (X1, X2, X3 etc.)
Graph the data	Scatter plot (p145)	Matrix plot (p149)
Check for correlations	Use Pearson coefficient (p195)	Use Pearson coefficient (p195), and decide which factors to include in the regression (if in doubt include them)
1st Regression	Simple Linear Regression *Minitab function: Fitted Line Plot*	Multiple Regression *Minitab function: Regression*
Evaluate regression	Check R-Squared and analyse residuals (p200)	Check R-Squared and analyse residuals (p200)
Re-run regression if necessary	Re-run with different model if necessary (Quadratic or Cubic)	Remove terms that are not significant if necessary and re-run
Use the results!	**Control critical process inputs, select best operating levels etc.**	

Correlation and the Pearson Coefficient

Once scatter plots have been used to look for correlations the Pearson coefficient can be used to measure the strength of any correlations found.

The Pearson coefficient (r) is used to measure the degree of linear association (correlation) between sets of Continuous data. The coefficient ranges from +1 (a strong direct correlation), to zero (no correlation), to -1 (a strong inverse correlation), and reflects not only the direction of the slope (if any), but the degree to which the data points are tightly clustered.

Using the scatter plot examples from pages 145/146 (that look at the time to answer calls at a call centre), several Pearson coefficients are shown here alongside the scatter plots they represent.

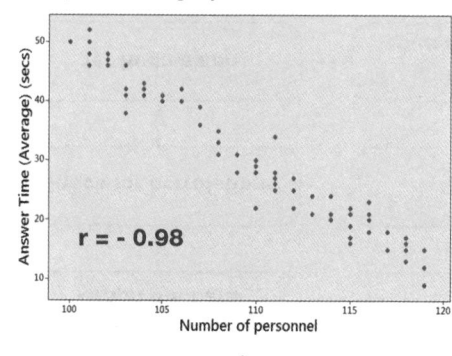

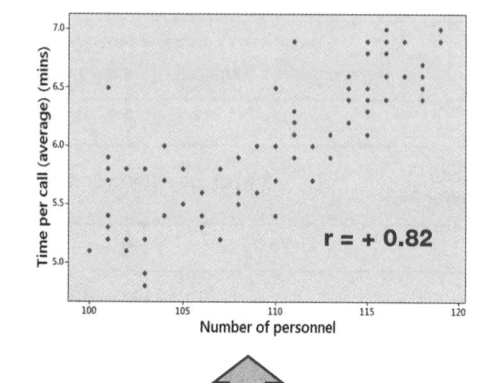

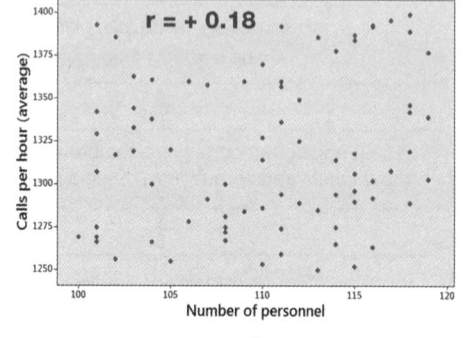

This scatter plot shows a strong (clustered) downwards (inverse) relationship, and so the Pearson coefficient is very high but negative (-0.98), to reflect the downward slope. It suggests the more personnel available the quicker the calls are answered.

The scatter plot between *number of personnel* and *time per call* shows a reasonably strong direct (upwards) relationship, and so the Pearson coefficient is positive and high (0.82). It suggests that the more personnel available, the longer they spend on each call.

There is clearly no relationship between *number of personnel* and the volume of *calls per hour*. Accordingly the Pearson coefficient is very low (0.18).
Note that it is rare to have exactly zero, even when no correlation exists.

Pearson Coefficient – Interpreting the Results

The statistical significance of your Pearson coefficient must be assessed before you can use it.

Because of the random nature of data, it is possible for a scatter plot to **suggest** a correlation between two factors when in fact none exists.

In particular, this can happen where the scatter plot is based on a small sample size. So, having calculated a Pearson coefficient, we also need to evaluate its statistical significance by considering the sample size it is based on. In other words – is it real?

For this reason, Minitab also calculates a p-value for the Pearson coefficient, based on the Null Hypothesis that there is **no** correlation (see right).

Example: Consider the relationship between the *number of personnel* and the *number of calls* received (where we already know there is actually **no** correlation). If we had taken a much smaller sample size (say 5), there is a chance that – just by chance – they would have fallen in a way that **suggested** a correlation (as shown below).

The Pearson coefficient can be calculated by Minitab, and can be found at:

Minitab Menu: Stat > Basic Statistics > Correlation

The results are recorded in the Minitab Session window because they are just text output (no graphics).

Interpreting p-values (with 95% confidence):

- If the p-value is less than 0.05, then you **can** be confident that a correlation exists, and use the Pearson coefficient to help quantify it.

- If the p-value is more than 0.05, then it's possible that **no** correlation exists, even if your Pearson coefficient suggests one.

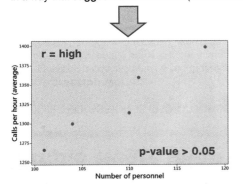

The question is, should we believe it with such a small sample?

The Pearson coefficient is high, but the p-value is also above 0.05, indicating that there might be no correlation.

In this particular case, having collected more data (sample size of 80), the correlation disappears (see right), proving we were correct to be suspicious.

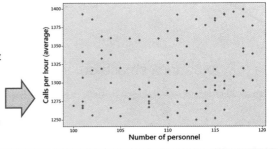

Simple Regression

Simple regression is the process of developing a mathematical model that represents your data.

How regression works:

The regression process creates a line that best resembles the relationship between the process input and output. As can be seen from the scatter plot on the right, it would be impossible to find a line that passes **exactly** through all of the data points, (unless they were on a very specific path).

Instead the best line is the one where the total of the errors between the data points and the line itself are minimised. Mathematically, it is the total of the squares of the errors that is minimised, and so the line is called the **'line of least squares'**.

Different types of mathematical model:

The regression process can fit several different shapes of line, since the linear relationship shown on the right won't be applicable to all situations. The alternatives are:

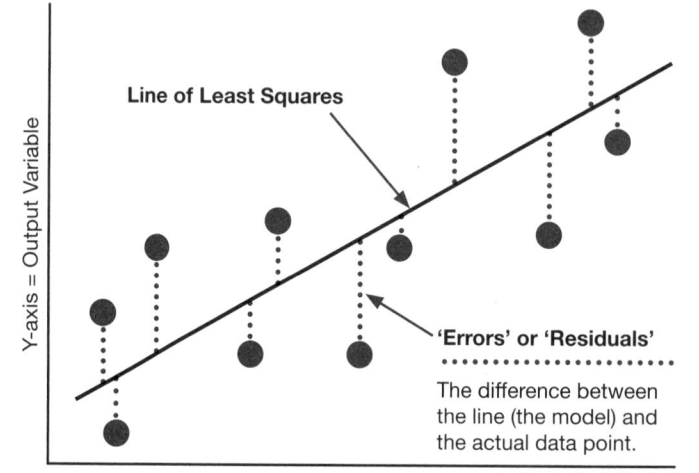

Line of Least Squares

'Errors' or 'Residuals'
. . . .
The difference between the line (the model) and the actual data point.

Y-axis = Output Variable

X-axis = Input Variable

Linear: A simple, common relationship that has the simplest mathematical model: **Y= m(X) + c** (where m and c are constants).

Quadratic: A more complex mathematical model that includes an x^2 term. This can be used to model process relationships that rise and then fall again.

Cubic: A rarer situation, where the process relationship rises, falls, then rises again (or vice versa).

Residual Errors:
While the residual errors between the data and the model are minimised by the 'line of least squares', they remain an indication of how accurately the model will be able to predict the process output. The residuals can also be analysed to check that the model line is a good fit for the shape of the relationship it is intended to represent, as explained on page 200.

Minitab Fitted Line Plot – Data Input

Fitted Line Plots are the Minitab function for performing simple regression.

The Scatter plot on page 195 suggests a positive correlation between the number of personnel in the call centre and the (average) time spent on each call.

Simple regression can be used to model the relationship between these variables, using Minitab's **Fitted Line Plot** function.

In this case:

- The *Time per call* is the process output: the **Response (Y)**.

- The *Number of personnel* is the process input: the **Predictor (X)**.

Type of regression model:
Select the model most appropriate to your data, based on the Scatter plots you have seen. If in doubt, start with **Linear**, and move to a more complex model if the Linear model exhibits problems.

 **Correlation.mpj**

Minitab: Stat > Regression > Fitted Line Plot

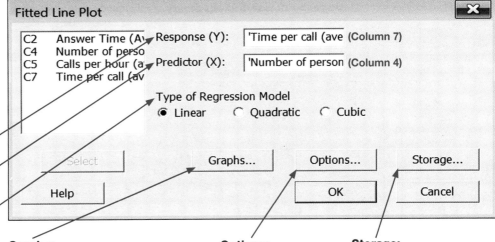

Fitted Line Plot

C2	Answer Time (A)	Response (Y):	'Time per call (ave (Column 7)
C4	Number of perso	Predictor (X):	'Number of person (Column 4)
C5	Calls per hour (a		
C7	Time per call (av		

Type of Regression Model
⦿ Linear   ⦾ Quadratic   ⦾ Cubic

Select   Graphs...   Options...   Storage...

Help   OK   Cancel

Graphs:
This refers to graphs of the residual errors from the model – see page 200 for details of analysing residuals.

Selecting **Regular** residuals (the default) will keep them in the same units as your data. Check **Four in one** to see all of the residuals plots.

Options:
Check both **Display Confidence Interval** and **Display Prediction Interval** in order to see both the intervals shown overleaf.

Storage:
A number of numerical outputs, including residuals, can be stored in your worksheet for further analysis.

Leave these blank until you need them or your worksheet will fill with data very quickly!

Minitab Fitted Line Plots – Interpreting the Results

The regression line is placed on a Scatter plot showing the line of best fit that was calculated.

In addition, two further sets of lines are shown either side, as follows:

Prediction Intervals (outer lines) indicate the interval within which you can expect 95% of the process output (individual data points) to occur.

Confidence Intervals (inner lines) indicate the interval within which you can be 95% confident that the process **average** will occur.

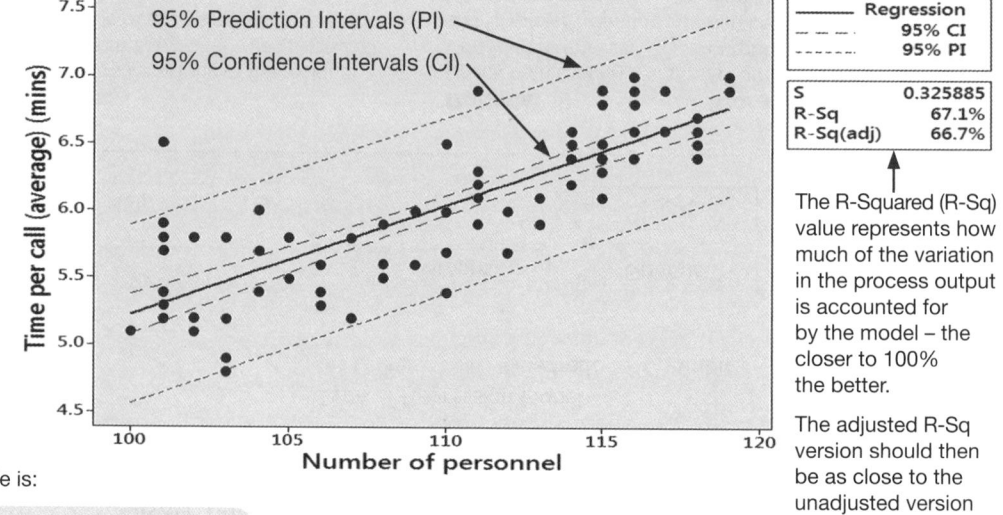

The R-Squared (R-Sq) value represents how much of the variation in the process output is accounted for by the model – the closer to 100% the better.

The adjusted R-Sq version should then be as close to the unadjusted version as possible.

The regression equation for this example is:

$$\text{Time per call (average)} = -2.888 + (0.08119 \times \text{No. of Personnel})$$

This can be used to predict the average *Time per call* that will be achieved for a specific *Number of personnel*.

The constant 0.08119 represents the average increase in *Time per call*, for an increase of one person in the *Number of personnel*.

⬇ **Correlation.mpj**

Using the regression equation:
Be careful when using the regression equation to predict process performance. The equation predicts the **average** results from the process, but **individual** results could fall anywhere within the prediction intervals shown.

In addition, you should not use the model beyond the bounds of the data used to create it. In other words, for this example, the model should not be used to predict the *Time per call* with less than 100 or more than 120 personnel.

Checking the Model – Analysis of Residuals

Confirming that your regression model is a reasonable fit can be done visually with simple regression, because you are able to see the Fitted Line Plot. However this is not possible with multiple regression since it is more than two dimensional. Instead, the residual errors between the model and the data points can be analysed in order to decide if the model is a good fit for the data. This is possible because the behaviour of residuals for a 'good fitting' model is well established, as described below.

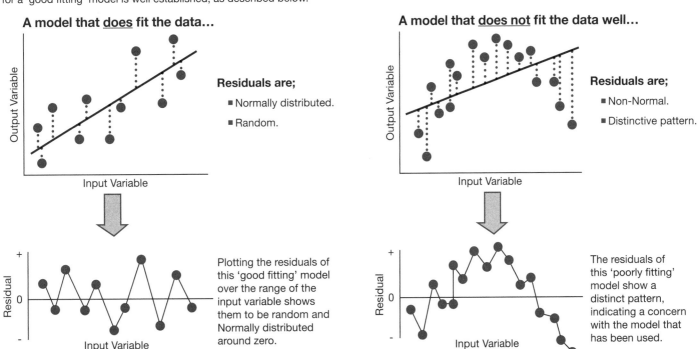

A model that <u>does</u> fit the data...

Residuals are;
- Normally distributed.
- Random.

Plotting the residuals of this 'good fitting' model over the range of the input variable shows them to be random and Normally distributed around zero.

A model that <u>does not</u> fit the data well...

Residuals are;
- Non-Normal.
- Distinctive pattern.

The residuals of this 'poorly fitting' model show a distinct pattern, indicating a concern with the model that has been used.

Multiple Regression – Overview

In reality, the output of a process rarely has a simple relationship with just one input, but is instead a more complex result of several factors.

The purpose of multiple regression is to identify the 'critical Xs' (those inputs that have a significant effect on the process), and to mathematically model their relationship with the process output.

To reflect the process thinking employed in Six Sigma you will often hear phrases such as '*Y is a function of the process Xs*', which is written mathematically as:

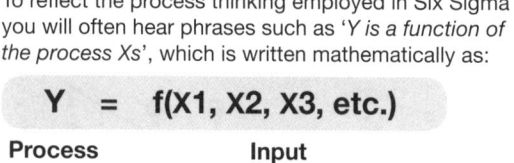

$$Y = f(X1, X2, X3, etc.)$$

Process Output	Input Variables		
Answer Time (secs)	Number of personnel	Calls per hour	Time per call (mins)
26	111	1357	6.1
24	114	1265	6.2
27	111	1336	5.9
16	118	1319	6.7
21	115	1290	6.4
22	112	1325	5.7

Correlation.mpj

Minitab: Stat > Regression > Regression > Fit Regression Model

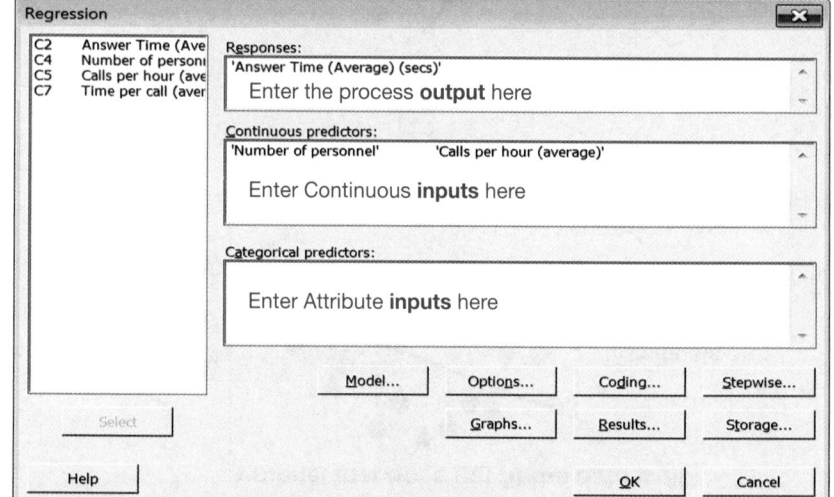

Which input (predictor) variables should be included in the regression?
If you think they could be important – all of them! But, in reality, the matrix plots will have given you some clues as to which ones to include.

❗ The input variables should be independent:
Because we know that the *Time per call* and the *Number of Personnel* are correlated (from the simple regression on page 199), we should only include one of them in the multiple regression, as shown above.

Multiple Regression – Session Window Output

This regression equation defines the relationship between both the *Number of Personnel* and *Calls per hour* (the inputs), and the resulting *Answer Time* (the output).

Interpreting the equation constants:

- Every extra person produces a **decrease** of 1.98 seconds in the average *Answer Time* (because it is negative).

- Every extra call per hour produces an **increase** of 0.0018 seconds in the average *Answer Time* – not very much!

Interpreting the p-values with 95% confidence (far right):

- If the p-value is less than 0.05, then the input variable (predictor) **does** influence the process output.

- If the p–value is more than 0.05, then the input variable (predictor) **does not** influence the process output.

So, for this example:

- The *Number of personnel* (p=0.000) affects *Answer Time*.

- The *Volume of Calls* per hour (p=0.783) does **not** affect *Answer Time*.

Regression Analysis: (edited)
Regression Equation

Answer Time (Average) (secs) = 245.78 – (1.98 * Number of personnel)
+ (0.00180 * Calls per hour)

Coefficients

Term	Coef	SE Coef	T-Value	P-Value	VIF
Constant	245.78	9.33	26.33	0.000	
Number of personnel	-1.9834	0.0503	-39.42	0.000	1.03
Calls per hour (average)	0.00180	0.00651	0.28	0.783	1.03

P-values

Model Summary

S	R-sq	R-sq(adj)	R-sq(pred)
2.50601	95.42%	95.30%	95.07%

Analysis of Variance (results not shown here – see appendix F)
Unusual Observations (results not shown here)

The **R-Squared** value indicates that the input variables in the regression account for 95.4% of the variation in the *Answer Time*, so it appears that we have found the most important input factors to the process.

However, since the calls per hour is not significant (see p-values explanation left), it must be just the *Number of Personnel* that is creating most of the variation in the *Answer Time*.

In summary:
It is always important to summarise the findings from statistical analysis in day-to-day language, such as:

- The number of personnel has a dramatic effect on the average answer time. It **decreases** by around two seconds for each extra person added to the shift.

- The number of incoming calls per hour has **little effect** on the answer time.

Binary Logistic Regression – Overview

Sometimes the output of the process is measured in Attribute data such as Pass/Fail or Yes/No. This requires a completely different regression approach, called **Binary Logistic** Regression.

Example: A project is looking at whether the Quality Approval status (of a call centre) and the average Wrap Up Time (per call) are critical inputs in generating Customer Satisfaction (the process output) across a number of call centres. In this case, customer satisfaction has been measured (in a customer survey) as just Low or High, and so we need to use Binary Logistic Regression.

Minitab: Stat > Regression > Binary Logistic Regression > Fit Binary Logistic Model

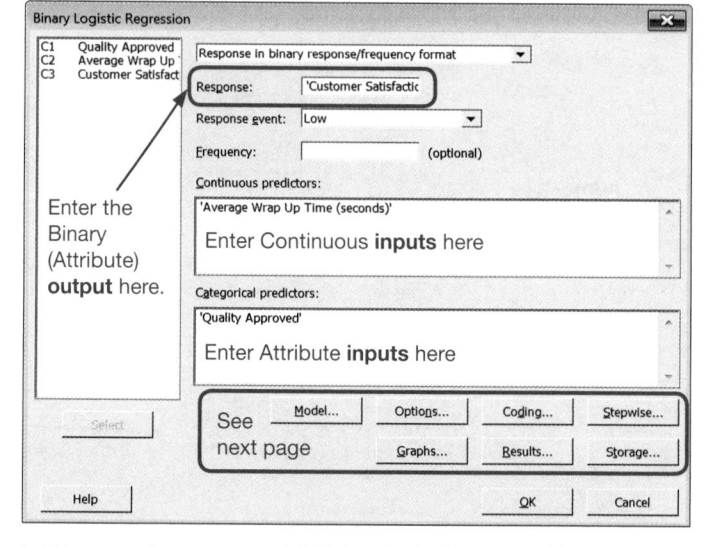

Enter the Binary (Attribute) **output** here.

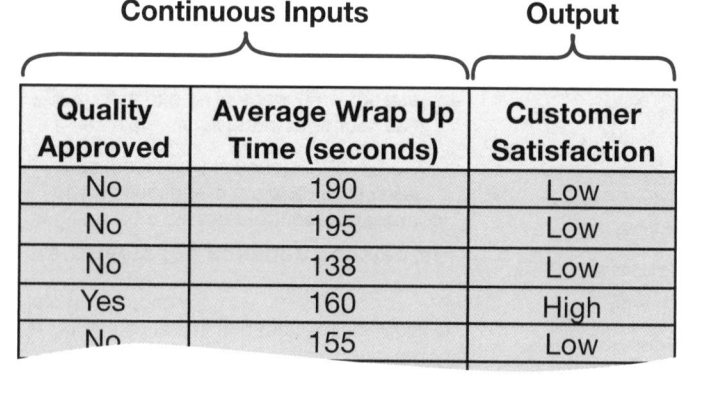

Attribute and Continuous Inputs   Attribute Output

Quality Approved	Average Wrap Up Time (seconds)	Customer Satisfaction
No	190	Low
No	195	Low
No	138	Low
Yes	160	High
No	155	Low

Binary Logistic Regression.mpj

This data file is based upon the Minitab data file: EXH_REGR.MTW

In this example, the data is in **Binary Response/ Frequency** format (see data file).

Minitab sets the **Response Event** (the reference level) as the last event alphabetically (in this case, **Low** Customer Satisfaction). This can be overridden manually, from the drop down list.

Binary Logistic Regression – Model, Graph & Coding Options

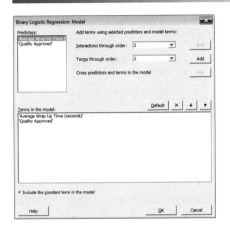

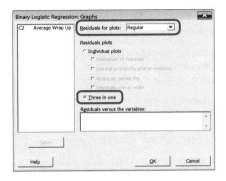

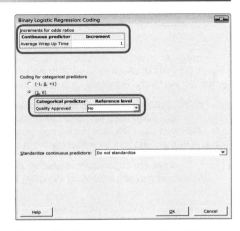

The Model dialog box is used to select the predictors (inputs) that that you want to include in the BLR model. The available predictors are shown top left (*Average Wrap Up Time* and *Quality Approved* in this example) and the default setting (used in this example) is for only the predictor variables to be included in the model.

If required, power and interaction terms can also be added to the **Terms in the Model** box, by using the **Add** buttons shown.

The Graphs dialog box is used to select the type of residuals plots that are required. Residuals plots are helpful in assessing the fit of the model to the data, as explained on page 200.

If in doubt, select **Three in one** (or **Four in one** if your data is in Event/Trial format) in order to see all the residuals plots available.

Minitab can provide three different types of residuals; **Regular, Standardised** or **Deleted**. Regular residuals are the differences between the model's predicted results and the actual results, and ideal for regression models, so used in this example.

The Coding dialog box is used to set the increments for odds ratios (for continuous inputs) and the reference level for categorical (Attribute) inputs.

Odds ratios are explained on the next page, but the increments (unit) for the odds ratio can be set here. In this example, the default of 1 second is acceptable; the odds ratio will be calculated based upon a change of 1 second in the *Average Wrap Up Time*.

The reference level for categorical inputs can also be adjusted manually, but in this example the default reference level of 'No' is acceptable.

Binary Logistic Regression – Session Window Output

Response Information

Variable	Value	Count	
Customer Satisfaction	Low	70	(Event)
	High	22	
	Total	92	

Firstly the session window summarises the output values used in the regression. In this example, customer satisfaction was recorded as either **Low** or **High** (the binary output), and there were 70 Low results out of a total of 92 customers. Low is defined as the reference **Event** - this was set in the input screen on page 203.

Deviance Table

Source	DF	Adj Dev	Adj Mean	Chi-Square	P-Value
Regression	2	7.574	3.787	7.57	0.023
Average Wrap Up Time (secs)	1	4.629	4.629	4.63	0.031
Quality Approved	1	4.737	4.737	4.74	0.030
Error	89	93.640	1.052		
Total	91	101.214			

The Deviance table contains the p-values for the regression inputs, both of which are less than 0.05. This indicates that we can be confident that both *Wrap Up Time* and *Quality Approved* status have a statistically significant effect on *Customer Satisfaction*.

So, now that we know they are significant, we should look to the coefficients to understand their relationships with the output.

Coefficients

Term	Coef	SE Coef	VIF
Constant	-1.99	1.68	
Average Wrap Up Time (secs)	0.0250	0.0123	1.12
Quality Approved			
Yes	-1.193	0.553	1.12

The coefficient of 0.025 for *Average Wrap Up Time* indicates that as wrap up times increase, the chances of **lower** *Customer Satisfaction* increase.

The coefficient of -1.193 for *Quality Approved* indicates that call centres that are quality approved tend to have **higher** customer satisfaction. The coefficient is negative to indicate that as *Quality Approved* changes from *No* to *Yes*, *Customer Satisfaction* tends to move **away** from the reference (*Low*) to *High*.

Odds Ratios for Continuous Predictors

	Odds Ratio	95% CI
Average Wrap Up Time (secs)	1.0253	(1.0010, 1.0503)

Odds Ratios for Categorical Predictors

Level A	Level B	Odds Ratio	95% CI
Quality Approved			
Yes	No	0.3033	(0.1026, 0.8966)

Odds ratio for level A relative to level B

The Odds Ratio of 0.30 indicates that, all other things being equal, the odds of a quality approved call centre having **Low** customer satisfaction are 30% of the odds of a **non**-quality approved call centre having **Low** customer satisfaction.

Interpreting the Goodness-of-Fit Tests:
These tests are used to check that the regression model is a reasonable fit for the data. We **do not** want the tests to reject the model (as a good fit), and therefore we are looking for p-values **greater** than 0.05.

Goodness-of-Fit Tests

Test	DF	Chi-Square	P-Value
Deviance	89	93.64	0.348
Pearson	89	88.63	0.491
Hosmer-Lemeshow	8	4.75	0.784

In this example, all the p-values are above 0.05, indicating that we can assume that the model is a reasonable fit.

Binary Logistic Regression – Graphical Output

Deviance Residual Plots for Customer Satisfaction

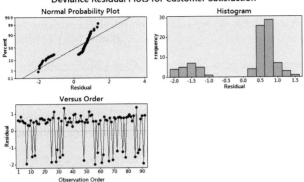

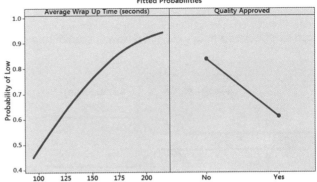

Main Effects Plot for Customer Satisfaction
Fitted Probabilities

Graphical Output: Three in one Residuals Plots

The Normal probability plot (top left) does not show a straight line and instead shows two distinct groups of residuals. This means that the residuals are clearly not normally distributed around the models' predicted values. The histogram (top right) also shows the same two distinct groups of residuals.

So, while the input factors have been shown previously to be statistically significant, this analysis shows that we should be careful how we interpret any extended results that rely on the residuals being normally distributed, such as confidence intervals.

The chart of residuals versus observation order (lower left) shows no particular trends in the residuals over the observation order (i.e. over time). This is a positive sign; in a 'good' model, we are looking for the residuals to be random, with no particular trends over time.

Additional Graphical Output: Factorial Plots

The factorial plots shown above are not created automatically by the Binary Logistic Regression (BLR) function, but can be created **after** a BLR model has been developed in Minitab. They are created by using the following function and entering *Customer Satisfaction* as the response and both input factors (*Wrap Up Time* and *Quality Approved*) as the variables to include in the plots:

Stat > Regression > Binary Logistic Regression > Factorial Plots

The factorial plots map the probability of **Low** customer satisfaction against the input factors, using the model created. The plots reinforce the session window output and show that the probability of **Low** Customer Satisfaction:

- Increases as *Wrap Up Time* increases.
- Decreases for call centers that are *Quality Approved*.

Design of Experiments (DOE) – Overview

This text contains a basic introduction to the Design of Experiments (DOE) approach, focusing specifically on Factorial designs. DOE is a large subject area and therefore readers looking for in-depth knowledge or other approaches to DOE (such as Response Surface or Taguchi) are recommended to consult a specialist text or training event for further advice.

What is Design of Experiments (DOE)?

DOE is the acronym given to a range of experimental techniques in which the process is experimented on in a controlled manner, and the results observed and analysed.

The aim is to identify the important inputs to the process (critical Xs) and to understand their affect on the process output. The maths behind DOE is similar to that for Regression.

What's the difference between Regression and DOE?

- Regression techniques are generally used to analyse **historical** data that is taken from the process in its 'normal mode'.

- Designed experiments are used to create and analyse **real time** data that is taken from the process in an 'experimental mode'.

Where is DOE used?

Designed experiments are more prevalent in Six Sigma projects that are technically orientated (manufacturing etc.) since this environment tends to have processes that can be modified and adjusted in a controlled real time manner.

The principles are relevant to transactional (service) projects but the ability to control an experiment in an office environment tends to be limited, and so the application of DOE is less frequent.

Example: A project is looking at controlling the thickness of steel emerging from the rolling process shown below. There are lots of input factors (e.g. input thickness, roller pressure, roller speed, lubricant, steel temperature) that might affect the output thickness and an experiment is planned to find out which ones are most important, and to quantify their affect.

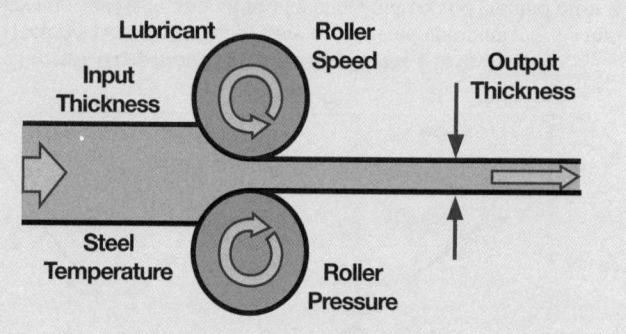

What approach would you take to understand this process?

A common approach to experimentation is to only change one factor at a time (e.g. firstly change the roller pressure, then steel temperature etc.).

This can be very time consuming, and therefore very costly, and also this approach does not allow for interactions between the process inputs.

DOE provides a range of efficient, structured experiments that enable all the factors to be investigated at the same time with a minimum of trials.

Design of Experiments (DOE) – Routemap

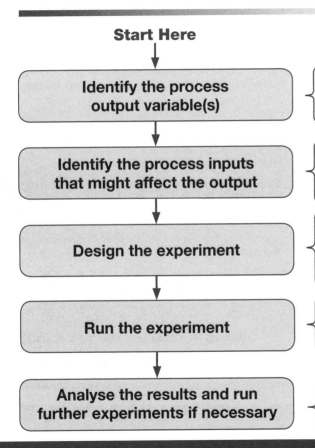

Start Here

Identify the process output variable(s)

Identify the process inputs that might affect the output

Design the experiment

Run the experiment

Analyse the results and run further experiments if necessary

Things to consider...

- Clarify the process output that you want to control or improve (you may want to investigate more than one at the same time).
- Ensure that you can measure the process output effectively (see MSA – p58).

- Use brainstorming (p110) and fishbone diagrams (p111) to select the input factors that you think are most likely to significantly affect the process output.
- Remember, the more factors you choose, the more costly and complex the experiment could be.

- Consider the **resolution** (full versus fractional experiments) – see p226.
- Do you want to **replicate** the trials to gain statistical significance? – see p220.
- **Center points** can help to check for non-linearity in the process output – see p220.
- Consider **blocking** if your experiment will be run in separate stages – see p212.

- Consider how to control the amount of **noise** from other input factors (that you're not investigating) during the experiment.
- **Randomise** your trials to negate the affect of lurking variables – p212.

- Analyse the statistical and practical significance of the results.
- Design further experiments if required.

2-Level Full Factorial Designs – Overview

A '2-Level Full Factorial Design' is the basic building block of Designed Experiments (DOE).

What is a 2-Level Full Factorial Design?

- **2-Level** means that every input factor is set at two different levels during the experiment; usually high and low.

- **Full** means that every possible combination of the input factors (at their 2 levels) is used during the experiment.

- **Factorial** means that the input factors are changed simultaneously during the experiment.

Standard Order	Run Order	Steel Temperature	Roller Pressure	Lubricant	Output Thickness
1	2	Low	Low	Low	?
2	7	High	Low	Low	?
3	3	Low	High	Low	?
4	4	High	High	Low	?
5	6	Low	Low	High	?
6	5	High	Low	High	?
7	1	Low	High	High	?
8	8	High	High	High	?

Example: The **2-level Full Factorial** experiment for the steel rolling process introduced on page 207, is shown here on the right.

Each row represents one trial that will be run during the experiment. Because there are three input factors, each set at two different levels, there are eight trials in total.

Setting the two levels for each input factor:

The values of the low and high levels for each factor should be chosen with care. While they should be different enough to produce a measurable change in the output (if applicable) they should not be set outside of the normal operating range of the process.

Running an experiment:

The experiment above is shown in its **standard order**, which shows a structured pattern for each input factor.

The **run order** (second column) provides a random sequence in which the experiment should be completed, in order that the results are statistically valid.

DOE Notation in Minitab:

The experiment above is shown using the coded notation **Low** and **High**.

Minitab uses an alternative code of **-1** (for Low) and **1** (for High), but the pattern will be the same.

DOE-Steel.mpj

2-Level Full Factorial Designs – Calculating Effects

For each input term in a DOE, the average effect of changing that term from low to high is calculated.

Calculating the effect of a DOE input term:

The effect of an input term is the average difference in results that occurs when the factor is changed from its low to high setting, as follows:

Average output result when input term is **high**	**−**	Average output result when input term is **low**	**=**	Average effect of the input term

Calculating the effect of a main effect factor:

As described on the left, the effect of an input factor is calculated by subtracting the average result for when the factor is low from the average result when the same factor is high. So, as an example, in the generic DOE example (lower left), the effect of the C factor is:

$$\frac{(18+14+15+17)}{4} - \frac{(12+10+9+11)}{4} = 5.5$$

Standard Order	A	B	C	Result	A*B Interaction
1	Low (-1)	Low (-1)	Low (-1)	12	+1
2	High (+1)	Low (-1)	Low (-1)	10	-1
3	Low (-1)	High (+1)	Low (-1)	9	-1
4	High (+1)	High (+1)	Low (-1)	11	+1
5	Low (-1)	Low (-1)	High (+1)	18	+1
6	High (+1)	Low (-1)	High (+1)	14	-1
7	Low (-1)	High (+1)	High (+1)	15	-1
8	High (+1)	High (+1)	High (+1)	17	+1

Calculating the effect of an interaction factor:

In order to calculate the effect of an interaction, you first need to work out when that interaction occurs during the experiment. This is done by multiplying the coded values (-1 and +1) of the factors involved, resulting in a new column that reflects the interaction. The effect of the interaction can then be calculated in the same way as for main effects.

So, in the generic DOE example (left), the AB interaction is calculated by multiplying the A and B columns, to provide the results shown. The effect of the AB interaction is then calculated as follows:

$$\frac{(12+11+18+17)}{4} - \frac{(10+9+14+15)}{4} = 2.5$$

Full Factorial Example – Creating the DOE Worksheet

Example: A project team decides that they want to complete the experiment introduced on page 209. The experiment aims to investigate the affect of three input factors (steel temperature, roller pressure and lubricant type) on the output thickness of the steel (measured in millimetres).

The team decides to complete a **full factorial** experiment, because they think that some of the input factors may interact with each other and affect the output thickness of the steel.

They also decide to **replicate** the experiment in order to gain statistical significance in the results (see page 220 for more information on replication).

Designs submenu: This menu provides a list of the available experimental designs, based upon the number of factors you have entered. In this case (of 3 factors), a Fractional Factorial design of 4 runs and a Full Factorial design of 8 runs are available. For this example:

- Select the **Full Factorial** design (8 runs).
- Select 2 **Replicates**.
- Leave the **Center points** at 0 and the **Number of blocks** at 1 (default values).

Minitab: Stat > DOE > Factorial > Create Factorial Design

Create Factorial Design

Type of Design
- ● 2-level factorial (default generators)   (2 to 15 factors)
- ○ 2-level factorial (specify generators)   (2 to 15 factors)
- ○ 2-level split-plot (hard-to-change factors)   (2 to 7 factors)
- ○ Plackett-Burman design   (2 to 47 factors)
- ○ General full factorial design   (2 to 15 factors)

Number of factors: 3 ▼

Display Available Designs...
Designs...   Factors...
Options...   Results...

Help   OK   Cancel

1) Select the top (default) option for a general **2-level factorial** experiment.

2) Select the **Number of factors** (inputs) that you wish to investigate.

3) Click the **Designs** box and select the required experiment design as described left.

4) Having completed the above, the **Factors** menu will be available – complete as below.

5) Leave the **Options** and **Results** menus at their default levels.

Create Factorial Design: Designs

Designs	Runs	Resolution	2^(k-p)
1/2 fraction	4	III	2^(3-1)
Full factorial	8	Full	2^3

Number of center points per block: 0 ▼
Number of replicates for corner points: 2 ▼
Number of blocks: 1 ▼

Help   OK   Cancel

Create Factorial Design: Factors

Factor	Name	Type	Low	High
A	Temp	Numeric ▼	800	900
B	Pressure	Numeric ▼	1500	1750
C	Lubricant	Text ▼	A	B

Help   OK   Cancel

Factors submenu: Enter the name, type (numeric/text) and low/high settings of each input factor that you will include in the experiment (in this example there are three input factors).

DOE-Rolling.mpj

Full Factorial Example – Running the experiment

Having designed the experiment using Minitab, each trial within the experiment is then carefully completed in a random order but under controlled conditions, and the results entered into Minitab.

Running the experiment:

DOE trials should be completed under controlled conditions, where variation in other process inputs is minimised. Essentially, this means that you should try and ensure that everything is held constant during your experiment, except of course for the input factors that you are deliberately changing.

In addition, in order to reduce the chance of an uncontrolled variable being confused with one of the controlled input factors, the trials are completed in a random order, known as the **Run Order** (C2 on the right).

Blocking:

To minimise the effect of variation over time, the trials should be run as close to each other as possible, in one **block**.

However, if each trial takes so long that the experiment has to be run over two shifts, then the experiment should be designed in two blocks in order for Minitab to be aware that the two blocks of trials were completed under different conditions.

The DOE Worksheet partially shown below is the result of the settings on the previous page:

	C1 StdOrder	C2 RunOrder	C3 CenterPt	C4 Blocks	C5 Temp	C6 Pressure	C7-T Lubricant	C8 Output Thickness
1	16	1	1	1	900	1750	B	21.2230
2	6	2	1	1	900	1500	B	22.7594
3	10	3	1	1	900	1500	A	22.8624
4	3	4	1	1	800	1750	A	22.9624
5	2	5	1	1	900	1500	A	23.1794
6	7	6	1	1	800	1750	B	23.2051
7	11	7	1	1	800	1750	A	23.1144
8	8	8	1	1	900	1750	B	20.9570
9	9	9	1	1	800	1500	A	23.9102
10	14	10	1	1	900	1500	B	22.9824
11	15	11	1	1	800	1750	B	22.8941

Standard/Run Order: Minitab can display the DOE in **Standard Order** or in a **Run Order** generated randomly by Minitab.

Factor Levels: Minitab displays the coded (-1/1) or uncoded (actual) values of the input factors for each trial here.

Recording the results: Enter the name of your process output and the trial results in a new column here.

Minitab DOE tips:
1) You can change how a DOE worksheet is displayed by using the following menu:

Stat > DOE > Display Design

2) You must use Minitab's Create Factorial Design (previous page) to create the DOE worksheet so that Minitab recognises the worksheet as a DOE (i.e. you cannot type a DOE directly into a worksheet).

Full Factorial Example – Interpreting the Results (1)

Having run the experiment, Minitab can be used to identify and quantify the critical process inputs.

Minitab: Stat > DOE > Factorial > Analyse Factorial Design

Terms: This menu allows you to select the terms that you want to include in the DOE analysis. The word 'terms' refers to the input factors and their interactions.

At first, you should include all of the available terms because you are not yet sure which terms have an effect on the process output. You can do this by selecting the highest number available in the top drop down box.

Later on, you can refine the DOE analysis (and the resulting model), by selecting specific terms that have been identified as statistically significant, using the right and left arrows.

Graphs:

Effects Plots provide a useful graphical summary of the statistical analysis, and demonstrate clearly which terms have a statistically significant effect on the process.

Residual Plots support the advanced analysis of a DOE model, but are not dealt with further in this text.

Example: This example is Full Factorial, using three factors. Therefore, the highest possible order term is three (the three way interaction between all three input factors). While it is rare for a three way interaction to occur, we should include it in the analysis at first (it can always be removed later).

In the next few pages, we discover that only the Temp (A), Pressure (B) and the interaction between them (AB) have a statistically significant effect on the process output. In reality, this analysis would therefore be repeated, with only the three significant terms included in the **Selected Terms** box. This would refine the process model produced by the analysis.

 DOE-Rolling.mpj

Full Factorial Example – Interpreting the Results (2)

Effects Plots help to identify which input factors have a statistically significant effect on the output.

The **Pareto** and **Normal** Effects plots on this page essentially show the same information. They demonstrate graphically which of the input terms have a statistically significant effect on the process output. These significant terms will exceed the threshold line on the Pareto plot (right) and are identified by name and by different symbols on the Normal plot (below).

In this example, both Effects plots indicate that the Temperature (A), the Pressure (B) and their interaction (AB) all have an effect on the process output (the thickness of the steel). Conversely, the results also indicate that type of lubricant (C) and any interactions associated with it (BC, AC, ABC) have **no** effect on the output.

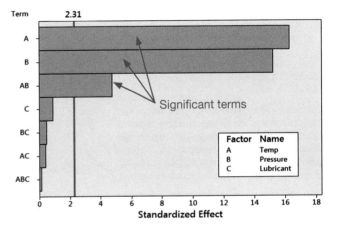

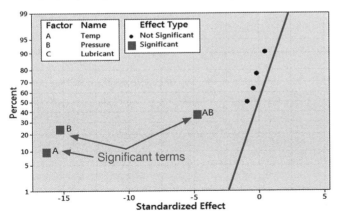

How does Minitab identify the important terms?

If you have used replication within your DOE, then Minitab compares the standardised effects (the t statistics) against a threshold t-value (taken from the t-distribution and based upon the degrees of freedom for the error term). Those t-statistics that are higher than the threshold t-value (indicated by the line on the Pareto plot at 2.31) are statistically significant, and will also have low p-values.

Without replication in your DOE, Minitab can estimate the significant terms and will still indicate them on the these charts (even though there are no t-statistics or p-values in the session window).

Full Factorial Example – Interpreting the Results (3)

Factorial Regression: Output Thickness vs Temp, Pressure, Lubricant

Model Summary

S	R-sq	R-sq(adj)	R-sq(pred)
0.181839	98.48%	97.16%	93.93%

Coded Coefficients

Term	Effect	Coef	SE Coef	T-Value	P-Value	VIF
Constant		22.7794	0.0455	501.09	0.000	
Temp	-1.4797	-0.7399	0.0455	-16.28	0.000	1.00
Pressure	-1.3816	-0.6908	0.0455	-15.20	0.000	1.00
Lubricant	-0.0809	-0.0404	0.0455	-0.89	0.400	1.00
Temp*Pressure	-0.4312	-0.2156	0.0455	-4.74	0.001	1.00
Temp*Lubricant	-0.0372	-0.0186	0.0455	-0.41	0.693	1.00
Pressure*Lubricant	0.0434	0.0217	0.0455	0.48	0.646	1.00
Temp*Pressure*Lubricant	-0.0115	-0.0058	0.0455	-0.13	0.902	1.00

Session Window Output (edited):
This page shows the critical information provided in Minitab's Session Window (excluding the ANOVA).

As with regression, a high **R-Squared** value indicates that the DOE model explains a high proportion of the process output. Minitab also provides a predicted R-Squared, which reflects how well the model will predict future process results.

The p-values that are less than 0.05 identify the terms that have a statistically significant effect on the process output. In this example, this confirms the results of the graphs on the previous page, in that *Temp, Pressure* and the interaction between them (*Temp*Pressure*) are shown as important inputs.

The p-value for the constant can be ignored – this is not a real process input.

The t-values are the standardised effects shown graphically on the previous page.

Effects and coefficients:
The effect figures are the average effect of moving a particular input from its low to high setting. So, in this example, the difference in the average steel thickness (the output) when the steel temperature was changed from low to high, was -1.47mm. Note that the effect was negative, so the steel thickness **reduces** as the steel temperature **increases**.

Later on, the coefficients will be used to create a process model (equation). At that point, it is important to be careful whether the coefficients you are using are in coded or uncoded units (the coefficients shown here are coded). See page 219 for more information.

Full Factorial Example – Interpreting the Results (4)

Minitab: Stat > DOE > Factorial > Factorial Plots

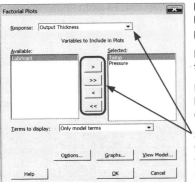

Factorial plots are useful for interpreting how the significant input factors affect the process output in real life.

Main Effects plots map one input against the process output (top right).

Interaction plots show how an interaction between two factors affect the process output (bottom right).

Select the process output (**Response**) to be plotted (in this case the output thickness of the steel) and then use the arrows to ensure that all of the input factors (**Variables**) that are significant are selected. For an Interaction plot, include all terms in that interaction.

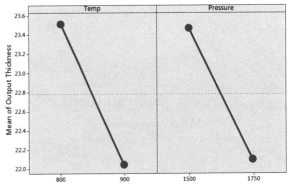

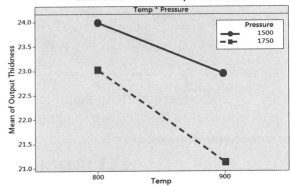

Interpreting the graphs:

The main effect plot (top right) shows that the average steel thickness reduced from around 23.5 to 22.0, when the steel temperature was increased from 800 to 900.

If the lines on an interaction plot (bottom right) are **not** parallel, it indicates that an interaction exists. In this case, this plot confirms the interaction, by showing that the reduction that occurs in the steel thickness when temperature is increased from 800 to 900, is **more pronounced** at higher pressures than at lower pressures (the dashed line is steeper than the solid blue line).

Full Factorial Example – Refining the model (1)

If during the first analysis it is found that some input factors do not affect the process output, the DOE analysis should be repeated without those terms, in order to further refine the process model.

Minitab: Stat > DOE > Factorial > Analyse Factorial Design

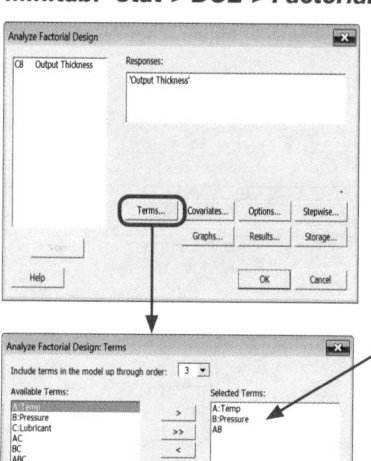

Refining the model:
During the first analysis, it was found that only the input factors *Temp* (A), *Pressure* (B) and their interaction (AB) were statistically significant in relation to the output steel thickness.

The analysis (not the experiment) should therefore be repeated with only these terms included.

Use the arrows within the **Terms** box to manually ensure that only the required terms remain (left).

The new graphical results on the right, show that with the non-significant factors removed, the input factors *Temp* (A), *Pressure* (B) and their interaction (AB) all remain statistically significant. This is indicated by the fact that all three factors exceed the threshold t-value (2.18) on the Pareto plot (top right), and all three effects are highlighted as distinct from the Normal line on the Normal plot (bottom right).

DOE-Rolling.mpj

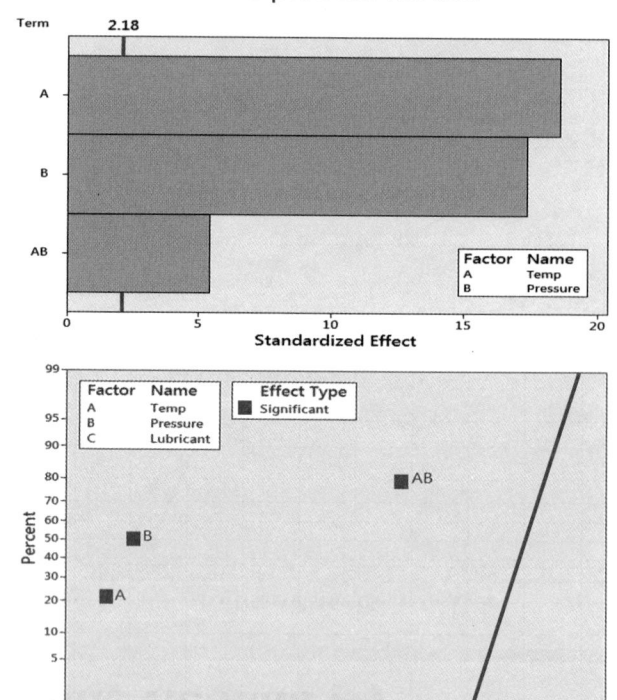

Full Factorial Example – Refining the model (2)

Once the insignificant terms have been removed, the numerical output is substantially reduced and will result in a more accurate model of the process.

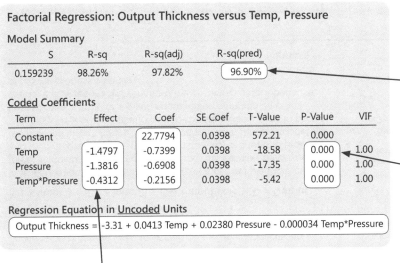

Factorial Regression: Output Thickness versus Temp, Pressure

Model Summary

S	R-sq	R-sq(adj)	R-sq(pred)
0.159239	98.26%	97.82%	96.90%

Coded Coefficients

Term	Effect	Coef	SE Coef	T-Value	P-Value	VIF
Constant		22.7794	0.0398	572.21	0.000	
Temp	-1.4797	-0.7399	0.0398	-18.58	0.000	1.00
Pressure	-1.3816	-0.6908	0.0398	-17.35	0.000	1.00
Temp*Pressure	-0.4312	-0.2156	0.0398	-5.42	0.000	1.00

Regression Equation in Underlined Units

Output Thickness = -3.31 + 0.0413 Temp + 0.02380 Pressure - 0.000034 Temp*Pressure

Session Window Output (edited):
This page shows the critical information provided in Minitab's Session Window (excluding the ANOVA). In this case, it shows the results of the second analysis of this DOE – **after** the insignificant terms (from the first analysis) were removed.

Most of the **R-Squared** values have not changed significantly from the first analysis on page 215 (they are still high). The exception is the predicted R-Squared, which has increased by around 3% from the first analysis. So, by removing the insignificant terms, this new model will better predict the process output.

The p-values are all less than 0.05 (in fact they are all zero!). This re-confirms the results from the first analysis, that the inputs *Temp, Pressure* and the interaction between them (*Temp*Pressure*) have a statistically significant effect on the process output (the steel thickness).

Again, the p-value on the first line for the constant can be ignored - this is not a real process input.

Effects and coefficients: As explained previously on page 215, the **Effect** figures are the average effect of changing a particular input from its low to high setting. So, in this example, changing the temperature of the steel from low to high (800 to 900) had the largest effect on the steel thickness – a reduction of 1.47mm. This was closely followed by the effect of Pressure (a reduction of 1.38mm) and finally the interaction between temperature and pressure had a lesser, but still statistically significant, effect.

The regression equation uses **uncoded** coefficients, and these are used (along with the **coded** versions from the table, highlighted) on the next page to create two process models.

Full Factorial Example – Calculating the Process Model

Within certain limitations, a process model (equation) that has been constructed from the results of a DOE can be used to predict the output of that process based upon the settings of the critical inputs.

Constructing a process model: The refined analysis from the previous page can be used to construct a mathematical model (equation) that represents the process. The generic form of the model is:

(C1 x Input1) + (C2 x Input2) + (C3 x Input3)etc. + C = Output

In this equation, each significant input (in this example there are three) is multiplied by its coefficient (from the session window), and then an overall mathematical constant (C) is added to provide the process output figure. It is important to note that the model will inevitably have some limitations, and the model only aims to predict the **average** output for a given combination of inputs. In other words, actual results will vary from the predicted output because of natural process variation.

Using the model: As described on the previous page, Minitab provides two sets of coefficients, for use with coded and uncoded units. So, for this example, the two different models shown below can be constructed (but it is important to remember which one is which!).

While the coefficients look quite different, the two models will provide the same result based upon equivalent inputs. To show this, the examples below show the calculations for the following settings, and both return the same output steel thickness of 23.044mm.

Temperature:	800 (uncoded)	or -1 (coded)
Pressure:	1750 (uncoded)	or +1 (coded)

The data file **DOE-Rolling.xls** enables you to enter different input values.

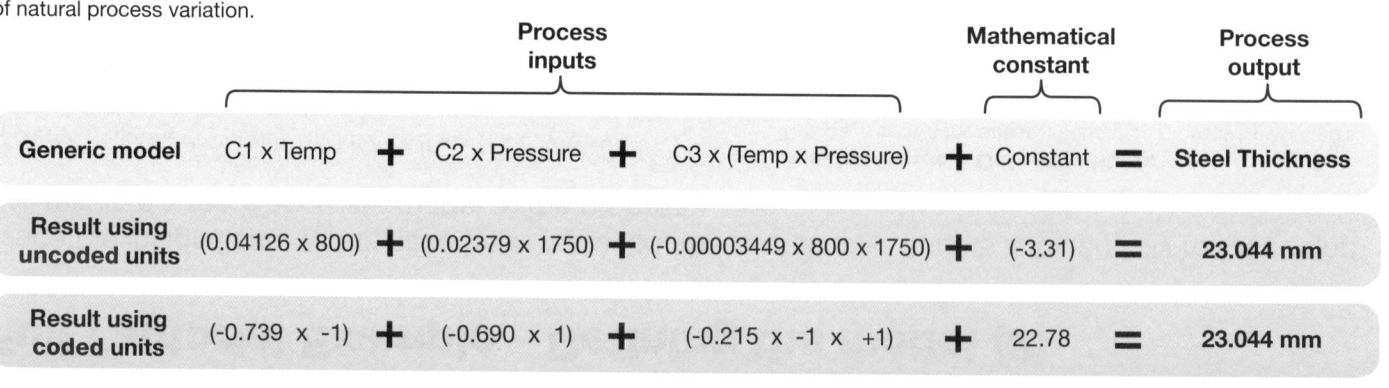

	Process inputs			Mathematical constant	Process output
Generic model	C1 x Temp **+**	C2 x Pressure **+**	C3 x (Temp x Pressure) **+**	Constant **=**	**Steel Thickness**
Result using uncoded units	(0.04126 x 800) **+**	(0.02379 x 1750) **+**	(-0.00003449 x 800 x 1750) **+**	(-3.31) **=**	**23.044 mm**
Result using coded units	(-0.739 x -1) **+**	(-0.690 x 1) **+**	(-0.215 x -1 x +1) **+**	22.78 **=**	**23.044 mm**

Fractional Factorial Designs – Overview

Using the '**Full** Factorial Design' as a starting point, designed experiments can become much more efficient by the careful use of **Fractional** Factorial Designs, combined with replication and centre points.

The downfall of **Full** Factorial Designs (introduced on the previous pages) is that the size of the experiment doubles for every additional input factor that is included in the experiment. So…

- Four input factors would require 16 trials;
- Five input factors would require 32 trials, and so on.

By selecting a (carefully chosen) fraction of the trials from a **Full** Factorial design, a **Fractional** Factorial experiment will often provide more information from the same number of trials (or the same level of information from fewer trials!). This can then enable Replication and Centre Point trials to be incorporated (see notes below).

Of course, there has to be a trade off – you can't get more information with fewer trials for free! The trade off is that the **resolution** of the experiment will be reduced. This means that some of the interactions will not be visible, because they will be **confounded** with other effects (see page 225). However, if this confounding is understood and managed, Fractional Factorial experiments are an effective tool.

Example: A Fractional Factorial experiment for the steel rolling example is contained within the **first four rows** of the experiment shown top right. A Full Factorial design for three input factors would require eight runs, but in this Fractional Factorial design only four runs are used.

	Standard Order	Run Order	Steel Temp.	Roller Pressure	Lubricant	Output Thickness
Fractional Factorial	1	3	Low	Low	High	?
	2	1	High	Low	Low	?
	3	4	Low	High	Low	?
	4	2	High	High	High	?
Replication	5	6	Low	Low	High	?
	6	7	High	Low	Low	?
	7	8	Low	High	Low	?
	8	5	High	High	High	?
Ct Pt	9	9	Mid	Mid	Mid	?

Replication:
Factorial Designs only run each trial once, so the sample size for each trial is one. In order to gain statistical confidence an experiment can be replicated, which means that the entire experiment is repeated. It makes sense that if the results are similar, then statistical confidence is increased.

Centre Points:
Because factorial experiments only study the results of a process at two levels (high and low), they cannot detect if the process output behaves in a linear manner between the two extremes. The use of a centre point (trial number 9 above) can be used to detect non-linear effects. Note that each input factor is set at a 'Mid' level for the centre point trial.

Fractional Factorial Example – Creating the DOE worksheet

Example: Imagine that the project team described on page 211 actually want to include four input factors in their steel rolling experiment.

With a **Full** Factorial design, four input factors would require 16 trials (even without replication). This is too expensive, and so the team select a **Fractional** Factorial design for four input factors that requires only eight trials. The team note that they will have to consider the confounding that will be present as a result of this Fractional Factorial design, when they analyse the results.

The team also suspect that the effect of some of the inputs on the thickness of the rolled steel (the output) may be non-linear, and therefore decide to add a Centre Point into their experiment (to test for non-linearity).

The team would also like to replicate the experiment to gain statistical significance, but this would double the number of trials. So, they decide to replicate just the Centre Point instead. This will help the Minitab analysis to assess the statistical significance of the results.

⊙ DOE-Rolling.mpj

Minitab: Stat > DOE > Factorial > Create Factorial Design

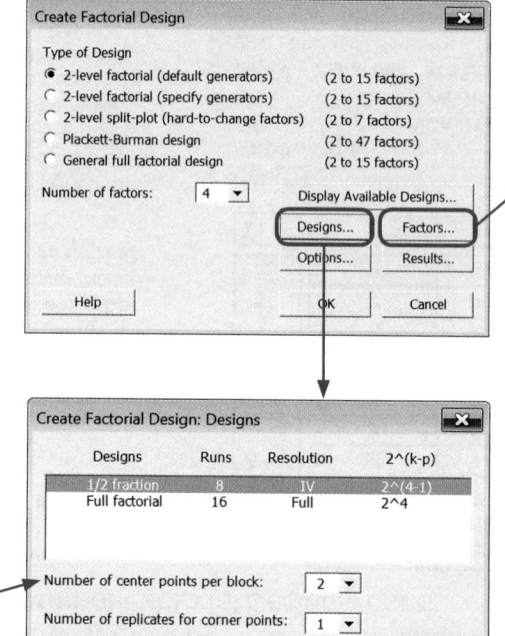

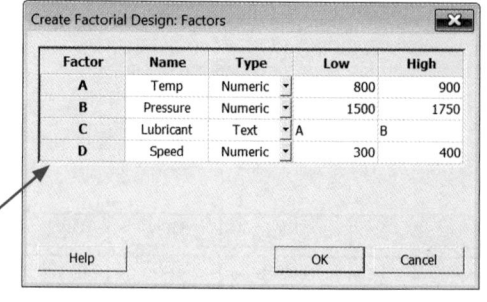

Factors submenu (above): The details of the four factors are entered here. Note that the *Lubricant* is a categorical input (so enter as **Text**).

In this case, the number of input factors is four.

Designs submenu (left): In this example of four factors, a Fractional Factorial design of 8 runs and a Full Factorial design of 16 runs are available. For this example:

- Select the ½ **Fraction** design (8 runs).
- Select two **Centre points per block** in order to replicate the centre point.
- Leave the **Number of replicates** and **blocks** at one.

Fractional Factorial Example – Running the experiment

Having designed the experiment using Minitab, each trial within the experiment is then carefully completed in a random order, but under controlled conditions, and the results entered into Minitab.

Running the experiment:

Page 212 provides information on running an experiment, the use of blocking, and some Minitab tips that are relevant to this example.

The Minitab worksheet on the right shows the Fractional Factorial design that is created by the instructions on the previous page. Each row represents one trial within the experiment, and shows the input factor settings that should be used for that trial.

The first eight rows contain the ½ Fractional Factorial design (for four input factors) that was selected on the previous page. Because this is a Fractional design, only a fraction of the possible input combinations are contained within the experiment. So, for example, the combination 800/1500/A/300 is present (and highlighted) but the combination 800/1500/B/300 is not included.

DOE-Rolling-Fractional Factorial.MTW ***

	C1	C2	C3	C4	C5	C6	C7-T	C8	C9
	StdOrder	RunOrder	CenterPt	Blocks	Temp	Pressure	Lubricant	Speed	Output Thickness
1	1	12	1	1	800	1500	A	300	24.05
2	2	4	1	1	900	1500	A	400	22.85
3	3	7	1	1	800	1750	A	400	22.99
4	4	5	1	1	900	1750	A	300	21.41
5	5	9	1	1	800	1500	B	400	23.90
6	6	6	1	1	900	1500	B	300	22.94
7	7	10	1	1	800	1750	B	300	22.92
8	8	8	1	1	900	1750	B	400	21.17
9	9	3	0	1	850	1625	A	350	22.93
10	10	11	0	1	850	1625	B	350	22.79
11	11	1	0	1	850	1625	A	350	22.73
12	12	2	0	1	850	1625	B	350	22.97

Confounding:

The input combinations used in the design are carefully selected in order to provide maximum information while still ensuring that the confounding of input factors is carefully controlled. The confounding within this experiment is explained further during the analysis.

Centre Points:

The last four rows of this design are the centre points that were specified at the design stage (previous page). However, only two centre points were specified, and yet the design contains four. This is because the *Lubricant* input is categorical (either A or B), and it's impossible to set the *Lubricant* half way between two different types. So, Minitab has created two different centre points (where all the inputs are at their mid-point) – one for each type of lubricant. Each of these centre points has been replicated twice (as specified), creating four in total.

Fractional Factorial Example – Interpreting the Results (1)

Analysing the experiment results:

Page 213 describes how to use Minitab's **Analyse Factorial Design** function, to set up the analysis of a DOE. The key difference for this example is the **Terms** submenu, below:

Minitab: Stat > DOE > Factorial > Analyse Factorial Design

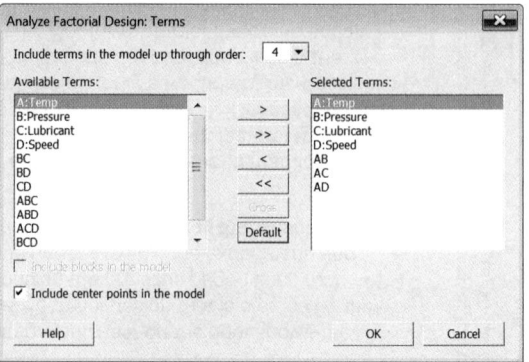

Because this is a **Fractional** design, Minitab has carefully pre-selected the key terms that should be included in the analysis (right hand side above) in order that they are not confounded with each other. So, although it might appear that there are many terms that are not included (on the left), you do not need to select these as they are confounded with one of the pre-selected terms (and therefore effectively already in the analysis).

For example, the BD term is not selected, because it is confounded with the term AC. Similarly the interaction BCD is confounded with the main effect A, and therefore should not be included.

! Don't forget to check **Include center points** if your design has them.

Analysing the graphical output:

The Pareto chart of the standardised effects (introduced on page 214 and shown below) indicates that the *Temp* (A), *Pressure* (B) and the interaction between them (AB) have a statistically significant effect on the process output.

It also indicates that the *Speed* (D) and the *Lubricant* (C) do **not** effect the process output – which is just as valuable to know!

At first glance, these results seem to replicate the conclusions of the Full Factorial example (previous pages). However, because this is a Fractional Factorial design, in real life you would need to manage and understand the confounding within the experiment, before reaching any firm conclusions based upon these results (see page 225).

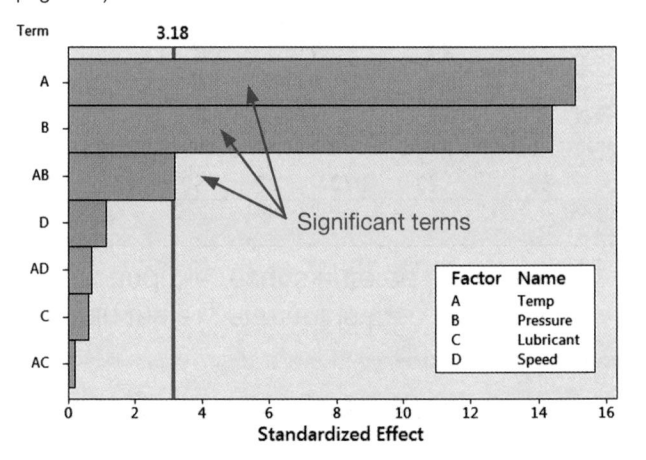

Fractional Factorial Example – Interpreting the Results (2)

Factorial Regression: Output Thick vs Temp, Pressure, Lubricant, Speed

Model Summary

S	R-sq	R-sq(adj)	R-sq(pred)
0.128760	99.34%	97.56%	63.91%

Coded Coefficients

Term	Effect	Coef	SE Coef	T-Value	P-Value	VIF
Constant		22.7787	0.0455	500.37	0.000	
Temp	-1.3725	-0.6862	0.0455	-15.07	0.001	1.00
Pressure	-1.3125	-0.6563	0.0455	-14.42	0.001	1.00
Lubricant	-0.0450	-0.0225	0.0372	-0.61	0.588	1.00
Speed	-0.1025	-0.0513	0.0455	-1.13	0.342	1.00
Temp*Pressure	-0.2925	-0.1463	0.0455	-3.21	0.049	1.00
Temp*Lubricant	0.0175	0.0088	0.0455	0.19	0.860	1.00
Temp*Speed	-0.0625	-0.0312	0.0455	-0.69	0.542	1.00
Ct Pt		0.0762	0.0788	0.97	0.405	1.00

This page shows the Session Window output from the Fractional Factorial analysis on the previous page (excluding the ANOVA and Alias Structure – see next page). Page 215 contains a more general description of how to interpret DOE analysis output such as this.

The high **R-Squared** values (R-sq & R-sq(adj)) indicate that the DOE inputs account for a high proportion of the output variation. However, in this case, the Predicted R-Squared is much lower, indicating that the current model will not predict new results very well. This is because there are several inputs included in the model that are not significant.

Although not shown in this text, if the next steps (see left) are completed, the Predicted R-Squared value increases substantially to 96.87%, indicating that the revised model is highly accurate for predicting the process output (the rolled steel thickness).

In this case, the **p-values** that are less than 0.05 (and therefore have a statistically significant effect on the process output) are the *Temperature* (A), the *Pressure* (B) and the interaction between them (AB).

The p-value for the **Centre Point** (Ct Pt) is above 0.05, which indicates that it is not significant. In other words, it is reasonable to assume that the relationship between inputs and outputs is linear (within the limits of the input factors used in the experiment).

Next Steps for this analysis:
As for the Full Factorial example (page 217), the next step is to refine the analysis by completing it again with only the input terms that are statistically significant. So, in this case, Centre Points should be excluded and only the *Temp*, *Pressure* and their interaction included.

Having done this, and assuming that all of the input terms remain significant in the refined analysis, a process model can be developed using the mathematical coefficients.

Fractional Factorial Example – Checking the Confounding

When does confounding occur and what is it?

In a **Full** Factorial experiment, the effect of **every** input term can be calculated because every single possible combination of the factors has been used in the experiment. Remember that because of interactions, there are far more input terms than factors. For example, for a Full Factorial experiment on 4 factors, there will be 15 input terms (shown below).

Main Effects	Two way Interactions	Three way Interactions	Four way Interaction
A, B	AB, AC, AD	ABC, ABD,	ABCD
C, D	BC, BD, CD	ACD, BCD	

In a **Fractional** Factorial experiment, because fewer runs are used, it is not possible to calculate the effect of each individual input terms (there are simply not enough results to do so). It's important to remember however, that all of the input terms will still exist during the experiment (and affect the results if they are important), but it just won't be possible to calculate their effect individually.

Fractional Factorial designs sound dangerous!

Well, yes and no. In reality, higher order interactions (say three way interactions and above) are quite rare. So, while **Full** Factorial designs allow their affect to be measured, this is quite often a waste of time and cost in an experiment, because they are rarely significant.

Fractional Factorial designs are carefully designed in such a way that the main effects (the most likely to be significant) are confounded with the higher order interactions (the least likely to be significant). So, when a significant input term is found, it can be fairly safely assumed that it is the main effect, and not the higher order interaction.

Alias Structure (coded)	Alias Structure (uncoded - Minitab 16 only)
I + ABCD	I + Temp*Pressure*Lubricant*Speed
A + BCD	Temp + Pressure*Lubricant*Speed
B + ACD	Pressure + Temp*Lubricant*Speed
C + ABD	Lubricant + Temp*Pressure*Speed
D + ABC	Speed + Temp*Pressure*Lubricant
AB + CD	Temp*Pressure + Lubricant*Speed
AC + BD	Temp*Lubricant + Pressure*Speed
AD + BC	Temp*Speed + Pressure*Lubricant

Understanding the confounding for this example:

When the DOE is created for the Fractional Factorial example on the previous pages, Minitab provides an Alias Structure (coded) in the Session Window. The same Alias Structure is provided when this DOE is analysed as described on page 223. An Alias Structure defines the confounding that exists within a DOE analysis. So, for example, the highlighted line **A + BCD** (above) means that the main effect **A** is confounded with the three way interaction **BCD**. Similarly the two way interaction **AB** is confounded with the **CD** interaction (highlighted).

The Resolution of a Fractional Factorial experiment (see next page) is always one above the order of the interactions that will be confounded with the main effects. So, for example, in a DOE of Resolution Five, the main effects would be confounded with the four way interactions.

In this example, the Resolution is four, which means that the main effects are confounded with three way interactions (as shown above).

Minitab's DOE *Display Available Designs*

As explained throughout the previous pages, the options for optimising a designed experiment means that there are endless permutations for any one experiment. Choosing the right combination depends on the specific environment, which inevitably means that experience is a key factor. The key options to consider are:

- **Fractional Factorials** can be used to reduce the size of an experiment, but the resolution decreases at the same time.

- **Replications** can be used to introduce statistical significance to an experiment, but the size of the experiment (number of trials) increases.

- **Centre Points** can be used to check for non-linear relationships, but require additional trials (with the input factors set at 'mid' levels).

When a DOE is created (see pages 211/221), Minitab provides a **Display Available Designs** option, that provides a useful summary of the available factorial designs, as shown on the right.

For any specific number of (input) factors, the table summarises the factorial designs that are available, the number of trials they involve, and their resolution. So, for the highlighted example:

- For five input factors, a Full factorial experiment requires 32 trials.

- This can be reduced to 16 trials, but the resolution level of the experiment drops to five (V).

- The number of trials can be reduced further to eight, but the resolution drops to three (III), which is potentially unacceptable.

Minitab: Stat > DOE > Factorial > Create Factorial Design > Display Available Designs

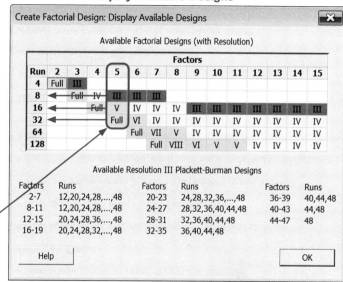

Resolution three is the lowest level available. **Resolution three** designs require careful application, but can be useful to **screen** for important input factors, which can then be experimented on in more detail.

For example, the table above shows a resolution three experiment for seven factors, which requires only eight runs. A second, more focused experiment would then usually be required.

Analyse – Checklist

Process Door:

☐ Has the process been mapped in detail (and as it really is)?

☐ Have the team gained first hand experience of the product or process in question?

☐ Have the key types of (or reasons for) failure been identified?

☐ Has Failure Mode Effect Analysis (FMEA) been used (if applicable) to identify the greatest areas of risk in the process/product?

☐ Have Brainstorming/5 Whys/Fishbone diagrams been used to identify possible root causes?

Data Door:

☐ Has the data been analysed graphically to investigate the clues contained within it?

☐ Has the data been stratified where possible to look for clues and benchmarking opportunities?

☐ Have hypothesis tests been used (where applicable) to verify observations made from the graphical analysis?

☐ Have correlation and regression techniques been used (where applicable) to understand and quantify the relationships between the critical process inputs and outputs?

☐ Have designed experiments (DOE) been used (where applicable) to find the critical process inputs?

Finally:

☐ Are you confident that you know the true root causes that produce the majority of your process failures?

Analyse – Review Questions

▪ What were your theories about the cause of the problem when you started the Analyse phase?

▪ Were those theories proven during the analysis?

Process Door:

▪ How was the process mapping done? Who was involved?

▪ How did the team get to know the process?

▪ What are the key ways in which the process or product fails?

▪ If an FMEA was completed, what risks were identified for reduction?

▪ Who was involved with the brainstorming/fishbone diagram activities?

Data Door:

▪ What graphs were used for analysing the data? Why?

▪ In what ways was the data stratified?

▪ What (if any) hypothesis tests were used? Why?

▪ If Designed Experiments were used, what process inputs were investigated? How was the experiment conducted?

Finally:

▪ What are the key root causes of failure or critical inputs to the process?

Improve – Overview

The Improve phase aims to develop, select and implement the best solutions, with controlled risks. The effects of the solutions are then measured with the KPIs developed during the Measure phase.

The flow through Improve:

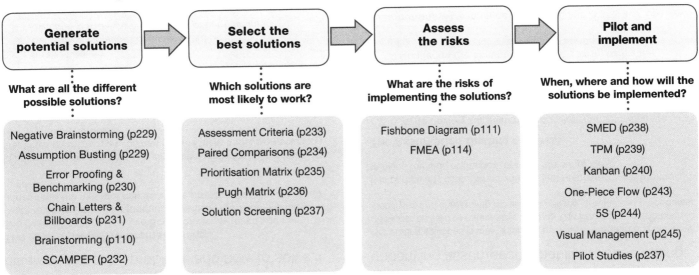

Generate potential solutions	Select the best solutions	Assess the risks	Pilot and implement
What are all the different possible solutions?	**Which solutions are most likely to work?**	**What are the risks of implementing the solutions?**	**When, where and how will the solutions be implemented?**
Negative Brainstorming (p229)	Assessment Criteria (p233)	Fishbone Diagram (p111)	SMED (p238)
Assumption Busting (p229)	Paired Comparisons (p234)	FMEA (p114)	TPM (p239)
Error Proofing & Benchmarking (p230)	Prioritisation Matrix (p235)		Kanban (p240)
Chain Letters & Billboards (p231)	Pugh Matrix (p236)		One-Piece Flow (p243)
Brainstorming (p110)	Solution Screening (p237)		5S (p244)
SCAMPER (p232)			Visual Management (p245)
			Pilot Studies (p237)

How is the success of the Improve phase measured?

During the Analyse and Improve phases, the data collection systems developed in Measure should remain in place, with the KPI charts being updated regularly and reviewed at the beginning of each project team meeting.

The success of the improve phase is not based upon the successful implementation of the selected solutions, but instead when the process measurements (KPIs) have improved and been validated with appropriate statistical techniques (graphs, hypothesis testing etc.).

Negative Brainstorming

Negative Brainstorming helps a team think very differently about a problem, and how to solve it.

The idea of Negative Brainstorming:

The concept behind Negative Brainstorming is that if you can deliberately create a bad product or service, then you probably understand the real root causes of the problem that you are trying to solve.

In addition, if you can come up with some ideas for deliberately creating a problem, then you can reverse them to develop solutions that *prevent* the problem.

How to use Negative Brainstorming:

Instead of asking your project team how best to *solve* the problem, ask them how best to *create* the problem.

So, instead of asking:
"How can we increase customer retention?", ask
"How can we make sure we <u>lose</u> all of our customers?"

And, instead of asking:
"How can we make a 100% perfect products?", ask
"How can we make sure we <u>have</u> a faulty product?"

You can facilitate a Negative Brainstorming event in much the same way that you would a normal brainstorming event. However, at the end, you must work with the team to reverse the suggestions and convert them into realistic solutions.

Assumption Busting

Assumption Busting forces you to recognise the underlying assumptions that limit your thinking.

Generating solutions is often inhibited by a set of assumptions that may no longer be valid or reasonable. Assumption Busting is an approach for identifying and challenging these assumptions (or rules and procedures).

It is particularly useful when your project team are having trouble thinking 'outside of the box' or have run out of ideas.

The Assumption Busting process:

1) Write down your assumptions. Ask yourself; what are the implicit limits that I have never normally challenged?

2) Identify the particular assumptions that are stopping or limiting you solving your current problem.

3) Challenge the assumptions. The 5 Whys technique (page 110) is ideal for challenging assumptions, as below:

Assumption: We cannot despatch products in less than one day.

Why? Because the whole process takes at least 30 hours.

Why? Because we can't prepare the shipment until finance has approved the sale and completed their paperwork.

Why? Because the shipping list is produced when finance create the invoice.

Why? Not sure! The shipping list could come straight to us from the sales department who take the order.

Error Proofing

What is error proofing?

Error proofing (also known as mistake proofing) refers to the use of solutions and improvements that either;

- Completely prevent or reduce the risk of a failure occurring by eliminating the root cause (preferable).

  or

- Detect a failure soon after it has occurred.

Error proofing solutions are particularly suited to repetitive manual tasks that rely on constant vigilance or adjustment. It is not the use of one, but the application of many error proofing solutions at every opportunity throughout a product or process, that will reduce the overall long term failure rate.

Examples: Every day examples of error proofing include:

- The use of different size fuel pipes and nozzles on vehicles in order to prevent the wrong fuel being used.

- Washing machines will not start or continue turning if the door is opened.

- A warning signal when a car's lights are left on and the door opened (when the engine is switched off).

These examples demonstrate that error proofing solutions work in several different ways. Some **shutdown** the process, others **control** the process to prevent a mistake and others provide a **warning** of a mistake that has already happened.

Benchmarking

What is benchmarking?

Benchmarking is a tool that can be used in several phases of a Six Sigma project.

- In the Measure phase, benchmarking involves identifying the best performance attained by similar processes in other organisations and industries. This evidence can be used to help assess if there is the potential to improve the existing process.

- In the Improve phase, benchmarking involves identifying and understanding best practices from other processes and organisations and adapting them to help improve your own process.

How do you benchmark?

Benchmarking is now a common and respected practice in the business world, and accordingly there are many organisations who facilitate and provide benchmarking visits and information. Alternatively, the internet is a valuable (and free) source of benchmarking ideas. Maximum value is usually gained from looking further afield than your direct competitors or industries, since the most innovative ideas and performance can often be found in similar processes that are operating within completely different environments.

Examples: Everyday examples of benchmarking include:

- A car manufacturer that would like to provide customised cars to order could benchmark with the pizza delivery or computer industries for ideas on rapid customisation and delivery.

- A supermarket online home delivery service could benchmark with other (non-competing) online retailers for ideas on best practice of website design or effective delivery operations.

Chain Letters

What are chain letters?

Chain letters are a method of generating ideas and potential solutions. They involve a letter being sent around a specific group of people, with a given objective and timeframe. Each participant is invited to review the previous suggestions and then make modifications, propose alternatives or develop new ideas. Like brainstorming, the aim is to encourage an atmosphere where there are no right or wrong suggestions.

How to use a chain letter:

- **Choose an appropriate format:** E-mail is an ideal format for chain letters but you should check that your organisation endorses this use of e-mail. Any format that allows people to view and build upon previous ideas will work.

- **Set a timeframe and facilitate:** Chain letters succeed through momentum. Set clear timeframes for responding and forwarding the e-mail – a larger volume of quick/short responses is often preferable to a few overly detailed suggestions. A chain letter therefore requires some level of facilitation to ensure it is progressing and the responses are focused.

- **Provide a clear, specific objective:** The chain letter should clearly state the objective that is being sought, such as '*providing quicker quotes*' or '*keeping the customer better informed*'. This helps to generate specific ideas because the participants are focused on achieving a specific outcome, rather than solving a broad problem.

Billboards

What are billboards?

Billboards are a similar method of generating ideas and solutions to chain letters. Both methods avoid the use of meetings and aim to tap the creativity of participants in their own time and environment.

Billboards can provide access to a large range of people, but therefore also require careful planning in order that the feedback received is focused and relevant.

How to use a billboard:

- **Prepare:** The location, size and format of the billboard all require careful consideration. Place it where it will be noticed, but also where people will feel comfortable stopping to contribute. Don't forget to provide a pen and paper if required.

- **Engage the audience:** The billboard should provide an introduction to what you are doing and why you are asking for suggestions. Always provide some background to the project and ensure that the objective of the billboard is very clear.

- **Set a timeframe and facilitate:** Billboards are similar to chain letters in that they require momentum to succeed. A billboard that has not changed in three months is clearly not part of a very active project and will not solicit many useful responses. Set a clear timeframe for removing the billboard and regularly review the feedback being received, updating the board as required.

- **Provide feedback:** Once you have collected and made use of the billboard suggestions, don't forget to provide feedback and thank people for contributing.

SCAMPER

SCAMPER is another useful idea generation technique. It provides a checklist that can be used to improve upon an existing design/product/service or to develop new ideas and solutions.

SCAMPER is an acronym that provides a framework of challenging questions. It helps you to take a structured approach to developing ideas and can be used to develop new solutions or refine existing ones.

It's particularly useful towards the end of your 'idea generation' phase, when ideas might be flowing slower and the team need re-invigorating!

How to use SCAMPER:
SCAMPER is best used by a team, but can still be used individually. Like many of the idea generation tools, if you are working with a team this technique requires good facilitation to be effective.

Good facilitation involves ensuring that you keep the team focused and that everyone has a chance to give input. As a facilitator, try and get the team to build upon other people's ideas, comments and suggestions in a positive way. This can be done by taking people's suggestions and turning them around using leading questions such as: *How? Why? Why not?* and *When?*

Work systematically and consider each element of a solution, product or service against the key words of SCAMPER in order to develop ideas for improvement.

S **Substitute** – Can you substitute people, components, materials or processes from elsewhere?

C **Combine** – Are there functions, elements, features or processes that you can combine to your advantage?

A **Adapt** – Can you alter or adapt ideas from different processes, products or industries to your advantage?

M **Modify** – Can you modify a feature or function, perhaps by increasing or decreasing it, or changing its shape or attributes?

P **Put to another use** – Can you put your product, service, solution or idea to a different use? Can you access a new market?

E **Eliminate** – What would happen if you removed an element or process? How would you work round it? Would it simplify things?

R **Reverse** – Can you turn things inside out or upside down? What would happen if you did things back to front?

Assessment Criteria – Development and Weighting

Developing agreed assessment criteria is the first step in selecting the best solution for a project.

Assessment criteria provide a constant basis of comparison within the solution selection techniques that are used next, and so it is important to get them right!

It's also important to involve a wide group of people in the development of the assessment criteria, to avoid missing any critical perspectives or having your selected solutions open to challenge later on.

Brainstorming is a good place to start for developing a list of criteria.

Some examples of common assessment criteria:

- Will it solve the problem or achieve the objective?
- Will it improve customer satisfaction?
- Will it impact the customer negatively during implementation?
- How easy is it to implement?
- Are there any potential problems or risks?
- What is the cost?
- Does it fit with the strategy of the business?
- Are there any potential regulatory or safety compliance risks?

Having agreed the assessment criteria, they are then weighted against each other.

There are two key approaches to weighting your assessment criteria:

1) Use the paired comparisons technique described on page 234 to compare and prioritise the different criteria. This technique is usually used to select solutions, but it can be used to weight criteria too.

2) Develop a team consensus using multi-voting in which you get your team members to apportion 100 points across the potential criteria. You then total up the scores for each assessment criteria, and this provides the weighting for that criteria (as shown below) for use later on.

Assessment criteria	Nathan	Simon	Melanie	Graeme	Miles	Weighted Totals
Can be implemented quickly	15	10	5	10	5	45
Will solve the problem fully	40	60	35	50	55	240
Costs less than 100K Euros	10	10	20	20	5	65
Won't impact the customer	20	15	25	15	30	105
No regulatory risks	15	5	15	5	5	45
	100	**100**	**100**	**100**	**100**	**500**

Paired Comparisons (a.k.a. Pairwise Ranking)

Paired Comparisons is a team based approach for ranking different options against each other. It is a particularly useful technique when there is little objective data to base a decision on.

Paired Comparisons is most commonly used to rank potential solutions or weight assessment criteria against each other. You need a team of people with knowledge of the process and effective facilitation skills!

How to complete a Paired Comparison:

1) Label the solutions or criteria that you are going to compare (A, B, C etc.)

2) Draw a comparison matrix, such as the one shown opposite.

3) Taking two solutions/criteria at a time, ask the team to compare them against each other and decide which one is better or more important.
NB: To compare solutions (rather than criteria), you will first have to define the criteria that you will use when making your decisions.

4) Write the result (the solution or criteria with the most votes) in the relevant box. So in the example on the right, when comparing solutions A and B, solution B was selected and written in the box (highlighted).

5) Rank the solutions, or weight the criteria as follows:

- If you are comparing solutions, rank the solutions in order of the number of times they were selected as the best of a pair.

- If you are weighting criteria, then work out the weighting for each criteria, by dividing the number of times it was chosen by the total number of decisions that were made.

Comparison Matrix	A	B	C	D	E
A	-	B	A	D	A
B	-	-	B	B	B
C	-	-	-	C	E
D	-	-	-	-	D
E	-	-	-	-	-

For ranking solutions

B	4	1st
A	2	2nd
D	2	2nd
C	1	3rd
E	1	3rd

For weighting criteria

B	4 / 10 =	0.4
A	2 / 10 =	0.2
D	2 / 10 =	0.2
C	1 / 10 =	0.1
E	1 / 10 =	0.1

Prioritisation (or Solution Selection) Matrix

A Prioritisation Matrix is a structured technique for selecting a solution from several alternatives. It combines the weighted criteria and list of possible solutions that the team have already developed.

A Prioritisation Matrix helps to weigh up the pros and cons of each possible solution using the weighted criteria and consensus of the team, and so provides a good chance of selecting the most appropriate solution.

How to complete a Prioritisation Matrix:

1) Finalise the selection of solutions that you will include in the matrix. Remove any clear 'no-go' solutions – those that the organisation just wouldn't accept at any cost.

2) Re-confirm that the team are happy with the assessment criteria and the weightings that will be used. In addition, you should ensure there is some element of cost/benefit assessment within the criteria.

3) Facilitate the team's scoring of the solutions, ensuring that a consensus is reached. Calculate the Final Weighted Scores and Overall Rankings.

4) Reality Check! You should verify that the team are all happy that the solution selected using the Prioritisation Matrix is the right one.

Where do the weighting figures come from?

The weighting figures are calculated from the multi-voting system described on page 233. For example, the weighting for the first criteria (which was *'can be implemented quickly'*) is calculated as follows:

$$\frac{\text{Weighted Total}}{\text{Total Available}} = \frac{45}{500} = 0.09$$

Criteria	Can be implemented quickly	Will solve the problem fully	Costs less than 100K Euros	Won't impact the customer	No regulatory risks	Final Weighted Score	Overall Ranking
Weighting	0.09	0.48	0.13	0.21	0.09		
Solution A	8	4	8	7	1	5.24	4th
Solution B	8	7	9	6	5	6.96	1st
Solution C	4	9	4	3	7	6.46	2nd
Solution D	4	5	3	10	4	5.61	3rd

How are the Final Weighted Scores calculated?

The final score for each of the solutions is the sum of each individual score multiplied by the weighting for that criteria. For example:

Solution A Final Weighted Score =

$(0.09 \times 8) + (0.48 \times 4) + (0.13 \times 8) + (0.21 \times 7) + (0.09 \times 1)$ **= 5.24**

Pugh Matrix

A Pugh Matrix is not only a method of **selecting** a solution, but a method for further **developing** and **refining** the potential solutions together, so that a '*best of all worlds*' solution can be found.

The Pugh Matrix works by comparing the different solutions against a chosen standard (in this case Solution C) for each assessment criteria. Further solutions can then be developed by mixing the positive aspects of a number of solutions, as described below:

How to complete a Pugh Matrix:

1) Finalise (with your team) the selection of solutions, assessment criteria and weightings that you will include in your matrix.

2) Choose a solution that will be your 'standard' for comparison.

3) Compare each solution against the standard for each criteria, making a note of whether you think it is better, the same, or worse in that respect.

4) Calculate the Weighted Sums (positive and negative) for each solution.

5) Focusing on the strongest solutions, look for opportunities to combine the best aspects of different solutions.

6) If required, re-run the Pugh Matrix again with the new solutions.

How to calculate the Weighted Sums:

The Weighted Sum of Positives is calculated by multiplying each positive sign by its weighting, as follows:

For Solution A: $(1 \times 1) + (1 \times 1) + (1 \times 2)$ **= 4**

The Weighted Sum of Negatives is calculated in a similar method.

Key:

+ = Better than standard
S = Same as standard
- = Worse than standard

Criteria	Solution A	Solution B	Solution C	Solution D	Weighting
Can be implemented quickly	+	+	S	S	1
Will solve the problem fully	-	S	S	-	5
Costs less than 100K Euros	+	+	S	S	1
Won't impact the customer	+	+	S	+	2
No regulatory risks	-	-	S	-	1
Weighted Sum of Positives	4	4		0	
Number of 'Sames'	0	1		2	
Weighted Sum of Negatives	-6	-1		-6	

Solution Screening

What is Solution Screening?
Solution Screening is a method of checking that the potential solutions developed during the Improve phase still meet the basic requirements of the project goal. It should be used as a final sanity check before selecting the solution(s).

A list of screening criteria are developed that reflect the basic requirements of the project goal, such as:

- Will the solution eliminate the root cause of the problem?
- Is the solution likely to be effective?
- Will the customer accept the solution?
- Will the solution be accepted by the business?
- Is the solution capable of becoming 'business as usual'? (see standardised processes, page 266).

Solution Screening is just one of a selection of tools that can be used during the Improve phase to help ensure that the solutions developed will be effective.

Affinity diagrams (p112) and fishbone diagrams (p111) can also be used to help organise and develop the ideas developed from chain letters or billboards (p231). Team voting can then be used to narrow down ideas, with solution screening providing a final check. Finally, pilot studies (opposite) can be used to check the effectiveness of a solution in practice, before full implementation.

Pilot Studies

What is a Pilot Study?
A pilot study is a localised, controlled trial of a solution in order to test its effectiveness before full implementation. There are many advantages to completing a pilot study, including:

- It validates the effectiveness of the solution.
- It promotes buy-in from key stakeholders.
- The final solution can be optimised (fine tuned) from the lessons learnt during the pilot study.
- Valuable implementation lessons can be learnt during the pilot study and incorporated into the full roll out plan.
- The risks and costs associated with a pilot study (versus full implementation) are low.
- The effectiveness of the solution can be measured, and checked against the goal statement or predicted results.

Planning a pilot study:

- **Where?** The scope and area of the pilot study should be chosen carefully and be as representative of the wider process as possible.
- **When?** The timeframe of the pilot study must be sufficient for the process to respond to the solutions implemented, and should also be clearly communicated to key stakeholders.
- **How?** A detailed data collection plan must be in place in order to capture the results of the pilot study. The amount of data must also be sufficient to reach statistically valid conclusions (see page 53).

Single Minute Exchange of Dies (SMED)

What is Single Minute Exchange of Dies (SMED)?

SMED is an approach that reduces set-up times. By reducing set-up times, the total changeover time involved with changing from one type of product or service to another, is also reduced. Although the acronym refers to the exchange of dies, it's worth noting that SMED techniques can be applied to all types of processes – you don't have to be changing dies!

Defining set-up time:

In practice, set-up time is measured as the total time it takes to changeover between products, since this is what is important from a production viewpoint. So, set-up time is measured from the last good part, to the first good part of the new product, as shown below:

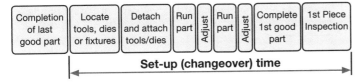

The benefits of SMED:

Reducing set-up times provides a range of benefits, including:

- **Flexibility** – fast changeovers enable organisations to rapidly respond to changes in customer demand.

- **Quicker delivery** – fast changeovers enable smaller production lot sizes, which means total lead time can be reduced for all products.

- **Better quality** – SMED reduces set up errors and adjustments.

- **Higher productivity** – faster changeovers enable more production time.

How to deliver SMED improvements:

A SMED programme should focus on bottleneck processes first, because they limit the overall production output. The set-up activities should be reviewed and categorised as either internal or external, as follows:

- **Internal activities** can <u>only</u> be performed when the process is stopped.

- **External activities** <u>can</u> be performed while the process is running.

SMED is then approached in three distinct steps, as follows:

1) Separate the internal and external tasks: Internal and external tasks should be identified and grouped together. The external tasks should then be completed while the process is still running.

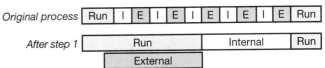

2) Convert internal tasks to external: A detailed review of the internal tasks will identify some that could be completed externally.

3) Change the internal and external tasks: Finally, it might be possible to redesign internal and external tasks, so that they can be completed more quickly, perhaps through redesigning tools and fixtures.

Total Productive Maintenance (TPM)

What is Total Productive Maintenance (TPM)?

TPM is a proactive approach to maintenance that aims to eliminate unplanned downtime and maximise equipment effectiveness. Traditionally, only maintenance workers are responsible for maintenance. Under TPM, all workers are responsible for continuous maintenance activities that are preventative rather than reactive. TPM activities can be divided into four key areas, as shown here:

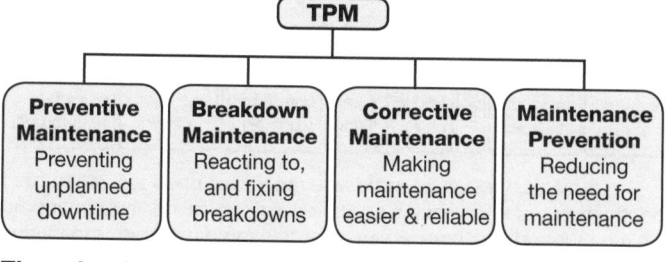

The role of the operator:

TPM relies heavily on operators, who take on the responsibility for maintaining their own equipment (known as Autonomous Maintenance). Through regular cleaning and inspection, operators are ideally placed to identify abnormalities early. With the support of maintenance specialists, issues can then be managed through planned maintenance, preventing an unplanned breakdown at a later stage.

Overall Equipment Effectiveness (OEE):

OEE is a measure that reflects the actual effectiveness of a piece of equipment (the calculation of OEE is explained in detail on page 39). It measures all losses, including those linked to equipment reliability, and provides a key measure for measuring the success of a TPM programme.

TPM versus Traditional Maintenance:

The diagram below represents a typical manufacturing shift under a traditional maintenance environment. The total production time available (6 hours) is significantly shorter than the 8 hour shift, because of a variety of reasons, that can be categorised into 6 key types:

- Breakdowns
- Slow cycle times
- Defects
- Set-ups
- Unplanned slowdowns/stoppages
- Start up losses

A traditional manufacturing shift:

| Begin shift | Quality issues | Minor stoppages | Set up | Minor stoppage | End shift |

Total time available = 6 hours
Shift = 8 hours

The diagram below demonstrates the intention of TPM, where a shift has two key planned stoppages, including planned routine maintenance at the end of the shift.

A TPM shift:

Daily production meeting   Cleaning and lubrication

Total time available = 7 hrs, 40 mins
Shift = 8 hours

Kanban

What is a Kanban?

A Kanban is a method of physically controlling the level and flow of the inventory that exists within a production system. A specific number of Kanban cards are used, and all inventory must be accompanied by a Kanban card. In addition, processes can only produce parts when there are unused Kanban cards available to accompany those parts. So, a Kanban system helps to control overall inventory levels, since unless a Kanban card is available, parts cannot be produced.

Moving from push to pull:

There are other advantages of a Kanban system too. Traditional production systems generally work on a 'push' basis. In other words, raw materials and parts are 'pushed' through the production system, according to a production schedule that is not directly linked to actual customer demand. Combined with poor quality, long changeovers and poor process reliability, traditional production systems typically over-produce parts 'just in case', creating high inventory levels and waste at every process step.

Kanban systems help to move to a 'pull' system, because parts are only produced when a Kanban card is available. When a customer 'demands' a product, then each previous process step responds by replenishing inventory levels. So, in effect, parts are 'pulled' through the process by customer demand, rather than being pushed by production schedules.

Two key types of Kanbans:

Production and Withdrawal Kanbans are the main two main types of Kanbans (see next page for more detail). Production Kanbans are used at process steps and for re-order points with customers. Withdrawal Kanbans are used between processes and for suppliers.

Key rules for a successful Kanban system:

- Kanbans work best where customer demand is relatively stable.
- The number of Kanban cards should be minimised whilst supporting expected demand rates (see page 242 for example calculations).
- The quantity of parts in each container should be minimised.
- Nothing should be produced or moved without a Kanban card.
- Bad parts should never be passed on.

What does a Kanban card look like?

An example of Production Kanban card is shown below. It details the part, the process step, and the quantity of parts that should be contained within each lot.

KANBAN CARD	
Part Number : 656-755-88B	
Description: Cables for Main Board	
Product Name: ELC-869	**Lot Quantity:** 30 (3 batches of 10)
Cont #: 2 of 3	
From: Warehouse	**To:** Final Assembly

Kanban System Flow

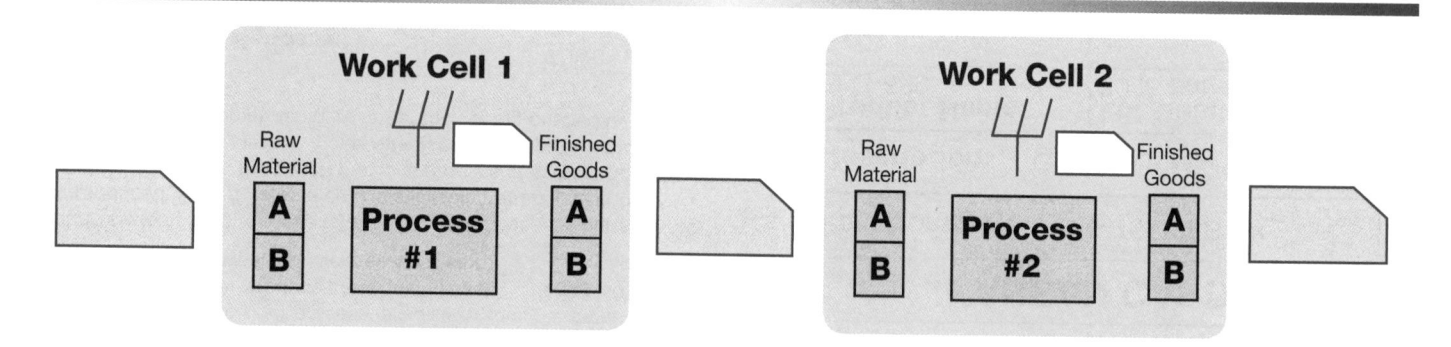

Two key types of Kanban:

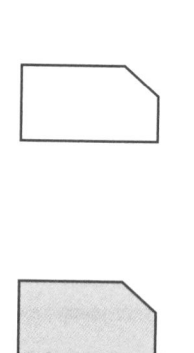

1) Production Kanbans control the actual production of products/parts. Production cannot take place unless there is a Production Kanban card available in the rack. The Production Kanban cards specify the type and quantity of parts that can be produced. When all the Production Kanban cards are attached to finished goods, production stops.

2) Withdrawal Kanbans control the movement of production parts from one work cell to the next. Parts can only be 'pulled' (taken) from the finished inventory of a previous process if there is a Withdrawal Kanban card available.

The flow of a Kanban system:

The steps below describe how the Withdrawal Kanban works between Processes 1 and 2 above, and how the Production Kanban for Work Cell 1 then replenishes the inventory that has moved on to Work Cell 2:

1) As parts are taken from the Raw Material at Work Cell 2, their Withdrawal Kanban cards are removed and retained.

2) Having available Withdrawal Kanban cards indicates that the Raw Material stocks at Work Cell 2 should be replenished from Work Cell 1.

3) As Finished Goods are taken from Work Cell 1, the Production Kanban cards from Work Cell 1 are removed (and returned to the Kanban rack in Work Cell 1) and replaced with the available Withdrawal Kanban cards.

4) The Production Kanban cards in the rack in Work Cell 1 indicate that parts should be produced to replenish the Finished Goods in Work Cell 1. They specify the type and quantity to be produced (see previous page).

Kanban – Card Calculations

How to calculate how many Kanban cards you need:

A key element of a Kanban based production system is how many cards are used within each individual Kanban. In setting the number of Kanban cards, it should be remembered that the aim of a Kanban system is to reduce inventory (Work in Progress).

So, while a high number of Kanban cards would reduce the risk of running out of stock, it would also lead to unnecessarily high inventory levels. Instead the number of Kanban cards should be calculated to minimise inventory, while ensuring that the risk of running out of stock is also carefully managed. The following equation takes account of these factors:

$$\text{Number of Kanban cards} = \frac{\text{ADD} \times \text{RT} \times (1 + \text{Safety Factor})}{\text{Standard Container Quantity}}$$

ADD: The Average Daily Demand (per day/hour/shift).

RT: Replenishment Time is the total time it takes to complete the single Kanban re-supply process, including the time for the signal to be sent and received, material to be queued, and parts built, transported and stored ready for use. Note that this time must be in the same units as the ADD.

Safety Factor: This optional additional multiplier creates additional capacity within the Kanban to allow for variations in demand or supply replenishment. While a safety factor might be necessary, it should be kept to a minimal level to avoid introducing excessive inventory.

Standard Container Quantity: The number of parts in a standard lot.

Kanban Example:

A Kaizen project team have decided to implement a Kanban system in order to move to a pull system and reduce inventory. The calculations of the Kanban size for one of the process steps are as follows:

Average Daily Demand: The average demand rate is *160 units per hour,* although there is some fluctuation in this.

Replenishment Time: The time it takes to re-supply a single Kanban, from signal to stock being ready for use, is 3 hours.

Safety Factor: In order to cope with the expected variations in demand, a safety factor of 0.5 has been chosen. This means that the Kanban will be 50% larger than is theoretically necessary. If, after the process has been running for sometime, the Kanban has never run nearly low, then this safety factor could potentially be reduced.

Standard Container Quantity: The lot size will be 40.

Calculating the Number of Kanbans (size):

$$\text{Number of Kanbans} = \frac{160 \times 3 \times (1 + 0.5)}{40}$$

$$= 720 / 40$$

$$= 18$$

The team implement a Kanban with 18 cards, and review periodically.

One-Piece Flow

What is One-Piece Flow?

One-Piece Flow refers to a system in which products (or services) are processed individually and flow between process steps without waiting.

As shown in the diagram below, this is the opposite of a traditional 'batch production' system, in which products (or services) are processed as batches and then stored between process steps as they wait to move on to the next step for processing.

The benefits of One-Piece Flow:

- Reduced response (lead) times and higher on-time delivery.
- Increased flexibility and productivity.
- Lower inventory (WIP) and associated storage space.
- Improved quality.

How to create One-Piece Flow:

Before implementing One-Piece Flow, you should consider whether it is suitable. Existing issues such as long changeover times, high scrap rates or excessive downtime may mean that it is more practical to move to 'fast lot production' first, as an interim step towards One-Piece Flow.

There are two key stages to creating One-Piece Flow, as follows:

1) Understanding the current state through tools such as Value Stream Mapping, in order to measure customer demand (i.e. Takt time) and identify the value add steps.

2) Designing the future state with balanced process steps (designed around the Takt time), non-value add steps removed and utilising efficient production cell layout in order to improve flow. U or C shape production cells reinforce One-Piece Flow by removing inventory stations and arranging all processes in sequence.

From traditional batch production...

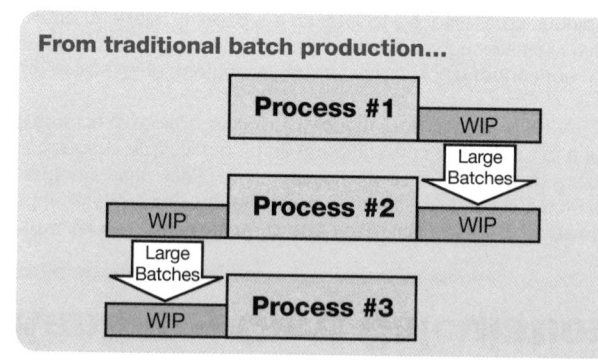

To One-Piece Flow...

Raw Material	Process #1	Process #2	Process #3	Finished Goods

Continuous One Piece Flow →

5S (a.k.a. Good Housekeeping!)

The 5S tool provides a useful structure for improving workplace environments, but the real benefits arise when excellent housekeeping becomes embedded as a key priority in an organisation's culture.

Why is housekeeping so important?

If you visit an office or manufacturing plant that has a proven track record of high quality and safety, you will often notice how clean and tidy everything is. This is no coincidence! Good housekeeping is both an indicator and a propagator of quality and safety. It both underpins and reflects a culture where procedures are followed, processes carefully controlled, quality and safety are respected and employees at all levels are motivated and diligent.

What is 5S?

5S provides a structured approach to improving and maintaining workplace housekeeping. As the name suggests, it involves 5 steps (described here on the right) that all start with S. While 5S is often categorised as part of the Kaizen and Lean toolkits, good housekeeping should be viewed as an essential priority for everyone in all industries (regardless of whether they use Lean or Six Sigma techniques). In particular, this is because good housekeeping practices are essential for safe working environments.

Service versus manufacturing environments:

5S is one of the Kaizen tools that is also immediately relevant to the service sector. The process of removing clutter and maintaining organised workplaces through improved systems and changed culture can be applied to offices, hotels, restaurants, and call centres through to computer hard drives, email accounts and databases.

Sort (Seiri): Get rid of the clutter! The objective of this first step is to de-clutter by ensuring that only items that are needed regularly are kept in the immediate workplace. Everything else is removed (obsolete items thrown away, infrequently used items archived, broken items fixed). Red tags can be used to track if specific items are ever used, and if so by who.

Straighten (Seiton): Find everything a place! The work environment is then organised so that everything has a defined place and the most frequently used items are most at hand, promoting efficiency. Labels are used to identify objects/areas and to communicate the system.

Shine (Seisō): Keep everything clean and tidy! Maintaining the new workplace organisation needs to be part of a routine. While employees should aim to keep things organised all of the time, many organisations also have regular, routine clear ups (e.g. at the end of each shift) that ensure the workplace is routinely put back in order.

Standardise (Seiketsu): Develop a system! The newly organised workplace needs to be integrated into the organisations systems (i.e. through written procedures, job descriptions, responsibility charts etc.)

Sustain (Shitsuke): Keep it going! Sustained senior level commitment to good housekeeping and safety through 'leading by doing' is the only way to support lasting behavioural change at all levels.

! 5S is not just about having a good old clean up!

Visual Management

Visual Management refers to the use of graphical methods to display and communicate how a workplace or process is managed, controlled and performing, in real-time wherever possible.

Just as graphs can make it easier to understand data, and graphical road signs are easier to understand than written ones, visual techniques can be very effective in improving performance and safety.

Visual Management encompasses a wide range of techniques that help make all aspects of a workplace, and the processes that take place within it, more visually apparent. It includes visual techniques that help to:

- Organise the workplace.
- Control and standardise process inputs.
- Manage the storage and flow of products/services.
- Monitor processes (often in real time).
- Communicate process performance.
- Improve safety.

Visual Management and Lean Six Sigma:

Visual Management integrates with many components of a Lean Six Sigma improvement programme, and can be used to:

- Improve housekeeping as part of a 5S program.
- Increase quality as part of an error proofing programme.
- Minimise Work In Progress through visual Kanbans.
- Reduce accidents as part of a safety programme.
- Improve control through visual, real time dashboards.

Visual Management examples in the service sector:

- A check sheet in a restaurant restroom that indicates when they were last cleaned, and by whom.

- A sign in a hotel lobby that tells you;
  'Your shift manager today is...'

- The colour coding of storage containers in hotel kitchens that indicate different food types (e.g. raw and cooked meat).

- *'Keep clear'* floor markings for access to fire exits and extinguishers.

- A sign that displays *'Currently serving number...'* at the supermarket delicatessen.

- A display board in a call centre (see below) that shows real time information and performance data such as the incoming call rate, the number of calls currently queuing, answer time performance etc.

Visual Management (cont.)

Visual Management examples in manufacturing:

- **Andon lights** can be installed on production machines to indicate their current status. Each colour on the light represents a particular state (e.g. operating, stopped, maintenance, error, awaiting parts etc.).

- **Visual standards** such as photos of good and bad parts can be used to improve defect detection rates and enable more consistent inspection decisions (i.e. higher GR&R – see page 58).

- **Process indicators:** Colour coding (e.g. Red/Amber/Green) can be applied to gauges or other measuring devices in order to monitor (visually) whether critical process inputs are within an acceptable or safe range.

- **Area information boards** are useful in communicating updates on projects, personnel, quality issues, housekeeping and performance.

- **Kanban cards:** A Kanban system (see p240 for more detail) provides a visual method of inventory control and supports a pull (versus push) approach to production scheduling. Typically, Kanban cards are attached to production containers and unused Kanban cards are stored in a Kanban rack, which then provides a visual summary of how much inventory exists (lots of Kanban cards in the rack means that there are not many containers of parts in stock, and vice versa).

- **Floor markings** can be used to improve workplace layout and management and to secure safety critical areas.

- **Transparent machine covers and guards** enable operators and maintenance teams to see processes working (which in turn means that processes are stopped less frequently).

Visual Tool Control:
The toolbox shown below has shaped cut-outs for specific tools with integral labels and coloured background foam. This ensures that the tools are protected, kept clean, identified clearly and that any missing tools are immediately obvious.

This visual approach helps to improve tool control, supports good housekeeping and reduces the risk of '*Foreign Object Damage*' (tools left in machinery during routine maintenance activities).

In addition, colour coded sleeving can be applied to the tools themselves, identifying all of the tools within a particular kit (or that belong to a particular team/area) with the same colour. This can help to reduce time spent looking for lost tools, in turn reducing equipment repair times etc.

Improve – Checklist

- ☐ Have alternative improvement ideas been generated for each of the root causes?

- ☐ Have structured techniques been used to ensure that the alternative improvement ideas are innovative and will create a step change in performance?

- ☐ Have the improvement ideas been assessed and compared using relevant criteria such as ease, speed, cost, benefit etc.?

- ☐ Before implementing improvements, have the risks been assessed in a structured way (e.g. FMEA)?

- ☐ Have the improvements been proven in pilot studies before full implementation (if appropriate)?

- ☐ Have the improvements been fully implemented and become *'business as usual'*?

- ☐ Have the KPIs been monitored and the performance improved?

- ☐ Have the improvements in the KPIs been validated graphically and statistically?

Improve – Review Questions

- How were the different improvement ideas generated?

- Who was involved in this process?

- How were the potential improvement ideas assessed and compared?

- How were the risks of the various improvement ideas assessed?

- Why did you choose your selected improvements?

- How much of an improvement is expected from the selected solutions?

- Were the solutions piloted before full implementation? If so, where, when, how, and why? etc.

- When was the full implementation? Is it still ongoing?

- How was the full implementation managed? (Project planning etc.)

- Has the process improved? Can we see the KPI charts?

- Has the goal statement been achieved?

- How are the KPIs being monitored and reviewed?

Control – Overview

The Control phase aims to ensure that the solutions that have been implemented become embedded into the process, so that the improvements will be sustained after the project has been closed.

The flow through Control:

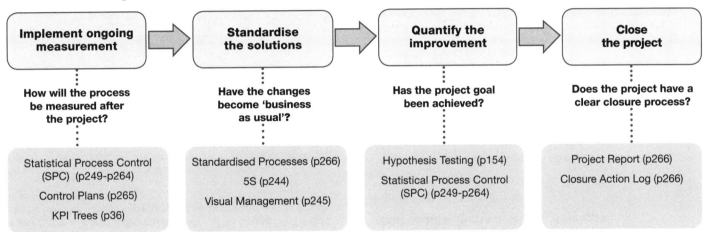

Implement ongoing measurement	Standardise the solutions	Quantify the improvement	Close the project
How will the process be measured after the project?	Have the changes become 'business as usual'?	Has the project goal been achieved?	Does the project have a clear closure process?
Statistical Process Control (SPC) (p249-p264) Control Plans (p265) KPI Trees (p36)	Standardised Processes (p266) 5S (p244) Visual Management (p245)	Hypothesis Testing (p154) Statistical Process Control (SPC) (p249-p264)	Project Report (p266) Closure Action Log (p266)

Ongoing measurement of the process:
Processes must have rigorous data collection systems in place before a project can be closed. This involves defining who is responsible for collecting and reviewing the data, as well as ensuring that the measurements have been integrated into the organisation's KPI Trees and dashboards.

Closing projects is a critical element of a successful Lean Six Sigma programme. There are often opportunities to apply the lessons learnt from projects to different areas of the business, which requires clear action plans and a 'knowledge management' approach to documenting projects.

Statistical Process Control – Overview

Statistical Process Control (SPC) charts are essentially a sophisticated form of Time Series plot that enable the stability of the process, and the type of variation involved, to be understood.

The traditional role of SPC charts is that of a real time process tracking tool in a production environment. In Six Sigma, SPC charts can be used for a much wider range of purposes and are applicable to all industries.

An example of an SPC chart is shown below. It plots the performance of a process over time and shows the control limits (not specification limits) that the results will fall within, if the process is stable and 'in-control'.

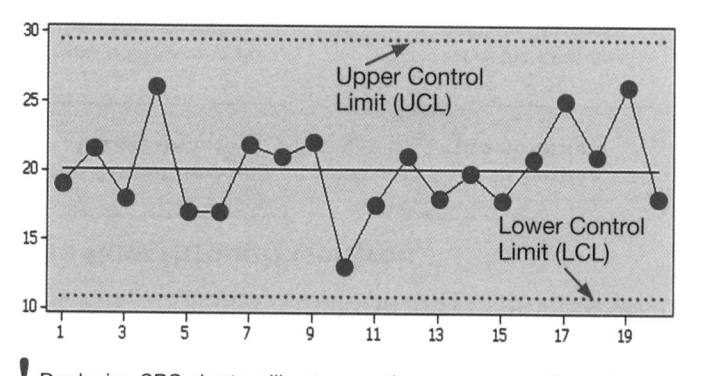

! Deploying SPC charts will not mean that processes will suddenly become 'in-control'. What they can do however, is help you to measure and understand processes, and provide a rigorous approach for deciding when a process has changed and/or needs intervention.

What do SPC charts detect?... Changes!

- Changes in process average.
- Changes in process variation.
- One-off changes such as special causes.

These changes are explained further on the next page.

When are SPC charts used?

Because of their name, SPC charts are usually placed within the Control phase of Six Sigma, where they are used for **Ongoing Control;** the real time analysis of process performance that aims to detect and react to process changes.

However, they are useful throughout the Measure and Analyse phases as well, where they can be used for **Historical Analysis;** the analysis of historical data to assess process stability.

These two approaches are explained further on page 252.

! **SPC Charts need maintenance!**
SPC control limits require regular review in order to make them relevant and meaningful. This in turn requires a quality control system to be in place, to control the review process itself.

What do SPC Charts Detect?... Changes!

There are many types of changes that can occur in a process, but they can usually be characterised as one of (or a combination of) the following three different types of change:

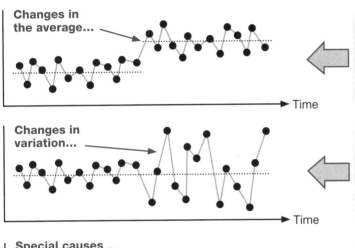

Changes in the average...

A change in process average:
The time series chart to the left shows a clear increase in the process average. While this example is visually very obvious, SPC charts can detect much smaller changes that wouldn't normally be obvious to the human eye. This might represent an uncontrolled change in the process or be the result of a deliberate improvement to the process.

Changes in variation...

A change in process variation:
The time series chart to the left shows a clear increase in the amount of variation in the process (note that the average doesn't necessarily change). Again, this example shows a very marked change, but SPC charts can detect much smaller changes in variation that wouldn't normally be obvious.

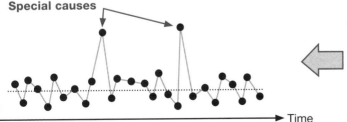

Special causes

One-off events (Special Causes):
The time series plot to the left appears to be relatively stable and 'in-control' (see process stability on p79), with the exception of two points that are significantly higher than the rest. These two points are known as special causes because they fall outside of the expected variation range of the process, and are therefore likely to be as a result of a specific 'special cause'. SPC charts help to detect these special causes, which can then be investigated to identify their root cause.

How do SPC Charts Detect Changes?

As shown in the SPC Routemap on page 253, there are a range of SPC charts to choose from depending on the application and type of data. However, they all work in roughly the same way, as follows:

1) The performance of the process is plotted as a Time Series plot.

2) The level of (historical) variation in the process is assessed.

3) Control Limits are drawn on the plot based on the variation measured.

4) Each data point on the chart is then assessed against a number of tests (see below for more detail on the tests).

5) Any data points that fail the tests are highlighted for investigation.

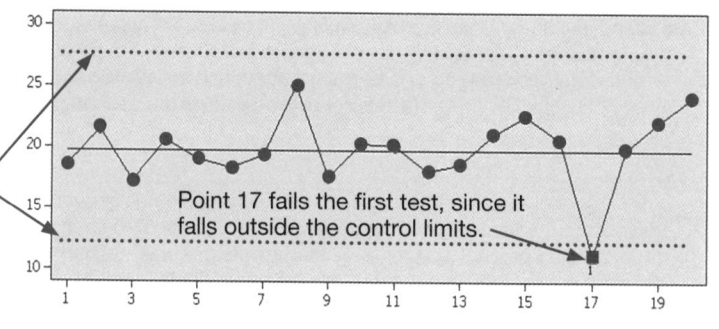

Point 17 fails the first test, since it falls outside the control limits.

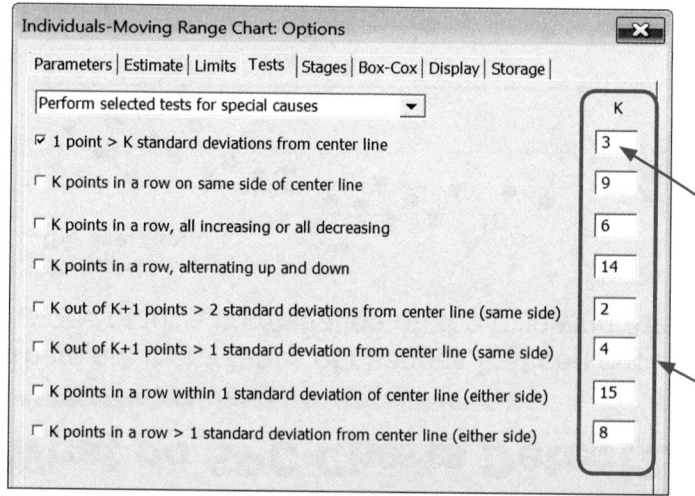

SPC Chart Tests are designed so that they are **unlikely** to be broken if the process has **not** changed. Each type of SPC chart has a set of tests (found under Minitab's Options) that are applied to each data point.

There are 8 tests for the 'Individuals' type of SPC chart shown above, and the Minitab Options screen that lists the tests is shown on the left.

The first most common test is that if any of the data points fall outside of the Control Limits (+/- 3 Standard Deviations) then they are considered to be 'special causes'. As an example, data point 17 on the chart above fails this test. The remainder of the tests are more complex, but all of them are designed to detect changes in the process.

The tests can be customised in Minitab by modifying the K values shown here. So, the first test **could** be changed to detect single data points outside of two standard deviations from the centre line, by changing the K value to two. However, if in any doubt, these K values should be left at their default levels shown here.

When are SPC Charts Used?

Historical Analysis:

SPC Charts can be used in the Measure and Analyse phases to understand how the process has been behaving in the past. They help to assess whether the process was stable or not and the type of variation that was present (i.e. common or special cause – p79), which both have implications for the type of changes that will be required to improve the process.

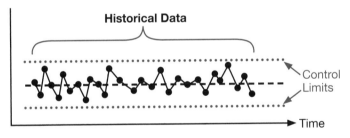

In this case, the control limits are set up based upon **all** the data points that are in the chart (i.e. all the historical data).

Ongoing Control:

Once the process has been improved, the Control phase aims to ensure the improved process is reviewed on an ongoing basis to check that the process performance does not deteriorate again. SPC charts can be used for this purpose since they provide a clear indication of whether the process has changed or not.

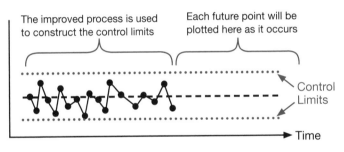

In this case the control limits are set up based upon the **improved process** data that you have, and are extrapolated forward. Each future result is then assessed against those control limits.

All of the different types of SPC charts described on the subsequent pages have the ability to be used both for Historical Analysis or for Ongoing Control. If required for Ongoing Control, the statistics of the improved process are entered manually into Minitab (as an average or standard deviation for example) and Minitab then sets up the future control limits based on these statistics.

Statistical Process Control – Routemap

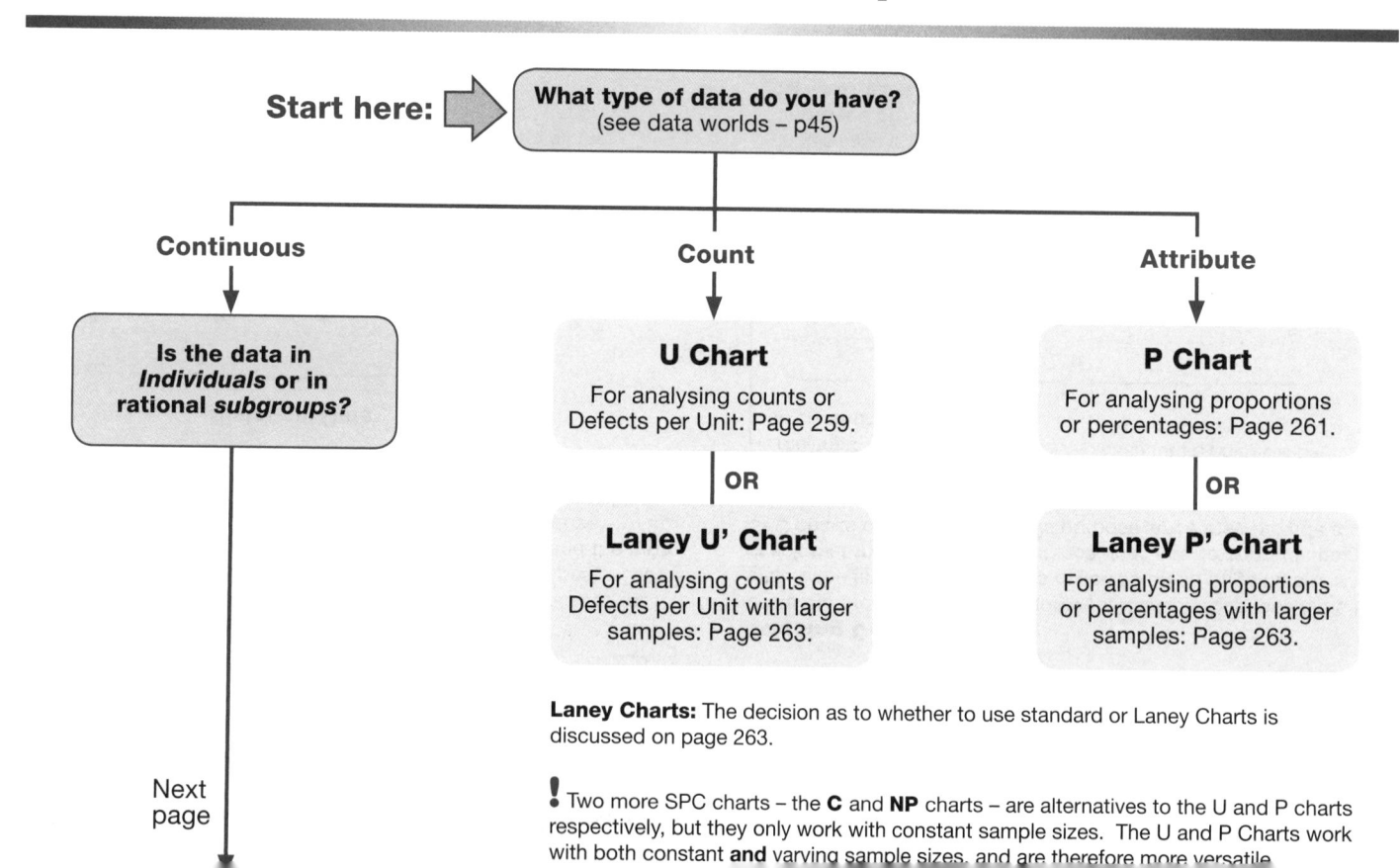

Start here: → **What type of data do you have?**
(see data worlds – p45)

Continuous

Is the data in *Individuals* or in rational *subgroups*?

Next page

Count

U Chart

For analysing counts or Defects per Unit: Page 259.

OR

Laney U' Chart

For analysing counts or Defects per Unit with larger samples: Page 263.

Attribute

P Chart

For analysing proportions or percentages: Page 261.

OR

Laney P' Chart

For analysing proportions or percentages with larger samples: Page 263.

Laney Charts: The decision as to whether to use standard or Laney Charts is discussed on page 263.

❗ Two more SPC charts – the **C** and **NP** charts – are alternatives to the U and P charts respectively, but they only work with constant sample sizes. The U and P Charts work with both constant **and** varying sample sizes, and are therefore more versatile

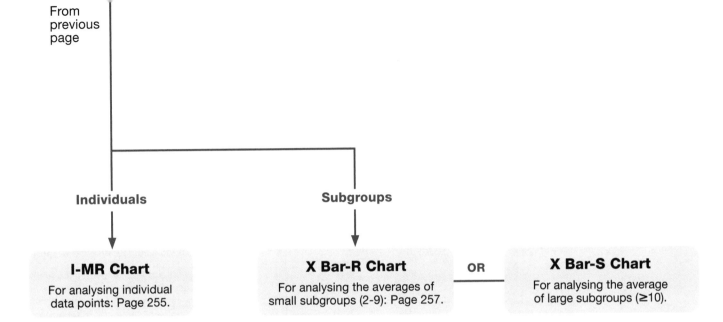

I-MR Chart (Individual - Moving Range) – Data Input

I-MR Charts are for use with Continuous data that does not have any rational subgroups. In other words, all the data points have been collected individually.

❗ I-MR Charts work best with data that is Normally distributed. If your data is Non-Normal, then the I-MR chart may produce invalid results because some of the tests will be failed when they should not be. You could try using an XBar-R Chart, which works with Non-Normal data because it plots averages, not individual data points.

Example: A building materials company is investigating the amount of sand its filling process puts into each bag. A data file containing the historical data of 50 bags is available to help understand if the process is 'in-control' (stable).

The **Scale, Labels** and **Multiple Graphs** functions all contain self explanatory options for the formatting of your graphs and are normally left as default.

Data Options allows you to use only a specific set of rows from your data in the I-MR chart.

Minitab: Stat > Control Charts > Variables Charts for Individuals > I-MR

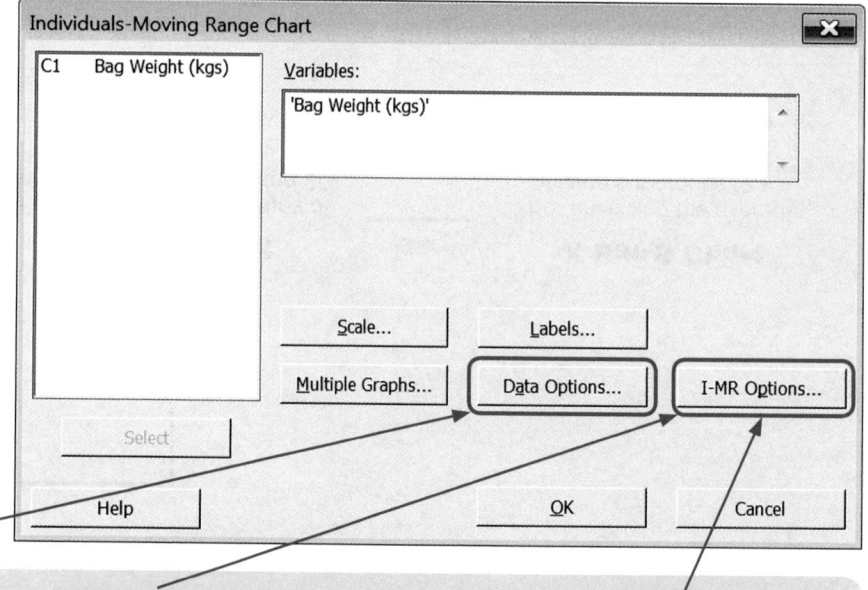

I-MR Options contains several important settings that control how the I-MR chart is completed. The two most commonly used, **Parameters** and **Tests** are described in more detail here.

I-MR Options > Parameters gives the option of manually entering the average and standard deviation of the process. If this is done, then the I-MR will use these values to construct the control limits, instead of calculating them from the data. Page 257 gives an example that uses this option.

I-MR Options > Tests allows the selection of the statistical tests that will be used (see page 251). If in doubt, select **Perform all tests.**

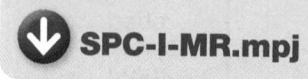

SPC-I-MR.mpj

I-MR Chart (Individual - Moving Range) – Output

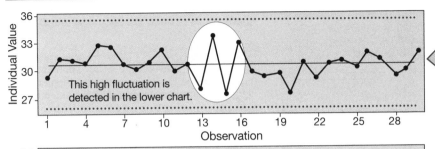

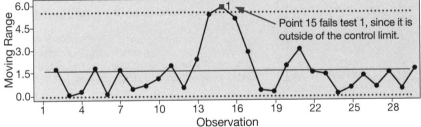

I-MR Charts are a combination of two SPC charts, as shown on the left and described below.

The Individuals (I) chart (top) shows a Time Series plot of the data with control limits. The control limits are set at +/- 3 Sigma (3 standard deviations) away from the average (middle line).

On this chart, the process appears to be stable around about 31 kilos, and it does not go outside of the control limits. Accordingly, none of SPC tests (p251) have been broken.

The Moving Range (MR) chart (bottom) shows the moving range of the data in the top chart. So for example, data point 3 on the lower chart is the range (the difference) between data points 2 and 3 on the top chart, and so on.

The range of a process is a reflection of the amount of variation in the process, and so an MR chart can be useful for detecting changes in variation (but not for detecting changes in average).

On the MR chart shown here, the process variation appears relatively stable, with some exceptions around point 15, which highlights a temporary increase in the process variation (not average) on the top chart (highlighted).

Example: As explained on the page above, these charts represent the weight of sand in a sample of 50 bags at a building materials company.

The top chart indicates the process average is stable, because none of the tests are failed. However, data point 15 on the lower **Moving Range** chart has failed a test because it is outside of the control limits. This indicates a local increase in range (variation), which can actually be observed in the top chart – where there is a large fluctuation (highlighted).

So, although the **average** is stable, there is an indication that the **variation** is not.

SPC-I-MR.mpj

X Bar-R Chart (Average - Range) – Data Input

X Bar-R Charts are used with small subgroups of Continuous data. Unlike I-MR charts, the raw data does not have to be Normally distributed for X Bar-R charts.

Example: A share trading company has completed a project that has reduced the average time it takes for its share/stock instructions to be traded, down to an average of 20.6 minutes.

They are now monitoring the new, improved process by randomly selecting five consecutive trades each day and plotting them on an SPC chart to check for process changes.

The X Bar-R chart is a suitable choice of chart because they have small subgroups of Continuous data being collected over a longer time period.

This particular example is using the SPC chart for 'ongoing control' purposes (as explained on p252), and therefore the control limits on the chart need to be set around the new average of 20.6 minutes, as described here:

! **Sub-group size does not need to be constant.**
This example has a constant subgroup size of 5, but the XBar-R chart can deal with subgroup sizes that change.

SPC-XBar-R.mpj

Minitab: Stat > Control Charts > Variables Charts for Subgroups > Xbar-R

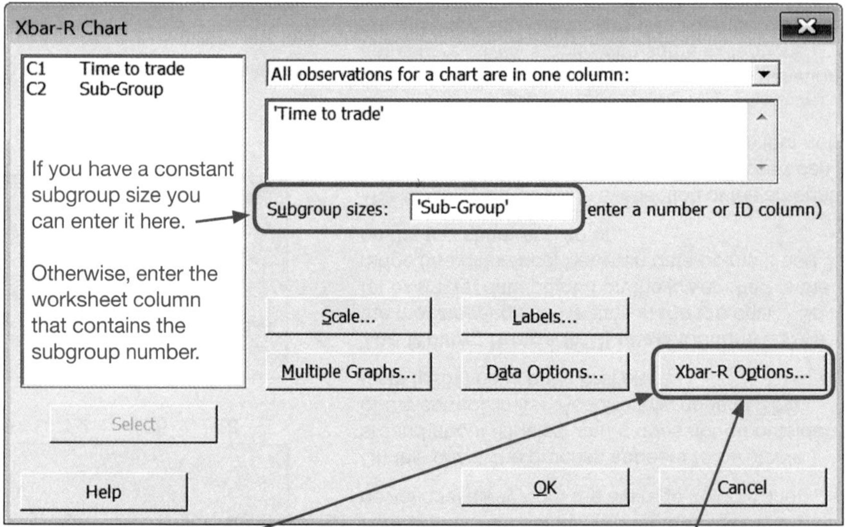

Xbar-R Chart

| C1 | Time to trade |
| C2 | Sub-Group |

All observations for a chart are in one column: ▼

'Time to trade'

If you have a constant subgroup size you can enter it here. →

Subgroup sizes: 'Sub-Group'   (enter a number or ID column)

Otherwise, enter the worksheet column that contains the subgroup number.

Scale...   Labels...

Multiple Graphs...   Data Options...   Xbar-R Options...

Select

Help   OK   Cancel

Xbar-R Options > Parameters gives the option of manually entering the average and standard deviation of the process.

In this example the new, improved average of 20.6 can be entered, in order to centre the control limits on the chart around this value.

Xbar-R Options > Tests allows the selection of the statistical tests that will be used (see page 251).

If in doubt, select **Perform all tests**.

X Bar-R Chart (Average - Range) – Output

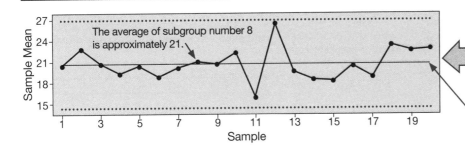

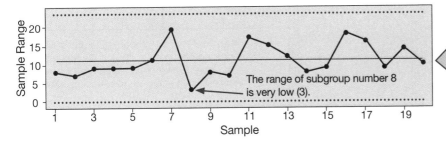

X Bar-R Charts are a combination of two SPC charts, as shown here on the left and described below.

The X Bar chart (top) shows a Time Series plot of the averages of the subgroups, with control limits. The control limits reflect the variation in the subgroup averages.

In this case, the average line is at 20.6 minutes, because this was defined at the data input stage (previous page). No tests have been failed, and so the process appears to be stable and does not appear to have moved from the new average trading time of 20.6 minutes.

The Range (R) chart (bottom) shows the range of the data that is within each subgroup.

The range of a process is a reflection of its variation and so the R chart can be useful to detect changes in variation, but it does not detect changes in average.

Subgroup 8 is explained in detail on the chart as an example.

Example: As explained on the page above, these charts represent the time taken from instruction to completion of a trade on the stock exchange.

No statistical tests have been failed on either chart, and so in this case, both the average and the variation of the process could be described as stable or in-control.

 **SPC XBar-R.mpj**

U Chart – Data Input

U Charts are for use with Count data, such as counting defects, counting phone calls, or counting hospital operations.

Example: A human resources department is looking at the number of internal applications they receive for each vacancy that they advertise.

They have 15 weeks of historical data available for analysis (sample shown below) in order to understand if the number of internal applications per vacancy is stable (in-control) or changing over time.

C1	C2	C3
Week Number	Number of applications	Number of posts advertised
1	12	4
2	13	6
3	1	2
4	6	3
5	6	5

❗ Subgroup size does not need to be constant.
The number of vacancies (posts) advertised each week is not constant, but the U Chart can accommodate this because it analyses the number of applications **per vacancy** (post).

 **SPC – U Chart.mpj**

Minitab: Stat > Control Charts > Attributes Charts > U

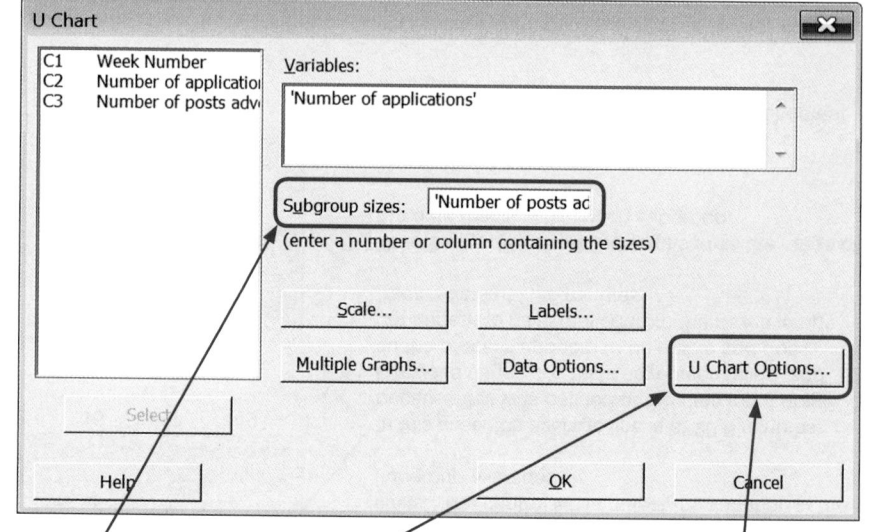

If you have a constant subgroup size, you can enter it here. Otherwise, enter the worksheet column that contains the subgroup number (C3 in this example).

U Chart Options > Parameters gives the option of manually entering the average Defects per Unit (DPU).

In this example, the SPC chart is being used to analyse historical data, so there is little reason to stipulate an average DPU.

U Chart Options > Tests allows the selection of the statistical tests that will be used (see page 251).

If in doubt, select **Perform all tests**

U Chart – Output

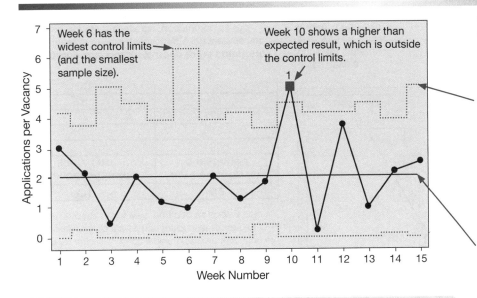

Week 6 has the widest control limits (and the smallest sample size).

Week 10 shows a higher than expected result, which is outside the control limits.

y-axis: Applications per Vacancy

x-axis: Week Number

The U Chart shows a Time Series plot of the average DPU (Defects per Unit), for each subgroup. In this example, the DPU is the number of internal applications per vacancy, and each subgroup represents a week.

Because the subgroup size (the number of vacancies posted each week) varies, the control limits adjust from week to week to reflect the different subgroup sizes.

For example, week 6 has the lowest sample size (only one vacancy was posted that week) and so the control limits expand to reflect this. This is because a much higher or lower result for week 6 is more likely given the low subgroup size.

The middle line is the overall average DPU. In this case the average number of internal applications per vacancy advertised, over the 15 week period, is 2.

Example: As explained on the previous page, this chart shows the average number of internal applications per vacancy advertised over a 15 week period.

The chart shows no clear rise or fall in the results, but week 10 shows an unexpectedly high result (outside of the control limits), which should be investigated further.

C Charts work in a similar way to U charts, but they require the subgroup size to be constant.

If the number of job vacancies posted was a constant number each week, then a C Chart **or** a U Chart could have been used.

SPC – U Chart.mpj

P Chart – Data Input

P Charts are for use with Attribute data (usually summarised as proportions or percentages).

Example:

A car breakdown service has noticed an increase in the proportion of vehicles that do not have a functional spare tyre over the summer months.

The team has 20 weeks of historical data from spring to autumn for analysis. Each week a random selection of drivers were asked if they had functional spare tyre in their car, and the result was recorded as shown below.

C1	C2
Number without spare tyre	**Number of drivers questioned**
7	59
5	47
7	48
6	67
10	46

! **Subgroup size does not need to be constant.**
The number of drivers questioned each week is not constant, but the P Chart can accommodate this because it analyses the **proportion** of cars without a spare tyre.

⬇ **SPC – P Chart.mpj**

Minitab: Stat > Control Charts > Attributes Charts > P

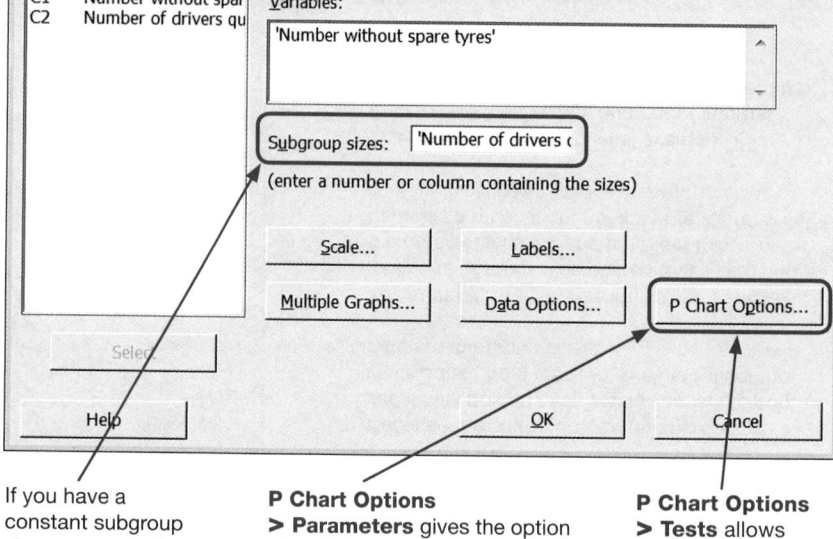

If you have a constant subgroup size, you can enter it here. Otherwise, enter the column that contains the subgroup number (C2 in this example).

P Chart Options > Parameters gives the option of manually entering the overall proportion. In this example, the SPC chart is being used to analyse historical data so there is little reason to enter an historical proportion value.

P Chart Options > Tests allows the selection of the statistical tests that will be used (see page 251). If in doubt, select **Perform all tests.**

P Chart – Output

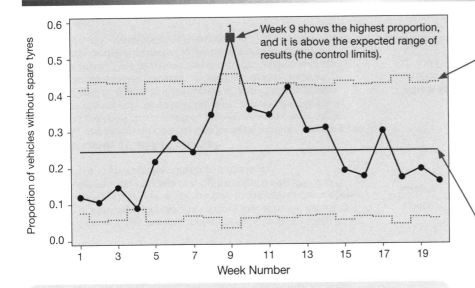

Week 9 shows the highest proportion, and it is above the expected range of results (the control limits).

Proportion of vehicles without spare tyres
Week Number

The P Chart shows a Time Series plot of the proportion for each subgroup (each week).

Because the subgroup/sample size (the number of drivers questioned) varies, the control limits adjust from week to week to reflect the different subgroup sizes.

For example, week 9 has the lowest subgroup size (only 38 drivers were questions that week) and so the control limits expand slightly to reflect this. This is because a much higher or lower result for week 9 is more likely, given the smaller subgroup. (Taken to an extreme, if only one driver were questioned, the result could only be 0% or 100%!)

The middle line is the overall proportion of vehicles without functional spare tyres (over the entire 20 week period), which in this case is 0.247 (24.7%).

Example: As explained on the page above, this chart shows the proportion of vehicles without functional spare tyres over a 20 week period. The chart shows a very clear rise and fall in the results which supports the team's original hypothesis that there is an increase in the proportion of vehicles without spare tyres during the summer months. This is supported (statistically) by the fact that the data point for week 9 is outside of the control limits.

NP Charts work in a similar way to P charts but they require the subgroup size to be constant.

If the number of drivers questioned each week had been the same, then an NP Chart **or** a P Chart could have been used.

 SPC – P Chart.mpj

Laney U' and P' Charts

The problem with standard U and P charts:

With larger sample sizes (particularly common in service environments), U and P charts often indicate that all of your data points are 'out of control', when you know that they're not! This is because they have a built-in assumption that all of the variation in the results is due to the fact that you're sampling. This is not a realistic assumption however, since we know that real processes also shift and drift as part of their day-to-day (common cause) variation – it does not mean that they are out of control!

With small sample sizes, this assumption does not present a significant problem, but with larger sample sizes it does, because the sampling errors become much smaller in comparison to the day-to-day (between sample) variation. You then see very tight control limits on U and P charts, with all of your results outside of those limits!

What are Laney U' and P' charts?

Traditionally, the recommended solution for large attribute sample sizes has been to use I-MR charts instead. However, these charts cannot account for varying sample sizes in the data, and so David B. Laney invented U' and P' charts. In short, Laney U' and P' charts assess and allow for day-to-day (between sample) variation by widening the control limits. They also have variable control limits based upon sample sizes, **and** they present the results in the same units as standard U and P charts for easy interpretation.

Attribution and references:

Laney charts were presented by David B. Laney in the paper: *Improved Charts for Attributes*. Quality Engineering, 14(4), 531-537 (2002). There is also an excellent reference article entitled *On the Charts: A Conversation with David Laney*, available at minitab.com.

Laney Charts in Minitab:

Laney U' and P' charts can be found alongside standard U and P charts in the Minitab menu shown here:

Stat > Control Charts > Attributes Charts

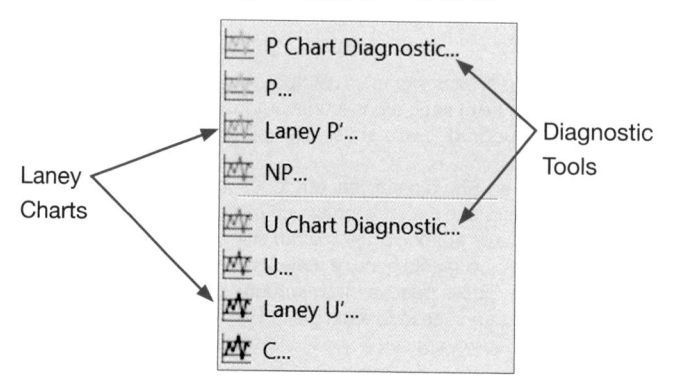

When to use Laney Charts:
Given that they provide a robust solution for all sample sizes, one approach is to always use Laney U' and P' charts instead of standard charts.

However, if you would prefer to use standard U and P charts where possible, and Laney charts where necessary, Minitab provides the U and P Chart Diagnostic functions shown in the menu above.

These functions assess your data and indicate whether a Laney chart would be more appropriate than a standard U or P chart. Data entry is exactly the same as for the standard U and P chart instructions on the previous pages.

Laney U' and P' Charts (cont.)

Laney U' Chart example:

Using the human resources example from page 259, regarding the number of internal applications for each vacancy, the **U Chart Diagnostic** function (previous page) returns the conclusion:

Using a U chart may result in an elevated false alarm rate. Consider using a Laney U' chart instead.

This indicates that a Laney U' chart would provide a more reliable assessment with less false alarms. This can be completed using the following function, in exactly the same way as for a standard U chart.

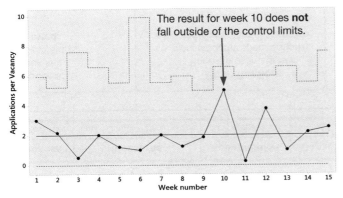

The result for week 10 does **not** fall outside of the control limits.

The Laney U' chart above shows that no results fail any tests, and in particular, that the result for week 10 does not fall outside of the control limits (whereas it did on the standard U chart). This is because the control limits on the Laney U' chart allow for the normal, week-to-week variation.

Laney P' Chart example:

Using the car breakdown service example from page 261, regarding the proportion of vehicles without a spare tyre, the **P Chart Diagnostic** function (previous page) returns the conclusion:

Using a P chart may result in an elevated false alarm rate. Consider using a Laney P' chart instead.

This indicates that a Laney P' chart would provide a more reliable assessment with less false alarms. This can be completed using the following function, in exactly the same way as for a standard P chart.

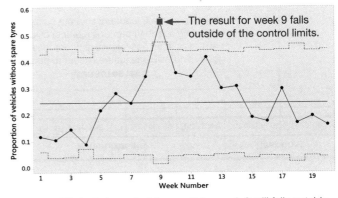

The result for week 9 falls outside of the control limits.

The Laney P' chart shows that the result for week 9 still falls outside of the control limits, even though they have been widened (very slightly) by the Laney P' chart. Having used the Laney P' chart however, we can be more confident that week 9 is a genuine special cause that requires investigation.

Control Plans

For each process step, a control plan defines the characteristics that are measured, their specification, historical capability, measurement method used and a response plan if out of specification.

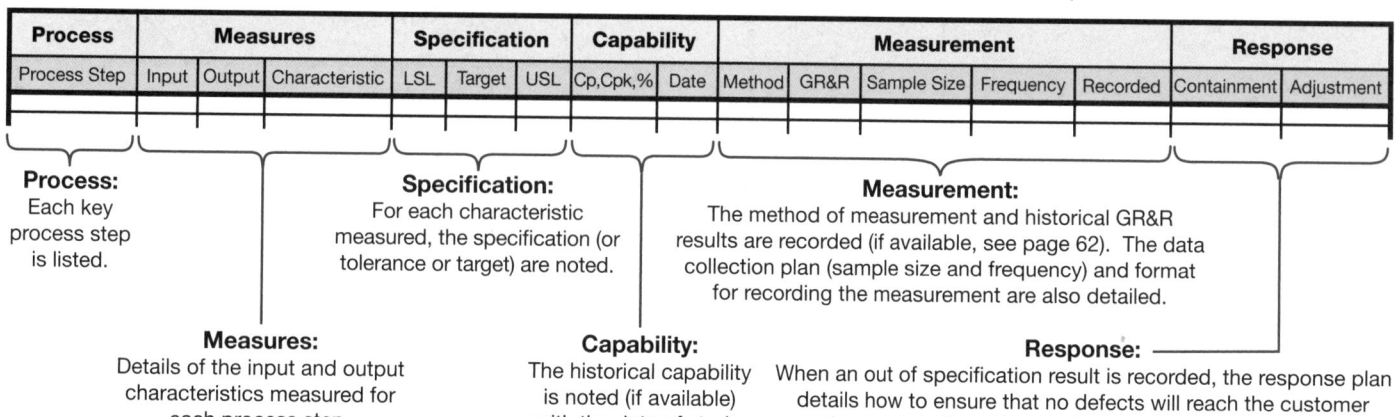

Process	Measures			Specification			Capability		Measurement					Response	
Process Step	Input	Output	Characteristic	LSL	Target	USL	Cp,Cpk,%	Date	Method	GR&R	Sample Size	Frequency	Recorded	Containment	Adjustment

Process:
Each key process step is listed.

Measures:
Details of the input and output characteristics measured for each process step.

Specification:
For each characteristic measured, the specification (or tolerance or target) are noted.

Capability:
The historical capability is noted (if available) with the date of study.

Measurement:
The method of measurement and historical GR&R results are recorded (if available, see page 62). The data collection plan (sample size and frequency) and format for recording the measurement are also detailed.

Response:
When an out of specification result is recorded, the response plan details how to ensure that no defects will reach the customer (containment) and how to fix the process (adjustment).

What is a control plan?
A control plan is a process management document that summarises the measurement details (what? where? when? how? etc.) for each process step.

The components of a typical control plan are shown above, and can be seen to summarise many of the essential Six Sigma tools (process mapping, process measures, Voice of the Customer, process capability, GR&R, sampling, etc.)

FMEA and Control Plans:
A control plan has similar elements to a Failure Mode and Effect Analysis (FMEA, page 114), but both documents have a distinctly different role to play as process management tools.

FMEAs are used to identify and assess risks, and to document existing controls in a process. Control plans provide increased detail on the measurement controls that will remain in place as 'business as usual' after a Six Sigma project is closed.

Standardised Processes

Successful solutions must become 'business as usual' in order to remain effective over the long term.

Standardised Processes is the phrase given to ensuring solutions have been embedded into the organisation's methods and procedures. A standardised process provides more consistent results since the variation is reduced by ensuring a task is always done the same way.

How to standardise your project solutions:

1) Understand the organisation's existing systems for standardising processes. These may by written instructions, visual examples, training programs, drawings, revision controls etc.

2) Challenge the existing systems before using them. There is no point standardising a process into systems and procedures that do not currently work. Identify the methods and procedures that are successful in your organisation and use them.

3) Document your project solutions. Ensure the new process and procedures are clearly explained, with no ambiguity.

When developing your standardised processes, do not forget to...

- Be innovative! – develop new systems if necessary.
- Ensure clear ownership.
- Use visual/practical systems wherever possible.
- Ensure any legal or auditing obligations are met.

Project Report & Action Log

Successful projects have a clear, timely and controlled closure. Knowing when to close a project is a balance between making sure all the actions are completed and maintaining a focus on the pace of a project.

Successful Six Sigma programs have clear visibility on the status of projects (open or closed) and a strong emphasis on transferring the lessons learnt from projects to provide gains elsewhere in the organisation. This is sometimes referred to as 'leveraging'.

Components of a Project Report:

- Clear storyboard through the DMAIC phases of the project, with summaries of the key conclusions, decisions and solutions.
- Keywords (for successful archiving and knowledge management).
- Lessons learnt (for transfer).
- Clear records and access to data used (Minitab files etc.).
- Closure Action Log (see below).

Closure Action Log:

- All outstanding actions should be documented at project closure with clear responsibility and target dates for completion.
- A review of the action log should be planned for 3-6 months.
- Ownership of the process in the short term should be clear, with identified handovers.

Control – Checklist

☐ Have ongoing KPIs been developed to monitor performance?

☐ Have they been integrated into the organisations KPI structure (dashboards/scorecards etc.) where possible/necessary?

☐ Have data collection plans for the ongoing KPIs been implemented as 'business as usual'?

☐ Do the KPIs and data collection plans have clear owners?

☐ Have relevant graphical and statistical techniques been implemented to help the new owners monitor and review process performance? (SPC, histograms, run charts etc.)

☐ Have the improvements been documented, 'standardised' and become 'business as usual'?

☐ Have the improvements in the KPIs been quantified, and new baselines established?

☐ Have the project savings been calculated and signed off with finance department agreement?

☐ Has the project report been completed, and lessons learnt communicated to other relevant areas?

Control – Review Questions

■ How were the ongoing KPIs selected?

■ Have the temporary data collection plans for the project been removed?

■ Who owns the KPIs now? Who will be monitoring them?

■ Have the new KPI owners been helped to understand how to monitor the KPIs?

■ How will we know if the process performance deteriorates? What alarm bells will ring?

■ What has been done to ensure the improvements have become business as usual and won't 'fall over' after the project closes?

■ By how much did the problem (and COPQ) reduce?

■ What are the validated project savings?

■ Where did the savings eventually come from? (efficiency, cash flow, cost of capital, scrap, reduced costs etc.)

■ What next? Is there anywhere else in the organisation that the lessons learnt from this project can be used?

Managing an improvement programme

A challenge of managing any improvement programme is finding the means to organise and standardise the way projects are executed. **Companion** by Minitab® was designed to help.

What is Companion by Minitab®?

Companion by Minitab® is software for managing your company's entire continuous improvement programme. Continuous improvement can be challenging. Typically, practitioners use a variety of disjointed software applications to track and document their project work. As a result, they spend more time managing files and consolidating data for reports, and less time moving their projects forward. To be successful, project teams need easy access to the right problem-solving tools so they can execute projects more efficiently. Executives and stakeholders need the ability to quickly assess the status and financial benefits of an initiative, as well as the individual projects that support it.

Companion's desktop app and web app (see right) work together to meet these needs. The desktop app provides smart and integrated tools to help teams work faster. The web app provides a cloud-based dashboard that gives leadership real-time visibility into a programme, a secure and central project repository, and a design centre for maintaining standardisation.

> **Learn more about Companion and download a free trial at:**
>
> *www.minitab.com/powerofcompanion*

The desktop app and the web app:

Companion by Minitab combines a powerful desktop app and a secure web app, as shown in the picture below.

- **The desktop app** (below right) is used by project teams to execute projects. It is their day-to-day tool for managing individual projects. An individual project is a single Companion file that contains all aspects of a project.

- **The web app** (below left) provides a dashboard that is used by executives, sponsors and other stakeholders (as well the project teams themselves) to gain instant insight into the status of the programme and projects.

Companion web app

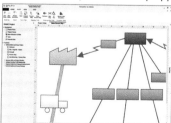

Companion desktop app

Companion Desktop App – Overview

The Companion desktop app helps teams to complete projects more efficiently, use consistent methodologies and metrics, and devote more time to completing value-added project tasks. It delivers a comprehensive set of integrated tools in an easy-to-use interface.

Project leaders use the Companion desktop app as their day to day work tool for managing their improvement projects. It helps to bring all of the components of a project together into one place, where they can be easily reviewed by all team members.

Team members use the desktop app to collect key metrics, review and deliver upon their actions for the project, and to keep track of the overall project status. Having this information available in one file keeps a project moving, provides clarity to team members, and reduces the need for time-consuming project meetings. What's more, this important information from multiple projects is rolled up to the dashboard, where it is summarised in reports to provide invaluable real-time progress of the entire deployment.

The three main areas of the desktop app are shown on the right.

- **The management section** is where team members enter important project details and metrics (see next page).

- **The Roadmap**™ outlines the methodology team members follow as they execute their project (see p271).

- **The workspace** is where team members work with individual tools. The workspace always displays the currently active tool.

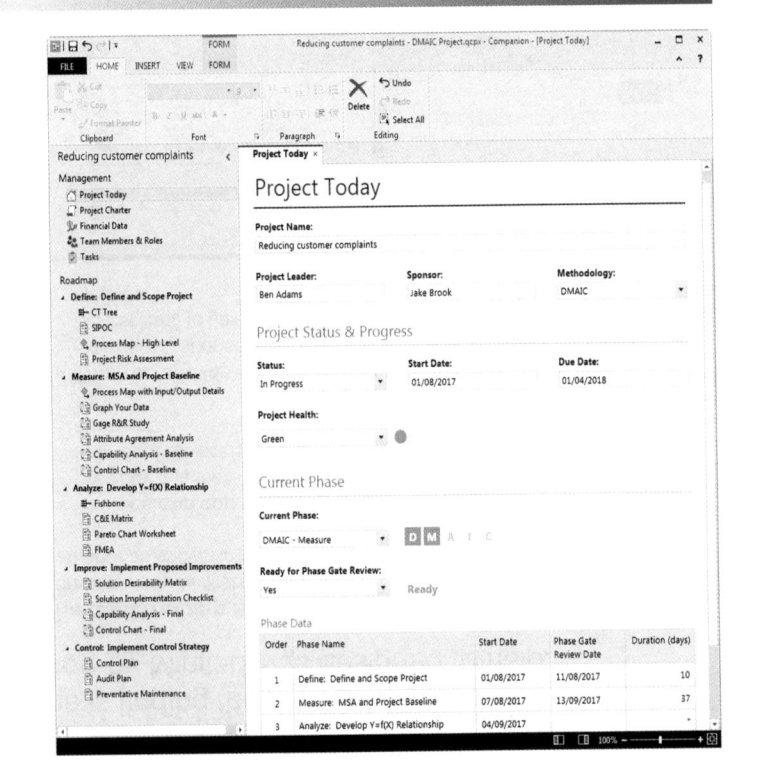

Companion – Management Section

A challenge of managing any improvement programme is finding the means to organise and standardise the way projects are executed. **Companion** by Minitab® was designed to help.

Many of the metrics your organisation wants to track are collected in the forms in the management section (right). New management forms can be added and existing ones customised at an organisational level through the design centre in the web app (p285). When management forms are added, edited, or removed, the management section of every project and project template in the live site is updated the next time site wide changes are published. By default, the management section contains the following forms:

Project Today: Provides a snapshot of overall project status, health and phases. The Project Today form contains the status and dates of each phase of a project, and provides a visual summary of the current phase and overall health of a project.

Project Charter: Defines the project and its benefits. As explained on page 32, the Project Charter is a critical form for most project templates because it often contains key metrics and important project information.

Financial Data: Records the project's financial impact in terms of annualised or monthly hard and soft savings.

Team Members and Roles: Compiles contact and role information for each member of the project team. Easily imports contacts from Microsoft Outlook and from your Companion subscription user list.

Tasks: Outlines the actions required to complete the project. It enables team leaders to identify and assign responsibilities, set priorities, and establish due dates.

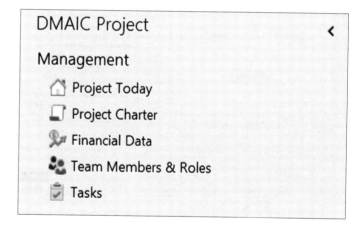

Because the management section is the same in every project, it helps to standardise project execution and important dashboard data.

Companion Roadmap

The Companion **Roadmap** offers an organised way for you to execute projects and document the tools used in each of the phases.

Companion's Roadmap™ gives teams a clear path to execute and document each phase of their projects. Companion includes pre-made Roadmaps based on common continuous improvement methodologies, including DMAIC, Kaizen, QFD, CDOV, PDCA, and Just Do It.

The Roadmap shown opposite is the standard DMAIC project Roadmap available within Companion. This can be customised at an organisational level via the design centre (p285) to suit the exact needs of an organisation. For example, tools can be moved to different phases or renamed to match exact terminology.

At a project level, you can add or remove forms and tools in the Roadmap. When you double-click a tool in the Roadmap, the tool opens in the workspace area on the right, where you can enter data, develop maps, or brainstorm ideas.

As an example, the image on the right shows that the CT Tree has been selected from the Define phase and is ready for completion. There is no need to individually save each tool after editing – the tool can be closed in the workspace without losing the latest edits, because the changes you make to any tool are saved in the project file. To start a new project, choose the project template that contains the Roadmap you want to use, in the menu below:

Companion: File > New Project

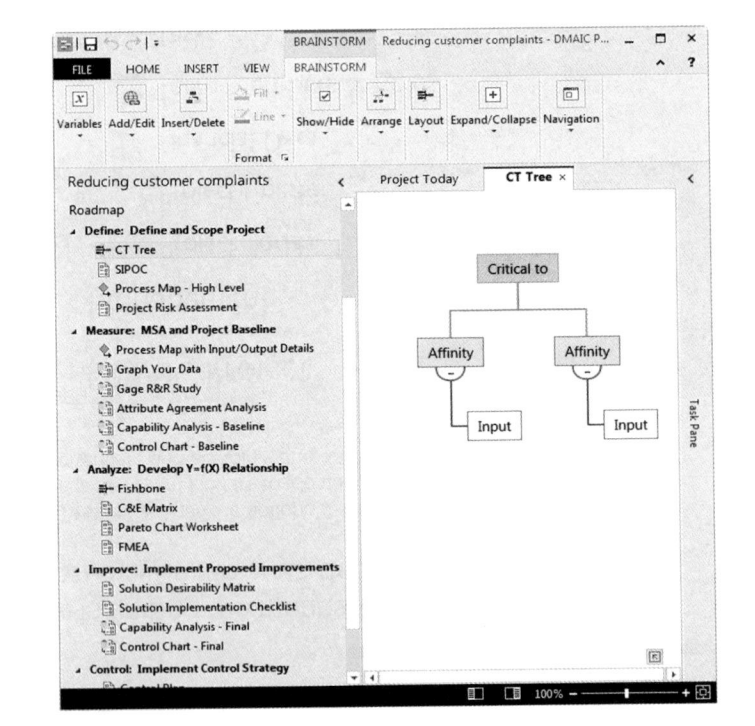

Companion – Tools

Companion contains a full set of integrated, easy-to-use and ready-made tools, such as:

- Process mapping tools (including normal and cross-functional)

- Value stream maps

- Forms based tools (over 50 standard forms including FMEA, Project Charter, C&E Matrix, SIPOC) – see page 278 for more on Forms

- Analysis Capture tools that enable a project team to document the results of data analysis from Minitab

- Brainstorming tools (fishbones, idea maps, and CT trees)

- Monte Carlo simulation

As teams add specific tools to their project file, the tools appear within the selected phases of a Roadmap. Everything you add to your project, including the tools, forms, data, and any external files, are stored in a single project file making it easy for teams to share, review, and stay focused on the project.

Within this single project file, the tools and forms share data with each other to reduce data entry and more importantly share critical status and benefit information to the Companion dashboard.

To insert a new tool into a project Roadmap, just right-click anywhere in the Roadmap and choose **Insert Tool**, or select the tool from the **Insert** menu.

The **Insert Tool** dialogue box (shown below) will open, enabling the user to select the required tool, which is then added to the Roadmap and opened in the workspace for creating or editing.

Companion Tools – Process Map

Process Maps help you to understand and communicate the activities within a process as well as the relationships between inputs and outputs and key decision points.

Companion offers two types of Process Maps as follows, and as shown in the dialogue box below:

A **Process Map** offers a blank workspace on which to draw your processes.

A **Cross-functional Process Map** includes Phases and Departments (also called 'swim lanes') to help you get started.

Companion: Insert > Process Map

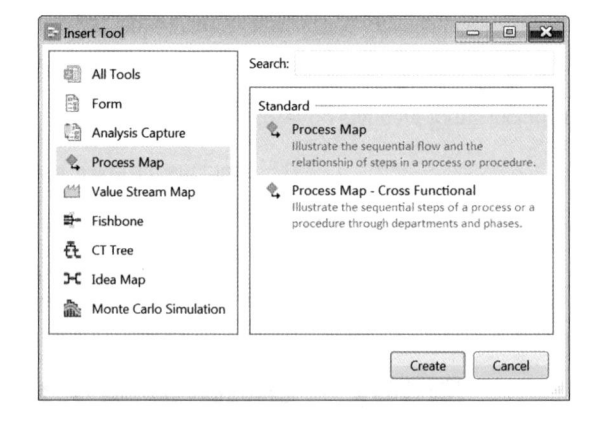

The shapes and connectors from the Process Map toolbar can be inserted or dragged onto the blank workspace, and formatted if required, as shown in the example below.

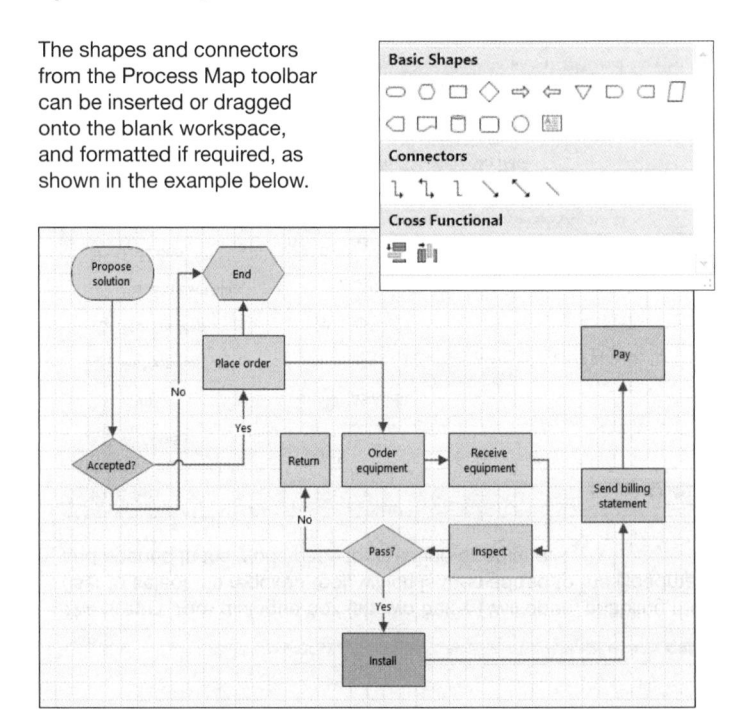

Companion Tools – Process Map (cont.)

The real power of Companion process maps is the ability to add X and Y variables as well as Process and Lean data to any shape (process step) on the map.

Right-click the relevant shape and select **Shape Data > Add Variables**. Then, click the tab in the task pane and enter the data that pertains to the process step.

X and Y variables appear next to process steps by default, as shown below. You can add and show other data by right-clicking a shape and selecting **Shape Data > Select and Arrange Shape Data.**

Cross-functional process maps:

If you want to create a cross-functional process map, you can start by selecting **Process Map – Cross Functional** specifically, or you can add Department and Phases to a basic process map.

An example of a cross-functional process map is shown below. It shows the various Departments and Phases involved with processing a service call.

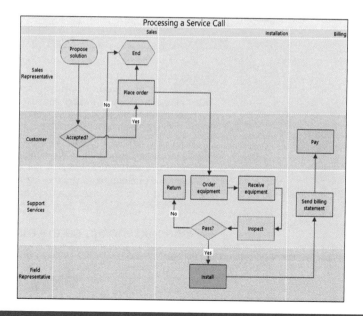

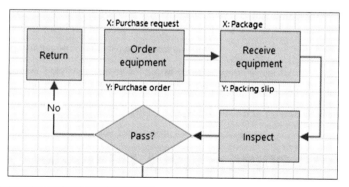

Companion Tools – Value Stream Map

You can add multiple VSMs to record Current and Future states of your process.

To add a Value Stream Map, right-click the desired phase, choose **Insert Tool**, and then select **Value Stream Map** or choose:

Companion: Insert > Value Stream Map

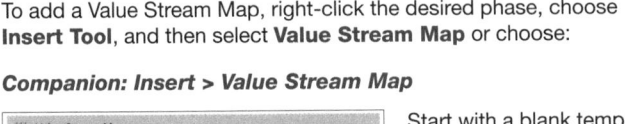

Start with a blank template to build your map from scratch, or get a head start by selecting a 4 or 7 process template.

The VSM task pane provides access to important shape, layout, calculation and map data features.

Companion's VSM shapes follow the principles of Lean and allow you to document a process, understand queue, set up, process and transportation times.

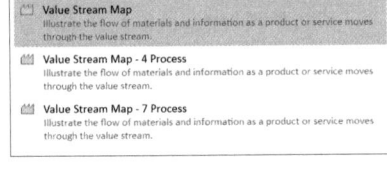

You can add shapes from the VSM Map menu.

On the **Map** tab in the task pane (right), you can enter facility data to automatically calculate customer demand and takt time. You can also choose whether to use takt time or cycle time in the map's inventory time calculation.

To customise the task pane, click **Add and Arrange Data Fields** (bottom right). You can then add, remove, and arrange the data that appears in the task pane (below).

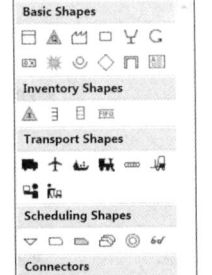

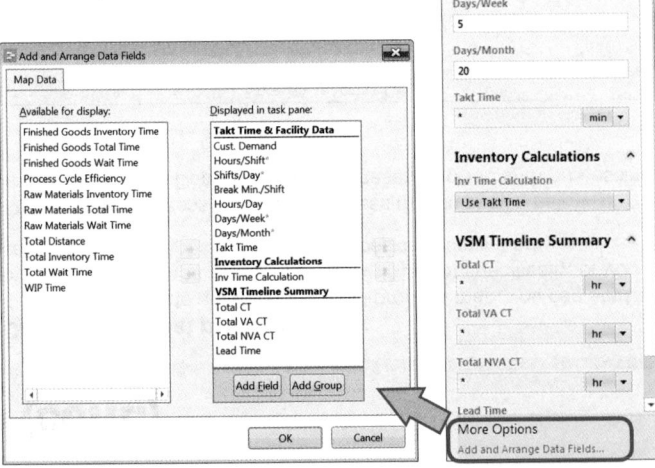

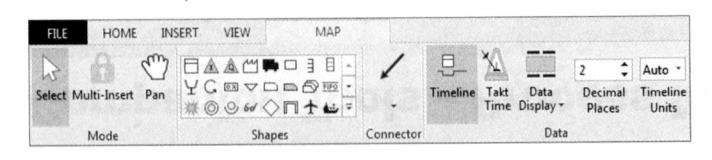

You can add multiple VSMs to record Current and Future states of your process.

As you add data to the shapes on a value stream map, Companion automatically calculates metrics about your process and displays them as a series of peaks (inventory time) and troughs (cycle time).

Takt time is calculated from customer demand and facility data.

The **timeline** is calculated from process shape data and inventory shape data that you have entered.

The **timeline summary box** keeps a running total of the values on the timeline.

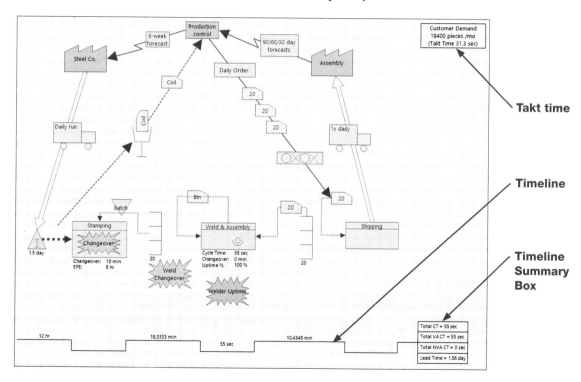

Takt time

Timeline

Timeline Summary Box

Companion Tools – Fishbone

Companion has three key types of tools to support brainstorming activities – Fishbone diagrams, Idea Maps and CT Trees. These can all be arranged to demonstrate a clustering of ideas or themes.

To add a Fishbone diagram to your project, right-click the Roadmap and select **Insert Tool > Fishbone**, or from the main menu, select:

Companion: Insert > Fishbone

There are 4 pre-made Fishbone templates available (4S, 8P, Fishbone and Man Machine Materials), but all can be customised so it is not critical which one you choose. A new, standard Fishbone diagram is shown below. To start editing the diagram, just right-click and insert an Affinity, Sibling or Child using the sub-menu shown below:

Once the data has been entered, Fishbone diagrams are easily formatted and customised. In fact, you can even change the layout to a CT tree or an idea map without affecting the levels and relationships of your original fishbone.

The layout of the diagram can be modified using the **Fishbone > Type** menu shown right:

The level of information on the diagram can be changed by expanding and collapsing levels using the menu shown below:

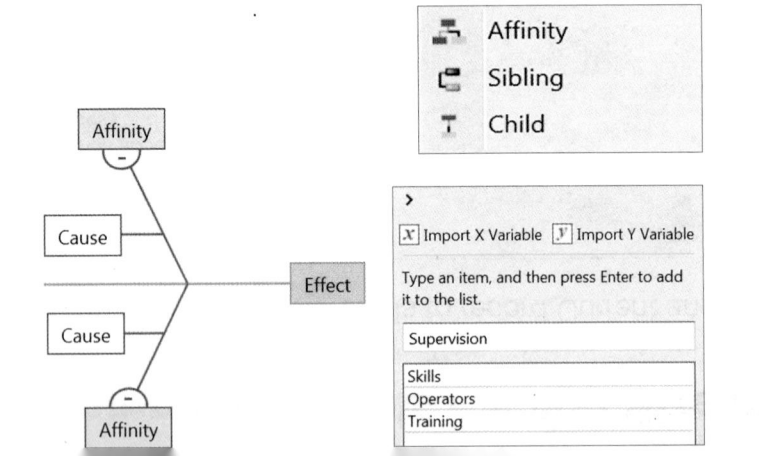

You can also generate a brainstorm list by typing items in the task pane or importing variables from your process maps (shown left). Then, you can drag the items from the list to shapes on the Fishbone diagram.

From the task pane, you can also import X and Y variables from other forms and maps in the project.

Companion Forms and Analysis Capture

You can record, calculate, prioritise, graph and capture data using **Forms** and **Analysis Captures**.

Companion contains over 50 different standard, built-in Forms including:

- C&E Matrix
- Control Plan
- Five Whys
- FMEA
- Project Charter
- Pugh Matrix
- RACI

- SIPOC
- Stakeholder Analysis
- Project Prioritisation Matrix
- Project Risk Assessment
- Lean Metrics Comparison
- Kanban & Supermarket Sizing
- Line Balancing - VSM

To add a form to your project, right click the Roadmap and select **Insert Tool > Form**. Or, from the main menu, select:

Companion: Insert > Form

Analysis Captures:
Companion's Analysis Captures are forms that help summarise the analyses you perform in Minitab Statistical Software. They highlight the assumptions that should be verified to validate your output.

To add a new analysis capture tool, choose:

Companion: Insert > Analysis Capture

Note: All Companion forms and analysis captures can be customised at the organisational level using the web app's design centre (p285).

Reducing data duplication:
Project data is shared across forms, thereby improving consistency and reducing mistakes.

For example, the top of the Project Charter form shown on the left already has key project information that was entered in the Project Today form shown on page 269.

Companion Forms and Analysis Capture (cont.)

Sharing process data across forms and tools:

As well as sharing data across forms, Companion also integrates forms with other tools so that relevant process data can be shared. For example, for the C&E Matrix (form) shown on the right you can import the process variables that were added to a process map. Then, as you complete the C&E Matrix by rating the importance of the process inputs relative to the outputs, Companion calculates the results and builds a Pareto chart simultaneously.

Summarising data in the dashboard:

Some forms contain data that is used by the dashboard in the Companion web app. As you collect this data, the values you enter automatically roll up to the dashboard and are displayed in reports. For example, the recorded **Location** of individual projects (right) can be shown in summarised format in the dashboard (below).

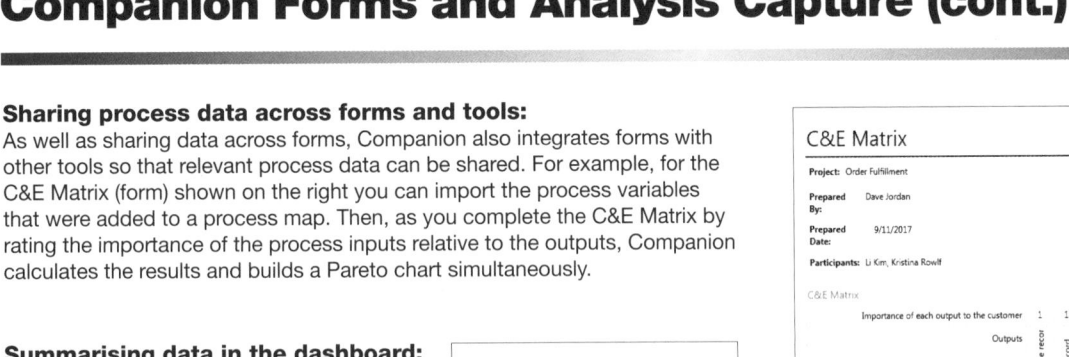

Recorded location of a single project on a form.

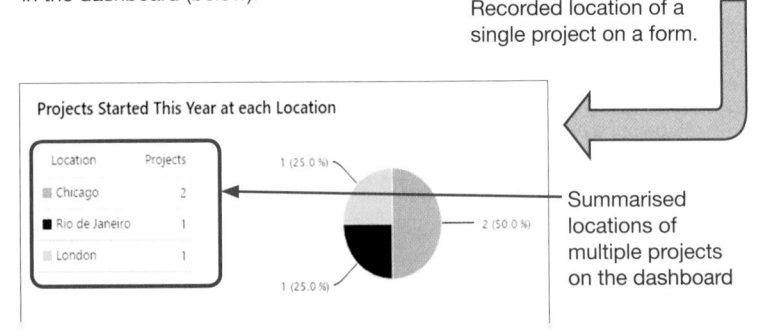

Summarised locations of multiple projects on the dashboard

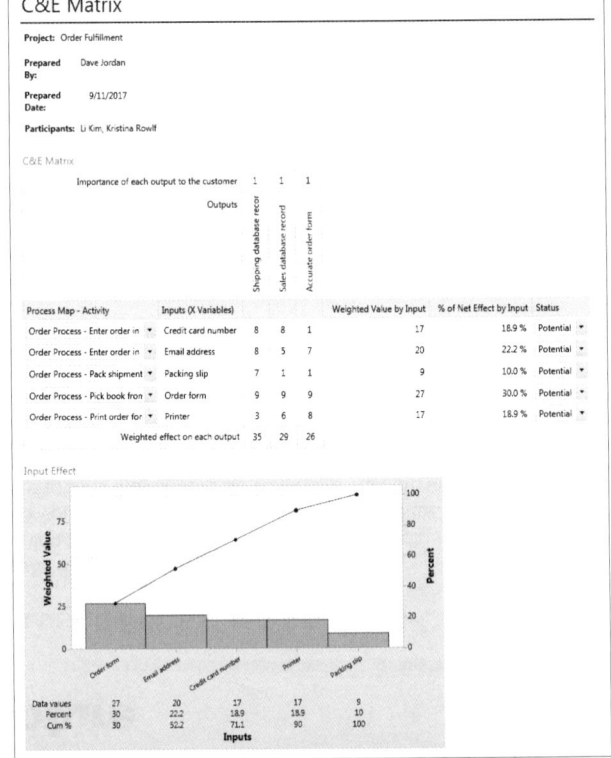

Monte Carlo Simulation

Monte Carlo simulation uses a mathematical model to account for the risk and uncertainty of a system due to variability. The system may be a new product, a manufacturing line, finance and business activities, and so on.

In Companion's Monte Carlo simulation, you add inputs and output equations that describe your system. You can also create groups and verify them by model or function.

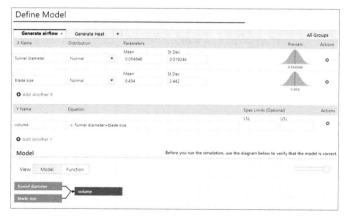

To add a Monte Carlo Simulation, right-click the desired phase, choose **Insert Tool**, and then select **Monte Carlo Simulation**, or choose:

Companion: Insert > Monte Carlo Simulation

After you define and simulate your model, Companion displays a histogram and summary statistics, including expected output values and an estimate of their variability.

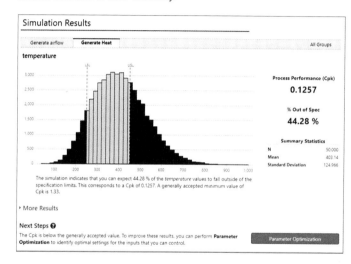

Under the histogram, click **More Results** to see Capability, Summary Statistics, Percentiles and Model Assumptions.

Based on the results, Companion provides guidance and next steps. You can also perform a parameter optimisation and sensitivity analysis in this tool.

Companion Web App – Overview

The Companion web app works with the desktop app to maximise the benefits of your improvement initiative and deliver real-time key performance indicators, such as project status, benefits and financials. The web app consists of three components:

- Dashboard (introduced here)
- Project repository (page 284)
- Design centre (page 285)

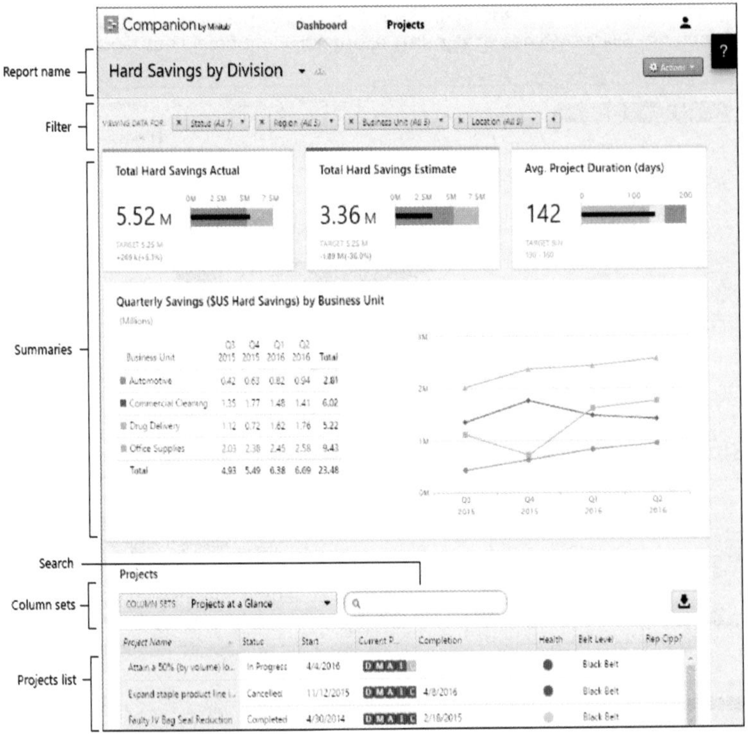

The dashboard:

Companion's dashboard (right) uses data from projects that are stored in the project repository to provide a dynamic graphical summary of your initiative. You can see financial information, status reports, project impacts, progress toward set targets and more. You can view your entire initiative, or select and focus on specific projects, teams or divisions.

Public reports are created at an organisational level so everyone in your subscription can have the same views of the information that is important to your organisation. Any user can create private reports to see information that is important only to them.

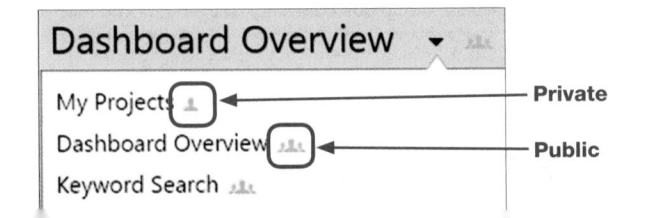

Companion Web App – Overview (cont.)

A Companion report is a collection of filters, summaries, and column sets.

Filter: Allows you to focus on a subset of projects based on a condition such as region, location, or project status.

Summary: Displays aggregate project data such as the number of projects in each division, the average duration of projects, or the total project savings by quarter.

Column Set: Determines the fields that are displayed for each project in the projects list.

Projects List: Displays a list of all the projects that meet the current set of filters.

Search: Allows you to perform a keyword search against the projects list.

Users can create personal reports or modify a copy of a public report by clicking the **Actions** button. They can also choose which report appears when they open the dashboard or save a report as a PDF to archive or send to other users.

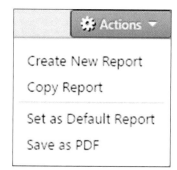

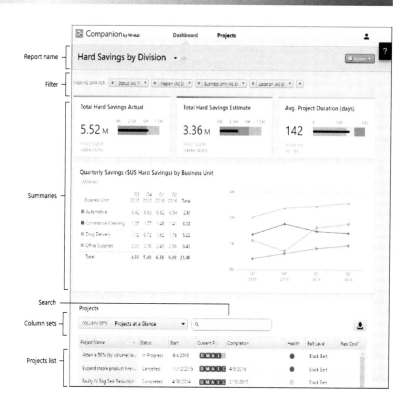

Companion Web App – Flexible Reporting

You can create any number of dashboard reports to show different aspects of your initiative. For example, you can create a high-level report for executives such as the one shown below:

Or, you can create a detailed report that shows savings by quarter or by year for your finance department, such as the one shown below:

Companion Web App – Project Repository

The project repository:

Companion's project repository is a secure, centralised storage system that contains your organisation's individual improvement projects.

When a user saves a project in the desktop app, it is automatically saved to the project repository so the dashboard has access to the project data for its reports.

With all projects in the same place, you can be sure that the reports are as accurate and as up-to-date as the projects.

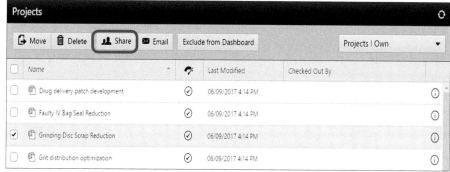

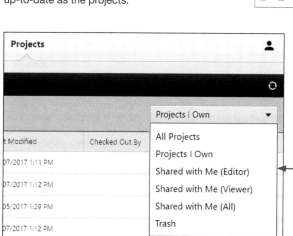

Including projects in reports:

While all projects are saved to the repository, not every project is included in dashboard reports. You must specify when to include a project in the dashboard.

A project is included when you see this symbol in the dashboard column in the project repository:

Sharing projects:

You can use filters (shown left) to show all projects, projects that you own, or projects that have been shared with you, making it easy for you to find and review projects. Sharing projects also makes it easier to collaborate with team members and keep key stakeholders informed.

To share a project, select the project in the repository and click **Share** (shown top).

Companion Web App – Design Centre

In a Companion subscription, data architects manage data fields and templates in the design centre.

The design centre:
Your data architects can manage all site wide changes through the Companion design centre. The design centre provides data architects with the tools they need to set up and customise your subscription. This allows data architects to update project templates, data definitions, and forms with zero downtime for your users.

Before you can edit data fields and templates, you must first create a sandbox, which is a copy of your live site. From the web app, click **Design**, and then **Create Sandbox**.

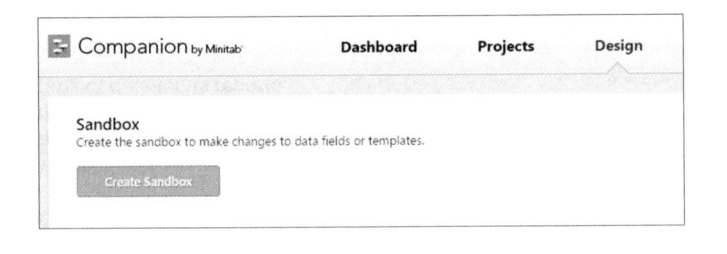

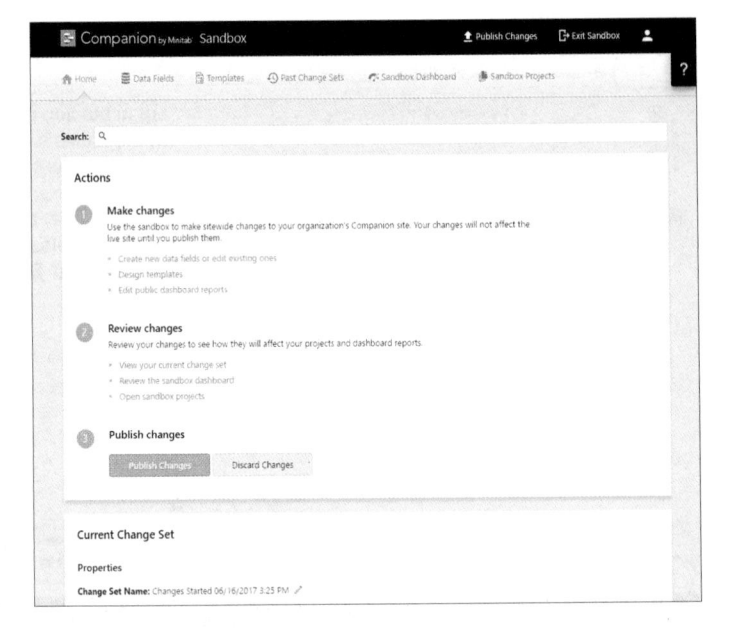

From the sandbox, data architects can create or edit data fields, design templates, create public dashboard reports, and test their changes without altering the live site. When changes are published, every affected project and template is updated.

Appendices

Recommended Resources and Partners

There are a large range of business improvement products and service providers on the market, so it can be a time consuming process selecting the right one. As a leading provider of resources for business improvement, OPEX Resources can recommend the following partners and resources:

For **free articles, example data files** and **support** from the publisher of this text…  **OPEX Resources**
www.opexresources.com

For **Lean Six Sigma Software & Services** trusted by the world's quality practitioners…  **Minitab Inc.** (p289)
www.minitab.com

For an **interactive guide to Lean Six Sigma** that complements this text…  **Six Sigma Tool Finder app** (below)
www.opexresources.com/app

FREE Lean Six Sigma Tool Finder app

The **Lean Six Sigma Tool Finder app** is a free, interactive app that helps you to find the right tool at the right time, including:

- DMAIC Routemap

- Over 90 tool definitions

- Terms and acronyms

- Hypothesis Testing & SPC Routemaps

The app is the perfect companion to this book, providing a high level summary of each tool and technique, accessed through an interactive DMAIC routemap that follows the same DMAIC sub-steps as in this text.

Available for iPhones & Android phones:

Find out more at:
www.opexresources.com/app

Learn and refresh your knowledge of statistics online.

  Quality Trainer®

Use our e-learning course to build the skills and confidence you need to analyze your data with Minitab. Work through animated lessons that bring statistics to life. Study and refresh your knowledge anytime you are online.

- ▸ Engaging Instruction
- ▸ Integration with Minitab
- ▸ Interactive Quizzes
- ▸ Hands-On Exercises
- ▸ Dynamic Table of Contents
- ▸ Searchable Index and Glossary
- ▸ And much more

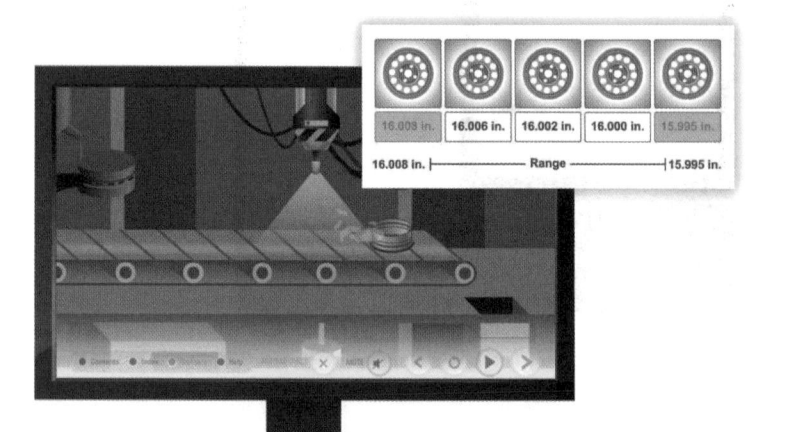

www.QualityTrainer.com

Only **30%** of improvement initiatives succeed.

TACKLE YOUR PROGRAM'S #1 CHALLENGE.

What if you could give your stakeholders automatic, real-time insight into how your projects affect the bottom line? And what if, at the same time, you could maximize the efficiency of your improvement process itself? And what if you could set it up in just minutes?

INTRODUCING

 Companion by Minitab®

Learn more and try Companion free for 30 days at
www.minitab.com/powerofcompanion.

Quick Guide to P-Values (based on 95% confidence)

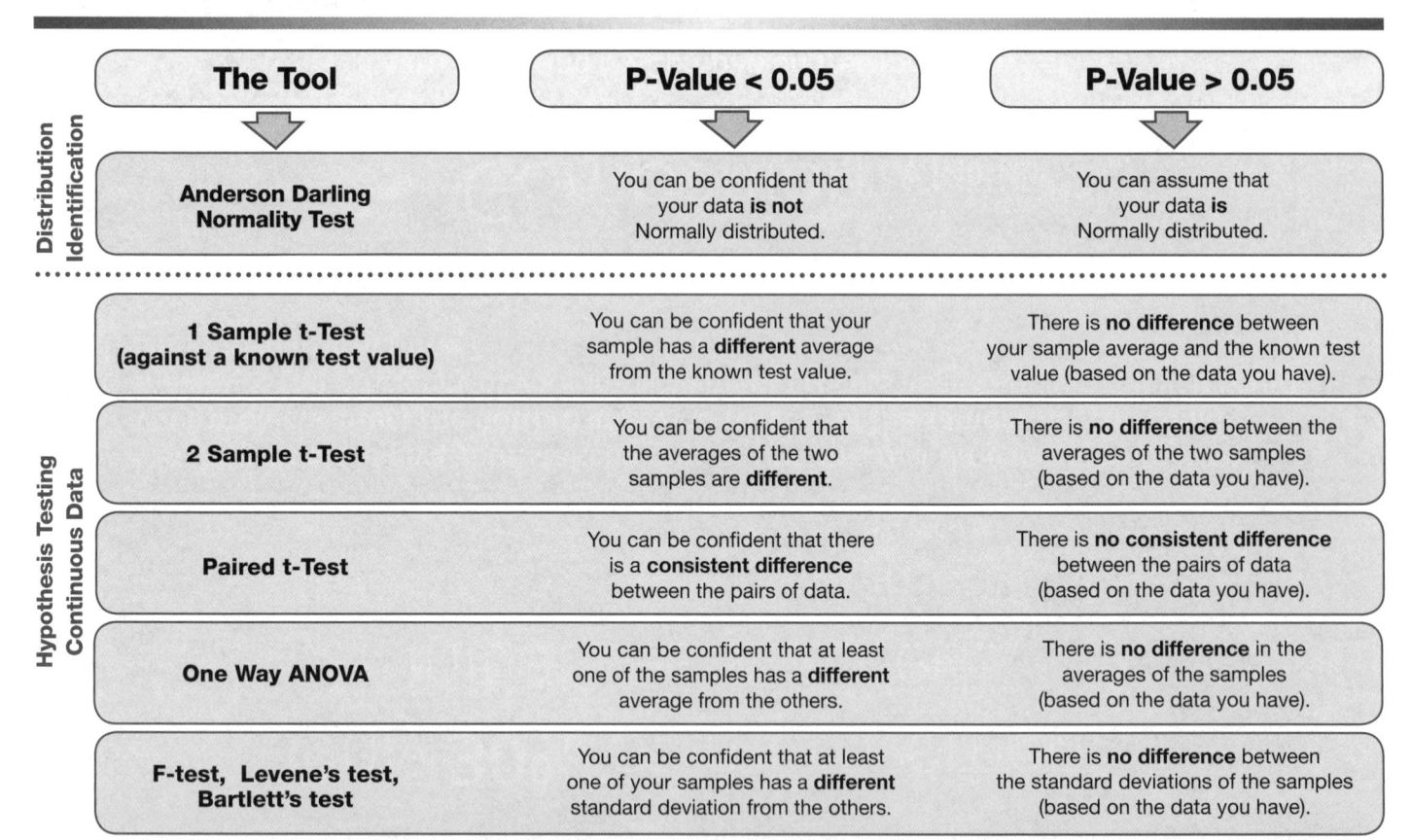

Distribution Identification	**The Tool**	**P-Value < 0.05**	**P-Value > 0.05**
	Anderson Darling Normality Test	You can be confident that your data **is not** Normally distributed.	You can assume that your data **is** Normally distributed.
Hypothesis Testing Continuous Data	**1 Sample t-Test (against a known test value)**	You can be confident that your sample has a **different** average from the known test value.	There is **no difference** between your sample average and the known test value (based on the data you have).
	2 Sample t-Test	You can be confident that the averages of the two samples are **different**.	There is **no difference** between the averages of the two samples (based on the data you have).
	Paired t-Test	You can be confident that there is a **consistent difference** between the pairs of data.	There is **no consistent difference** between the pairs of data (based on the data you have).
	One Way ANOVA	You can be confident that at least one of the samples has a **different** average from the others.	There is **no difference** in the averages of the samples (based on the data you have).
	F-test, Levene's test, Bartlett's test	You can be confident that at least one of your samples has a **different** standard deviation from the others.	There is **no difference** between the standard deviations of the samples (based on the data you have).

Hypothesis Testing Continuous Data	**One Sample Sign Test** (against a known test value)	You can be confident that your sample has a **different** median from the known test value.	There is **no difference** between your sample median and the known test value (based on the data you have).
	Kruskal Wallis & Mood's Median Test	You can be confident that at least one of the samples has a **different** median from the others.	There is **no difference** in the medians of the samples (based on the data you have).
Hypothesis Testing Attribute Data	**1 Proportion Test** (against a known test value)	You can be confident that your sample has a **different** proportion from the known test value.	There is **no difference** between your sample proportion and the known test value (based on the data you have).
	2 Proportion Test	You can be confident that the proportions from the two samples are **different**.	There is **no difference** between the proportions from the two samples (based on the data you have).
	Chi-Square Test	You can be confident that at least one of the samples has a **different** proportion from the others.	There is **no difference** in the proportions from the samples (based on the data you have).
Correlation and Regression	**Correlation** (Pearson Coefficient)	You can be confident that there **is** a correlation (Pearson coefficient is not zero).	There is **no correlation** (based on the data you have). (Pearson coefficient could be zero)
	Regression	You can be confident that the input factor (predictor) affects the process output.	There is **no correlation** between the input factor (predictor) and the process output (based on the data you have).

FREE OPEX Customised Minitab Menu

Minitab allows you to easily customise the layout of the menus (or even to add your own one), which means that you can group together your favourite tools into one menu.

The **OPEX Customised Minitab Menu** is a free, ready made menu that brings together all of the tools described in this guide. The structure of the OPEX menu is shown on the next page.

The menu is contained within a file which can be downloaded online. The file should be imported as a profile file into Minitab as described below. In doing so, please note that:

- All of the standard Minitab menus will be unaffected.

- The OPEX menu can be easily switched off if you do not require it anymore by removing the profile from the active list.

- Although this file has been downloaded and installed successfully by thousands of users, OPEX Resources accepts no liability for any issues associated with installing this file.

Installing the OPEX Customised Minitab Menu:

- Download the profile file (opposite) and save to your local disk.

- In Minitab, open the **Manage Profiles** function (opposite).

- Click **Import** and navigate to the file. Click **Open**.

- The '*OPEX Customised Minitab Menu*' profile should now be shown in the **Available profiles** list.

- Transfer it to the **Active profiles** list.

- Ensure the OPEX profile is at the **top** of the **Active profiles** list by using the arrows indicated. Click **OK**.

Minitab: Tools > Manage Profiles

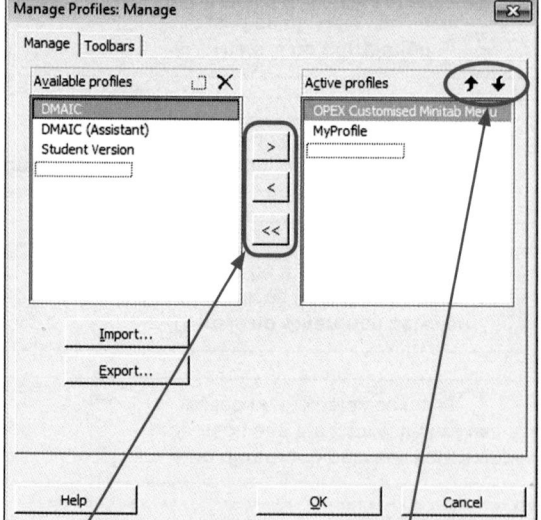

The OPEX profile will appear under **Available profiles** when first imported. Use the arrows to transfer it to **Active profiles**.

Move the OPEX profile to the top of the **Active profiles** list, using these

⬇ **OPEX Customised Minitab Menu.reg**

Download available online at www.opexresources.com

FREE OPEX Customised Minitab Menu

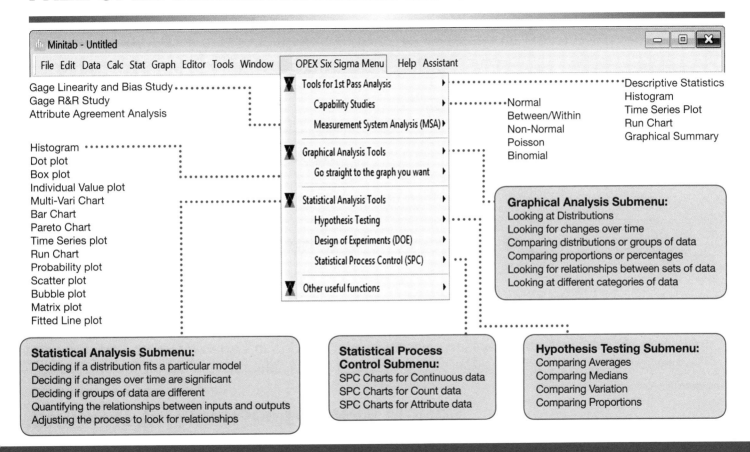

Minitab - Untitled

File Edit Data Calc Stat Graph Editor Tools Window **OPEX Six Sigma Menu** Help Assistant

Gage Linearity and Bias Study
Gage R&R Study
Attribute Agreement Analysis

Histogram
Dot plot
Box plot
Individual Value plot
Multi-Vari Chart
Bar Chart
Pareto Chart
Time Series plot
Run Chart
Probability plot
Scatter plot
Bubble plot
Matrix plot
Fitted Line plot

Tools for 1st Pass Analysis
Capability Studies
Measurement System Analysis (MSA)

Graphical Analysis Tools
Go straight to the graph you want

Statistical Analysis Tools
Hypothesis Testing
Design of Experiments (DOE)
Statistical Process Control (SPC)

Other useful functions

Normal
Between/Within
Non-Normal
Poisson
Binomial

Descriptive Statistics
Histogram
Time Series Plot
Run Chart
Graphical Summary

Graphical Analysis Submenu:
Looking at Distributions
Looking for changes over time
Comparing distributions or groups of data
Comparing proportions or percentages
Looking for relationships between sets of data
Looking at different categories of data

Statistical Analysis Submenu:
Deciding if a distribution fits a particular model
Deciding if changes over time are significant
Deciding if groups of data are different
Quantifying the relationships between inputs and outputs
Adjusting the process to look for relationships

Statistical Process Control Submenu:
SPC Charts for Continuous data
SPC Charts for Count data
SPC Charts for Attribute data

Hypothesis Testing Submenu:
Comparing Averages
Comparing Medians
Comparing Variation
Comparing Proportions

Different Terminology for Data Worlds

The terminology for the different data worlds within Six Sigma is not applied consistently across consultancies, training providers or books. Some of the alternative terminologies are described here:

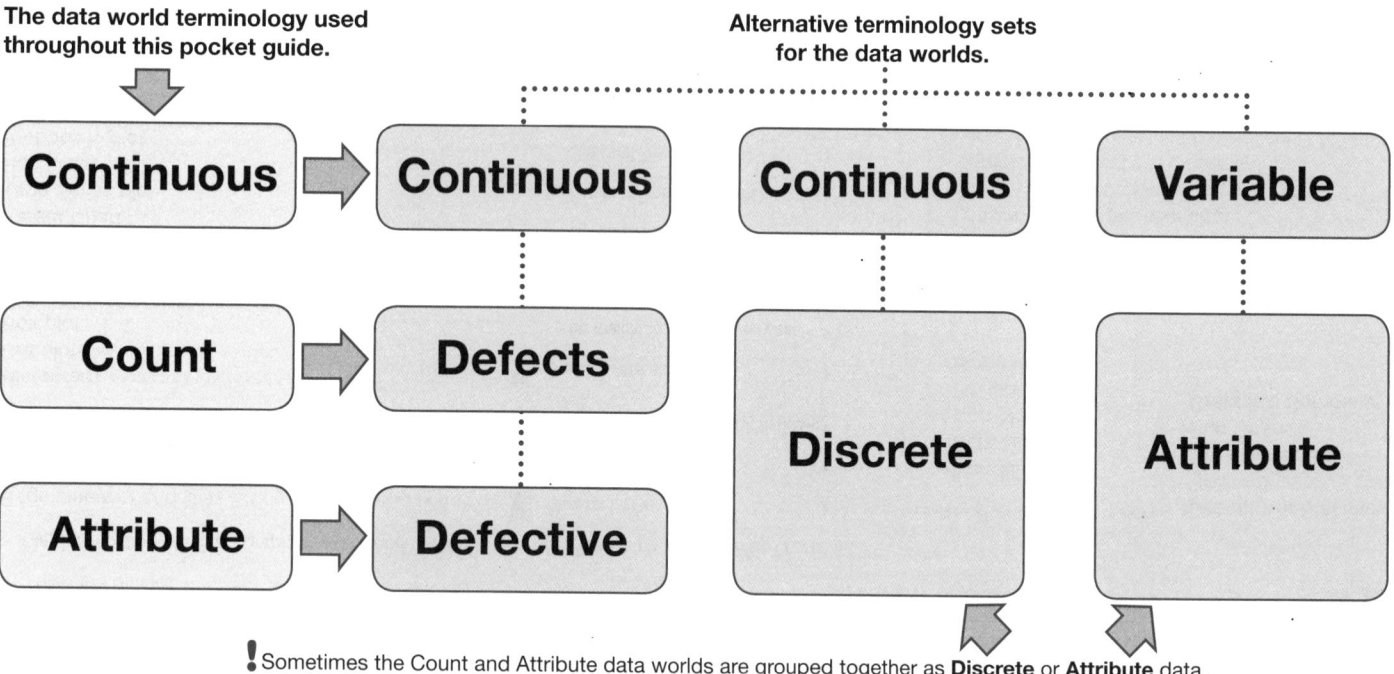

The data world terminology used throughout this pocket guide.

Alternative terminology sets for the data worlds.

Continuous	Continuous	Continuous	Variable
Count	Defects	Discrete	Attribute
Attribute	Defective		

! Sometimes the Count and Attribute data worlds are grouped together as **Discrete** or **Attribute** data. However, this ignores the fundamental differences between these two data worlds, and the statistical models on which they are based.

Central Limit Theorem

What is the Central Limit Theorem?
The Central Limit Theorem (CLT) is a useful statistical theory that works behind the scenes of several Six Sigma tools and techniques.

The theorem says that if you take lots of subgroups of data from a population and plot their averages, the averages will always be (approximately) Normally distributed, regardless of the shape of the population distribution.

So, even if the population is skewed to the left or the right, the subgroup averages will be Normally distributed as shown on the right.

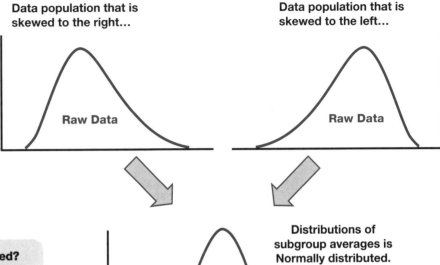

Data population that is skewed to the right...

Raw Data

Data population that is skewed to the left...

Raw Data

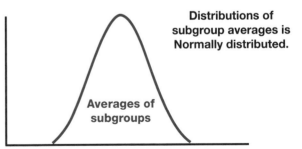

Distributions of subgroup averages is Normally distributed.

Averages of subgroups

Where is the Central Limit Theorem (CLT) used?
The Central Limit Theorem is not used as a tool in its own right but it is at work behind the scenes of some of the Six Sigma tools in this text. For example:

- When calculating Confidence Intervals for an average, the CLT means that the interval is symmetrical.

- In Statistical Process Control the CLT means that the XBar-R chart (which plots averages of subgroups) can be used with non-Normal data.

Analysis of Variance (ANOVA)

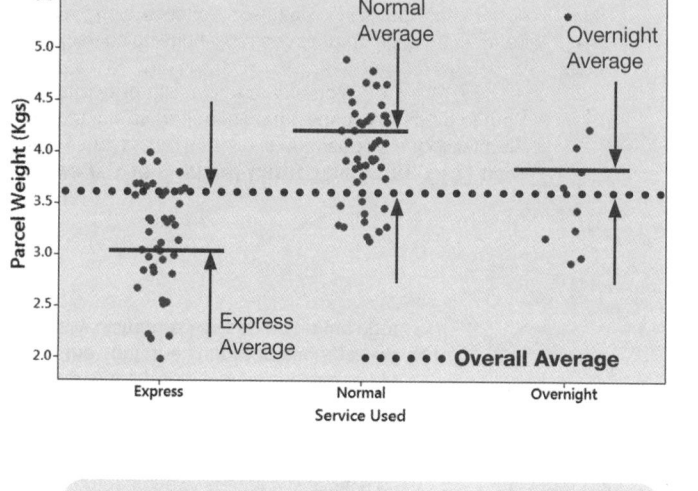

What is Analysis of Variance (ANOVA)?

ANOVA is a mathematical technique that separates out the different sources of variation within a sample of data.

Using the example from pages 141 & 143, the parcel weights for different types of courier service are shown on the left.

ANOVA can be used to find out how much of the total variation in parcel weight is attributable to the different service types, and how much is left over (the 'residual' variation).

How does ANOVA work?

ANOVA works on the following principle:

| Total variation in parcel weight. | = | Variation **between** the service types. | + | Variation **within** the service types. |

The variation **between** the service types is calculated by studying the variation of the subgroup averages around the overall average (as indicated on the Individual Value plot top left).

The variation **within** the service types is calculated by studying each subgroup separately.

Where is ANOVA used?

ANOVA is at work behind the scenes in many of the tools and techniques of Six Sigma.

- In GR&R it is used to identify the relative variation caused by the gauge and the appraiser.
- In Regression it is used to identify the relative variation caused by the different process inputs.
- In DOE it is used to assess the relative variation caused by input factors and their interactions

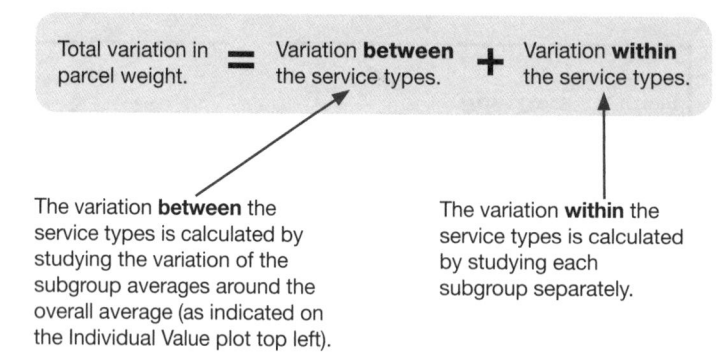

⬇ **Courier-Process.mpj**

Data Transformation

What is Data Transformation?
If your data is not Normally distributed it can restrict the use of certain tools and techniques. Data Transformation is a method for mathematically converting a data set so that it becomes Normally distributed (for the purpose of analysis only). Decisions and analysis can then be completed on the transformed data.

How does Data Transformation work?
Data transformation techniques apply a mathematical function to the data in order that (hopefully) the resulting 'transformed' data is Normally distributed. Minitab offers two types of data transformation; the Box-Cox and the Johnson transformations. The next page introduces these transformations in more detail.

Real data:
This real data (below) is quite clearly **not** Normally distributed. This means that the Z-table cannot be used to predict the percentage of defects that are above the specification limit (among other things).

Transformed data:
The data transformation creates a Normal distribution from the data. The Z-table can now be used to predict the area above the specification limit.

! The Upper Specification Limit must go through the transformation as well, if the Z-table is to be used to predict the proportion of defects.

Mathematical Transformation
Each unit of raw data is 'transformed' according to the selected technique (Box-Cox or Johnson).

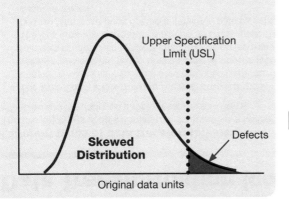

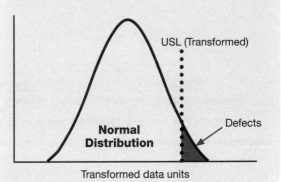

Data Transformation (cont.)

Different types of data transformations:

The two key types of data transformation available in Minitab are the Box-Cox and the Johnson transformations, as follows:

- **The Box-Cox transformation** is a mathematical 'power transformation' that involves a constant called lambda. Various values of lambda are tested until an optimal value is found where the transformed data has the best chance of being Normally distributed. The Box-Cox transformation is simpler to understand and so should be tried first, but it does not work if the raw data includes zero or negative values.

- **The Johnson transformation** is a more complex but more powerful method that can also transform raw data that includes zero or negative values.

When to use data transformation:

If your data is Non-Normal and you want to use a tool that assumes Normality, then you have three options (in order of preference):

1) Find a similar tool that does not require Normality; such as Non-Normal Process Capability (p87) and nonparametric hypothesis tests (p172).

2) Transform the data; then check to see if the transformed data is Normally distributed and if so, proceed with your original tool.

3) Carry on regardless and get meaningless results (not recommended!).

This text does not provide detailed information on data transformation beyond this appendix, but if you have exhausted all other options, then you should ensure you are comfortable with data transformation techniques before using them.

Where to find data transformations in Minitab:

Stat > Control Charts > Box-Cox Transformation

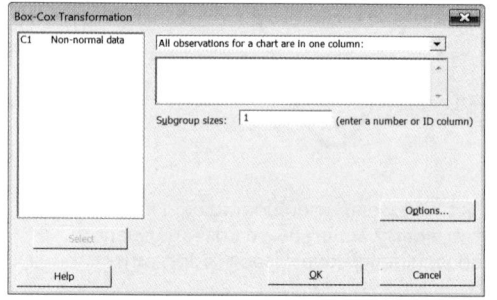

Stat > Quality Tools > Johnson Transformation

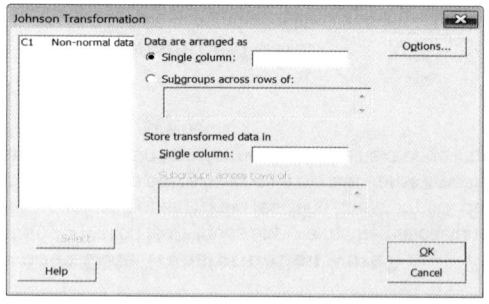

In addition, data transformations are available as options within the Individual Distribution Identification (p191), Normal Capability Analysis (p85) and Control Chart (p249) functions in Minitab.

Why Normality?

The Normal distribution is a common concept throughout Six Sigma and so it is important for it to be fully understood. Some tools and techniques rely upon an assumption that the data is Normally distributed and will return invalid results if this is not the case.

It is therefore important to check the distribution of a data set using a Normality test (p189) or Minitab's Individual Distribution Identification function (p191).

Despite the fact that some techniques require Normality, there are still plenty of tools for analysing Non-Normal data, and this is considered in appendix I on the next page.

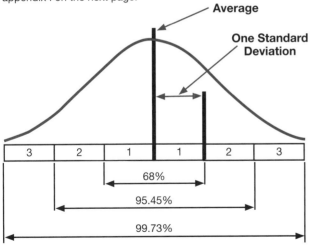

Where and how the Normal distribution is important:

For Capability Analysis:
If we know the Normal distribution is behind a sample of data, then we can make predictions about the process capability over the longer term, using tools such as the Z-table.

For Confidence Intervals:
The mathematics behind the calculation of a Confidence Interval for the average of a sample is based upon the Normal distribution.

For Hypothesis Testing:
Many hypothesis tests are based on the assumption that the data is Normally distributed. If this assumption is not correct then the results of these hypothesis tests may be invalid.

For Correlation and Regression:
The validity of a regression model can be assessed by analysing its residual errors. If they are Normally distributed it indicates the regression model fits the data well.

For Statistical Process Control:
Certain SPC charts require the data to be Normally distributed in order to be valid.

For Design of Experiments (DOE):
During the analysis of a DOE, the important input factors (critical X's) are identified by looking for standardised effects that do not conform to the Normal distribution.

My data isn't Normal!

First of all, don't panic!

If you find that a sample of data is **not** Normally distributed (with a capital N), it's really not a big deal. Too many Six Sigma courses give their delegates the impression that data that is not Normally distributed is not good data. This is quite clearly not true, and Non-Normal data will only slightly limit the tools and techniques that you can use in your projects.

Lots of process measures (particularly in the service sector) are not Normally distributed (so it's perfectly normal!). For example, the following types of measures would typically be Non-Normally distributed:

- Process lead time – most lead times are Non-Normal because if anything goes wrong with the process, you get a delay which creates a long tail in the distribution.

- Time to failure – the distribution of the service life of mechanical components are typically Non-Normal.

- Some physical measures are typically Non-Normal because of a natural limit or feature of the process. For example, tyre pressures are typically Non-Normal, because only a few people over-inflate their tyres, but lots of people forget to check their tyres regularly, and let them deflate.

Count data: When considering Normality, we're typically looking at Continuous data. If your data is Count data, then you wouldn't generally expect it to be Normally distributed and there are some specific tools you should be using in any case (e.g. U charts for SPC).

Transforming data – the last resort: It is possible to transform Non-Normal data into Normal data using data transformation (p298), but this technique is not covered in detail in this text because it is an advanced technique that requires an experienced statistician.

Non-Normal data really isn't that bad:

In the Define Phase:
- Non-Normal data doesn't prevent you using any of the tools.

In the Measure Phase:
- You can complete all the key steps.
- You can use Minitab's Non-Normal Process Capability function.
- You won't be able to use the Z-table, but you can still work out Sigma Levels (if you really want to! – see page 93).

In the Analyse Phase:
- You can use **all** of the process door tools (p99, process mapping etc.) and **all** of the graphical tools (p116).
- You can still use hypothesis tests, but you will have to select a test that does not require Normality (of which there are several).

In the Improve Phase:
- Non-Normal data doesn't prevent you using any of the tools.

In the Control Phase:
- You can use all of the tools with the exception of Statistical Process Control (SPC) charts, where you may have to use an XBar-R chart instead of an I-MR chart.

As you can see, there's no reason to stop your project just because you have Non-Normal data!

Power and Sample Size

Power, risk and confidence in hypothesis testing:

The approach taken to hypothesis testing in this book (and in most training courses because it's the simplest approach) is to focus on **proving** differences between sample statistics with a reasonable level of **confidence**. In doing so, the risks we tend to consider are the risks of deciding there is a difference when there's not (incorrectly rejecting the Null Hypothesis).

Accordingly, we tend to want lots of confidence (usually 95%) to decide there is a difference, and we do this by setting the Alpha Level at 0.05 (in order to limit the risk of **incorrectly** deciding there is a difference to 5%).

But, as with many things, there is another side of the coin! Incorrectly deciding there is a difference is just one possible mistake in a hypothesis test – the other possible mistake is failing to prove a difference when there is one. The ability of a hypothesis test to find differences that really exist (i.e. to correctly reject the Null Hypothesis when it should do) is known as its **power**.

It often helps to think about a real world example; a legal court room, where the Null Hypothesis is that the defendant is innocent (a presumption of innocence) and the alternative is that they are guilty.

The worst thing (**error**) that could happen in a court case is to find an innocent person guilty (incorrectly rejecting the Null Hypothesis). So, in order to limit this **risk** and have **confidence** in convictions, the evidence required to convict someone must be substantial ('beyond reasonable doubt' in many countries). However, taking this approach means that we limit our **power** to find guilty people guilty (to correctly reject the Null hypothesis).

Minitab's Power and Sample Size functions:

Often, we use existing data samples when carrying out a hypothesis test, which means we are accepting the predetermined power of the test to find a difference if there is one. If we want to design a hypothesis test that has a certain level of power to find a specific size of difference, we would have to be able to calculate the sample sizes required and collect that amount of data.

Minitab's Power and Sample Size functions enable you to enter two of the following three variables, and they then calculate the third:

- **Sample size**(s).
- The **difference** that you want to be able to detect.
- The **power** of the test to detect a difference if it exists.

Example: A test is required that has a power of 90% to find differences of 2 or more (units not specified) between two samples, from a process that has a historical standard deviation of 6.

The results (in the Session window, not shown) show that each sample would need to have 191 data points to achieve the required power.

Stat > Power and Sample Size > 2-Sample t

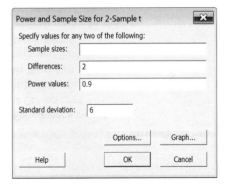

Acronyms

ANOVA	Analysis of Variance
BB	Black Belt
BNVA	Business Non Value Add
BPR	Business Process Re-engineering
CAP	Change Acceleration Process
CI	Confidence Interval
CLT	Central Limit Theorem
COPQ	Cost of Poor Quality
CTQ	Critical To Quality
DFSS	Design for Six Sigma
DMADV	Define Measure, Analyse, Design, Verify
DMAIC	Define, Measure, Analyse, Improve, Control
DOE	Design Of Experiments
DPMO	Defects per Million Opportunities
DPU	Defects per Unit
FMEA	Failure Mode and Effect Analysis
FTY	First Time Yield
GB	Green Belt
GR&R	Gauge Repeatability and Reproducibility
Ha	Alternative Hypothesis
Ho	Null Hypothesis
IDI	Individual Distribution Identification
IVP	Individual Value Plot
JIT	Just In Time (scheduling)
KPI	Key Performance Indicator
LCL	Lower Control Limit
LSL	Lower Specification Limit
MBB	Master Black Belt
MSA	Measurement System Analysis
NVA	Non Value Add
OEE	Overall Equipment Effectiveness
OFD	Opportunities for Defects
PCE	Process Cycle Efficiency
p(d)	Probability of a Defect
PPM	Parts Per Million
QFD	Quality Function Deployment
SD	Standard Deviation
SIPOC	Suppliers, Inputs, Process, Outputs, Customers
SMED	Single Minute Exchange of Dies
SPC	Statistical Process Control
TPM	Total Productive Maintenance
UCL	Upper Control Limit
USL	Upper Specification Limit
VA	Value Add
VOC	Voice of the Customer
VOP	Voice of the Process
VSM	Value Stream Mapping
WIP	Work In Progress

Glossary (excluding tools detailed in this guide)

Accuracy: A type of measurement system error, also referred to as Bias.

Alpha Risk: The risk of (mistakenly) deciding there is a difference in a hypothesis test, when there isn't.

Alternative Hypothesis (Ha): An alternative hypothesis is used during hypothesis testing, and usually starts with '*there is a difference between*'. (Opposite to the Null Hypothesis).

Attribute Data: A type of data world that contains only 2 different categories of results (e.g. Good / Bad, Pass / Fail, On time / Not on time.)

Average: The arithmetic average aims to represent the middle position of a sample of data. It is calculated by adding all the results and dividing by the sample size.

Baseline: A value that represents the existing performance of a process, typically before an improvement project starts.

Bias: A type of measurement system error, Bias refers to any consistent differences between the true value and the measured value.

Binomial Distribution: The statistical distribution behind the attribute data world. The results of a dice or a pack of cards conform to the Binomial distribution.

Black Belt (BB): A (usually full-time) Six Sigma practitioner who has completed 3-4 weeks of training and delivered several successful Six Sigma projects.

Business Non Value Add (BNVA): A process step that adds no value to the product or service but is required for business purposes.

Business Process Re-engineering (BPR): The process of analysing and re-building business processes in order to reduce complexity, remove non value add work and deliver more customer focused products and services.

Categorical Data: Non-numeric data that has distinct categories, such as different root causes or failure types etc.

Central Limit Theorem: A statistical theorem that states that the distribution of subgroup averages will be approximately Normal.

Champion: A sponsor of Six Sigma, responsible for gaining buy-in and facilitating a successful Six Sigma program at a senior level.

Common Cause Variation: Random variation that is predictable within a specific range, and indicates a stable process.

Confidence Interval (CI): Based on a sample statistic, a CI is a range within which you can be confident (to a specified confidence level – usually 95%) that the real population statistic is within.

Contextual Data: Non-numeric information about where and when a piece of data came from (e.g. serial numbers, dates, machine numbers, location, customer etc.)

Continuous Data: A type of data world that contains numeric data which has been 'measured', (such as temperature, time, distance etc.).

Cost of Poor Quality (COPQ): The negative financial effects of a defect occurring are termed the Cost of Poor Quality.

Count Data: A numeric data world that contains results from 'counting' things. The Count data world only contains whole numbers (integers).

Critical to Quality (CTQ): The features of a product or service that are critical to its quality from the voice of the customers perspective.

Data Door: A phrase given to a selection of graphical and statistical techniques used in the Analyse phase that focus on gaining clues from the data available.

Glossary (excluding tools detailed in this guide)

Data Worlds: Different types of data, each with distinctive qualities that determine the type of analysis and tools that should be used, (see the Continuous, Count and Attribute data worlds).

Defect: A feature of a product or service that does not meet the customer's requirements.

Design for Six Sigma (DFSS): The use of Six Sigma tools and techniques in the design of products, services and processes. DFSS follows the DMADV flow.

Design of Experiments (DOE): A wide range of controlled experiments that are used to understand the relationship between the inputs and outputs of a process.

Discrete Data: The Count and Attribute data worlds are both 'discrete', because they can only be whole numbers (integers).

Entitlement: The difference between the process capability in the short and long term is referred to as the entitlement of the process, since a large difference indicates the process could be improved.

Goal Directed Project Management: A structured team based approach to planning and controlling projects.

Green Belt (GB): A (usually part-time) Six Sigma team member who has completed around five to ten days of training and participated in several successful Six Sigma projects.

Hypothesis Testing: A structured approach that quantifies statistical confidence when making decisions based on data. A range of different hypothesis tests are available, depending on the situation and type of data.

In-Control: A process that is stable and under the influence of common cause variation only.

Jitter: The sideways scattering of data points on an Individual Value plot in order to prevent them overlapping (graphically).

Long Term: A time period during which all the inputs to the process have a chance to vary and affect the process.

Master Black Belt (MBB): A (full-time) Six Sigma practitioner who has completed Black Belt training and additional coaching/facilitation training. Typically also trains and coaches Black Belts.

Mean: An alternative word for Average.

Measurement System Analysis (MSA): The process of challenging the quality of data through analysis of the measurement system, using tools such as Gauge R&R.

Median: The middle value of a sample of data; 50% of the data points fall above the median and 50% below. (The same as the 50% percentile).

Milestone: A key event within a project plan, a milestone has clear deliverables and is usually marked with a tollgate review.

Non Value Add (NVA): A process step that adds no value to the product or service (e.g. inspection).

Normal Distribution: A commonly occurring distribution that is symmetrical and 'bell-shaped'.

Null Hypothesis (Ho): A null hypothesis is used during hypothesis testing, and usually starts with 'there is no difference between'. (Opposite to the Alternative Hypothesis).

Outlier: A data point that is outside of the expected range of results, and is therefore likely to have been caused by special cause variation.

Out-of-Control: A process that is un-stable and under the influence of both common and special cause variation.

Glossary (excluding tools detailed in this guide)

Poisson Distribution: The statistical distribution behind the Count data world.

Population: A statistical term that represents the entire population from which a data set was sampled.

Precision: A type of measurement system error; precision refers to the level of variation/errors (in the data) that is caused by the measurement system itself.

Process Capability: The capability of the process to fulfil the customers requirements.

Process Door: A phrase given to the selection of tools used in the Analyse phase that focus on gaining clues from the process itself (process mapping etc.).

Process Stability: The extent to which a process has a predictable range of output or results over time.

Range: The difference between the highest and lowest values.

Resolution: The smallest difference that a measurement system is able to record (or discriminate).

Root Cause: The fundamental reason why a defect occurred.

Sample: A collection of data taken from a process.

Sample Size: The number of data points in a sample.

Short Term: A short time period during which only a few process inputs have a chance to vary and affect the process.

Sigma Level: The Six Sigma measure of process capability.

Sigma Shift: The difference between the short and long term Sigma Levels.

Special Cause Variation: Variation that is not predictable and usually caused by specific events. This type of variation creates an unstable process.

Specification: The limits of acceptability, as defined by the voice of the customer.

Standard Deviation: A measure of variation. Standard deviation represents the average variation of a sample of data points from their own average.

Stratification: The division of data into different subgroups based on categorical data (such as different locations or different products).

Subgroup: Often used interchangeably with 'sample', a subgroup should be used to refer to a small sample of data that has some connection or that was collected at the same time.

Tollgate: A structured review meeting used to ensure a project has completed a specific set of deliverables.

Unstable: A process that is unpredictable over time, usually due to special cause variation.

Value Add (VA): A process step that directly increases the value of a product or service, from the customers perspective.

Voice of the Customer (VOC): A Six Sigma phrase that refers to the range of results that are acceptable to a customer, whether in the form of a numeric specification or verbal feedback.

Voice of the Process (VOP): A Six Sigma phrase that refers to the range of results that are produced by a process.

Z: The distance (in standard deviations) between the process average and the upper specification limit.

Index of Tools and Techniques

Index of Tools and Techniques (cont.)

Index of Tools and Techniques (cont.)